P9-AGE-121

CHINA'S
UNINTERRUPTED
REVOLUTION

The Pantheon Asia Library

New Approaches to the New Asia

No part of the world has changed so much in recent years as Asia, or awakened such intense American interest. But much of our scholarship, like much of our public understanding, is based on a previous era. The Asia Library has been launched to provide the needed information on the new Asia, and in so doing to develop both the new methods and the new sympathies needed to understand it. Our purpose is not only to publish new work but to experiment with a wide variety of approaches which will reflect these new realities and their perception by those in Asia and the West.

Our books aim at different levels and audiences, from the popular to the more scholarly, from high schools to the universities, from pictorial to documentary presentations. All books will be available in paperback.

Suggestions for additions to the Asia Library are welcome.

CHINA'S UNINTERRUPTED REVOLUTION
From 1840 to the Present

Edited by VICTOR NEE and JAMES PECK

PANTHEON BOOKS
A Division of Random House, New York

Library of Congress Cataloging in Publication Data
Main entry under title:

China's Uninterrupted Revolution.

   (The Pantheon Asia Library)
   Includes bibliographical references.
   1.   China—Politics and government—1949-   —Addresses, essays, lectures.   I.   Nee, Victor, 1945-
II.   Peck, James, 1944-
DS777.55.C44924   1975   320.9′51′05   74-4770
ISBN 0-394-46863-5
ISBN 0-394-70924-1 pbk.

Manufactured in the United States of America

First Edition

*To Edgar Snow and other American
friends of the Chinese people*

Acknowledgments

This book has involved many people in its making. We have appreciated and benefited over the years from conversations and discussions with many friends.

To Susan Gyarmati and Brett de Bary Nee we express special gratitude.

Contents

CHINA'S
UNINTERRUPTED
REVOLUTION

INTRODUCTION: Why Uninterrupted Revolution?

The essays in this book share a common assumption that the Chinese Revolution is a protracted and continuous historical process which grew out of the Chinese response to the impact of Western expansionism in the mid-nineteenth century. The long struggle to free China from foreign domination and the search for the way to transform the Chinese nation in a world undergoing rapid change and upheaval encompassed a century. After the victory of the revolution in 1949, the commitment of generations of Chinese to building a modern, just, and independent China did not abate even as the seizure of power introduced new concerns and issues for continuing the revolution. This book seeks to explain why viewing China's modern experience from 1840 to the present through the perspective of uninterrupted revolution provides the key to understanding both the China of today and the complex historical processes which formed it.

FROM THE OPIUM WARS TO THE REVOLUTION OF 1911

In the early nineteenth century, the waves of an expanding Western capitalism broke upon China's shores, giving rise to an epochal crisis in Chinese history. China's relative isolation from the rest of the world approached its end, widespread corruption in the government spread, administration deteriorated, peasant rebellions broke out, and the state public works projects began to break down. In addition, the unprecedented growth of population was a new and ominous sign of a crisis at the heart of traditional Chinese society. Even before the British victory in the First Opium War (1839–1842), a deepening internal crisis was interwoven with, and profoundly aggravated by, Western economic penetration. No longer was it a question of barbarian threats from the northern and northwestern frontiers which the Chinese could hope to assimilate. The new invaders came not only armed with superior weapons, but commanding a power unleashed by the Industrial Revolution in the West which was to undermine the foundations of China's self-sufficient agricultural economy and its traditional culture and values.

Initially, at the turn of the nineteenth century, the West traded with China for silk, porcelain, and, above all, tea. China, with its diverse economy, sought few Western goods. Thus the Western nations, foremost among them Britain, had to pay with large amounts of silver. Only with the sale of Indian opium to China was this outflow reversed. Indeed, British commercial expansion depended on it. British India counted on opium sales for up to ten percent of its revenues. Between 1820 and 1825, some 9700 chests of opium a year were smuggled into China; by 1830 it was 35,400. In 1838, opium constituted fifty-seven percent of China's imports.

The effects of the opium trade were devastating: growing addiction, smuggling, and official corruption. The exchange rate began to rise between the copper cash used in everyday transactions in China and silver, used largely for remitting taxes and for government financial operations. Growing peasant destitution resulted from many causes, but the larger sums of copper needed to meet taxes undoubtedly increased it. Widespread insistence on banning the opium trade, the threat to the health of the nation, the danger to the finances of the country, and the reduced revenues for the Ch'ing government finally forced the emperor to take steps to stop the trade. The First Opium War was the result. It marked the beginning of modern Chinese history, the first important struggle against the imperialist onslaught.

When Lin Tse-hsü was sent to Canton by the emperor in 1839, he quickly took steps to destroy the opium supplies and ban trade. He built fortifications to prepare against attack. When the war came, there was resistance by local gentry and militia against the British. But when the British seized Chusan Island south of Shanghai and began to menace Tientsin in the north, the Manchu government hurriedly dismissed Lin and eventually sued for peace. Even so, popular resistance continued. British units were harassed; warships were attacked. In 1841, in the village of Sanyuanli, peasants from scores of villages fought the British, a battle which to this day is enshrined in the history of the revolution.

Though the First Opium War was launched to defeat Chinese attempts to ban the opium trade, the British also wanted to "open" China to Western trade and commerce on terms acceptable to them. The result of the war was the Treaty of Nanking, followed in quick succession by treaties with France and the United States which radically transformed the Western role in China and began the process of instituting the unequal treaty system through which Western interests were to flourish. The Chinese were forced to pay a large indemnity to the British, to concede territory (Hong Kong), to open up five major ports, and to exempt Westerners from Chinese law. The Chinese government was prevented from levying more than a five percent import tax on foreign goods, opening the way for the rapid influx of cheap goods in the decades which followed. And the "most favored nation" clause meant that all the Western powers would share in the legal concessions granted by the Manchus.

The Chinese defeat in the First Opium War was a setback

for those who had advocated a policy of banning the opium trade and fighting for China's rights. The dominant Manchu faction feared that further military action by the British would weaken their ability to cope with the growing criticism of Ch'ing rule and the danger of peasant uprisings. As an alien dynasty, they worried about the threat to their position from Han Chinese, hesitating to entrust them with political and military power. In addition, the activities of foreign firms and the smuggling involved in the opium trade had created a network of clients and a pattern of mutual interests between the Western powers and some court officials, merchants, and local mandarins.

The Opium War greatly aggravated the problems confronting the Manchus. It demonstrated their weakness and helped to shatter the dynasty's prestige and image of military invincibility. Economic conditions deteriorated, exacerbated partly by the opium trade (52,000 cases in 1850), growing Western economic inroads, the payment of the indemnity, and the breakdown of the monetary system. This was especially true in South China, and contributed to the outbreak in 1851 of the greatest peasant upheaval in Chinese history, the Taiping Revolution.

Peasant unrest had broken out in dispersed and marginal ways at the end of the eighteenth century, cresting between 1850 and 1870 in the Taiping Revolution. Countless millions rose in revolt; twenty million perished. Nearly all of China's eighteen provinces were torn by brutal conflict. Such fierce peasant uprisings have dominated the entire history of imperial China, but they had always failed to break the hold of the feudal economic relations and the Confucian political system. At some point they were used by segments of the gentry to bring about dynastic change. While peasant uprisings thus dealt blows to the prevailing feudal regime, the political and economic fabric of Chinese society remained basically unchanged.

The Taiping revolutionaries were very much a part of China's 2000-year history of peasant uprisings. They attacked the traditional adversaries of the Chinese peasant, the landlords and the officials, drawing their strength from the bitter social warfare and class struggle in the villages where alternatives to grinding rural misery and exploitation were desperately needed. Their primitive rural collectivism, their attack on the tyranny of the educated Confucian élite which had dominated the history of imperial China, their drive for equality and women's liberation, expressed concerns which have been at the heart of China's inland peasant revolution ever since. An intensely national movement against the Manchus, they were also a forerunner of the later mass-based nationalism.

The Taiping Revolution, however, was in many ways different from previous peasant struggles. The heterodox borrowing from Christianity by some of its leaders symbolized a search for the "secret" behind the superiority of Western power. Hung Hsiu-ch'üan, the Taiping leader, had lived in Canton among missionaries and was acquainted with the productiveness of Western industry. In their attack on the traditional feudal land system and in the expressed willingness of some of the Taiping leaders to promote proto-capitalist developments, the Taipings frontally assaulted the traditional Confucianists who derogated economic growth and used the state bureaucracy to regulate all economic life in the nation. These antigentry, anti-Confucian peasant revolutionaries introduced the notion that the Confucian tradition was not *the* Chinese tradition, but gentry tradition. Some of their articulate leaders advocated the introduction of steamships, railroads, a modern postal system, and banks, and the transformation of the educational system, knowing that this would undercut the Confucian ideology and its traditional agrarian base.

Seizing the opportunity to turn the crisis faced by the Manchus to their advantage, the Western powers initiated the Second Opium War (1856–1858). The Manchu government concluded that it could not fight domestic rebels and foreign invaders at the same time. Threatened with imminent collapse by the Taipings, it feared internal insurrection even more than it feared the foreign powers. To fight upheaval at home, it eventually sought to establish external peace, and even to gain some assistance from abroad by making further concessions. The government's defeat in the Second Opium War was thus followed by the granting of sweeping new privileges to the foreign powers: the right to legally import opium, the right for their vessels to traffic on inland waterways, permission for businessmen and missionaries to travel throughout the country. The policy of passive bureaucratic footdragging followed after the First Opium War gave way to an active policy of conciliation and collaboration.

Western assistance to the Manchus helped to defeat the Taipings in 1864. However, internal weaknesses contributed their part. Strikingly modern elements in the Taiping ideology did not prevail over internal dissensions and other difficulties which had flawed peasant uprisings in the past. Yet though the Taipings were defeated, the fear of peasant revolution dominated the actions of the gentry and the imperial regime throughout the rest of the nineteenth century, and partly explains the facility with which the Western powers were able to impose their will upon China. In none of the wars—the Sino-French War, the Sino-Japanese War, even the siege of Peking—did the Western powers or Japan actually reduce China to a state of total military surrender. Operations were quite localized and remarkably short in duration. The reason the imperial government surrendered so quickly on these occasions, giving away an increasing number of territorial, financial, and political rights, was largely that it feared instability in the provinces. The unwillingness of the government to support a mobilized population at the time of the First Opium War proved prophetic. After the Second Opium War, neither Manchu nor Han officials considered launching widespread, protracted struggle, for their own interests had become enmeshed with those of the foreigners. Nor could they easily have led such a resistance if they dared, for this type of protracted conflict against the foreign presence would entail a new social relationship between leaders and led, peasant and intellectual, which denied the very privileges and role they fought to preserve.

After 1860, as the Manchu government formalized its conciliatory stance toward the Western powers and they, in turn, gained a vested interest in supporting the government with which they had made so many favorable agreements, a fierce debate broke out among the traditional Confucian scholar-officials over how to cope with the spread of Western power. On one side of this debate were members of the "self-strengthening" movement, who sought to understand Western military might and advocated the building of an armaments industry. They soon found themselves forced, however, to probe ever deeper into the nature of the West's economic dynamism. In the 1870s, they were succeeded by another generation, whose slogan was "wealth and power" through the development of a textile industry, communications, and mining.

On the other side, "traditionalists" argued that such changes were unleashing economic forces which the Confucian ethos and the imperial bureaucratic system had always carefully sought to regulate and control. They warned that it could get out of hand and destroy the agrarian base of Chinese society. The debate suggests how weak the commitment to building a powerful economic base really was. Both sides wanted to preserve the *ancien régime* and contain internal enemies rather than to promote fundamental changes.

Indeed, the weakness of indigenous capitalism in the face of feudalism and imperialism is graphically evident in comparisons with Meiji Japan. In Japan, the economic power of the landlord-merchant groups and the political prestige and experience of representatives of the feudal class complemented and reinforced each other, enabling the Meiji government to launch a radical economic transformation of the nation and to move in the direction of capitalist development. In China, commercial groups were so pitifully weak that the self-strengtheners themselves opposed unfettered growth and sought to use traditional bureaucratic methods to manage the economy.

Nonetheless, China did become more and more incorporated into the Western capitalist system, as machines, weapons, and ideas of the industrial West poured in. And the Western powers themselves advanced their interests by supporting much that was politically conservative, oppressive, and backward in China. To resist revolutionary change and the growth of indigenous Chinese capitalism, they joined forces with the self-strengtheners, who sought to preserve Chinese feudalism.

Gentry conservatism contained the seeds of its own destruction. Attempts to restore the old order, to move slowly and with extreme caution, only temporarily thwarted the ineluctable forces of change at work deep within Chinese society. Imperialism, stimulating China's social economy, was producing new groups and social forces which, though essential for its ongoing penetration of Chinese life, were also the basis for a growing opposition to it. These new groups, drawn neither to the conservatism of the traditional Confucianists nor to the social vision of the Taipings, sought new alternatives for directing China's course.

One of the most conspicuous of China's new social elements was its bourgeoisie, which became a significant force around the beginning of the twentieth century. The opening of the treaty ports had provided new opportunities for merchants, and their numbers grew steadily. As the power of the gentry began to crumble, many of them saw the advantages of modern enterprise. Overseas Chinese, too, joined the ranks of this class of entrepreneurs, businessmen, financiers, and industrialists.

The new bourgeoisie gained economic power and social status within Chinese society, but it found itself subordinate to and dependent on foreign capital. The unequal treaty system which gave competitive advantage to foreign products and foreign enterprise blocked the road to successful industrialization by indigenous capitalists. This spurred the rise of nationalist sentiment among the Chinese bourgeoisie at a time when nationalism was spreading rapidly among many classes of Chinese. By the turn of the century, a majority of the bourgeoisie wanted a strong central government to assure the conditions in which a national market could develop, a uniform national currency be established, and a modern commercial code be enforced.

Although it sought to implement nationalistic goals, the defining characteristics of China's bourgeoisie were still its intimate links to international capitalism and to the landlord-gentry class in the countryside. But the beginning of the twentieth century saw the growth of social groups not quite so closely tied to the imperialist powers. With the spread of modern schools and the return of growing numbers of Chinese students who had studied abroad, an active and dynamic political force emerged which called for a radical break with tradition. These new intellectuals came to play a pivotal role in attacking imperialism, as would the young military leaders who were training in the new, foreign-modeled military academies.

China's nascent railroad, mining, and textile industries gave birth to a third new social group, the industrial working class. They lived and toiled in unbearable conditions, comparable only to the worst experienced by the British working class in the early stages of the Industrial Revolution. Though small in numbers, this class was to become a potent force for change. The industrial workers later put teeth into the protest movements which spread after the turn of the century.

All of these new groups were in positions to be acutely sensitive to the heavy toll imperialism was exacting from China. All were in positions where action seemed possible. All had little stake in preserving the traditional Confucian state.

In 1898, in the wake of China's defeat in the Sino-Japanese War of 1895, the first genuine reform effort was attempted, largely by traditional social elements. Led by K'ang Yu-wei, Confucian reformers sought to transform the archaic Manchu government into a modern state instrument. Against the inertia and conservatism of the gentry, however, these reformers proved helpless. They sought change from the top down with no thought of mobilizing peasant support, and their failure opened the gate to revolution by the new social elements ready to assume a central role.

By the turn of the century China had become a semicolony for all the international powers. The unequal treaties had given them the right to station land and sea forces in China, control of the trading ports, even direct control of the concessions. The foreigners ran China's customs service and controlled the revenue from it, operated the postal system, and controlled most of the modern communications systems. Extraterritoriality allowed nationals of the treaty powers to escape the jurisdiction of Chinese courts. Inland rivers were patrolled by foreign gunboats. The Chinese had to rely on foreign shipping to carry much of their products, even in their own waterways. The foreign powers dominated China's banking and financial community; war indemnities and loans to the government led to its subservience in financial matters. Chinese goods were taxed internally while foreign goods were exempted. Protectionist measures were prohibited. After 1895, the foreign powers moved in to build their own modern industries, taking advantage of cheap Chinese labor and raw materials. They began to divide China into spheres of influence, obtaining mines and railway concessions.

With the savage Allied pillage of Peking in the wake of the Boxer uprising in 1900, fear spread among the Chinese that their country would be partitioned among foreign powers and that they would disappear as a people. There was now no question that China could be saved only through new and far-reaching measures. The call went out for the creation of a modern centralized nation-state capable of forcing back imperialism and advancing the nation's economic, political, cultural, and social regeneration. The beliefs that had underlain the political foundations of Chinese society for millennia finally lost their sway. Die-hard conservatives who had blocked the reforms of 1898 were swept aside in a desperate last-gasp attempt of the late Ch'ing leaders to come to terms with the grave situation in China. Even the conservative Empress Dowager advocated a series of reforms that in early years would have been unthinkable. The imperial examination system was formally abolished in 1905. More modern military schools were established. New schools teaching mathematics, science, geography, and above all, nationalism, proliferated rapidly. It was hoped that utilization of such skills on a massive scale would create the weapons to meet the imperialist threat to the existence of the Chinese nation.

Bitter dissension and clashes divided the different factions and parties that advocated drastic changes for China, but all looked to the West and Japan for their models. Most shared the belief that China would be made over in the image of Western capitalism. The basic split between the late Ch'ing reformers, the radical reformers, and the republican revolutionaries centered on the question whether China was to have a constitutional monarchy or a republican form of government. Chang Chih-tung and the conservative court reformers made a belated attempt to emulate the Japanese Meiji Restoration, working desperately to save the enfeebled dynasty; the reformer K'ang Yu-wei, remaining loyal to the Kuang-hsü emperor, continued to advocate the cause of constitutional monarchy; and Dr. Sun Yat-sen's band of revolutionaries worked with overseas Chinese and secret societies to overthrow the Manchus and establish a Western-style republican government. Although concern was voiced for avoiding some of the abuses of the Western experience in capitalist economic development, neither reformers nor revolutionaries sought to overturn the existing social structure. Even Sun, who called for the policy of "land to the tiller," nevertheless assumed that the Chinese economy would operate along capitalist lines. Both reformers and revolutionaries attacked the direct manifestations of Western imperialist and Japanese military presence, but the less obvious threads of imperialist power eluded them. Indeed, the reforms they advocated would only enmesh China more completely into the international capitalist economy. The growth of the "modern sector," improved communications, the modernization of China's customs service, and the growth of a Chinese banking system were all necessary for the increasingly sophisticated imperialist system which was evolving.

As was true of the self-strengtheners, those who sought to learn from the West were dominated by it. The dilemma remained: how could the country free itself from foreign domination and gain independence while using the reform methods and ideology of Western capitalism? The 1911 revolution which overthrew the Manchu dynasty exposed the bankruptcy of merely adopting the "new learning" of the West. Even after the establishment of the Chinese Republic, no class or group rose to power that was capable of directing the transformation of the country, of solving the agrarian crisis, of regaining national independence and building the strength necessary to resist imperialist incursions.

After the 1911 revolution, the republican revolutionaries found themselves without the organizational means, popular base, or military support to consolidate their victory. They watched helplessly as the new republic floundered in the morass of warlord politics. The constitutional government which they helped to establish was not an organ of real power, but window dressing for the warlords. Yüan Shih-k'ai's revival of the monarchy and Chang Hsun's march into Peking to restore the Ch'ing dynasty made a mockery of constitutional government. As the warlords battled among themselves, secretly selling out China's national rights to foreign powers and plundering the land, the plight of the peasants became ever worse. The nation continued to disintegrate as the centrifugal forces grew more pronounced. Agricultural production declined. Floods, droughts, famines, banditry, and all of the ancient curses of social disorder exacted their toll on the Chinese people. China of the early twentieth century was, as Lu Hsün described it, an "iron room without windows, absolutely indestructible, with many people fast asleep who will soon die of suffocation."[1] The vast majority of the Chinese people continued to live, toil, and die unaware of the new ideas and issues that were at the center of intellectual debates and political controversy.

THE MAY FOURTH PERIOD
AND THE ORIGINS OF CHINESE MARXISM

The crushing defeats of the nineteenth century and the failure of the 1911 republican revolution contained the seeds of victory for the long-developing Chinese Revolution. In Peking a new generation of Chinese intellectuals gathered. After studying abroad, in Japan, France, and the United States, their return to China brought them face to face with the depressing reality of their country. They were painfully conscious of China's low international standing, extreme material backwardness, and suffocating cultural stagnancy in contrast to the dynamism they had found in the West and Japan. Fired by intense patriotism, they took on the challenge of China's national regeneration. The task before them was awesome. Reform within tradition and revolution according to the Western model of constitutional government had both proved unable to break the seemingly inexorable course of events leading to continued internal disintegration and increasing subjugation by imperialist powers. Moreover, the legacy of these repeated defeats and failures was a general mood of despair. Talk of the possibility of national extinction was widespread in intellectual circles. Never before in the long history of the Chinese nation had intellectuals faced a crisis of civilization of such proportions. The new intellectuals began to see the need for a total transformation of Chinese culture and society.

For intellectuals like Chen Tu-hsiu and Hu Shih in the years preceding the May Fourth movement, this meant the wholesale westernization of China. But international and domestic events worked to undermine that position. The First World War and the carnage and devastation left in its wake stirred in China ripples of disillusionment with the West. The war symbolized the spiritual bankruptcy of Western civilization; it also seemed to suggest that the West had begun to decline. Revolutionary currents unleashed by the European War and the news of the Bolshevik seizure of power in backward Russia offered new ideas and sources of hope and inspiration. Both the disillusionment with the West and the nascent appeal of the October Revolution spread quickly among young Chinese after the Versailles Peace Conference. To patriotic students, the flagrant betrayal of Chinese national sovereignty at Versailles by the ceding to Japan of the German concessions in Shantung peninsula revealed dramatically the hollowness of Wilsonian idealism and the hypocrisy of Western democracies.

On May 4, 1919, thousands of Chinese students in Peking poured into the streets to demonstrate against the decision of the Allied Powers at Versailles. The demonstration ended in an attack upon the homes of key members of the Peking warlord government who were notorious for their collaboration with Japan in selling out Chinese national rights. From Peking the student movement swept like fire to the major cities of China, igniting a massive wave of anti-imperialist nationalism and culminating in widespread workers' strikes, demonstrations, riots, and nationwide boycotts. Encouraged by the broad popular support given to the movement, students reached out of their universities to establish ties with the classes that could provide the social basis for the new revolution. Following the outbreak of the student movement and the emergence of a politically conscious urban proletariat, Marxist study groups sprang up one after another, leading to the introduction of revolutionary Marxism into Chinese radical circles. In 1921 the Chinese Communist Party was established in Shanghai.

The May Fourth period marked the watershed in modern Chinese history. Out of its political and intellectual ferment emerged the key concerns which underlay the course of the Chinese Revolution all the way through the Great Proletarian Cultural Revolution. Whereas the Taiping peasant revolutionaries, the landlord self-strengtheners, the westernizing reformers, and the republican revolutionaries all had failed to provide the intellectual synthesis needed to guide China along the path of national regeneration, the radical intellectuals of the May Fourth period succeeded in making the critical intellectual breakthroughs. Their significance was not that they formulated a step-by-step blueprint for the Chinese Revolution. This they did not do. What they accomplished was to ask the right questions and suggest orientations that could lead to the resolution of the central contradictions confronting those who were committed to the task of national regeneration. The ideas and concerns of two of the leading intellectuals of the May Fourth period in particular, Li Ta-chao (1888–1927) and Lu Hsün (1881–1936), both "returned students" from Japan, proved seminal to the future development of the Chinese Revolution. Their writings (including those that extended beyond the May Fourth period) greatly influenced the thoughts of a whole generation of Chinese students, including especially the young Mao Tsetung. Li Ta-chao's and Lu Hsün's influence on Mao's intellectual and political development is reflected in the major themes and concerns of Mao Tsetung Thought.

Among the most important of the intellectual breakthroughs of the May Fourth period was the realization that the powerful historical forces that had collided against China since the Opium War grew out of a worldwide process of expanding capitalism. Previous generations of Chinese had looked to Western military technology, political institutions, thought, science, and culture for the source of the West's "wealth and power." But they failed to solve the paradox of why the West, which they looked to as the model for China's regeneration, seemed always to be committing aggression against its pupil. Why did the West oppose every effort to bring about fundamental change in China and instead support the social forces that sought to stem the tide of change? In the May Fourth period, influenced by Lenin's theory of imperialism, radical intellectuals for the first time linked the expanding web of international capitalism with the forces of domestic reaction. If imperialism and warlord-feudalism joined hands to rule China, obstructing its path to national regeneration, then the new revolution must mobilize the social forces that could overthrow the warlords and roll back the tide of imperialist aggression. Radical intellectuals came to believe that only through social revolution involving the masses of Chinese people could China experience its national rebirth. Thus the May Fourth period saw the beginning of the rejection of the Western capitalist model and the rise in China of revolutionary Marxism.

Li Ta-chao, the first of the May Fourth intellectuals to write on the significance of the October Revolution, played a critical role in the early attempts to adapt Marxism to the Chinese situation. Like much of his interpretation of the Marxist tradition, Li's writings on imperialism were filled with implications for China's path to revolutionary transformation. Li believed that all of the major economic changes that occurred in China following the onslaught of imperialism were imposed from the outside and that they had led to the virtual incorporation of the Chinese economy into the Western-dominated international capitalist system. He argued that the exploitation and oppression of China within this system was comparable to that of the proletariat in the advanced centers of capitalism, only much more severe. The Chinese, according to Li, suffered from both domestic and external oppressors, whereas the proletariat of the West were exploited only by their native bourgeoisie. Thus, Li contended, although the urban proletariat represented only a small percentage of the total Chinese population, China's position within the world capitalist system qualified it as a "proletarian nation." Not only was China well prepared to join the world proletarian revolution, but owing to the enormous size of its population, nearly a quarter of mankind, the Chinese Revolution would play a central role in the world revolutionary process unleashed by the October Revolution.

Li's theory of "proletarian nation" had far-reaching implications for the role which China's peasantry could play in the revolutionary process. Only domestic oppressors—"evil gentry," compradors, and bureaucrats—were excluded from the proletarian ranks, as agents of international capitalism. But even before Li formulated this theory, he had assigned to the Chinese peasantry a pivotal role in China's rebirth. In "Youth and the Villages," written in his pre-Marxist days, Li stated: "Our China is a rural nation and most of the laboring class is made up of peasants. If they are not liberated, then our whole nation will not be liberated; their sufferings are the sufferings of our whole nation; their ignorance is the ignorance of our whole nation; the advantages and defects of their lives are the advantages and defects of all of our politics."[2] After becoming a Marxist, Li continued to look to the peasantry as the single most important force in the Chinese Revolution. Veering sharply away from the classical Western Marxist tradition, which relegated peasants to petit-bourgeois status, he believed that because of China's position within the world capitalist economy, the Chinese peasantry shared with the urban proletariat the potential for proletarian consciousness. It only required the revolutionary Marxist intellectual to awaken that consciousness.

If the preconditions for proletarian revolution had been created by the impact of imperialism and if, as Li believed, the Chinese Revolution was an integral part of the most progressive trends of world history, then China could bypass the stage of capitalist economic development. Li believed that the immediate task of the Chinese Revolution was to awaken the masses and mobilize them in a revolutionary struggle against both imperialism and the domestic exploiting classes, thus ridding China in one stroke of her semicolonial, semifeudal status. Having achieved national independence, China could establish a socialist government, and with the national destiny in the hands of the producers, move directly to the stage of socialist construction.

Li's interpretation of Marxism, while taking into consideration the importance of the economic base in determining the superstructure, tended to stress the role of the human will and conscious political action in history. Thus, for Li, the question of what type of attitudes and consciousness should guide human action was critically important, so important that he tended to view ethics almost as a transhistorical social force not tied to a particular class base: "This spirit of mutual aid, this ethic, this social instinct, is able to cause human progress." Li held that "the ethics of men has been a powerful social instinct since the most ancient period of human life; there has developed in the human heart a voice of authority that down to the present day still echoes in our own hearts."[3] This aspect of Li's thought is what rooted him in the ethically oriented Chinese cultural tradition. Yet like the other new intellectuals of the May Fourth period, Li believed that the ethical principles of Confucianism could no longer serve the needs of modern China and that a new ethical system had to be created. Li's emphasis on direct political action tempered his involvement in the New Culture movement, setting him in opposition to those who believed that the creation of a new culture must precede political and social transformation. But Li did believe (as Lu Hsün did later in his life) in the importance of creating a new proletarian culture by drawing from the emerging "proletarian culture" of the West and the Soviet Union, as well as from progressive elements of traditional Chinese peasant culture.

Li did not share the intense antitraditionalism of other May Fourth intellectuals such as Lu Hsün, China's first great modern writer, whose call for creating a new culture grew out of a passionate rejection of the Confucian tradition. Lu Hsün believed that Confucian morality formed the core of China's cultural heritage. As the official ideology of the landlord class, it was used to legitimate and perpetuate a highly exploitative and oppressive social system, an "accursed place," where "we calmly burn, slaughter, rape and plunder, doing things to our fellow-countrymen which barbarians would never do to their own people."[4] The waste of human lives, the untold suffering and oppression of the masses, and the wretched, stunted lives of men and women which Lu perceived at the lower levels of Chinese society were the price for upholding Confucian morality and China's cultural heritage. "Our vaunted Chinese civilization is only a feast of human flesh prepared for the rich and mighty," Lu wrote. "And China is only a kitchen where these feasts are prepared. Those who praise China because they do not know this are excusable, but the rest deserve to be condemned forever."[5] In his first short story, "Diary of a Madman," Lu states passionately that the essence of the Confucian tradition amounts to license for cannibalism. His "madman" has a paranoiac obsession that his relatives and fellow-villagers are plotting to eat him. "How can I possibly guess their secret thoughts—especially when they are ready to eat people. . . . I recollect, in ancient times, people often ate human beings, but I am rather hazy about it. I tried to look this up, but my history has no chronology, and scrawled over each page are the words: 'Virtue and Morality.' In any case, I could not sleep, so I read half the night, until I began to see words between the lines, the whole book being filled with the two words, 'Eat People.' "[6]

Lu believed that the still pervasive influence of the Confucian world view diverted contemporary Chinese from facing up to the stark reality that confronted China. "Our sages long ago taught men: 'Avert your gaze from all that is unseemly!' "[7] Thus Chinese, rather than confronting the ravages of foreign aggression and the virtual breakdown of their society, rather than responding vigorously to the awesome tasks facing the nation, "at the crucial moment when an abuse is about to be exposed . . . hasten to declare that 'all is well,' and close their eyes."[8]

Lu condemned as a fatal national disease the obsessive concern of many, especially the old-style intellectuals, to defend the Chinese cultural heritage at the cost of perpetuating China's intellectual isolation from the world. He believed that this was yet another regressive influence of the backward-looking Confucian historical perspective. It gave rise to a deadening conservatism and stubborn refusal to adapt to new ways and new conditions for fear of "offending the ancestors." Moreover, "to boast of our ancient culture" at a time when China was facing the threat of national extinction fostered a ludicrous sense of moral superiority whereby defeats and failures could be rationalized as psychological victories for China. Thus the Chinese "contrive ingenious lines of retreat," wrote Lu Hsün. "Content to go down hill from day to day, we imagine we are advancing from glory to glory."[9]

While Lu's essays seethe with outrage at the crippling grip of Confucian tradition on Chinese intellectual and political life, his short stories show the extent to which he believed Confucian values and concepts had permeated the culture of the oppressed. They give a penetrating picture of the Chinese countryside and the lives of poor peasants at the turn of the century, revealing not so much the spirit of rebellion that emerges from Mao's report on the peasants of Hunan province, as a picture of quiet suffering, decline, and people being ground down by both material poverty and psychological oppression. Confucian morality is for Lu Hsün the opiate of the masses, for it leads them to identify with their oppressors and to take on their values; it binds them psychologically to a system of oppression that leads to their ruin; it numbs their consciousness and renders them unable to voice their true feelings, thoughts, and sufferings.

If Confucian morality represented all that was backward, repressive, and unscientific in Chinese culture, and if the whole of the Chinese cultural heritage had been poisoned by it, then the cure was to root out every vestige of the diseased culture.

The new culture, Lu believed, must define new ethical principles and provide new customs and ideas by which modern Chinese could live their lives. Its aim was to bring about the moral and spiritual regeneration of the nation, and ultimately to create a new man.

Lu called on Chinese to "break out of the cordon around us" and draw fresh inspiration and new ideas from the dynamic cultures of the world. Unlike many of the May Fourth intellectuals, however, Lu did not find inspiration in the literature of the bourgeois West. "Stories of detectives, adventurers, English ladies and African savages can only titillate the surfeited senses of those who have eaten and drunk their fill," he wrote. Instead he searched for the "insurgent" literature of oppressed people and nations, and found it in Eastern Europe and Russia. In Russian literature, he wrote, "we can see the kindly soul of the oppressed, their sufferings and struggles."[10]

While the Russian, Eastern European, and Japanese literary traditions deeply influenced Lu Hsün's literary sensibility, Lu maintained that the new culture should be Chinese in both content and form. He opposed the use of "foreign stereotypes," criticizing both westernizing intellectuals like Hu Shih and leftist intellectuals who advocated dogmatic imitation of Soviet literature and art. The new culture must be based instead on the experience of modern Chinese and give expression to their sentiments, opinions, suffering, and hope. In order to have broad popular appeal and sink roots in native soil, it must also draw from Chinese folk and traditional forms, but only in such a way as to "result in a new form, a change."[11]

From the time of his involvement in the New Culture movement in 1918 to the end of his life, Lu was primarily engaged in literary activity, giving leadership and content to China's cultural revolution. It was only toward the latter part of his life, when the logic of events convinced him that there was no other realistic path for China, that he came to accept Marxism-Leninism. Yet throughout his literary career Lu believed that his purpose in writing was to promote radical social and political change. He disagreed with those who advocated that cultural transformation must precede political and social revolution, arguing that "politics comes first, and art changes accordingly. If you fancy art can change environment, you are talking like an idealist."[12]

In Lu Hsün's vision, the regeneration of China could only come from a fundamental transformation of the lives of the masses. Without this, however revolutionary the developments in thinking among intellectuals, they were doomed to ultimate futility. Lu's short stories, written in the May Fourth period, develop this theme. They present a profoundly searching and realistic picture of the Chinese peasantry, bleak, yet not without hope. Lu shows that despite its overthrow of the Ch'ing dynasty and the creation of a façade of constitutional government, the goals, ideas, and programs of the 1911 revolution failed to sink roots in Chinese society. In "Medicine," for example, he unsparingly depicts the masses on the eve of the revolution as so locked in backwardness and superstition that a man takes the blood of a revolutionary martyr to use as medicine for his consumptive son. Lu faults the revolutionaries for having failed to go among the masses to win popular support for the revolution. The villagers in the story are indifferent: some consider the martyr a fool, some just scoff contemptuously. Even his mother does not understand his death. She is a simple, superstitious countrywoman, completely ignorant of the revolution.

The sardonic caricature of the poor peasant in Lu's famous "True Story of Ah Q," which also describes the period of the 1911 revolution, is even more unsparing. The buffoonlike Ah Q, beaten by scholar and ruffian alike, clings through thick and thin to the pathetic belief in his own superiority. When village idlers yank his pigtail and bash his head against a wall, Ah Q walks away convinced he has won a psychological victory. Priding himself on being a man of strict Confucian morality, Ah Q stands on the street corner scoffing at those who seem in any way unconventional. He detests the revolutionaries because he thinks the revolution would make life difficult for him and enjoys watching the beheading of some of them in a nearby town. Yet the satirical portrait of Ah Q does not deny his revolutionary potential. Despite his distorted consciousness, Ah Q's objective interests are tied to revolutionary change. When he observes that the local gentry are frightened by the news of the revolution, he is impressed by its power. "Finish those bastards . . . they're distasteful! hateful! . . . I would like to go over to the revolutionaries myself."[13] But in the end, Lu reveals how very far Ah Q is from a genuinely revolutionary consciousness. Ah Q, who imagines himself killing the local gentry, taking their belongings, seizing their women, embodies Lu Hsün's sober and unflinchingly realistic understanding of the Chinese masses awaiting liberation in the early twentieth century.

Lu believed that the failure of the 1911 revolution lay not so much in the limitations and primitive consciousness of peasants like Ah Q as in the inability of the revolutionaries to find a place for them in their movement. Rather than educating Ah Q, they barred him from the revolution. Thus when the revolution finally comes to the village, it brings with it no change. The local gentry and westernized intellectuals hastily join, the county officials remain in power, changing only their titles. Some "bad revolutionaries" go about cutting off people's pigtails. And when Ah Q comes to join in, he is told, "Get out!"[14]

Both Li Ta-chao and Lu Hsün believed that the role of the intellectual as the bearer of advanced consciousness was as indispensable to the revolutionary process as the involvement of the masses. But if intellectuals are to carry out their revolutionary mission and awaken the masses, if they are to transcend their own class origins and identify themselves with the cause of the oppressed, then they must themselves undergo transformation.

Anticipating Mao's call for "educated youth" to go out and settle in the countryside and hinterlands, Li appealed to the young intellectuals of the May Fourth period to leave the cities and go to the rural villages to thoroughly integrate themselves with the lives and concerns of the peasants. Li contended that "all of the awakened members of the intelligentsia ought to destroy the very concept 'intelligentsia,' throw themselves into the world of labor, and completely join together with the laborers."[15] He maintained that only after the young intellectuals had sunk roots in the countryside could they become effective leaders of the oppressed peasantry. "We need to know who these suffering people are, what kind of thing their suffering is, and the cause of their suffering. We need to think about what methods to use to eliminate their suffering."[16]

While Li Ta-chao saw the role of revolutionary intellectuals in terms of their capacity for conscious political action, Lu Hsün emphasized their role as creators of revolutionary literature and art. Lu believed that the revolutionary artist must be foremost a realist who probes deeply in society. It was not enough simply to be angry and to write searing condemnations of society. "Even those writers who merely attack the old society may do harm to the revolution unless they see abuses clearly and understand the root of the trouble."[17] Lu cautioned revolutionary artists from harboring any illusions about the nature of revolution. Otherwise when they confront the reality, which is a "bitter thing, mixed with filth and blood, not as lovely or perfect as poets think,"[18] their ideas will be shattered and they might then betray or desert the revolution. Thus revolutionary artists cannot afford to dream idly, and must write realistically about the great difficulties and suffering that the revolution will entail. Lu wrote:

> Although some dream of "food for all," others of a "classless society" or "universal equality," very few indeed dream of what is needed before building such a society: the class struggle, the White Terror, air-raids, men tortured to death, boiled capsicum poured down nostrils, electric shocks. . . . Unless men dream of these things, that better world will never materialize, no matter how brilliantly they write. It will remain a dream, an empty dream. And describing it will simply teach others to dream this empty dream.[19]

Lu argued that unless intellectuals "share the life of the revolution or keep their fingers closely on its pulse," however traumatic and bitter the experience, they will be unable to create revolutionary literature and art. He cautioned that it is easy for a "left-wing" writer to turn into a "right-wing" writer if he becomes isolated from the revolution and loses touch with social conflict. Intellectuals, Lu believed, no matter how impoverished, are by virtue of being able to afford an education still privileged members of society. Thus, drawing from their own experience, they can write about the decadence of the old society, or about the revolt of petit-bourgeois intellectuals. An intellectual "cannot do this, though, in connection with the working class and characters with which he has no contact, or he will paint a wrong picture."[20] Only by prolonged periods of living with peasants and workers, studying and analyzing their customs and traditions, might the revolutionary artist be able to write perceptively and accurately about the masses. Only then might there develop a revolutionary literature and art that portrays the life and concerns of the masses. But Lu believed a "real" people's literature would not develop until the masses themselves began to write.

Lu appealed to revolutionary intellectuals to acquire an ethic of selfless service to the people. He urged writers to overcome the illusions that they are superior beings, that their work is nobler than any other, and that when the revolution comes to power they will be able to lead a privileged life in reward for their services.

THE DEVELOPMENT OF MAO TSETUNG THOUGHT

The scope and depth of Lu Hsün's and Li Ta-chao's insight into the nature of China's condition far surpassed those of other intellectuals of the May Fourth period. They pointed to contradictions that had to be confronted if China's revolutionary objectives were to be attained. But they did not provide the concrete strategies or tactics needed to resolve them. They lived, moreover, in an intellectual world where few established intellectuals wanted to pursue a revolutionary path at all. Traditionalists were aghast at their ideas, while the majority of the new intellectuals, those educated in the modern schools, felt more at home with policies of gradual reform. The emphasis placed on the revolutionary potential of the peasants by both Li Ta-chao and Lu Hsün was left largely in abeyance in the early years of the Chinese Communist Party. Nor was this particularly surprising.

The Russian Revolution, which had inspired almost all Chinese revolutionaries, brought with it the conviction that classic European models of urban-based revolution could be applied to China as well. The peasants had risen in Russia, but it was through organizing the cities that the Bolshevik party had gained control of the nation. This vision of a revolution in which the urban proletariat comes to power in a swift and violent upheaval, generating the energies for transforming the entire country, was particularly attractive to the young, inexperienced Chinese Communist Party. Not only did they believe that the cities could more easily be organized than the peasant hinterlands, but the early members of the party—the radical students and professors of the May Fourth movement—came largely from upper-class backgrounds and were steeped in a cultural tradition that viewed the peasant masses with disdain. With few exceptions, they viewed the cities as the center of the modern world of industry, commerce, and culture which, though created and dominated by imperialism, represented all that was progressive and hopeful in China, and associated the peasantry with much that was backward and culturally inferior. This predisposition combined with the Russian example of urban insurrection to produce an even stronger bias against organizing in the countryside. Ch'en Tu-hsiu, the chairman of the Chinese Communist Party, argued that only the workers in the large industrial cities could constitute the main force of the revolution. "In a country such as China, over half the farmers are petit-bourgeois landed farmers who adhere firmly to notions of private property," he wrote. "How can they accept communism?"[21]

The leader of the historic movement of the Chinese Revolution from its urban preoccupation to the countryside was Mao Tsetung, of peasant origin himself. In relative isolation from the mainstream of party activity in the cities, he sought the methods for winning China's national liberation. "In the past, and especially at the beginning," he wrote in 1958, "all our energies were directed towards revolution, but as for how to make revolution, what we wanted to change, which should come first and which later, and which should wait until the next stage—for a fairly long time none of these questions were properly understood."[22] Through observing and participating in the peas-

ant movement in his native Hunan province, Mao's
theoretical understanding of revolutionary Marxism began
to move beyond that of his comrades in the cities to incorporate the peasantry into the forces of the Chinese Revolution. In 1925, when he returned to his home in the Hunan
countryside, Mao discovered a dramatic upsurge of peasant
unrest in the wake of the nationwide resurgence of anti-
imperialist sentiment in the May Thirtieth movement of
1925. Whereas formerly, as secretary of the Hunan Party
Committee, he had organized miners, railway workers, and
municipal employees in Changsha, he now threw himself
into establishing the early party nucleus of the peasant
movement in Hunan. "Formerly I had not fully realized the
degree of class struggle among the peasantry, but after the
May 30th Incident (1925), and during the great wave of
political activity which followed it, the Hunanese peasantry
became very militant."[23] From that time on, Mao devoted
himself to organizing the peasants, and sought to convince
his fellow party members of their enormous power and
revolutionary potential.

In 1926, as head of the newly set up peasant department
of the Communist party, Mao returned once again to
Hunan from Shanghai. He found on his arrival that the
peasant movement had grown by leaps and bounds. Excited
by what he saw in the villages during this inspection tour,
Mao wrote his famous "Report on an Investigation of the
Peasant Movement in Hunan," and urged his party to
adopt a new line on the peasant question. Out of the
devastated, famine-ridden Chinese countryside, he wrote
in 1927, "several hundred million peasants will rise like
a mighty storm, like a hurricane, a force so swift and violent
that no power, however great, will be able to hold it
back."[24] The challenge for a revolutionary party was not to
fear or doubt the capabilities of the aroused peasantry, but
to learn how to lead and organize them. "There are three
alternatives. To march at their head and lead them? To trail
behind them, gesticulating and criticizing? Or to stand in

their way and oppose them?" The gentry and landlords, Mao wrote, were naturally terrified by the peasants' revolt, which had unleashed a torrential force and would destroy the foundations of the feudal-landlord system. But there were also revolutionaries who would say that the masses were "going too far" and committing grievous "excesses." Such people, he warned, could not lead a revolution or understand what leadership of the masses requires. They could not assist the peasantry to consolidate and develop the peasant associations which Mao saw as new centers of political power. They could not help the peasants to free themselves from the feudal bonds of state, clan, and superstition, and, for women, the bond of male oppression. They could not seriously believe in the peasant demand for education and the desire to raise their cultural level. And they could not see, in the fury and terror unleashed by the peasants' revolt, values and cooperative forms of social relations upon which a new order could be built in the countryside. "Every revolutionary comrade should know that the national revolution requires a great change in the countryside," he wrote. "The revolution of 1911 did not bring about this change; hence its failure."[25]

Even while there was a growing interest in the peasant question within the Communist party by 1926, the peasant movement was always subordinated to the immediate tactics and strategies of urban insurrection by the industrial working class. To help to win peasant support for the Northern Expedition against the Peiyang warlords, which was to unify the country and roll back imperialism, Communist rural organizers intensified their propaganda work along the anticipated path of advance of the Kuomintang Expeditionary Army. But as millions of poor and middle peasants rushed to join peasant associations, and the peasant movements in Kwangtung, Fukien, and Hunan quickly gained in momentum, the young military officers in the Kuomintang army, most of whom came from landlord families, began to demand the suppression of the peasants' revolt.

Anxious to preserve the united front with the Kuomintang and under pressure from its Comintern representatives, the Communist party responded by seeking to restrain peasant "excesses."

Nevertheless, increasingly alarmed by the rapid growth of communist influence in the Kuomintang as well as by the militancy of the peasant movement, and the threat of workers' uprisings in the cities, the Kuomintang right redoubled its effort to end the alliance with the Communist party. The social classes which the KMT right represented—the landlords and the comprador bourgeoisie—opposed any radical change in either the cities or the rural areas. Despite the Communist effort to appease them, Chiang Kai-shek purged Communists from the army in 1926, before the Northern Expedition left Kwangtung. In April he further shattered the uneasy alliance with his ruthless suppression of the Communist-led workers' insurrection in Shanghai. The terror unleashed by Chiang's counterrevolution ranged far and wide. The labor movement was decimated; a wave of white terror swept through the countryside, destroying the peasant movement; large numbers of the Communist party's best cadres were put to death and others went into hiding. The attempt to complete the bourgeois-democratic revolution begun in 1911 ended in yet another failure. And though the Communists struggled desperately in the following years to rebuild their base in the cities, the forces of Kuomintang reaction allied with those of imperialism overwhelmed every attempt to revive a militant workers' movement. But out of this bloody defeat of the strategy of urban proletarian insurrection grew the recognition that it was only by tapping the revolutionary tradition of the inland peasantry, which had spawned the Taiping Revolution of half a century before, that the Chinese Revolution could develop.

Confronted after 1927 with the desperate situation of leading a revolutionary struggle in the peasant hinterlands, Mao began to work out a new strategy for the Chinese

Revolution, drawing upon the breakthroughs of the May Fourth period and deepening them through his study of Marxism-Leninism. While no Chinese revolutionary doubted after the May Fourth movement that the revolution had to be directed against both imperialism and internal feudal oppressors, it was Mao who successfully elaborated the conception of China as a "semicolonial, semifeudal" nation. This was no abstract search by Mao for a formal definition of China's plight. The revolutionaries' survival depended on their ability to correctly identify enemies and friends, to form united fronts, and to understand the weaknesses and strengths of their enemies and themselves. This required an analysis of the status of classes in Chinese society, their attitudes toward revolution, and their relation to the operations of imperialism in China. At a time when so many intellectuals despaired of finding ways to realize their hopes and aspirations, Mao was able to explain why red political and military power could exist in the hinterlands of China, the protracted nature of the coming revolutionary war, and how the Chinese Revolution could win political power.

With his characteristic ability to see weakness transformed into strength, Mao explained how semicolonialism could assist rather than retard the Chinese Revolution. Disunity and rivalry among the imperialist powers, he argued, contributed to disunity among the ruling groups in China. Red political power could survive the encirclement of a divided and therefore less menacing white rule. The forces of imperialism could successfully extend their power only in the cities and lacked centralized control over the rural hinterland. National capitalism was less able to develop in China than it would be under a single colonial rule. Thus the persistence of the "localized agricultural economy" in most regions of the country created a virtually independent alternative and a separate wellspring of popular mobilization. In view of these conditions, Mao believed that the center of gravity of the revolution could be in the countryside until the final stage when the cities would be surrounded and liberated.

Mao established a base area for the Chinese Revolution among the peasantry in the border region of Hunan-Kiangsi, but the search for how to organize rural revolution was extraordinarily difficult. The period after 1927, when the soviet base areas were constantly under siege from without, was one of great hardship and bitter struggle. Heavily outnumbered and armed with old rifles and spears, the Communists fought off five extermination campaigns launched by Chiang Kai-shek. When they left Kiangsi in 1934 and started the Long March, they had both suffered great defeats and learned invaluable lessons. Settling down two years later in Shensi province after the nearly 6000-mile trek across China's roughest terrain, Mao brought past lessons together in the new context of promoting a united front with the Kuomintang against the Japanese invaders, reaching a fresh synthesis in his developing theory of the Chinese Revolution.

Although the basic themes and line of analysis were already present in his earlier writings, in Yenan, as leader of his party, Mao formulated the methods for organizing the masses which enabled the Communist party to win victory in a peasant revolutionary war. The theoretical summation of the Yenan period is what is recognized today as the main corpus of Mao Tsetung Thought.

Mao's general theory of revolution was in many ways similar to that of Li Ta-chao; where it differed was in the great precision of Mao's class analysis, his conception of the stages of the revolution, and his explanation of why revolution was a protracted process. Like Li, Mao believed that the chief enemy confronting the Chinese people was imperialism. But imperialism could rule China only with native assistance, and the landlord class was imperialism's essential base of support. Locked in a symbiotic embrace, imperialism and feudalism colluded with each other to strangle every attempt to bring about fundamental change.

This is why the national bourgeoisie possessed a dual character, making it at best an unreliable ally of the national revolution. Fettered in its drive to develop national capitalism, the national bourgeoisie at times would enthusiastically side with the cause of anti-imperialism and anti-warlordism; but it was politically and economically "flabby," and unable to lead the bourgeois-democratic revolution. Though large in numbers, the national bourgeoisie was only a small percentage of Chinese bourgeois capital. Though few, the comprador bourgeoisie, the direct agents of imperialism in China, controlled over eighty percent of Chinese capital. They had betrayed the national revolution in 1927, actively collaborated with the landlord class on behalf of imperialism against the Chinese Revolution, and supported the Kuomintang.

Since China was a semicolonial, semifeudal country, the revolution had to be directed primarily against the landlord class, the compradors, and the forces of imperialism. Domestic capitalism was not the enemy of the revolutionary movement, as in the advanced industrial nations; the character of this phase of the Chinese Revolution, therefore, was "bourgeois-democratic." This Chinese Revolution, however, was qualitatively different from the aborted "bourgeois-democratic" revolution in 1911. Like Li Ta-chao, Mao believed that with the advent of the Russian Revolution and the proletarian-socialist movements in the West, the Chinese Revolution was part of the world revolutionary current, fighting the same enemy— international capitalism. "The victory of China and the defeat of the invading imperialists will help the people of other countries. Thus in wars of national liberation patriotism is applied internationalism."[26]

Like Li, Mao held that although the Chinese Revolution was still bourgeois-democratic, its success would not lead to the establishment of a capitalist society with the bourgeoisie playing the dominant political role. A proletarian party, he argued, would lead the revolution and eliminate the necessity of a capitalist stage. Moreover, in a world marked by war and revolution, where capitalism was clearly on the decline and socialism was the symbol of the future, it would be foolish for the Chinese to want to establish a capitalist society after the bitter struggle to overthrow feudalism and imperialism. During the stage of New Democracy, Mao stated, China would socialize the major industries, banks, and communication systems, while not immediately abolishing free enterprise in the noncritical industries and private ownership in agriculture. Anticipating his concept of "people's dictatorship," he wrote that the new state would be led by the "joint-dictatorship of the revolutionary classes," not by the bourgeoisie.

From the time of his Hunan report, Mao was unwavering in his conviction that the poor and middle peasantry were the key to the Chinese Revolution. In Yenan he continued to insist that the main force of the revolution was the peasantry and the "biggest motive force" the poor peasants. Since imperialism and the forces of reaction occupied only the major cities, revolutionaries could turn the backward villages into powerful base areas where the revolution could build up its strength for the final struggle to liberate the cities. Since the landlord class was the "main social base" of imperialist rule, the rural revolution would destroy imperialism's essential prop. Only by helping the peasants to overthrow the landlord class, Mao contended, would it be possible to build up the revolutionary forces capable of defeating imperialism. The Chinese Revolution was "essentially a peasant revolution."

> We are now living in a time when the "principle of going up into the hills" applies; meeting, work, classes, newspaper publication, the writing of books, theatrical performances—everything is done up in the hills, and all essentially for the sake of the peasants. And essentially it is the peasants who provide everything that sustains the resistance to Japan and keeps us going. . . . As every schoolboy knows, 80

per cent of China's population are peasants. So the peasant problem becomes the basic problem of the Chinese revolution and the strength of the peasants is the main strength of the Chinese revolution.[27]

Mao's study of the history of peasant uprisings, however, made him familiar with their patterns and failures. In summing up the lessons of the past, Mao wrote: "Every peasant revolution failed, and the peasantry was invariably used by the landlords and the nobility, either during or after the revolution, as a lever for bringing about dynastic change."[28] A fatal weakness of peasant uprisings was that they lacked the kind of strong and disciplined leadership that the Communist party provided the contemporary peasant revolution. While pointing to the weakness of the urban proletariat (numbering only 2.5 to 3 million), Mao believed in the historic role of the proletariat led by the Communist party. For "if the masses alone are active without a strong leading group to organize their activity properly, such activity cannot be sustained for long or carried forward in the right direction, or raised to a high level."[29] Like Lu Hsün in his depiction of Ah Q, Mao believed that simply unlocking the revolutionary impulse of the peasants through expropriating the land and possessions of the landlord was not enough. "It is only through the cadres that we can educate and guide the masses,"[30] he wrote. This demanded a fundamentally different conception of leadership from that of the bureaucratic ways of the Confucian tradition and a radical redefinition of the role of the intellectual. It required a new relationship between leader and led in which leaders merge with the masses, learn their thoughts, their demands, and their language.

The social composition of the cadres in Yenan was diverse, but few came from an urban-based proletariat. The revolutionary cadres who belonged to the Communist party either came from peasant backgrounds, joining the revolution during the Hunan-Kiangsi soviets and in the years at Yenan, or they were students and young intellectuals who either had joined the party in the Twenties, or had flocked to the wartime capital of Yenan to serve the cause of national resistance to the Japanese invasion. They came largely from privileged backgrounds, the sons and daughters of landlord, bourgeois, and petit-bourgeois families. Their dedication and enthusiasm, however, were not matched by ideological consciousness. They needed to be educated in the basic elements of Marxist theories, and at the same time to learn to break out of the mechanical and subjectivist application of Marxism-Leninism which had been rampant in the party ever since it was established in 1921.

These concerns led to the *cheng-feng* rectification campaign of 1942–1944. Through this campaign, Mao extended the cultural revolution which had begun in the May Fourth period to the conditions of waging peasant warfare in the countryside of North China. Out of it emerged a sinification of Marxism-Leninism, a theoretical formulation of the mass-line method of leadership, a theory of literature and art, and a conception of economic development.

One of the most persistent problems which Mao sought to overcome was the tendency of cadres to view the Chinese Revolution from the perspective of the urban experience of the Russian Revolution. This problem lay at the heart of his controversy with Wang Ming and the Moscow-trained "returned students," as well as with the young intellectuals from the cities who were recent converts to Marxism-Leninism. These young Marxists brought with them the viewpoint and assumptions of urban life. "They approach rural affairs from an urban viewpoint and often run their heads against a brick wall because they draw up many inappropriate plans subjectively and enforce them arbitrarily."[31]

Lacking roots in the masses, such intellectuals also tended to "parrot things foreign" and to blindly imitate the style of Soviet Marxist writing. "They become gramophones and forget their duty to understand and create new things."[32] The May Fourth movement had helped to free Chinese from the bondage of the "old dogmatism." But this "stereotyped party writing," Mao believed, still had roots deep in China's bureaucratic tradition, in the lifeless, cramped, and unimaginative essay style of the Confucian orthodoxy. This isolation from the realities of their own country meant for Mao that these cadres could not apply the universal principles of Marxism-Leninism to their concrete situation. He urged them to study the history and present-day conditions of China. "There are some who are proud, instead of ashamed, of knowing nothing or very little of our own history," he wrote. "What is particularly significant is that very few really know the history of the Communist Party of China and the history of China in the hundred years since the Opium War. Hardly anyone has seriously taken up the study of the economic, political, military and cultural history of the past hundred years."[33]

Mao's opposition to the mechanical application of Marxism-Leninism was not only that it brought great harm to the revolution. The defeats and failures of the Twenties and Thirties stood as mute testimony to this. He also felt that, just as the notion of wholesale westernization had been rejected by the peasant masses, so would they ultimately turn down the wholesale importation of Soviet Marxism. If the peasants disliked the foreign-style schools because the content of education was urban and had nothing to do with the rural situation, they would also reject Marxism-Leninism unless it became a method of coping with the problems of their daily lives. Theory ultimately had to be rooted among such people for the same reason that the Ah Q's of China had to participate in the revolution. This is what Mao meant when he spoke of "from the masses, to the masses." "Take the ideas of the masses (scattered and unsystematic) and concentrate them (through study turn them into concentrated and systematic ideas), then go to the masses and propagate and explain these ideas until the masses embrace them as their own, hold fast to them and translate them into action, and test the correctness of these ideas in such action."[34]

No revolutionary leadership, he held, even one which

has correctly identified the needs and wishes of the masses, should try to impose change upon them bureaucratically. "It often happens that objectively the masses need a certain change, but subjectively they are not yet conscious of the need, not yet willing or determined to make the change," he wrote. The party must wait until the majority of the people have become conscious of the need and are willing to carry out the change. "Otherwise we shall isolate ourselves from the masses. Unless they are conscious and willing, any kind of work that requires their participation will turn out to be formality and will fail."[35] Leaders should always allow the masses to carry out for themselves the changes that will transform their lives. " 'Draw the bow without shooting, just indicate the motions.' It is for the peasants themselves to cast aside the idols, pull down the temples to the martyred virgins, and the arches to the chaste and faithful widows; it is wrong for anybody to do it for them."[36]

This emphasis on the creative role of consciousness and human will in the dynamic relationship between leader and led brought Mao during the Yenan years to explore literature and art as agencies of revolutionary change, as Lu Hsün had done earlier. If conscious action on the part of both leaders and led is essential to the revolutionary process, then the question of consciousness is of critical importance. The idea of the self-conscious remaking of an entire culture, the definition of a new ethics and morality to guide action, and the problem of the relationship of cultural transformation to political and economic revolution were areas pioneered by the May Fourth intellectuals. It is not surprising, therefore, that Lu Hsün, more than any other thinker, influenced Mao's ideas and writings on the question of culture. No other man had explored so profoundly and contributed so much to China's cultural revolution.

Lu Hsün's influence is evident in Mao's writing from 1940 to 1942, especially in "Talks at the Yenan Forum on Literature and Art," an essay which has defined the Maoist view of the role of the intellectual and the process of literary and artistic creation up to the present day. In them he distilled Lu Hsün's major insights on the question of creating a new culture for China and added to them the mass-line perspective which had emerged so prominently during the Yenan years. Mao agreed with Lu on the political nature of literature and art and its role in molding consciousness; on the need to critically assimilate the literature and art of foreign lands; and on the need to overthrow the Confucian tradition. But Mao went further in defining the masses as the primary audience for revolutionary literature and art and in stressing the need for popularization and the importance of selectively drawing from the Chinese cultural heritage to develop a new national culture. The dominant theme, however, was Mao's conviction that writers and artists could create the new culture only by remolding themselves through fusing their thoughts and feelings with the masses and drawing from them the raw material for literary and artistic creation.

> China's revolutionary writers and artists, writers and artists of promise, must go among the masses; they must for a long period of time unreservedly and whole-heartedly go among the masses of workers, peasants, and soldiers, go into the heat of the struggle, go to the only source, the broadest and richest source, in order to observe, experience, study and analyze all the different kinds of people, all the classes, all the masses, all the vivid patterns of life and struggle, all the raw material of literature and art. Only then can they proceed to creative work. Otherwise, you will have nothing to work with and you will be nothing but a phony writer or artist, the kind that Lu Hsun in his will so earnestly cautioned his son never to become.[37]

"From the masses to the masses" underlay not only Mao's sinification of Marxism-Leninism and his views on literature and art, but his understanding of economic development as well. These principles of economic growth, like all Mao's theories, were formulated out of practical problems confronting the revolution. The highly effective Communist-led war mobilization, based on the policy of uniting with all classes to wage a war of national resistance to Japan, had brought the Japanese high command to direct a greater part of their war effort against the base areas in North China. The rapid expansion of the Eighth Route Army from its 45,000 in 1937 to 400,000 in 1940 and the spread of communist influence throughout North China and increasingly in Central China as well also greatly alarmed the Kuomintang. Following the powerful Hundred Regiments Offensive launched by the Communists in 1940, the Japanese concentrated their military efforts on the base areas in North China and carried out "mopping-up operations" and their ruthless "three-all" policy (burn all, kill all, loot all). This policy had a devastating impact, reducing the population in the base areas from a reported 44 million to 25 million. At the same time, the united front with the Kuomintang was rapidly crumbling as clashes between Kuomintang and Communist troops increased. Reeling from the combined impact of the Japanese three-all policy and the virtual destruction of the new Fourth Army by the Kuomintang, the Communists returned quickly to their policy of strategic defense as their base areas rapidly contracted and the Eighth Route Army shrunk to 300,000 soldiers. In coordination with the Japanese, the Kuomintang moved quickly to impose a tight blockade on the base areas, which caused enormous economic hardship for the resistance movement in the Shensi-Kansu-Ninghsia border regions. It was in this context that Mao developed his basic concepts of economic development.

To overcome this economic crisis, he turned once again to the energy of the masses. "The gist of this policy is to organize the masses, to mobilize and organize into a great army of labor all the available forces without exception— the people, the army, the government and other organizations and the schools—all men and women, young and old, who can contribute their labor power on a part-time or full-time basis."[38] Every effort, Mao held, must be made to link leadership to the masses, for leadership divorced from the masses could never learn how to mobilize their creative energies and initiative. The greatest threat to rapid economic development was bureaucratic methods of leadership, which he defined as an inevitable result of isolation from the masses. Mao was opposed to bureaucracy not only in the party and the army, but in government organizations as well. With the policy of "better troops and simpler administration," he called for an emptying of the bureaucracies and reassignment of cadres to production-related posts, leaving government organs with the minimum staff to carry out essential administrative tasks. This policy, combined with that of "unified leadership and decentralized management," led to a strengthening of party leadership and a far-reaching administrative decentralization. Collective and cooperative efforts were quickly developed and a spirit of self-reliance was fostered. The mobilization of all available resources and people to carry out production, Mao said, was a prerequisite for expanding the economy in the face of the Kuomintang blockade. He criticized conservative economists whose response to the economic crisis was to push for a tight fiscal policy instead. The policies which Mao developed in the wartime situation in Yenan have been the hallmark of his economic thinking.

Out of the years in Yenan emerged a style of leadership that sought to prevent any clamps being placed on the revolutionary momentum from below. Mao's commitment was to a type of development that would promote cooperative relations, bring the masses into decision making about all aspects of their daily lives, and thus unleash the creativity and resourcefulness at the local level so necessary to build a new China. Out of these years came a conviction on Mao's part that revolution was an ongoing process, entailing the combined, intertwined transformation of both the economic base and the superstructure and rooted in the profound demands for change among the Chinese masses.

UNINTERRUPTED REVOLUTION

In 1949, with the establishment of the People's Republic of China, over a century of upheaval and revolution was crowned with the attainment of national liberation. From this vantage point, the long and protracted efforts of generations of Chinese to defeat imperialism and feudalism no longer seemed a record of constant defeat. The collapse of traditional Chinese society had given birth to a revolutionary force prepared to build a new and powerful China. The Chinese people had emerged from a century of humiliation and struggle with an understanding both of China's plight and of the methods to overcome it, led by a party rich in experience. In looking back on those who had fought for so long, Mao wrote in August of 1949: "They fought, failed, fought again, failed again, fought again and accumulated 109 years of experience, accumulated the experience of hundreds of struggles—great and small, military and political, economic and cultural, with bloodshed and without bloodshed—and only then won today's basic victory."[39]

The revolution did not end, however, in 1949. Indeed, the next quarter-century was to see its continuation through a progression of mass campaigns that culminated in the Great Leap Forward of the 1950s and the Great Proletarian Cultural Revolution of the 1960s. Out of this experience came a theory of uninterrupted revolution, an explanation why even under socialist conditions revolution must continue. But like the methods employed in the bourgeois-democratic phase of the revolution, this theory emerged only after a period of protracted experimentation and revolutionary practice.

In 1949, few leaders of the Chinese Communist Party

thought of "continuing" the revolution. No model of revolution, certainly not the Russian, suggested that it be continued and deepened through a prolonged period of contention and struggle. Revolution was the act of seizing power. The building of a new society would require entirely different methods. The extent to which Mao shared this view in 1949 is not known, but certainly these assumptions were inherent in the Soviet model of socialist development which the Chinese attempted to follow in subsequent years.

There were many reasons why the Chinese turned to the Soviet Union for a model in the 1950s. It was a society which had achieved both industrialization and collectivization, key objectives of all leaders of the Communist party. It offered a model for the organization of the cities, an area where the CCP felt itself lacking in experience. At a time of intense American hostility and a U.S.-backed blockade of its coast, it was quite natural for China to lean toward the Soviet Union in defense and economic policy. Yet perhaps the most decisive factor was that in those early days it was not yet clear that there was an alternative form of socialist development, one that did not rely on élite-planned and bureaucratically administered programs of economic development which subordinated the needs of the countryside to the demands of heavy industry.

While the Chinese Communist Party seemed relatively united on the first steps of the transition toward socialism, beneath the surface were questions which became increasingly prominent in the years that followed. Was the aim of the revolution merely to build up China's "wealth and power," or was it to entail the creation of a new socialist man as well? Was a professional party, equipped to lead China's industrialization through its mastery of planning and scientific technology, the proper motivating force for building a socialist society? Or was that force the creativity of the masses, liberated by new social, political, cultural, and economic relationships?

Though lack of experience and expediency were partially

responsible for the choice of the Soviet model in the early 1950s, as the years passed it became more compelling to some Chinese leaders. The reasons for this illuminate the disputes which have shaken the Chinese Communist Party since the mid-1950s. Those who sympathized with the Soviet model or sought a more flexible adaptation of it shared its assumptions of how to build a socialist society. They saw the party leadership as the motive force for change in society and conceived that change in terms of building up the backward forces of production. All efforts, therefore, were to concentrate on production, using similar managerial, motivational, and organizational means to those used in Russia and with the same consequences—privileged élites, bureaucratic hierarchy, and extensive reliance on individualistic material rewards. Once the traditional class forces had been defeated in the rural areas and the cities, it was reasoned, the transition to socialism could begin. Class struggle would end.

Those who sympathized with the Soviet model quickly turned their back on the legacy of Yenan. They dismissed it as the tactics of guerrilla war, irrelevant to the problems of building a modern industrial society. They insisted that a large industrial base was necessary to create the mechanized agriculture required for collectivization. Consequently, the mass line in the rural areas was anachronistic. The educational methods explored in Yenan, the attempts to relate intellectuals to the masses, were clearly inappropriate. Underlying all this was a conviction that the energy capable of transforming society came not from a spirited, actively participating population, but from the party, with its industrial, organizational, and scientific techniques.

In 1949, Mao had justified the "leaning to one side" and the reliance on the Soviet model. He warned that the task ahead was enormous, that only a *basic* victory had been won. "Our past work is only the first step in a long march of 10,000 li,"[40] he wrote—"a brief prologue to a long drama."[41] Governing the entire country was a completely new experience for the party. "We shall soon put aside some of the things we know well and be compelled to do things we don't know well. This means difficulties."[42] It is possible that at this time Mao had concluded that many of the methods the CCP developed in coming to power were no longer adequate or appropriate. "From 1927 to the present the center of gravity of our work has been in the villages— gathering strength in the villages, using the villages in order to surround the cities and then taking the cities. The period for this method has now ended."[43] Yet Mao never wavered in his conviction that the task of the revolution was to transform the life of China's peasants, to break the hold of material poverty and old customs. "The serious problem is the education of the peasantry," he wrote in 1949. Industrial and technological progress was essential to overcome rural backwardness. Yet for Mao, though the peasants needed assistance from the cities, they were not inferior to them. They, as well as the workers, were capable of being organized, of confronting their immediate problems, and of coping creatively with their lives. This belief accounts for much of his conflict with other party leaders in subsequent years and his profound disenchantment with the Soviet model of socialism.

In evaluating the application of the Soviet model in the 1950s, Mao began to see dangerous implications that threatened the revolutionary transformation of the nation. The growing gap between town and countryside reinforced ingrained habits of looking down on those engaged in manual labor, especially peasants, an attitude that in turn nurtured bureaucratic and élitist methods of leadership. Mao feared that the growing reliance on technical development at the expense of social revolution would exacerbate the very contradictions that had to be overcome to transform the rural areas. The diverse problems which figured in Mao's growing uneasiness included the role of contradictions in a socialist society, the nature of democratic centralism in the operation of the Communist party, the relationship of heavy industry to agricultural development, and the balance between coastal and inland development.

Yet it would be a mistake to describe Mao as having a clearly worked out alternative to the Soviet model during these years. Nor did he view the tendencies emerging in the early Fifties with anything approaching the sense of alarm he was to feel in later years. The differences within the party were often ones of emphasis, not of principle; of tactics and strategy rather than of the general line. Disputes still seemed to take place within the shared conception of building a socialist society.

The differences became more evident in July 1955 when Mao supported the acceleration of agricultural collectivization. In doing this, he was returning to the experience of working among the peasants that had come to practical and theoretical fruition in Yenan. In his editing of *Socialist Upsurge in China's Countryside,* as in his Hunan report more than a quarter-century before, he found that he had to convince a doubting party of the capabilities, creativity, and latent force for change that existed among the peasantry. Mao saw a great revolutionary movement in progress at the grass roots led by many of the local rural cadres who had come out of the period of land reform. "It is as if a raging tidal wave has swept away all the demons and ghosts," he wrote.[44] Yet this promising upsurge of creativity at the base was met by the constant criticism, carping complaints, and doubts of timid bureaucrats. "Some of our comrades are tottering along like a woman with bound feet, and constantly complaining, 'You're going too fast.' "[45]

The difficulties of carrying out rural transformation, however, were not simply a result of bureaucracy or the tenacious opposition of the old class forces. There is a practice, Mao warned, "prevalent almost to the point of being universal: right opportunists in the Party, working hand in glove with the forces of capitalism in society, are preventing the broad masses of poor and middle peasants from taking the road to the formation of cooperatives."[46]

This was the first appearance of a theme which re-emerged in Mao's thinking on the Great Leap Forward and crystallized in the conception of the "capitalist roader" during the Great Proletarian Cultural Revolution.

It was in the complicated period of struggle and conflict that led from the upsurge in the countryside to the Great Leap Forward that the vision of a new course for the development of China began to take shape. For the first time, the idea of revolution as an uninterrupted, continuous process appeared, in the context of creating the communes. "China's 600 million people," Mao wrote in 1958, "have two remarkable peculiarities: they are, first of all, poor, and secondly, blank. That may seem like a bad thing, but it is really a good thing. Poor people want change, want to do things, want revolution. A clean sheet of paper has no blotches, and so the newest and most beautiful words can be written on it. . . ."[47] Mao made this notion of the latent energy of the masses the basis for his formulation of a step-by-step, stage-by-stage deepening of the revolution. In so doing, he built upon the conceptualizations of the Yenan period and insisted on finding new ways to apply them to the building of a socialist society. He synthesized the lessons of Yenan—self-reliance, decentralization, and the involvement of the masses directly in all aspects of social activity. For the first time, Mao began to speak of successive steps in the revolution after the initial victory of the establishment of a socialist state. In 1949, Mao had spoken of a continuity and tradition in the Chinese Revolution since 1840, a series of struggles through which experience had been gradually accumulated. Now he described the revolution in the rural areas after 1949 also as a deepening, continuous process, pointing to its stages: from mutual aid teams and low-level cooperatives, to high-level cooperatives, finally, to the communes.

"One revolution must follow another, the revolution must continually advance,"[48] he urged. This did not mean, however, a reckless pushing ahead. Mao showed how each step in the development of socialism after 1949 had been achieved against the opposition of various privileged groups. There were those who doubted the ability of the masses; those who had fixed notions of industrial management and party leadership; and those who simply feared the uncharted course of revolution, its openness to experimentation and the risks of failure. To Mao, an understanding of why these groups had emerged to oppose the revolution was inseparable from the recognition of its stage-by-stage nature as a process which constantly sought to give the masses a greater and greater role in the life of the country.

None of this was easy. Indeed, however much the Great Leap Forward drew on the past, it was also a leap into an unknown future. It was an attempt to extend within a new context and on an enormous scale throughout Chinese society the antibureaucratic mass line formed in Yenan. This meant reconsidering the role of education and of intellectuals, finding ways to bring worker participation into factory management, and profoundly reassessing the functions of the cities. These years saw a shift from centralized to decentralized decision making, from one-man factory management to greater roles for the party committees and greater initiative by the workers, from the extensive use of material incentives to increased reliance on social responsibility. China began to "walk on two legs" as rural and local industry using traditional or intermediate technology was developed along with heavy industry.

Though much was accomplished by the Great Leap Forward in laying an invaluable groundwork for later changes, the country was wracked by failures and difficulties—crop failures, flood damage, drought, the abrupt withdrawal of Soviet technicians and assistance. Serious mistakes had also been made in the implementation of the Great Leap policies, exacerbated no doubt by divisions within the leadership. The "three hard years" which followed, 1959–1962, were a time of retrenchment and consolidation. They were also a time when division between the leaders of the Communist party sharpened. What were once tactical conflicts now began to be differences of principle. In the years after 1959, critics of the Great Leap Forward within the party began to claim that it was not the implementation of the policy but its very conception which was responsible for its failures. Though some of them had supported it at the time, they now concluded that the methods of mass mobilization, the legacy of Yenan, were no longer relevant. Experimental projects in education, factory management, and commune organization were largely set back. This did not result in a full swing back to the rigid application of the Soviet model. Agriculture was still more heavily emphasized; small- and medium-sized industry continued to grow in the hinterlands.

Nonetheless, the methods evolved in these years to restore the economy had unmistakable resemblances to the Soviet system of administration. The Liuists believed that development was possible only through orderly, bureaucratic methods. Human motivation, accordingly, was most effectively brought into play within an organization which provided both individualistic material incentives and an intricate system of rules and regulations. Without such strict regulations, the people would be unproductive. They would work hard only if they knew their tasks and were adequately supervised. From this perspective, the idea of relying on mass initiative to create enthusiastic participation in production or mass supervision of local cadre work seemed utopian. Technical experts were needed to solve the problems of production. Party cadres must run administration. Liu believed that the dangers of bureaucratization were to be found less at the top levels than in the corruption of local cadres and the cultural backwardness of the masses.

As these policies and methods began to take shape in the early 1960s, Mao became greatly alarmed. In 1962, he told his colleagues that "class differences do exist in socialist countries and class struggle undoubtedly exists."[49] In analyzing the lessons of the Great Leap and the response of so many of his associates to it, Mao no longer focused on the old classes as the primary threat to the continuation of the revolution. New groups had come to the fore, threatening to block the revolution through their positions in the party and the bureaucracy. The right-wing opportunist current Mao had spoken of in the 1950s during the upsurge in the countryside had emerged full-blown as revisionism, just as in the Soviet Union. "Right-wing opportunism in China should be renamed," he said in 1962. "It should be called Chinese revisionism."[50] As Mao saw it, conflicts within the party were reaching the point where they entailed different class interests. He warned in 1963 that underlying differences in principle and work style were becoming so acute that China's Marxist-Leninist party would soon be a "revisionist party or a fascist party." Unless the party was committed to developing methods to break these tendencies, a new privileged class would emerge.

But how could a new privileged class arise in a socialist society and gain access to power at the very heart of the Communist party? What methods were appropriate to deal with such a problem? It was to take Mao more than a decade to work this out theoretically. In the years before the Great Proletarian Cultural Revolution, as the conflict within the party leadership intensified, he sought to understand the dangers facing the Chinese Revolution by studying the Soviet Union as a "negative experience." He analyzed the implications of the Russian emphasis on economic development as the basis for social transformation and the bureaucratic methods it ultimately produced. Such a system quite logically entailed the extensive use of material incentives, the existence of vast differences in income, and a rigid hierarchy of political control. Convinced that their methods were economically rational and scientific, the new Russian élite could hardly be expected to launch revolution on ideological, cultural, or political fronts. Such campaigns were predicated on the creative participation of the masses, which was suppressed in Russia.

The lessons Mao drew from the Soviet Union were consistent with the view of revolution he had advocated since the 1920s. Just as in Hunan and Yenan he had insisted that the revolution arouse the fullest potential of the masses, he now urged that even under conditions of socialism, economic change must be accompanied by thoroughgoing revolution on all fronts. The productive forces alone were utterly inadequate to solve the problems which the Chinese Revolution had faced for generations. The Soviet system of high salaries for a few had to be abolished in China. The gap between the incomes of the leadership of the party, the government, the enterprises, and the rural communes and the incomes of the masses of the people must be rationally and gradually narrowed. Continuous efforts must be made to increase the involvement of the poor and lower middle peasants in the affairs of their own communities, in the organization of their schools, in the management of the commune and the investment of its resources. Workers must be brought more and more into the operations of the factories. Masters of their own productive destiny, the workers and peasants would perform well, find effective forms of organization, and create new leaders from their midst. The greatest danger to the revolution comes from above, Mao concluded on the eve of the Great Proletarian Cultural Revolution, from a leadership that turned its back on the principles and values of the revolution. He called these leaders "capitalist roaders," and warned that they would find a ready reception among various groups and interests in society.

Mao saw the immediate task of the Great Proletarian Cultural Revolution as the removal of these capitalist roaders. But its long-term aim was to promote the new proletarian world view demanded at this critical juncture in China's revolutionary history.

Indeed, cultural revolution has been emphasized at all

pivotal moments in the history of the revolution when the Chinese took stock of past experiences to gain an understanding of the alternatives confronting them. The May Fourth movement led to a conscious espousal of revolution to overcome China's plight. The *cheng-feng* movement in the 1940s summarized the experience of two decades and consolidated the foundations of Chinese Marxism.

The Great Proletarian Cultural Revolution was the summing up of the experience of socialist construction since 1949. It became necessary when Mao recognized that socialism cannot develop automatically through economic and social changes, that powerful spontaneous tendencies toward capitalism exist in a socialist society and must be consciously fought at all levels. The struggle to build a proletarian world view to counter bourgeois consciousness became the hallmark of the Great Proletarian Cultural Revolution.

Out of the Cultural Revolution came the theory of "continuing the revolution under the dictatorship of the proletariat" which for the first time addressed the growth of new classes in socialist society. Revisionism and opposition to a continuing revolution were no longer understood as mere remnants of old values and old classes. Retrogressive forces were seen to spring as well from the social system in its present stage of development. It was recognized that a developing socialist society cannot abolish immediately all the inequalities of the past. The hierarchical division of labor continues to exist and will continue to be reproduced in enterprises and governmental organizations.

Mao's ultimate aim, like that of his revolutionary predecessors, is to overcome the three great contradictions in Chinese society—between manual and mental labor, between city and countryside, and between workers and peasants. This is a process that will take generations. Inequalities will continue to exist long into the future, as will social groups with interests to protect or promote. Uninterrupted revolution is thus not a process of automatic advance. The obstacles are great and the course is uncharted. At times it will be slow, at times fast, and always there will be the dangers of failure and backsliding. The problem, as Mao speaks of it today, is to understand the contradictions as essentially between bourgeois right and morality, and proletarian consciousness. But revolution must continue, for only through struggle can the contradictions in China be confronted and a better society created.

Victor Nee
James Peck

NOTES

We are grateful for the criticisms and suggestions of the following people: Sam Noumoff, Moss Roberts, Theda Skocpol, Dian Smith, and Ernest Young.

1. Lu Hsün, Preface to "Nahan," in *Lu Hsün ch'üan-chi* (Peking, 1973), 1:274.
2. Li Ta-chao, "Ch'ing-nien yü nung-tsun," in *Li Ta-chao hsüan-chi,* pp. 146–7.
3. Li Ta-chao, "Wu-chih pien-tung yü tao-te pien-tung," in Shih Tsün, *Chung-kuo chin-tai ssu-hsiang-shih ts'an-k'ao tzu-liao chien-pien* (Peking, 1957), p. 1120.
4. Lu Hsün, "Ma-shang chih jih-chi," in *Lu Hsün ch'üan-chi,* 3:318.
5. Lu Hsün, "Pi-man hsia teng," in *Lu Hsün ch'üan-chi,* 1:201.
6. "K'uang-jen jih-chi," in *Ibid.,* p. 281.
7. Lu Hsün, *Selected Works of Lu Hsün* (Peking, 1964), 2:185.
8. *Ibid.,* p. 186.
9. *Ibid.*
10. Lu Hsün, "Wen-chih tzu wen ê-chong zhu," in *Lu Hsün ch'üan-chi,* 5:55–58.
11. Lu Hsün, *Selected Works,* 4:38.
12. Lu Hsün, *Selected Works,* 3:45.
13. Lu Hsün, "Ah Q cheng-chuan," in *Lu Hsün ch'üan-chi,* 1:395–96.
14. *Ibid.,* p. 405.
15. Li Ta-chao, cited in Maurice Meisner, *Li Ta-chao and the Origins of Chinese Marxism* (Cambridge, Mass., 1967), p. 88.
16. Li Ta-chao, "Hsien-tai ch'ing-ning huo-tung ti fang-hsiang," in *Li Ta-chao hsüan-chi,* p. 161.

17. Lu Hsün, *Selected Works,* 3:125.
18. Lu Hsün, "Tui-yu tso-i, tso-chia lien-meng ti i-chien," in *Lu Hsün ch'üan-chi,* 4:239.
19. Lu Hsün, *Selected Works,* 3:125.
20. *Ibid.,* p. 186.
21. Ch'en Tu-hsiu, *Hsin Ch'ing Nien,* no. 4 (1924), p. 22, cited in *Mao Tse-tung,* Stuart Schram (New York, 1966), p. 70.
22. Mao Tsetung, "On Democratic Centralism," in *Chairman Mao Talks to the People,* ed. Stuart Schram (New York, 1974), p. 173.
23. Edgar Snow, *Red Star Over China* (New York, 1961), p. 160.
24. Mao Tsetung, *Selected Works of Mao Tse-tung* (Peking, 1965), 1:23.
25. *Ibid.,* p. 27.
26. Mao Tsetung, *Selected Works,* 2:196.
27. *Ibid.,* p. 366.
28. *Ibid.,* p. 309.
29. Mao Tsetung, *Selected Works,* 3:118.
30. *Ibid.,* p. 83.
31. *Ibid.,* p. 190.
32. *Ibid.,* p. 20.
33. *Ibid.,* p. 19.
34. *Ibid.,* p. 119.
35. *Ibid.,* p. 186.
36. Mao Tsetung, *Selected Works,* 1:46.
37. Mao Tsetung, *Selected Works,* 3:82–88.
39. *Ibid.,* p. 153.
39. Mao Tsetung, *Selected Works,* 4:426.
40. *Ibid.,* p. 422.
41. *Ibid.,* p. 374.
42. *Ibid.,* p. 422.
43. *Ibid.,* p. 363.
44. Mao Tsetung, ed., *Socialist Upsurge in China's Countryside* (Foreign Languages Press, 1957), p. 160.
45. Mao Tsetung, "On the Question of Agricultural Cooperation" (Foreign Language Press, 1955).
46. Mao Tsetung, ed., *Socialist Upsurge in China's Countryside,* p. 159.
47. Mao Tsetung, quoted in *The Political Thought of Mao Tse-tung,* ed. Stuart Schram (New York, 1969), p. 352.
48. Mao Tsetung, "Speech at Chengtu: The Pattern of Development," in *Chairman Mao Talks to the People,* ed. Stuart Schram, p. 94.
49. Mao Tsetung, "Speech at the Tenth Plenum of the Eighth Central Committee," in Schram, *Chairman Mao Talks to the People,* p. 189.
50. Mao Tsetung, "Speech at the Tenth Plenum," in Schram, *Chairman Mao Talks to the People,* p. 192.

REVOLUTION VERSUS MODERNIZATION AND REVISIONISM: A Two-Front Struggle

James Peck

For much of the last quarter-century, the world's two superpowers have reacted hostilely toward China's revolutionary transformation. Both Russians and Americans portrayed the Great Leap Forward and the establishment of the rural communes in the late 1950s as economic madness. Both ridiculed the Great Proletarian Cultural Revolution in the 1960s as irrational. Neither could seriously entertain any conception of the Chinese Revolution as a continuous, deepening process leading toward radically new ways of organizing society and motivating people.

The perspectives on the Chinese Revolution and Mao Tsetung Thought created by American and Russian government officials and intellectuals are deeply rooted in the attitudes each brought with them. As with any outlook or ideological position, much is revealed about the values and assumptions of its formulators. What they emphasize, what they ridicule, and how they do it are shaped by various historical, ideological, and social traditions.

The United States emerged from World War II as the center of the international capitalist system. Ever since, numerous government spokesmen and intellectuals have justified and analyzed America's global role through "modernization theory." To these Americans, the United States was the champion of anti-imperialism; "self-determination" was a progressive way to reorganize a "developing" world after the collapse of the European colonial system. In this new world, there were certain prescribed ways to develop and as the most modern nation, America was in a privileged position to know them and thus to help others. American-guided "nation-building," foreign "aid," the meaning of "modernity" itself, are all aspects of an ideology of "modernization" deeply rooted in the needs of empire and the prevailing values and beliefs of postwar America. The People's Republic of China and the Chinese Revolution are to this day still analyzed largely through its assumptions.

As Washington saw itself the center of the capitalist world, so Moscow saw itself the center of the socialist world, and considered its ways universal. In the late 1950s, as American-Russian détente grew, Russian-Chinese relations deteriorated. Like all empires historically, Russia thought that other nations should follow its "rational" methods, and spoke of the "irrationality" of the Chinese when they departed from these. The Russian perspective on the Chinese Revolution and the arguments they use are often politically expedient. Yet criticizing another nation's revolution is perhaps the surest way of revealing what are considered the important qualities in one's own. How the Russians describe the Chinese Revolution reveals a set of assumptions about bureaucracy, mass participation in decision making, and the role of intellectuals and experts grounded in a view of their own revolution.

In 1949, the Chinese, having stood up against Western and Japanese imperialism, looked to Russia for alternatives to discredited capitalist ways. Through planning and heavy industry, the Russians argued and many Chinese believed, Russia had successfully challenged the anarchistic and uncontrolled forces of capitalism and imperialism, industrialized and collectivized agriculture ("socialism in one country"), and triumphed against the Nazi holocaust. The very existence of Russia at that time reduced for China the pressure of capitalist encirclement and provided a storehouse of socialist experience.

Sixteen years after Liberation, the Great Proletarian Cultural Revolution was launched partly to shatter what remained of China's reliance on the Soviet model. Yet underlying this seemingly striking shift in China's development was an ideology that had grown out of a century of revolutionary struggle—what Mao in the late 1950s spoke of as "uninterrupted revolution" and the Chinese today call "continuing the revolution under the dictatorship of the proletariat." Like modernization theory and the Soviet conception of socialism, it is an ideology, a way both of understanding and of justifying certain social goals and the methods appropriate to realize them. What the Chinese mean by uninterrupted revolution and why so many Russians and Americans attack it are the central questions of this essay.

AMERICAN MODERNIZATION THEORY

In 1945 the United States stood at the center of the world. Its technology and science unsurpassed, its economic strength unequaled, its hopes and visions global, America abruptly emerged as the most powerful nation in a charred and leveled world. Yet America's leaders were uneasy about the future. The specter of revolution, civil war, and chaos haunted them everywhere overseas. Europe was decimated. Russia's armies were in Eastern Europe, and local Communist parties were strong in Western Europe. Throughout the rest of the world the conclusion of the war set in motion a process of social upheaval and decolonialization that was to become the most profound transformation of the postwar period.

Domestically, the fear of a future economic crisis gripped practically every leader of the Roosevelt and Truman administrations. As the ghost of Munich haunted Washington's foreign-policy corridors, so did the shadows of the Great Depression darken the outlook of those preoccupied with the American economy. American officials feared that the peace so many fought for might result once again in a crisis of capitalism. Upheaval abroad and possible economic depression at home required policies capable of dealing with both at the same time.

The international economic crisis of the 1930s dealt a shattering blow to the American economy. The United States found its role in the collapsing world market system rapidly contracting. As the Depression accentuated the division of the world into increasingly self-sufficient trading blocs, the largest centering on the British sterling area, America's share of world trade plummeted by almost half. A negative balance of trade lasted for most of the 1930s. Vast agricultural surpluses found no markets. Trading zones threatened to tie up critical raw materials essential for a deficient American economy. In the view of many New Dealers, this destruction of the international economic system was a prime cause of the rise of fascism and militarism in Germany and Japan and their policies of economic nationalism.

By itself, the New Deal offered no solution to the economic disaster of the 1930s. The rough edges of depression were smoothed, but neither a process of "normal recovery" nor governmental measures had restored the system's health. Before the onset of massive, war-induced spending, some nine million people were unemployed; the temporary upswing of the economy after 1933 ended with the sharp recession of 1938. Amidst the collapse of the world financial and commercial system in the 1930s, the New Deal offered sometimes sweeping but essentially defensive domestic measures to shore up American capitalism and to alleviate the suffering of some of the hardest-hit victims.

The reform of a ferociously nationalistic world racked by depression, war, and revolution became for the economic leaders of the Roosevelt administration an absolute precondition for the long-term prosperity of the United States. Franklin Roosevelt's vision of the postwar world has often been interpreted as an extension of his New Deal to the world at large. More accurately, it was an answer to the New Deal's weakness at home. The way to counter economic depression and possible social turmoil at home was to restructure the capitalist world system through the "international" institutions and needs of a globe-spanning American imperialism.

The scope and depth of the debate during the war over the new economic order was immense, but almost without exception government spokesmen agreed that the world financial system had to be restructured, trading blocs and financial barriers eliminated. The challenge was to rapidly raise America's share of world trade, to maintain the high wartime profits, to provide markets for American goods and farm products, to obtain needed raw materials, and to utilize a labor force temporarily absorbed in the military services and the defense industries. This link between the transformation of the world economy, American exports, the availability of cheap raw materials, and full employment was stated with the utmost clarity by American officials. What the United States required were foreign markets in which to sell the products pouring out of its factories, the materials and cheap oil to fuel these factories, and the competitive edge against rivals.

Two developments were of crucial importance in America's attempt to transform world capitalism. Domestically, the New Deal and the war had created a system of executive and bureaucratic power capable of running a global empire. From this powerful base, those "internationalists" committed to restructuring world capitalism gained a distinct advantage over their domestic critics. Internationally, the war left Britain broke, its sterling bloc vulnerable to American pressure. Germany and Japan, the two industrial powers in their respective parts of the world, were defeated, occupied, and largely subject to an American-directed transformation of their economies. Russia was still economically weak and faced with the immense task of rebuilding. And the old colonial empires were crumbling.

The most impressive ideological achievement as America set out to build a new capitalist world order was the speedy dressing of its vision in the garb of universal order and benevolent self-sacrifice. This task needed, among other things, a battery of thoughtful planners and scholars, funded by the government itself, to prove that the emperor was indeed well dressed and a presentable sight for the people to look at. Especially needed was a new theory to replace the "white man's burden" and the *mission civilatrice,* something more suitable to "postcolonial" times.

What the planners and scholars developed was an "international" American world view. Modernization theory was trumpeted by its formulators as a new, progressive way to transform the poor and backward nations of the world. Traditional European colonialism, modernization theorists argued, relied largely on feudal and reactionary groups, thus ensuring a coalition of all but the most reactionary in the fight against it. The extension of spheres of influence and colonial possessions at the end of the nineteenth century had transformed capitalism into a world system, but one dangerously torn by rivalry among the colonialist powers and the bitter antagonism between feudal-reactionary forces and progressives groups in the colonies themselves. The emergence of a native bourgeoisie, the beginnings of a proletariat, the awakening of national consciousness, and the spread of movements for independence were the historic results of the traditional policies of colonialism and European imperialism.

How to cope with this new situation was the problem modernization theorists set for themselves. For after 1945 they recognized that colonialism could hardly stem the tide of revolutionary change or hope to channel the demands for radical change. That was to be the task of reformist élites operating within the newly restructured international capitalist system. These were the leaders, it was argued, who could reform their nations while facing west, men who could gradually build their nations through trade, aid, and foreign investment. Because American power was committed to political independence and sympathetic to the attack on feudalism, many of the national bourgeoisie could respond with enthusiasm. By so doing, any alliance between the revolutionaries and the "reformists" could be broken, and massive American support given to those committed to a path between feudal reaction and revolutionary transformation. What turned out to be basically new about modernization theory, therefore, was its class base and its ideological wrapping of capitalist assumptions. In essence it was the ideological formulation of the needs and demands of American capitalism as it entered the stage of global American imperialism.

It is interesting to note how modern even the word "modernization" is. The term was not widely used until it was publicly associated with the goals of American foreign policy in the Point Four Program in 1949. Its quick and widespread use thereafter is testimony to its success in creatively explaining America's new global role in the Third World. Traditional imperialism had used the language of power, conflict, and exploitation—empire was empire, conquest was conquest. The conquered, it was often argued, were probably better off living under the rule of the civilized than left to themselves. Modernization theory, however, spoke of international order and universal processes of worldwide "development" and foreign aid. It argued that American power, manifest after 1945 in military bases and nuclear might, was unique in its nonexploitative quality. Its focus was presented as not self-serving but international. The international organizations America created—the United Nations, the International Monetary Fund, the World Bank—would simply help overcome the chaos of global war and serve as regulators of a new world order that would enable all free nations to develop peacefully.

To a growing number of American theorists, government officials, and non-Western leaders, such views seemed a refreshing and progressive alternative for a world already devastated by two world wars. Such views also constituted the most sophisticated formulation internationally of the ideology of the New Deal. The essence of the New Deal ideology was that liberal spending through government-created and -administered programs would preserve order and security, and thus the fundamentals of American capitalism. Aid to the poor nations after 1945 would be similar to social-welfare programs within the United States. It would give those nations security to overcome chaos and thus prevent them from becoming revolutionary. They would be drawn inextricably into a revived world market system and, in the process, they would become more re-sponsible—just as American labor unions had drawn in some of the poor in the 1930s and then demonstrated their responsibility during the war. If you help the Western-inclined élites of underdeveloped nations to modernize their societies, and if you urge reforms that undercut the appeal of revolutionaries, and draw such nations into the interna-tional marketplace, then revolutionary solutions and com-munism will lose their appeal. It was, in essence, the Freud-plus-Santa-Claus theory of foreign relations: Persuade countries that underdevelopment is *sui generis* to a society rather than sustained by a world system; then portray a benevolent, charitable United States bestowing aid and technical assistance.

In this new world system, the role of "modernizing élites" was seen as pivotal. With the collapse of their colonial masters, they were now described as the conveyors of modern ways to their backward peoples. Still somewhat tradition-bound themselves and faced with the awesome task of over-coming archaic traditions, especially among the peasants, these élites were portrayed as needing all the aid and assis-tance America could provide.

This conclusion, however, posed a most painful dilemma for modernization theorists. As they saw it, the modernizing élites had no choice but to adapt the universal techniques of industry, science, technology, and administrative efficiency historically developed in the West; yet these Western methods created excruciatingly difficult problems of national identity, acute psychological and cultural traumas. Rebellion in the form of anti-American or anti-imperialist rhetoric was understandable, modernization theorists often admitted; but it was nonetheless a most regrettable and extremely dangerous flight from reality into emotionalism and xenophobic nationalism. It often led to a search for ideological and simplistic answers, which the Communists were all too ready to provide. Thus the dilemma: how to treat the various emotionally or culturally distraught élites before they ended up in the communist straitjacket.

No theme is more pervasive in modernization literature than the psychocultural problems of Third World nations. If modern American ways are rational, how can opposition to them be other than fundamentally irrational? It was assumed that industrialization and technological sophistication require strict organizational hierarchy within which a few lead while the less able, less knowledgeable, and less well paid obey; that modern society is incompatible with a radical egalitarianism and with an increasing integration of man's manual and mental capabilities; that men are largely motivated by self-interest rather than the collective good; that development requires the fullest possible integration into the international capitalist system rather than self-reliance. Just as America was the center of the capitalist world after 1945, so were its industrial methods made the center of modernization theory. No Chinese ever meant quite so much when speaking of China as the Middle Kingdom.

Such confidence in the progressive nature of American power rested upon a consensus about America formed by the early 1940s (especially among liberals) and then enshrined during the war against fascism. Modernization theory could hardly have flourished earlier when doubts about capitalism were widespread. As the New Deal became more and more idealized, it justified a growing optimism about America's future world role. What was once doubted became unchallenged orthodoxy. Serious intellectual questioning in the early 1930s of the causes of the Great Depression in terms of the chaos of capitalism, the anarchy of the marketplace, and the breakdown of institutions gave way by the end of the decade to growing emphasis upon the need for order, the dangers of insecurity, and the value of social control. Earlier calls for new ways of organizing industry and agriculture led only to regulation of excesses in order to preserve fundamentals. Economic recovery, not the nature of capitalism, became the preoccupation. For liberals especially, this involved support for the centralization of power in the executive branch, a faith in the presidency, and confidence in the beneficence of large national bureaucracies.

The progressive change that the New Deal came to symbolize at home and in modernization abroad was predicated upon order and administrative authority. In time this reliance on administration and regulation, on bureaucracy and the technical leadership it required, on the interpretation of political issues as technical questions, on an extraordinary expansion of the state's role in economic and social processes was widely preferred to any mass political movement—whether from the right or the left, fascist or communist.

Paralleling these changes was a significant shift in domestic attitudes toward the quality of American life. In the early 1930s, amidst deepening depression, competition and acquisitiveness were often seen as eroding the nation's social foundation. The quality of life under capitalism seemed to offer men no sense of community or common experience. Even though people's attitudes remained individualistic, some argued that society had grown more corporate and interdependent, and thus a new view of man as an inherently social being and new forms of community were essential.

Yet by the end of World War II the feeling that American life was too fragmented, too competitive and individualistic was aborted. Instead there was more a passionate recommitment to existing values than the creation of an alternative ethic—a sanctification of the old liberal values as the American way. If, in the early 1930s, intellectual debates often centered on socialism versus capitalism, by the end of the decade they had shifted to democracy versus fascism. The shift was important. The former required serious questioning about America; the latter served to feed a manichaean division of the world into good and evil.

Of course, not all the earlier concerns were cast aside. The feeling of individual powerlessness in the face of large and impersonal institutions, the view of work as a source of anomie, the dangers of subordinating life to the imperatives of moneymaking remained important concerns. But they were stripped of the widespread assumption that the purpose of social revolution "was to create a new man as well as new institutions"—an assumption that had given that special fervor and intensity to those discussions in the early 1930s.[1] The loss of such belief led after World War II to innumerable criticisms of revolutionary attempts to create a new man or a new society abroad. The United States came to be portrayed as the "arsenal of democracy," the only viable model for efficient and orderly change.

Most of the modernization theorists who later became prominent in sociology, economics, history, political science, and comparative politics emerged from the growing numbers of trained technicians and specialists needed to win the Allied war effort. Large numbers joined the OSS, military intelligence groups, or civilian advisory groups to the government. This left them more inclined to adopt the role of official spokesmen in a national cause, to combine their views of America's postwar role with a comfortable relationship with the government. The rapidly changing nature of the university and the availability of massive foundation and government funding enhanced their postwar emergence as a privileged élite. They became the often tough-minded tacticians of anticommunist diplomacy and were an indispensable font of ideology in an increasingly bureaucratic and managerial empire. In return for their "expertise," they were given a new status and new pretensions and were becoming the well-adjusted servants of the modern American empire.

From this group came the founders of the major research centers at the élite universities—Harvard, Columbia, Berkeley—first, in the 1940s, on Russia, Eastern Europe, and communism; later, in the 1950s, on China, Japan, and Asia. Though their analysis of the Chinese Revolution provides only a window to postwar history, it is nonetheless a most revealing one. For at the very moment that America's global position was being consolidated in the late 1940s, the success of the Chinese Revolution challenged every major assumption underlying America's role in the world, including those of the modernization theory which had justified that role.

The American world of China observers was a world of many parts—scholars at the China centers in the élite universities; government analysts and intelligence personnel; China watchers in Hong Kong, a crossroads for journalists, academics, and government intelligence personnel.

If American China observers often seemed mesmerized and hopelessly divided by the battles that raged throughout the 1950s and early 1960s between "conservatives" and "liberals," or by the struggle for survival against McCarthyism, their differences pale beside the shared assumptions and ideology through which the Chinese Revolution has become largely understood. A few dissenters like Edgar Snow, Jack Belden, and Anna Louise Strong opposed such views and lost their public voices during these early formative years. Some academics studied only traditional Chinese philosophy, language, literature, privately appalled by the application of modern social-science methodology to China. The success of modernization theory, however, was so great that even those who thought they were dissenting often found themselves ensnared in its finely woven, crisscrossing threads. For the sake of clarity, those who espoused modernization theory will hereafter be referred to as "American observers," "China scholars," or "China observers."

By the early 1950s, modernization theory was often quite consciously fashioned into a theoretical alternative to a jumbled, distorted version of Marxism which was reduced to a series of stereotypes and then attacked as crude, simplistic, and propagandistic. The particular form this process took among China observers flowed quite naturally from the American government's failures in China and the "lessons" this raised for its policy elsewhere in Asia. Many of the most passionate advocates of modernization theory, the real founders of modern China studies in American universities, had lived in China and witnessed the collapse of Chiang Kai-shek and the success of the Chinese revolutionaries. In the early 1950s they vowed with virtual unanimity that such a defeat would be avoided everywhere else in Asia.

At a conference organized by the State Department in 1949 shortly after the People's Republic of China was formally established, John Fairbank, Harvard professor and director for the next two decades of its East Asian Research Center, argued that "our objective there is to formulate an alternative to the Marxism which provides them [the Communists] with a world spiritual dynamic. . . . Our ideology is very rich and we are very much devoted to it, but we do not have it as an export product, it seems to me, in an organized form for the present day."[2]

A decade later he renewed his call for some picture of "the modern world and its history more meaningful than Marxism-Leninism. The non-communist explanation of the social process—of imperialism, colonialism, nationalism, economic growth, social order—must make more sense to Asians than the Communist explanation."[3]

This commitment to creating a counterideology to communism was to a large degree a consequence of the widely held belief that "the most spectacular failure we have suffered" in China was in the "battle of ideas."[4] Wrote Edwin Reischauer:

> We exerted far more military effort in China than the Russians; we gave economic aid, while they were plundering Manchuria; but the Communists outdid us on the third level [the ideological] and won. The

ideological war went to them, in large part by de-
fault, as more and more Chinese came to the conclusion that communism represented the only or at
least the best hope for a united and strong China.[5]

Scholars and intellectuals thus saw themselves as sharpening
America's ideological weapons for the Asian cold war.

The war, however, had two fronts. The bourgeoisie and
the Western-oriented reformists had to be persuaded to
accept those reforms that would bring their nations into the
newly organized, American-centered international capitalist system. This required that the United States work
"to get the allegiance or the alliance, and get into our
camp, the minds and beliefs of these Asiatics."[6] At the
same time, a sophisticated explanation of America's
international role was necessary to justify this role to
the American people. Domestic opponents of it had to
appear isolationist, selfish, and ungenerous in this crusade
against "backwardness," as well as simpleminded about the
nature of the communist threat.

The lessons China watchers drew from the Chinese Revolution brought both fronts together. For no lesson about
China's "loss" was more important than that modernization,
while undoubtedly a native process, "cannot be conducted
only by the native government concerned." Said John
Fairbank, "Containment of Communism, to keep it out of
countries undergoing social metamorphosis, is like containing a forest fire. It is better to build a backfire."[7] That meant
going "much further into non-Communist Asia at once and
on many levels, private as well as governmental, cultural as
well as economic, with ideas as well as arms."[8] China observers, liberals and conservatives alike, argued for a model
of social change that linked containment of communism,
American-sponsored "nation-building" programs, and "non-
totalitarian" types of change with a strong ideological commitment to "reforming" noncommunist élites. This was a
crucial ideological development. It meant that American
involvement in the internal affairs of other nations would
be viewed as basically progressive and well intentioned,

similar to the American government's deepening involvement in the social and economic life of America. As Marion Levy, a Princeton sociologist and specialist on China and modernization theory, stated in 1949 with a bluntless lacking in some of his colleagues,

> either the United States or Russia or both are currently interfering in the government of every major country in the world and most of the minor ones to boot. Furthermore, as the world is governed today, it is a matter of life and death that we do. We have too many dangerous tools, both psychological and physical, to do anything else. No matter what ideals we express, we shall continue to operate in this fashion. . . . Since we must sin, let us sin bravely and intelligently and if possible with goodwill toward all concerned.[9]

Modernization theory was the ideological answer to a world of increasing revolutionary upheavel and continued reaction among traditional political élites. For "revolution will endanger our liberal interest," most agreed, "yet reaction is even now destroying it."[10] The lesson of the "loss" of China was to learn how to back those reforming élites (the bourgeoisie) against traditional feudal groups (like Chiang Kai-shek) and the revolutionaries.

Descriptions of the victory of the Chinese Communists in the late 1940s almost universally bemoaned Chiang Kai-shek's feudal leadership. In the future, America had to reach much further than "the top layers of demoralized and sticky-fingered officials of the old regime."[11] It must penetrate into all levels of society and in the process build up the bourgeoisie and the pro-Western educated élite. America's dilemma in China during the 1940s was its inability "to find a social and political group . . . which had standing and power in the Chinese scene and which at the same time had some kind of affinity to the United States and all it stands for."[12] Indeed, America government policy had actively supported Chiang Kai-shek's brutal regime against America's weak, yet most important friends. Lamented one observer:

Why did not our policy support more vigorously those elements in Chinese society which really represented our principles? What did we do for modern Chinese private banking establishments like the Shanghai Commercial and Savings bank? What did we do, with our millions of American aid, for private Chinese educational institutions like Nanking University in Tientsin? What did we do to support the efforts of genuine democrats in the early Democratic League? . . . The answer is not one to be proud of.[13]

If this approach was overwhelmed in China by the Japanese invasion and American policy failures, these observers argued, it must be reformulated and applied with renewed vigor under the guise of modernization throughout the rest of noncommunist Asia.

The ideological warfare of the China scholars, however, was not confined to the domain of foreign policy. It was imbedded as well in the most influential intellectual portrait of modern Chinese history to emerge after 1949. China, this fashionable intellectual view argued, was once a proud and mighty civilization, a self-sustaining society with a self-sufficient culture that enabled the Chinese to view themselves as the "center of the world." But China's traditional civilization, confronted with the industrial methods and military power of the West in the nineteenth century, "let her down. The old ways were inadequate to modern times."[14] The "requirements of modernization ran counter to the requirements of Confucian stability."[15] To assert that "China was victimized by the foreign powers . . . leaves unanswered the basic and prior question—why did China not respond to foreign encroachment earlier and more vigorously?"[16] None of this denies, it is maintained, the "evil effects of Western expansion," but in the final analysis "circumstances made China the worst accident case in history," not Western imperialism. China was simply unable to adapt to Western power, to the modern ways of science, industrial organization, and technology which underlay it.

One noted observer, arguing before the Senate Foreign Relations Committee in 1966, said:

> I don't think [the Chinese] were victimized by us or even by the British. I think they were victimized by circumstances of history; namely, that the world civilization which is spreading around, beginning in and expanding from Europe and now expanding with us and others, found China to be the last remaining, separate, distinct, isolated country which had its own culture and hasn't joined up. And this is the background, therefore, of real "cultural conflict."[17]

Not surprisingly, American observers understand that such views will be "emotionally unsatisfying" to many Chinese. "It is like asking a man run over by a truck to blame it on a congested traffic pattern. He will say, 'No, it was a truck.' "[18] Thus Chinese intellectuals are portrayed as seizing upon Western imperialism and the evils of capitalism (the truck) as a response to modernization (the traffic pattern). Theories of imperialism appealed to the "racked" Chinese intellectuals. It "sank into minds that struggled to explain and to cure the ills of the country; and it sank into hearts that rejected the West and yet desired its methods."[19] Marxism-Leninism and the theory of imperialism is thus described as providing a partial *psychological* answer for the failures of traditional Chinese culture and for the humiliation suffered at the hands of the West. Here, China observers argue, are the roots of that "grievance against modern history . . . which underlies the current vogue of seeing imperialism as the cause of modern China's difficulties,"[20] and which creates "the need for an explanation of history in terms of evil and justice."[21] Instead of casting aside "all the dated Leninist theorizing about economic exploitation" and analyzing the "modern world's development and expansion,"

> Marxism offers a devil-theory to explain it; how "capitalist imperialism" combined with "feudal re-

action" to attack, betray, and exploit the Chinese
people and distort their otherwise normal development toward "capitalism" and "socialism." Thus a
great Communist myth of "imperialist" victimiza-
tion becomes the new national myth.[22]

The real "victim" for American China observers is an innocent United States which found itself the target of Chinese
psychological projections, with the myth of American imperialism a means used by the communist leadership to
explain China's problems. Myths, of course, are engendered
in the psyche, and so once again the emotional, cultural,
ideological, and psychological explanations of Chinese views
and policies are counterposed to the modern, rational, industrial ways to which they eventually must yield. To be
Chinese in this American perspective is to be "understand-
ably" maladjusted.

Not surprisingly, as this perspective became established
in the mid-1950s, providing the historical overview for the
modern Chinese Revolution and American foreign policy,
the stage was also set for modernization theory to describe
China's internal development and the nature of its revolutionary process. These two uses of modernization theory
were obvious correlates. The first denied the existence of
imperialism and disguised America's role in the Third
World. The other denied revolutionary possibilities for
changing society and individual motivation.

Viewing China's domestic transformation after 1949
through modernization theory, however, was not largely the
work of the first postwar generation of China observers.
Rather it was the work of a younger second generation of
social scientists whose writings first blossomed in the late
1950s and have remained dominant ever since.

The Chinese Revolution
Through Modernization Theory

Modernization theory passionately holds to the conviction that all revolutions, in the end, must give way to the

rational imperatives of development and immutable human nature. In short, they must die. Mao and some of his colleagues may struggle against the reality of death, but they will be no more successful than the Taoist mendicant in search of the formula for immortality.

Why must the Chinese Revolution die? First, because revolution, as portrayed by the American scholar-seer, is a cataclysmic, violent, emotional upheaval that overthrows the old ruling élite unable to respond effectively to the demands for change. Revolution tears down the old edifice and thus prepares the way for the new. But once in power, the methods of revolutionary struggle, guerrilla war, and sweeping experimental programs are no longer useful.

Here is a richly savored, much discussed irony pointed to by American observers of China. The very methods and values that led to the triumph of the Chinese Communists will inevitably jeoparadize their long-term ability to modernize. In this assumption lies the basis for the most popular scholarly image of Mao—that of a deeply frustrated visionary, applying revolutionary values to a postrevolutionary society. Thwarted by the Chinese people, opposed by many of his own Communist party colleagues for over two decades, Mao collides not simply with a peasantry mired in tradition, nor with a party mesmerized by the Soviet model, but ultimately with the imperatives of "administrative routine" and "technical specialization." Mao, "the poet of revolution," cannot adjust to the "prose of stable administration." Both the cause and failure of the Cultural Revolution are understandable in terms of a Mao "consumed by an obsessive urge to launch another revolution," in an anachronistic old man's last leap toward utopia.[23]

Thus China eventually will have to "move away from the idea of great utopian, apocalyptic, grand strategies; away from the radical revolutionary policies that Mao has tried to promote in the last few years."[24] From this perspective, the creation of the Red Guards and other mass organizations during the Cultural Revolution was a last "desperate gamble" to spare China "a gray, managerial bureaucratic fate; a final effort to prove that charisma, ideology, and youthful zeal could triumph over political prudence and economic incentives; a crude, terrible, yet high-minded attempt to rescue the permanent revolution from an agonizing death."[25] More pragmatic policies will be necessary to get China "back on the track of rational development," but to some observers "the prospect of rational development is blocked by a single hurdle—Mao himself."[26]

Observers less preoccupied with Mao the individual write of conflict in China as "divisions between technicians and bureaucrats on the one side and political zealots on the other, or between pragmatists and visionaries—between those who would rather be fed than red."[27] Busy academic wordsmiths write as if pragmatism were synonymous with economic progress and national strength through the accumulation of technical skills and orderly bureaucratic and administrative procedures, while visionaries and radicals cling to outmoded techniques of mass mobilization, egalitarian ideals, and innumerable irrelevant organizational methods. To some, Mao's very political system itself is "singularly inappropriate for . . . modernization."[28] Others accept some of the radical methods as useful for modernizing but not modernity, as short-term, stopgap measures whose time will shortly pass.

To almost all observers, however, revolutionary values stand opposed to the steady, ordered measures needed for building a new society. Great leaps and abrupt halts, the search for nonbureaucratic means to achieve economic development, the deliberate fostering of social tensions to arouse the populace, intensive efforts to change people's attitudes, the promotion of equality and collectivity instead of relying largely on self-interest and competition are labeled "Maoist" and judged ineffective ways to modernize.

In such views of China, 1949 is the "essential turning point." The "simplicities" of revolutionary struggle must give way to the "complexities" of managing a nation. Illusions of uninterrupted revolution could only interrupt ordered progress and organizational efficiency. In the language of American political science, China now had to move "from the relatively undifferentiated stage of radical social mobilization and revolution to the more organizationally complex stage of economic rationalization and technological innovation."[29]

What must wither away, then, is not the state but revolutionary values. Nowhere is this assumption so deeply embedded than in the widespread American academic tendency to speak of modernization as a process of rationalization. In the words of Harvard professor and China specialist Benjamin Schwartz, modernization "tends to mean something approximating Max Weber's conception of the process of rationalization in all those spheres of social action—economic, political, legal, educational—which lend themselves to the application of 'Zwecksrationalitat.' "[30] Rationalization means the spread of quantitative measurement, functional efficiency, and economizing attitudes through science, technology, accounting, and regulations to the entire conduct of life. It is fundamentally a theory of the division of labor that presupposes a social and mental universe in which science and religion, economy and polity, laws and customs are increasingly distinct and separate. As these realms separate, as every activity develops its own conceptual basis, each becomes the province of professionally trained experts and bureaucratic administrators.

Technical and industrial progress, in short, makes the higher tasks of production increasingly complicated, widening rather than narrowing the gap between them and the remaining tasks of manual labor. The division between those who *know* and those who *do* is the prerequisite of specialization and modern notions of expertise. Unequal distribution of rewards is accepted as an inevitable part of the division of labor, essential to recruit and reward competent people for the performance of important tasks. In such a society, choices and decisions must increasingly be made on "technical" and quantitative grounds, and the raising of more time-consuming, ideological considerations is deemed inefficient. Arguments supported by production, wage, and budget data become more pervasive as moralistic arguments decline. "The technician, and for that matter, the professional bureaucrat will be very conscious of the limits imposed by his material and by the imperatives of the situation within which he operates."[31] This "sober respect" by technicians and bureaucrats will eventually lead China's leaders to recognize that the revolution is dead, that Chinese society requires a certain premium of status and power for experts and administrators trained in modern ways. The value of a charismatic or father figure will decline. There will be a growing social need for autonomy in the nation's intellectual life. The natural sciences, indispensable for the country's economic and military progress, will be the first to win some independence from dogmatic ideological controls. As society becomes more complex, the need for sophisticated techniques of economic planning and coordination will facilitate the recognition of the "logic of the economic realm." As unplanned and unanticipated events occur, empirical social research must be encouraged to enable the rulers to recognize and respond to the population's needs. As the authority of the official faith declines, moral problems unforeseen by the canonical writers will emerge. And this will stimulate a desire for autonomous development and experimentation in the literary and artistic worlds for which the growing privacy of individuals in the cities provides a ready market.

Such is the description of the death of the Chinese Revolution. The "revisionism" Mao so strongly condemns is more often than not painted as a "latent function of modernization." Again, in the language of political science:

> On the one hand, modernization is positively valued as a social goal, for modernization means economic development, and economic development means national power. On the other hand, however, modernization entails bureaucracy, instrumentalism, and the

consequent attenuation and ritual sterilization of ideological principles. Damned if they do and damned if they don't, the leaders of the CPSU and the CCP have thus been forced to steer a not altogether happy course between the Scylla of modernization-cum-revisionism and the Charybdis of atavism-cum-orthodoxy.[32]

Another reason often cited for the coming death of the Chinese Revolution is "human nature." It is alleged that the reintroduction of ethics as a motivating force in society's economic and social life, the attempt to create a new socialist person, may temporarily motivate a tradition-bound people, but it is also ultimately utopian and anachronistic. Indeed, the systematic rejection of one component in the frequently used dichotomies of rationality and revolutionary ways, routinization and mass mobilization, competitive self-interest and public good assumes a view of modern man as egoistic, competitive, self-interested, motivated by material goods, status, and power. Such dichotomies, of course, draw on a long tradition in the history of Western sociology—Toennies' *gemeinschaft-geselleschaft,* Durkheim's mechanical-organic solidarity, Redfield's folk-urban worlds, Comte's three stages, and Weber's stress on the fundamental rationalism of Western development. But while some of the original formulators of these distinctions were appalled by the shattering of community their theories implied, and sought alternatives to the bleak future they foresaw, modernization theorists after World War II passionately embraced that future, judging it progressive, rational, and "modern." The intellectual doubts of the 1920s and early 1930s—about where progress lay, the search for ways to overcome the conflicts between culture and technology, "civilization and culture" as Lewis Mumford described it, human needs and economic well-being—were all swept aside by the simplicities of modernization theory.

Individual competition rooted in egoistic self-interest and rationalization were thus accepted as inseparable aspects of an industrial society. Weber's theories are particularly revealing in this context, for he clearly associated his theory of rationalization and bureaucracy with individualistic patterns of motivation. "Formal rationality" for Weber was capitalist rationality, the essential precondition for profitability, which in turn is oriented toward systematic, methodical calculation, "capital accounting." Such rationality, an essential criterion of modernity, requires the triumph of abstract, instrumental reason, a complete break between "emotional and abstract relationships," the sacred and the secular. This was what Weber saw Protestantism sparking with its overriding emphasis on the individual at the expense of all external ties, bonds, symbols, or works attributable to a community. His *Zwecksrationalitat* implies a society without collective effort, without community, a society where individuals see each other largely as means. But Weber, more bluntly than many of his followers, faced the consequences of his argument that the "formally most rational" mode of capital accounting is the one into which man and his purposes enter only as a variable in the calculation of gain and profit. "Capital accounting in its formally most rational mode thus presupposes the struggle of man with man."[33] Modern bureaucracy is directly tied to that struggle. Thanks to its "precision, steadfastness, discipline, rigor and dependability, in short, calculability for . . . the head [of the organization],"[34] bureaucracy is the most rational means of control of seemingly isolated individuals. It is this because it is "domination by virtue of knowledge," ascertainable, calculable, calculating knowledge—specialized knowledge, the very glue that binds together the sophisticated forms of the division of labor. An intensely egoistic, competitive notion of modern human nature feeds a certain conception of bureaucratic organization, rationality and power—and vice versa. In this mutually reinforcing set of assumptions lies the essence of modernization theory.

China observers, who pay ardent lip service to rationality and science, compare China with a theory (of bureaucratic rationality, of modernization) rather than with its concrete historical reality. Nor is this surprising, for genuine comparative study would challenge the explanation modernization theory provides of both China's and the West's industrialization. Applied to the classic model of Western industrialization, Great Britain, modernization theory transforms its most painful and exploitative characteristics into rational progress. What is rational and progressive for the beneficiary class, the British bourgeoisie, is miraculously transformed into progress for everybody.

The fact is, industrialization entails the destruction of older ways of life, often at the cost of enormous suffering. The effect of such disruption should be at the very heart of any discussion of modernization, yet it is usually ignored. Modernization theorists particularly like to overlook the reasons for the exceptional violence of eighteenth- and nineteenth-century British industrialization. That violence was a consequence of social pauperization, "the destruction of old ways of life without substitution of anything the labouring poor could regard as a satisfactory equivalent."[35] The experience of immiseration came in a hundred forms:

> for the field labourer, the loss of his common rights and the vestiges of village democracy; for the artisan, the loss of his craftsman's status; for the weaver, the loss of livelihood and of independence; for the child, the loss of work and play in the home; for many groups of workers whose real income·improved, the loss of security, leisure, and the deterioration of the urban environment.[36]

The physical suffering in the great industrial cities almost defies description. Cities cloaked in soot and smoke, impregnated with filth, lacked even the most elementary public services. People entirely unused to nonagrarian life were forced into bleak and overcrowded slums. Nowhere is the degradation of daily life more evident than in the life expectancy of the laborers. In Liverpool in 1840 the "gentry and professional persons" had an average life of thirty-five years; the "laborers, mechanics, and servants" only fifteen. In his classic study of Manchester, Engels described what the urban and factory conditions did to the workers.

> There are few vigorous, well-built, healthy persons among the workers. . . . They are almost all weakly, of angular but not powerful build, lean, pale, and of relaxed fibre. . . . Nearly all suffer from indigestion, and consequently from a more or less hypochondriac, melancholy, irritable, nervous condition. Their enfeebled constitutions are unable to resist disease, and are therefore seized by it on every occasion. Hence they age prematurely, and die early.[37]

It was not only the poverty and disease, however, but the destruction of meaningful work which cast such a black shadow over the years of British industrialization. In many countries the memories of a "golden age" were based not on the idea that material goods were more plentiful in the past, or disease less prevalent, but on remembered patterns of work and leisure. To replace these patterns with the pressure of long hours of totally unsatisfying work under severe discipline for alien purposes, as D. H. Lawrence noted, was a source of that "ugliness" which "betrayed the spirit of man in the nineteenth century."[38]

What modernization theorists have done is to take those very elements that directly contributed to the social costs of the British Industrial Revolution and turn them into the inevitable prerequisite for creating a modern, rational, industrial society. Preserving or building upon traditional forms of community became irrational; future collective forms were only utopian daydreaming. As Weber often stated, the development of modern economic power was marked by its "specific hostility to the idea of brotherhood."[39] No democratic participation by the workers was possible—the technical superiority of bureaucratic administration and its panoply of trained, privileged experts was too great; the rationality which could only result from separating the worker from the ownership of the material means to his activity too necessary. He was

> separated from the means of production in the economy, from the means of war in the army, from the material means of administration in public administration, from the means of research in the university institute and laboratory, from the financial means in all of them. It is the decisive foundation common to the capitalist private enterprise and to the cultural, political, and military activities of the modern power state.[40]

Many of Weber's American followers take this portrayal of violent technological and bureaucratic differentiation between work and life and turn it into a value. Such rationalization allows only the bourgeoisie to profit from industrialization. Indeed, Weber's analysis of the Puritan ethic and Tawney's concern with the origins of commercial capitalism are largely focused on the social development of the bourgeoisie (the former stressed the concept of "calling," the latter the values of freedom, self-discipline, acquisitiveness, and individualism). Intrinsic to both was the argument that Puritanism contributed to the psychic energy and social cohesion of the bourgeoisie. Both pointed to powerful ideological currents, particularly methodism in nineteenth-century England, which favored an atomistic individualism, one which justified forcing the individual, in Weber's words, "in so far as he is involved in the system of market relationships, to conform to capitalist rules of action"—turning man "into his own slave driver." Herein lay a significant part of the justification for the transformation of "human nature" demanded by the factory system. The "working paroxysms" of the artisan or outworker must be "methodized until the man is adapted to the discipline of the machine."[41] The ideology that rationalized this was deeply rooted in the bourgeoisie, but what it meant for them and what it meant to the workers was very different.

There is a tendency to see middle-class values as foreshadowing what all people can ultimately achieve rather than what reinforced the exploitation and cruelty of British industrialization. Yet what were praiseworthy values to the rising bourgeoisie were forms of suppression for the poor and the proletariat. The acquisitive individualism of the bourgeoisie denied the plausibility of collectivity in the work process. The radical separation of public and private shattered the relation between life and work. The pursuit of self-interest and private economic gain justified the destruction of traditional forms of community without replacing them with other forms of cooperation. "Progress" enriched the few at the cost of incredible suffering for the many.

The way modernization theorists preclude any serious consideration of the social costs of British industrialization suggests a shared perspective with those who traditionally benefited from it—the bourgeoisie. But if modernization theorists raised questions about the social costs of modernization, they would question their own social position. Like the contemporary bureacratic administrators, technocrats, scientists, corporate executives and intellectuals they consider so modern and progressive, they would have to be seen as beneficiaries of capitalism, as part of a class with specific interests, rather than spokesmen for an inevitable rational historic process. Indeed, such questions would challenge the application of modernization theory to the non-Western world since 1945. They would also challenge support for the bourgeoisie and the privileged Western-educated in the Third World, since their counterparts (in vastly different but comparable historic circumstances) can be shown to have been so instrumental in aggravating the social costs of industrialization in Great Britain.

If modernization theory can justify the social costs of British industrialization, it cannot, by its very nature, deal with China's efforts to avoid such costs. Thus, some of the most violent features of Western industrialization and capitalist development are made to appear rational, while

Chinese attempts to overcome them are made to appear irrational. In Britain, the justifications for capitalist management; the increasing complexity of the division of labor in which a few led, and others, less well paid, obey; the later privileged role for skilled technicians and scientists are accepted as eminently rational, although they are clearly what partly prevented worker participation in the factories, radically separated manual and mental labor, and made the work process so dismally exploitative. In China, therefore, any attempts to fundamentally bridge the gulf between manager and worker, professional and peasant, urban and rural areas, mental and manual labor are viewed, at best, as a useful short-term ideological way of preventing the premature spread of bureaucratism. It is not understood as fundamentally rational or related to the creation of long-term meaningful collective work relations. Collective work is also dismissed by American observers as hopelessly in conflict with acquisitive individualism and the competitive self-interest inherent in advanced forms of the division of labor. Chinese efforts to raise living standards through group activity, to achieve material improvements through cooperative effort, are dismissed as excessive ideological zeal.

Ironically, comparisons between Britain and China suggest that the former rather than the latter posited happiness in a religious ideology that denied minimal social and material rewards for work. Religion helped to accumulate surplus capital by making the pitiful wages and appalling standards of living more acceptable for the workers and farmers. If ever a society substituted "ideology" for material values, it was nineteenth-century England. Encased in their bulletproof ideological vests, however, American observers simply ignore experiences in their own tradition that contradict their beliefs, while vehemently denying even the possibility that the Chinese idea of rapid development might cost less in human suffering.

American observers often ridicule the Chinese confidence in self-reliance and in the creativity of local inventors and technicians. Yet once again modernization theory distorts the process of Western industrialization. Without the British artisans and outworkers' superb ingenuity with primitive tools, the inventions of the Industrial Revolution could scarcely have gotten off the ground. In the modern world, such skills are the province of technicians and specialists. To modernize, the Chinese are asked to use only these sophisticated methods, not the ones that proved so effective in the early stages of British industrialization. Such advanced modern methods, of course, contributed in the West to the reduction of artisan skills to relatively simple tasks which ensured that no individual worker or group could master the intricacies of either the production process or the market. The capitalist's centrality to the process of production and distribution, his ability to coordinate the relationships between the producers and the market, is thus assured and portrayed as the only rational course. This assumption underlies the view of experts and technicians in modernization theory as well. To analyze China through such assumptions, therefore, once again precludes any appreciation of its radically different approach to industrialization.

These comparisions again illustrate the bedrock assumption of modernization theory—the denial of any revolutionary alternative. The Chinese may be attacking many of the features of Western industrialization that made it so violent, yet their attack must ultimately be judged by American observers as utopian, ideological, and abstract because they challenge what modernization theorists insist is the ahistorical essence of rationalization and the division of labor. Ironically, looked at from the perspective of the classic British example of industrialization, such views of rationality and modernization appear intricately interwoven with violence. It is not only the rational which is real in the history of Western capitalism, but the violent which is rational.

UNINTERRUPTED REVOLUTION

The theory of uninterrupted revolution is as deeply embedded in Chinese history as modernization theory is in American. Its roots grow in many soils: in millennia of peasant uprisings, bitter social warfare and class struggle, and repeated failures to find alternatives to traditional Chinese society; in the uninterrupted assaults on Chinese territory, sovereignty, and cultural identity by Western imperialism since the Opium War of 1840; in over two decades of armed struggle through which the Chinese Communist Party gained power; in the need for the Chinese to understand and consciously adapt scientific, technological, and industrial methods developed in the West and to differentiate between these methods and their particular manifestations in European and American capitalist societies; and in the contradictions of Chinese society today, between urban and rural areas, mental and manual labor, peasants and workers.

To most China specialists in America, uninterrupted revolution suggests a continuation of the abnormal, the exceptional, the emotional. Predicated upon evolution rather than revolution, gradualism rather than struggle, controlled change through élites rather than mass participation, modernization theory signals a historic difference between the Chinese Revolution and the classic Western revolutions. Revolutions in the West, by and large, are viewed as momentary upheavals, great mass uprisings that occur like earthquakes—long in germination but sudden to those involved; of enormous shattering power but an accentuation of long developing (though often unnoticed) trends; quickly over as society returns to more normal ways of operating. To accept conflict and intense struggle as the norm, to see oneself as part of a process of revolutionary transformation going back well over a century, turns such assumptions about revolution upside down. It begins to suggest why understanding and learning to consciously shape struggle and conflict rather than deny them became so paramount to many Chinese. As one reform movement after another collapsed, many concluded that only revolutionary ways could overcome the traditional dilemmas of chaos versus rigid stability, violent upheaval versus bureaucratic domination, change versus stifling order, peasant egalitarianism versus bureaucratic hierarchy. In short, uninterrupted revolution became not a way to promote chaos but to overcome it.

Nothing is further from the truth than the portrayal of a peaceful, changeless, gracious China set ablaze by twentieth-century social and nationalist revolutions sparked by the Western impact; of China as a tranquil giant torn by foreign ideas from thousands of years of lethargy amidst a dazzling culture; of a stable, well-balanced society following a historical rhythm similar to a recurring seasonal cycle finally shattered by Western aggression. Underlying the grace and culture of the gentry and the rise and fall of dynasties was "one long chain of peasant revolts."[42] Indeed, "no country has had a richer and more continuous tradition of peasant rebellion than China."[43] Thus, bitter struggle and intense exploitation in China's long history were not the exception but the norm. Though official Chinese historians disguised and distorted this reality for millennia, it was experienced by China's rural millions and memorialized in the folktales celebrating heroic "bandits" and defiance of the cruel landlord. In this tradition, the Maoists argue, is the real history of the Chinese masses. Only within it does the traditional world of mandarin and bureaucrat assume its proper social and economic setting.

That world, of course, rarely appears in the official histories, for Chinese history "was written by officials for officials."[44] Between those who wrote and those who read there was little problem of communication, for they shared similar education, tastes, interests, and social functions. History was written largely as a guide to administrative practice, filled with examples of good and evil rulers, the rules of the bureaucratic game, the moral ways of emperorship. Moreover, though numerically weak, these scholar-officials were omnipotent by reason of their position and prestige; bureaucracy was the vortex of privilege, influence, education, and power. The scholar-officials had the power of the state behind them, imposed taxes, administered justice, and exercised control over the economy through such activities as the salt monopoly, the supervision of taxation and markets, and by public works. They carried out, in short, all mediating and administrative functions.

While such officials occasionally sided with peasant uprisings, their traditional role was essentially one of conformism or withdrawal, not revolt. The revolts came from below, as an elemental tidal force. If the peasant insurrection led to dynastic upheaval, some officials lent their skills to the new order, but in the process sought to quickly bring any popular forces "under control, canalized them, tamed them, and rendered them harmless."[45] Whereas the classic revolutions of the West have historically been associated with a rising class, the bourgeoisie, centuries of peasant uprisings in China truly came from the bottom, challenging officials and everyone else in the established order. The West has had its peasant struggles, but they did not constitute its revolutionary tradition. The classic revolutions remain associated with a rising, powerful class aligned with a progressive, well-educated segment of society. By contrast, in China the educated and the intelligentsia were so interwoven with the bureaucratic apparatus that the dichotomy between the masses and the officials was never bridged through newly emerging class forces. The dichotomy of élite and mass, leaders and led, mental and manual work thus have far more radical and profound implications in Chinese revolutionary traditions than in the West. Until the twentieth century, Chinese officials who tried to reduce peasant sufferings could hardly hope to break with the very system that engendered them. Nor could they hope to ally themselves with other rising literate classes. The rare reformist could not become a revolutionary.

The Chinese peasants also were never able to put China on a new historical path more favorable to their own interests. "They did not, nor were they able to, produce a revolutionary programme or a revolutionary solution."[46] Their political horizons did not extend beyond the boundaries of the district in which the goods they produced or consumed were found. Hampered by the endless personal struggle to acquire a little land, the peasants' vision of a good society was one in which everyone had food to eat, clothes to wear, a plot of land, or was part of a communal society. Yet small private holdings and primitive technique offered no way to prevent the old process of differentiation, which had originally produced landlord and tenant, from producing them all over again.

All this encouraged impetuosity in peasant uprisings. The imagery of outbursts, explosions, tidal waves, primitive violence captures important qualities of traditional peasant protest. Though partly motivated by ideals of egalitarianism, primitive socialism, and justice, these momentous uprisings throughout Chinese history led only to drastic but short-term action to divide the existing wealth rather than promoting a fundamental transformation of society. Almost alone, the Chinese Communists developed the theory and practice of revolution as a way of overcoming the traditional dynamics of chaos and violence or acquiescence and passivity. Almost alone, they found keys to unlock the traditional peasant world through mass mobilization rooted both in long-term goals and in a prolonged step-by-step, stage-by-stage conception of struggle. Throughout their long march to power, the Communists often had to fight to contain egalitarian and collectivist extremes, such as arise naturally in the villages, as they had to push to the left against conservatives. Successful revolution, they argued, could not be a temporary mass upheaval, a cataclysmic outbreak—that was the traditional Chinese road to failure. Revolution must entail not only destruction of the old but creation of the new. It was a long process, they said, not a single major act. As a result, when the Chinese Communists triumphed in 1949, revolution to many was not just the act of seizing power but a century-long process fueled by rich and varied traditions of learning to understand intense struggle and consciously molding them in a way to produce a better society.

Though traditional China faced an acute internal crisis in the nineteenth century, the forces unleashed by Western capitalism shattered that society beyond recognition. Modern Chinese history is conventionally dated from 1840, the year of the first Opium War between Britain and China. Earlier Western advances were dwarfed by what followed 1840. The intermingling of Western capitalism and the collapse of traditional Chinese society, the outbreak of the greatest peasant uprisings in Chinese history, led by the Taipings, entailed an almost total process of dissolution. By the end of the nineteenth century, Chinese society had become an archaic social system not quite able to die, sitting on a people barely able to live.

The modern Chinese Revolution was fueled by two aims: to free China from alien domination, be it Manchu or Western and Japanese imperialism, and to destroy the outworn social institutions and the ruthless system of rural exploitation. Yet even as Western capitalism weakened the archaic economic system, broke open the walls of the clans, changed the traditional patterns of conduct, and created classes in the coastal cities that had been largely absent from Chinese life, Western penetration did not weaken but rather temporarily strengthened the feudal and reactionary forces in China. This is so for the simple reason that the landlords, the usurers, and the bureaucrats were linked increasingly to compradors or government bureaucrats and warlords, who in turn were bound to foreign interests protected by extraterritoriality treaties, gunboats, military missions, and all the usual accouterments of imperialism.

Simply put, the Chinese Revolution had two distinguishable currents. One arose in the villages of inland China. The other was urban-centered. The first current drew deeply from class warfare; the second from the development of a middle class in response to the impact of imperialism and colonialism. The revolutionary current in the rural areas was antitraditional (hatred of the gentry and the traditional system), whereas that of the cities was intensely nationalistic and often anticolonialist. The Chinese Communists gradually came to understand that China was a semifeudal, semicolonial country, and that the struggle, therefore, was not for immediate socialism but for the liquidation of feudalism, to achieve social democracy on the one hand and national emancipation on the other.

The Kuomintang under Chiang Kai-shek never could change the system of rural authority, but compromised with it; never could break with Western imperialism, but relied on it even before the Japanese invasion. Because Chiang compromised, and in the end allied himself, with many of the most backward elements in Chinese society and with imperialist authority, he perpetuated the basic contradictions that had torn Chinese society asunder for a hundred years. Independence and rural revolution were intricately bound together, and these were precisely the realities addressed by the Chinese Communists.

The indigenous nature of industrialization in the West makes it especially difficult to comprehend this brutal interweaving of imperialism and feudalism. However violent, the combination of capitalism and industrialization never threatened the total social fabric in Western Europe and America as did the combination of feudalism and imperialism in China. No external challenges threatened Europe's and America's very existence. In the West, growth could be viewed as rational and evolutionary. Thus it was eminently logical for many European thinkers to argue that the real "revolution" in the West was industrial, scientific, or technological. There were, of course, intense debates over the break with traditional values, protests against the brutality of the capitalist transformation. Yet in England, as in much of the Western capitalist world, capitalism and progress seemed members, however quarrelsome, of the same family. Questions of "cultural identity," the "weight of history," the preservation of a cultural heritage were hardly the questions for Englishmen that they were for Chinese. History more often than not seemed linear, progress and civilization something more in the future than in a golden past. Ironically, even the values of the Tories, defenders of traditional aristocratic ways, were part and parcel of the success of British industrialization. Such Tory traditions as the marginal notion of "collective harmony" could "not have acquired reality in the age of Industrial Revolution in Britain without the actual nourishment that came from the more organic harmony of a medievalism that had not altogether disappeared."[47]

In short, in the development of Western capitalism a certain totality could be assumed; "change with tradition" applies far more to the West than it does to modern China. After 1840 China's very culture and existence were placed in peril, its ways brutally shown to be parochial. As alternatives failed over the years, as one reformer after another failed, it seemed apparent that a total transformation was needed, not a scientific, or industrial, or technological revolution, but all these and much more.

This essential difference between China and the West suggests why Chinese intellectuals struggled to understand China's problems in terms few Westerners could appreciate. Because China's disaster was so total, Chinese intellectuals increasingly sought answers that would deal with the disaster in its totality. Because the success of reforms and changes depended upon understanding the dynamics of Western civilization, generations of Chinese sought the laws, patterns, or principles of the development of imperialism and capitalism. Because so much had to be built anew, Chinese intellectuals sought the fundamental principles underlying the old society and those essential to build the new one. Because a totality could no longer be taken for granted in China, a "totalistic" response was increasingly accepted as a rational rather than an emotional answer to China's desperate plight. Theories predicated upon the interrelatedness of economic, social, political, and cultural questions grew not only out of traditional ways of posing questions but out of this total rational need.

Ironically, even those Chinese whom Westerners laud as opponents of such totalism, who spoke of pragmatism and solving problems one by one, offered only another variant of it. In opposing all "isms" and ideologies, men like Hu Shih sought to solve problems as though China were a giant picture puzzle to be assembled piece by piece, slowly and cautiously over great periods of time. Such methods, however, really constituted a total rejection of China's traditional ways, a "total Deweyanization of China, not . . . an authentic search for a Chinese cultural identity in the process of China's modernization."[48] Indeed, throughout the course of the Chinese Revolution appeals for "pragmatism" and "gradualism" have been the ideological alternative to uninterrupted revolution and the fundamental need for rapid, conscious change encompassing all aspects of a society's and an individual's life, propelled both by the need to overcome material backwardness and the desire to create a new public spirit. If the transition from feudalism to capitalism took place in an unplanned or haphazard way in the West, in China many came to argue that planning at both an economic and philosophical level was a necessity. In time the Maoists spoke of combining rapid economic advance and conscious, self-remolding in the social group. It is this double, intertwined, speeded advance toward what they regard as a higher stage in the revolution of mankind that underlies the Maoist view of uninterrupted revolution.

Maoist views of education illustrate such an approach.

The word "education," however, has a far different meaning to Westerners than it does to Chinese. Education is not just the acquisition of technical skills in order to make a living but includes moral behavior—attitudes toward others, relatives and country; public responsibility. To the Maoist the interrelatedness of economic, social, political, and cultural questions underlies the reorientation of values, the need to transform patterns of motivation, the struggle within each person between selfish and unselfish demands, the desire for personal gain and the need for collective advance. This expansive view of education has obvious roots in various Chinese traditions, as does the Maoist insistence upon predicating cultural and material changes upon an ever-deepening collective form of social organization.

But to many American observers of the Chinese Revolution, the emphasis on collectivity, groups, on the need to consciously understand and thus shape all aspects of material and philosophical change denies Western individualism and all the values so loosely associated with it. Such views are rooted in the history of European capitalism. The indigenous character of Western capitalism enabled Europe's bourgeoisie, as they emerged from feudal society, to see themselves as fighting for universal rights through law without appearing fundamentally antagonistic to society. Law combined both the universal and the particular, individual autonomy and social order. Various Western theorists have enshrined the individual as the very creator of social value, and even those who spoke more of groups and tradition praised individual autonomy and privacy as the source of creativity, initiative, and art. The individual bourgeois enshrined in popular theory, then, was an atom in a self-regulating universe.

Chinese intellectuals who looked at the West in the nineteenth and twentieth centuries, however, by and large saw not individuals but the highly organized, powerful nation-state of the West—navies, churches, highly organized companies and banking systems. What struck them was not the separation of individual and society but the consolidation of individual energies in factories, bureaucratic organization, and the complex machinery of nineteenth-century capitalism. As more and more Chinese concluded that a new society had to be built, Western individualism came to seem a pitifully useless guide. The "ideology of individualism" as applied in China appeared to do no more than justify privilege, luxury, and exploitation. Sons of the gentry who attended Christian schools in China, learned English and went abroad. Having studied Western concepts of liberty and individualism, they returned home and put them into practice as compradors, bureaucrats, or bank managers. Missionary schools in China seemed to train people to feel more at home in the West than in their own society. Thus to generations of radical Chinese the idea of the self-interested and autonomous individual standing outside groups became the antithesis of public values and community, unity, and organization. Such ideas were useful iconoclastic ways of attacking many traditional Chinese ideas, but ultimately the West seemed to belie the very individualism it propagated by the way it integrated all aspects of society into a drive for wealth and power. And only integration of all parts of Chinese life would provide liberation through the breaking down of barriers that would free women from men, the child from the father, the tenant from the landlord. All these relations had to be interfered with, made public, and politicized. All these private lives had to be "broken into." And when the Chinese Communists had learned how to do this, there burst into the world the revolutionary determination and the explosive dynamic from which emerged the cadres that would lead the revolution to victory.

Mao on Uninterrupted Revolution

"Uninterrupted revolution" not only describes important aspects of China's transformation since 1840, but of Mao

Tsetung Thought as well. When the term first became widely used in China in the late 1950s, it signaled a major break with the Soviet model of development, a decision to push the revolution in the rural areas by establishing the communes, and a renewed commitment to overcome the contradictions between mental and manual work, peasants and workers, urban and rural areas. The theoretical basis for uninterrupted revolution, however, had long been implicit in Mao's writings.[49]

Mao's best-known theoretical essays, *On Contradiction* and *On Practice*, express the two overriding themes in his thought, and the two least acceptable to China's traditional élite. "There is only one basic law and that is the law of contradiction," Mao writes. As it has been throughout Chinese history, struggle and not harmony is eternal. "The development of things is always out of balance," (two do not merge into one), and thus there is always a perpetual state of becoming, a constant shifting of forces, transformation, and change. "The contradictions between balance and imbalance exist in all fields and in all sectors of every department. They arise without interruption and they are resolved without interruption."[50] This is not unfortunate for "if there were no contradictions and no struggle, there would be no world, no progress, no life, there would be nothing at all. To talk all the time about unity is 'a pool of stagnant water'; it can lead to coldness. We must destroy the old basis for unity, pass through a struggle, and unite on a new basis. Which is better—a stagnant pool, or 'the inexhaustible Yangtse comes roaring past'?"[51]

If Mao's emphasis on struggle and contradiction frontally assaults the Confucian value of harmony, his emphasis on practice attacks their traditional bureaucratic role. "Discover the truth through practice," Mao writes, "and again through practice verify and develop the truth . . . in endless cycles, and with each cycle the content of practice and knowledge rises to a higher level. Such is the whole of the dialectical materialist theory of knowledge. . . ."[52] There is no innate wisdom. No knowledge precedes experience. No competence is possible before practical doing.

Abstraction alone, therefore, never shows the way to truth. One never understands without being a part of what is understood. To isolate oneself from a situation, to dwell within a world of abstract concepts, to escape into inner emotions and subjective feelings can lead only to idealism. In Chinese history, "isolation" has long meant privilege, the life of the mind over the harsh life of the peasant. In this division of labor lies the historic roots of the bureaucrat. Knowledge thus becomes power, an essential tool of the ruling class. This is just as true for Mao whether it is utilized by traditional Chinese bureaucrats, dogmatic Marxists, or those trained in certain Western academic ways.

Moreover, abstraction is inadequate by itself because knowledge always involves a process of "leaps." There is a leap from perceptual to conceptual knowledge, another "leap through the test of practice." For "it is this leap alone that can prove the correctness or incorrectness of the first leap in cognition, i.e., of the ideas, theories, policies, plans or measures formulated in the course of reflecting the objective external world."[53] Just as there is no continuum from perceptual to conceptual knowledge, so is there no step-by-step process from conceptualization to implementation. Leaps and imbalance, in short, are at the very core of Mao's notion of dialectics.

This is just as true of all social change. No blueprints from above for implementation below have any place in Mao's writings. "The Hunanese often say," Mao remarks, " 'Straw sandals shape themselves in the making.' "[54] Change is an inherently untidy process, for creative mass initiative always produces unanticipated results, "sprouts" pregnant with lessons and future possibilities which will be crushed or ignored if central leadership or an entrenched local élite is intent on implementing its own preconceived ideas. Just as no individual can stand outside the situation being analyzed, so no group of planners can anticipate and program the response and creativity of the people. "It cannot be argued that history is being created by the planners, and not by the masses."[55]

Whereas modernization theorists usually see knowledge concentrated in various élites, Mao insists that, though they have high culture and know the bureaucratic rules of power and survival, their understanding of reality is quite limited. Whereas modernization theorists see new ideas and ways of life disseminated down from élites whose eyes are turned outward toward the modern industrial world, Mao sees creativity less in abstract ideas than in the way they are utilized, understood, and incorporated into people's lives. In this sense creativity comes from below, for the political, economic, and social breakthroughs made by society are always germinated among the people. How modern science and technology are utilized depends ultimately on such creativity.

"According to the laws of the old society, the oppressed had a low culture, but," Mao insists, "they were more clever. On the other hand, the oppressors had a high culture, but they were more stupid."[56] Bureaucrats may have high culture, but they cannot be creative by themselves. No more fundamental lesson than this, Mao warns, can be drawn from Chinese history.

> In history it is always those with little learning who overthrow those with much learning. . . . Ever since ancient times the people who founded new schools of thought were all young people without too much learning. They had the ability to recognize new things at a glance and, having grasped them, they opened fire on the old fogeys. . . . Then those with learning oppressed them. Isn't that what history is like? . . . When we started to make revolution, we were mere twenty-year-old boys while the rulers of that time . . . were old and experienced. They had more learning, but we had more truth.[57]

Throughout Mao's writings, bureaucratic control by the few is associated with inertia, privilege, and class. It entails decay and exploitation, for bureaucrats cannot cope with the continuous nature of change except by resorting to domination. The notion of politics as a process, an ebb and flow of power constellations, an eternal conflict leading to splits, consensus, and coalition, is deeply rooted in Chinese consciousness. "Empires wax and wane; states cleave asunder and coalesce." So begins the Chinese classic, *The Romance of the Three Kingdoms*. Though Mao is very much part of this tradition, he insists that people can learn to understand and then shape the nature of change. Unlike traditional Chinese thinkers, Mao does not see change as circular in nature, flux without direction or purpose. Indeed, man's very creativity is predicated upon learning how to make change both uninterrupted *and* shaped, continuous *and* guided. That only became possible for the Chinese in the modern era when for the first time more and more people were drawn into a revolutionary process that required them to control the forces that shaped their lives.

Mao's advocacy of the mass line has been analyzed from many angles, but it is his emphasis on the creativity of the masses that is probably the least understood. The essence of revolutionary leadership is to "go to the masses and learn from them, synthesize their experience into better, articulated principles and methods, then do propaganda among the masses, and call upon them to put these principles and methods into practice so as to solve their problems and help them achieve liberation and happiness."[58] No élite isolated from the masses can ever be creative, for in time it will seek to block or abort any mass initiatives, as it has throughout Chinese history.

Conflict is for Mao the essence of reality; contradictions are the very motive force of politics; criticism and self-criticism are the methods of resolving contradictions; and their resolution propels society forward. Criticism not only entails discipline that comes through constant comparison with accepted models or goals of the group; it is also a way of bringing contradictory forces into direct confrontation so that they can act positively on each other. Society should gradually be reorganized to allow this process to take place continuously, for criticism and self-criticism can only work positively if the various elements that provide the basis for progress are brought together, interact, and reinforce one another. If struggle is denied, organization leads to one group or segment of society seeking to dominate all others. In Chinese history, bureaucracy has long represented that danger.

Creativity requires a leadership that allows the clash of interests inherent in any situation to fully manifest itself, for only in this way can it be both thoroughly investigated and molded toward an objective. Revolutionary leadership thus remains a necessary midwife whose purpose is to encourage, anticipate, yet constantly learn from the unexpected course of social change. Only such leadership can overcome the curse of traditional Chinese life—that oscillation between spontaneity and rigid organization, between the passionate but often blind peasant upheavals and the traditional bureaucratic authority which built upon their failures.

After decades of engaging in revolutionary practice, Mao has developed several rough guidelines for analyzing it. "The masses in any given place" he wrote in 1943, "are generally composed of three parts, the relatively active, the intermediate and the relatively backward." Leaders, "must therefore, be skilled in uniting the small number of active elements around the leadership and must rely on them to raise the level of the intermediate elements and to win over the backward elements."[59] More than a decade later, during the Great Leap Forward, Mao's view of the three groups that emerge in any process of change was much the same. "At least thirty percent of them are activists, thirty percent are passive elements, including landlords, rich peasants, reactionaries, undesirables, bureaucrats, middle peasants, and some poor peasants, and forty percent follow the stream." If properly led, "those who follow the stream" are also prepared to accept revlutionary change.[60]

Throughout his career, Mao has shown himself to be both a master analyst of the multiplicity of interests in any concrete struggle and a leader remarkable for his ability to build united fronts on the basis of a central task that defines one's friends and enemies (if the struggle is considered antagonistic) or the advanced and the backward (if it is non-antagonistic). In the maelstrom of revolutionary practice, leadership must correctly single out the major task, a principal contradiction. "In studying any complex process in which there are two or more contradictions, we must devote every effort to finding its principal contradiction. Once this principal contradiction is grasped, all problems can be readily solved."[61] If no central task is defined, there is no way to organize for its accomplishment, no way to understand which groups may oppose a policy and which can be brought into a united front to achieve it. Without it, there is no way of knowing whether a situation calls for advance and struggle or for consolidation and unity, or whether one section of society should be more involved than another in any particular movement.

The control of the revolutionary process is not, therefore, to be left to the spontaneous impulses of the people. Yet neither is it to be administratively or bureaucratically dominated. The social forces that are mobilized will have their own dynamic, the conflicts of interest and class can only be truly clarified through such mobilization. Thus, leaders must learn to accept conflict when it is opportune, promoting struggle with discipline when necessary.

The fundamental issue for Mao is not centralization or decentralization, but what *kind* of centralization will best promote local initiative. "The proletariat needs to have great coercive power," Mao insists. "But it must also oppose bureaucracy and it must not have an inflated establishment."[62] Indeed, Mao's emphasis on the dictatorship of the proletariat has often been invoked to ensure that the revolution remains committed to the peasants. He has staked a great deal on his wager that China's rural poor will be left behind unless strong central leadership recognizes the deep divisions and conflict of forces in Chinese society and seeks constantly to allow all a meaningful degree of participation in the fruits of the revolution. Unless powerful leadership is exerted, the urban-rural split and all it implies will destory the values of the revolution, reinforcing traditional bureaucratic tendencies now augmented by the privileges often demanded by an educated technical élite.

Inequality of power, authority, and influence will remain, however, even as the task of central authority is to see that steps are continuously taken to ensure the accountability of power through the mass line. Though the nature of the Communist party's vanguard role may be questioned at times, though different people and groups continue to emerge as the activists for change, the principle of leadership remains.

"What is centralism?" Mao asks. "First of all it is a centralism of correct ideas."[63] Such centralism, however, is rooted in a continuous process of summing up unforeseeable circumstances that arise in the course of practice. General ideological directives that encourage and ultimately require local experimentation and innovation—that is Mao's preferred way. General guidelines by their very nature cannot simply be implemented. Indeed, "to carry out a directive of a higher organ blindly, and seemingly without any disagreement, is not really to carry it out but is the most artful way of opposing or sabotaging it."[64] It rides roughshod over that same local participation that the policy ultimately depends on for its effectiveness.

Hence the counterpart of Mao's emphasis on ideological centralism is the growth of local self-reliance, and, in time, increasingly sophisticated forms of popular participation. His insistence on such an approach has undoubtedly been an essential factor in the growth over the last two decades of a still crude but practical form of mass participation which has created a extraordinarily articulate population in local affairs. The success of such participation does not depend on everyone joining in equally. Perhaps only a third of the workers in a factory will participate extensively, becoming the activists Mao sees in any group. Different people at different times will emerge to confront diverse problems. What is fundamental is that politics is structured to encourage such participation, and to build a context in which activists can mobilize others with whom they work who are less involved. This is the dynamic that still produces new revolutionary recruits and leaders to prevent the ossification of the mass line at the base.

At times Mao's approach may seem a costly process, as during the Great Leap Forward and the Cultural Revolution. But he insists it is better to err on the side of experimental movements, with their potential for mass creativity, than cling to the safety of routine. And once a movement begins, it should not be abruptly turned off by a leadership worried about its course. "We cannot pour cold water on this kind of broad mass movement," Mao told his colleagues during the Great Leap Forward. "We can only use persuasion and say to them: Comrades, your hearts are in the right place. When tasks are difficult, don't be impatient. Do things step-by-step."[65] Leaders at all levels of society must not trail behind, gesticulating and criticizing, but must try to lead the activists, help them build alliances with those who "follow the stream," and teach them how to overcome the opposition of the backward. In such great upheavals lies the real test of leadership.

The history of the "two-line struggle" in the Chinese Communist party, however, is itself eloquent testimony to the great conflicts over revolutionary change. To Mao, "the correct line is defined with reference to the erroneous line, the two constitute a unity of opposites. The correct line is formed in the struggle with the incorrect line. . . . That there should be only correct things, and nothing erroneous, is without precedent in history."[66]

Any situation involves intense conflicts of interest, since "wherever there are groups of people, they are invariably composed of the left, middle and the right." Vastly divergent social forces are liberated in any mass movement.[67] In the process, a zigzag course of development has become evident. "Events have their twists and turns and do not follow a straight line." It was not just with irony that Mao told Edgar Snow in 1970 that he was a "center leftist." Committed throughout his career to the left and struggling in a variety of ways to encourage the activists, he has also argued that a period of consolidation and unity had to follow each period of intense struggle. In periods of upheaval and great advance the danger is of going too far, too fast. If at times "proper limits have to be exceeded in order to right a wrong," this accentuates a tendency during necessary periods of consolidation for "rightists" to "go on consolidating for all time." But such long-term consolidation will "make inflexible the ideology reflecting this system and render people incapable of adjusting their thought to new changes."[68] The temptation to bureaucratically dominate change will grow. The right is historically prone to this bureaucratic dictatorship, while the ultraleft seeks to realize the impossible all at once, forgetting that development must also proceed by stages.

Mao's *Selected Works*, containing his writings from the 1920s to 1949, are the way the Chinese can learn to understand their revolutionary history during China's bourgeois-democratic phase. Indeed, they constitute the most remarkable writings on its course and development. They are a literal textbook of revolutionary experience—a record of successes and failures, of new problems raised and solved, a history of united fronts and the breakup of old coalitions, of widening experience. It is not a smooth history, for it entails the struggle within and without the party of those too willing to compromise with the enemy and those who refused to build a broad enough united front; of those who resorted to bureaucratism and commandism to gain the obedience of the masses and those who opposed almost all central leadership; of those who were tempted by bourgeois methods and those enamored of Russian ways. Nor are the *Selected Works* to be read as a blueprint containing the ABCs of engineering social change in post-1949 China. They are instead to be studied as the very embodiment of the history of a method of problem solving in its concrete historical setting. "Laws cannot explain themselves," Mao insists. "Laws cannot be defined clearly if one does not start from specific analysis in the historical process."[69] "One must go through concrete analysis before he can discover and verify the principles and tenets involved."[70]

The great challenge throughout the struggle to gain power was to distinguish the necessary stages in the revolution's development, to realize that everything was not possible at a given time, while at the same time not drawing boundaries between stages so tightly that they served as a pretext for inaction. Before 1949, despite disputes within the Communist party, the central leadership was relatively united on the need to push the revolution toward victory. When it was a question of fighting Chiang Kai-shek or land reform, Mao noted in 1958, the party was "comparatively unanimous," but beginning with the forming of cooperatives, opposition spread.[71]

In 1967 Mao told a visiting delegation of foreigners that the "capitalist roaders" were those Communists who had supported the first stage of the Chinese Revolution against the imperialists and the feudalists, but were less sympathetic about the struggle against bourgeois ideas. They favored the distribution of the land, but not the collectivization of agriculture. Speaking in 1958 at the start of the Great Leap Forward about the temporary setback his policies suffered in 1956, Mao commented:

> In 1956, something was blown away: the general line of achieving greater, faster, better and more economical results, the promoters of progress, the Forty Articles [on agricultural development]. There were three kinds of people with three kinds of reaction: distress, indifference, and delight. A mill-

stone had dropped from their neck and there would
be peace in the world. Of those exhibiting these three
attitudes, the ones in the middle were numerous,
while those at the two extremes were few.

The struggle within the party, therefore, was not just to
combat the conservatives but to win over those in the middle
who would respond if correctly·led. Mao's role then, as it
was to be in the Cultural Revolution, was as a "center
leftist." The danger he saw was that the leadership would
prove too cautious. Indeed, Mao clearly said he was part of
the minority in the two greatest movements of post-1949
China, the Great Leap Forward and the Cultural Revolution.

Even under socialist conditions, therefore, the danger
exists that the revolutionary process will be interrupted.
That was the essence of Mao's warning to his colleagues in
1962 that "classes do exist in socialist countries and that
class struggle undoubtedly exists."[73] Whereas modernization
theorists stress the conservativeness and backwardness of the
peasants, Mao insists that they will respond creatively and
dynamically to leadership coming from their midst. The
real dangers of interruption of the revolutionary process
thus do not come from below but from above, from the
tendencies toward élite rigidity, bureaucratic inertia, and
privilege.

To be sure, it is only natural that "when any new things
emerge, they will encounter obstruction probably as a result of people not being accustomed to them or not understanding them, or their being in conflict with the interests
of a segment of the people."[74] There will also be people
throughout the course of the socialist revolution who
would like to preserve backward production relationships
and outmoded social institutions. "In the rural areas, the
well-to-do peasants have their own viewpoints on many
questions. They cannot adapt themselves to new changes."[75]

Yet in a socialist society it is not just a question of newness
or of declining bourgeois remnants rooted in the historical

bourgeois class, but of "conservative strata" or "something resembling 'vested interest groups' " that will thrive on the contradictions between mental and manual labor, the split between urban and rural areas, between workers and peasants. "Man is a queer animal," Mao mused in 1961. "As soon as he possesses some outstanding conditions, he will give himself airs. . . . Not to give heed to this is very dangerous."[76] And again: "Man has one defect. It is despising people. People with a little achievement will look down on people with no achievement."[77] As he told André Malraux, "Humanity left to its own devices does not necessarily reestablish capitalism . . . but it does reestablish inequality. The forces tending towards the creation of new classes are powerful."[78]

Thus deterioration can occur on both an individual level (a process of "embourgeoisment") and on the social level ("capitalist restoration"), so that ideological struggle will necessarily continue at all levels of society. It is waged at all levels of the Communist party, and within each individual between his class background and new collective demands, between selfishness and the demands of unselfishness, the desire for personal gain against the need for collective advance.

Again and again throughout Chinese history, mobility for the few has led to their defense of bureaucratic privilege. In the early 1960s Mao warned of this tendency both among the veteran cadres of the revolution and their children. He saw that they constituted a powerful potential élite. In addition, "there are still 'academic lords' who are in control of scientific and research institutions" who "suppress new-born forces."[79]

On the one hand, Mao observed, "we believe in uninterrupted revolution, yet many comrades gave no thought to the timing of the socialist revolution or to what should be done after land reform. They closed their eyes to the sprouts of socialism, even after such forms had appeared."[80] No leadership, Mao insists, can create the new social forms and political and economic innovations out of its own head, then apply them through administrative decree in a way that the masses can willingly accept. But new forms and methods will emerge if cadres and the people are allowed to experiment, if they are mobilized and encouraged by a central leadership willing to learn from their potential breakthroughs. In the 1940s, under wartime conditions, the writer Jack Belden described the redefinition of leaders and led in the liberated areas. "Peasant and cadre were like a two-man patrol into enemy territory; they went forward into the unknown by a process of mutual encouragement, first one holding back, then the other, then both rushing forward together."[81] Today, in vastly different circumstances, it is still to this intimate relationship that Mao turns for mass initiative and creativity.

Precisely in order to continue this process and to sum up the creative potential of an aroused, active population, Mao spoke of uninterrupted revolution at the time of the Great Leap Forward.

> I stand for the theory of uninterrupted revolution. . . . In making revolution one must strike while the iron is hot—one revolution must follow another, the revolution must continually advance. . . . For example, after the Liberation of 1949 came the Land Reform; as soon as this was completed there followed the mutual-aid teams, then the low-level cooperatives, then the high-level cooperatives. After seven years the cooperativization was completed and productive relations were transformed; then came the Rectification. After Rectification was finished, before things had cooled down, then came the Technical Revolution.[82]

Mao's example of uninterrupted revolution combines his constant emphasis on stages and steps in any process of change and the need to continually push the revolution forward. While he accepts the zigzag course of change, his emphasis is clearly on the necessity to continuously support those groups within and without the party who at any given time wish to push the revolution beyond the last stage of consolidation.

This emphasis on one revolution following another, as has been noted earlier, is a theme running throughout the history of Chinese attempts to change China since 1840. It reflects the deep fears of those who for so long found their attempts to build a new China brushed aside as inadequate to the enormous challenges, of seeing once progressive changes falling by the wayside as insufficient, of one generation after another seeking to solve problems only to see their ways become a new orthodoxy which was then overthrown. Mao sees the process arising from the deeply rooted demand for change among the vast majority of the Chinese people. But unless the process of bureaucratization and the cultural and ideological rigidification historically associated with it is directly attacked, it would triumph even under socialist conditions. How to prevent this was a concern that haunted innumerable Chinese long before the Great Proletarian Cultural Revolution.

In a sense there is no final answer for this danger to the revolution. Each generation has to win that battle for itself, though their methods will in time become qualitatively different. Even communist society "will certainly be divided into stages,"[83] and "ideological and political struggles between men and revolutions will continue; they will never cease."[84]

Trotsky and Mao on Uninterrupted Revolution

"I stand for the theory of uninterrupted revolution," Mao said, but "do not mistake this for Trotsky's theory of uninterrupted revolution."[85] There is indeed little in common between the two theories but the name itself. Mao and Trotsky differ profoundly on the meaning of an uninterrupted revolutionary process, the forces that propel it, and the relationship between revolution at home and abroad.

Trotsky's theory sought a historical and political explanation for the simultaneous outbreak in Russia of two revolts, one rural, one proletarian. That "peculiar mixture" of the most backward, rural, feudal elements with the most modern, industrial, proletarian ones, Trotsky argued, was the key to the "fundamental riddle" of the Russian Revolution. Applying the classic European revolutionary formula to Russia, Trotsky wrote:

> If the agrarian problem, as a heritage from the barbarism of the old Russian history, had been solved by the bourgeoisie, if it could have been solved by them, the Russian proletariat could not possibly have come to power in 1917. In order to realize the Soviet state, there was required a drawing together and mutual penetration of two factors belonging to completely different historic species: a peasant war— that is, a movement characteristic of the dawn of bourgeois development—and a proletarian insurrection, the movement signaling its decline. That is the essence of 1917.[86]

Trotsky's theory of uninterrupted revolution sought to explain the combining of a bourgeois with a proletarian revolution, the moving without pause from one historic moment, the bourgeois, to another, the socialist. No leaping over stages here, only the possibility of "telescoping" them into "embryonic forms," of shortening what would otherwise be the work of centuries. The unique feature of the Russian Revolution is that it immediately placed the proletariat in the position of power, thus requiring that the revolution "grow over" into more advanced phases. The transformation of a still backward society became the prerogative of a new state power under the leadership of the workers.

Backwardness provides the momentum for this entire process. Both the peasants and the workers required revolutionary changes to confront their problems. However, only a tactical alliance growing out of mutual dependence was possible: agreement about what had to be destroyed but not about what was to take its place. Hence there was only a general commitment to upheaval and violent change, but no consensus at all about how to adapt to the modern industrial world.

Trotsky reasoned as follows: When the old political order has been overthrown, the workers will control the cities. Only a small segment of the bourgeoisie will have joined the revolution (and this only after the fact), but the bourgeois opposition will be weak and divided. The peasants, without whom the revolution would have been impossible, will initially accept proletarian leadership because of their traditional willingness to accept the organizational power of the cities and, more importantly, because the spontaneous grabbing of land in the wake of the revolutionary upheaval will receive official sanction. Feudalism will thus have been socially abolished. For a brief moment, the "proletariat in power will stand before the peasants as the class which has emancipated them."[87]

Without any genuine agreement between the workers and the peasants about the future, a dictatorship of the workers, the only force prepared and capable of carrying out development, becomes inevitable. Yet almost immediately the proletariat faces an acute contradiction with the peasantry. The peasants will have expropriated the large landholdings. Yet no long-term solution to Russia's agrarian problems is possible on the basis of small peasant landholdings. The industrializing needs of the cities are too great to be solved by the eighteenth-century agrarian solution of the French Revolution. Class differences will quickly reassert themselves in the countryside, providing a natural setting for the growth of capitalist and petty-bourgeois interests.

Though the proletariat will not begin with radical measures when it first seizes power, confronted with such contradictions it is forced into these measures, driven not so much by its will or ideology but by the need to cope with the concrete, day-to-day problems thrown up by the revolutionary process as it unfolds. As the proletariat is driven to ever greater measures of state control in order to handle both the spreading opposition and pressing social and economic problems, the alliance between the workers and the peasants breaks down.

Finally, the peasants will turn their "hostile face towards the proletariat." The "resulting political problems of continuing the revolution will now be joined by the problems of organizing 'social production.'" The poverty of the country, the lack of experience in planning and self-management, the problems of coordinating agricultural and industrial production, the shortage of technical know-how all undermine the new government's capacity to go beyond the most rudimentary stage of collectivism. A "number of oases" will be created, but on the whole, nothing that even approaches a socialist society.[88]

As the indigenous potential of the Russian proletariat reaches its limits, the second stage of the revolution exhausts itself. Having aroused the peasant masses, the new proletarian state is threatened by collapse. Russian backwardness, which first enabled the workers to seize power, now returns to wreak its revenge. To survive, the revolution must spill over into the international arena. Only the victory of the European proletariat will allow the Russian Revolution to progress further.

In his writings during the 1930s, Trotsky argued that the dictatorship of the proletariat had been established in Russia, the foundations of collectivism laid. Yet he concluded that further development in isolation was no longer possible. Economic scarcity threatened to undermine the rudimentary forms of the new society; the primitive foundations of the old society were reasserting themselves.[89]

Alone among the leaders of the Russian Revolution before 1917, Trotsky argued that the Russian proletariat could begin the process of going beyond the bourgeois-democratic revolution and inaugurate the transition to socialism. In 1905 Lenin spoke of uninterrupted revolution.

> We stand for uninterrupted revolution. We will not
> halt half-way . . . we will exert every effort to help
> the whole of the peasantry to make the democratic
> revolution in order thereby to make it easier for
> us, the party of the proletariat, to pass on as quickly
> as possible to the new and higher task—socialist
> revolution.[90]

Yet until 1917 Lenin maintained that only the completion
of the Democratic Revolution would create the preconditions for the proletariat's struggle for socialism. Only then
did he argue that the logical distinction between the
bourgeois and proletarian stages did not imply a chrono-
logical succession. The rule of capital could be overturned,
the transition to socialism begun, even as Russia's feudal
past was attacked. As he said on the fourth anniversary of
the October Revolution, "The first stage develops into the
second. The second, in passing, solves the problems of the
first. The second consolidates the work of the first. Struggle,
and struggle alone, decides how far the second succeeds in
outgrowing the first."[91]

Struggle and conflict permeate all of Lenin's writings
after 1917. The dictatorship of the proletariat is a constant
struggle—educational and administrative, military and
peaceful, cultural and economic, bloody and bloodless—
against the forces and traditions of the old society. Lenin
warned repeatedly of the strength and durability of the
bourgeoisie and the dangers arising from small production
which "engenders capitalism and the bourgeoisie continuously, daily, hourly, spontaneously, and on a mass scale."
He called for new forms of cooperation with the peasants, and he vehemently attacked the "deplorable" and
"wretched" condition of the state apparatus. Yet, though
an ardent opponent of bureaucratization, Lenin frankly
acknowledged that it was "a question that we have not yet
been able to study." While his last writings pointed to the
need to confront these and other problems, Lenin died
without developing a theoretical conception of the con-

tinuation of the revolution under the dictatorship of the proletariat.

If Lenin's writings leave open the question of continuing the revolution, Trotsky's clearly preclude this possibility. The revolution is uninterrupted only in the sense that it combines two stages analytically distinguishable in the history of Western capitalism. The immaturity of Russian capitalism makes the revolution "uninterrupted" in terms of the seizure of power and its initial moments, but then precludes for Trotsky the possibility of engendering within itself a proletarian ideology and a new culture capable of leading the transformation of the peasants and the workers. The ideological transformation Mao sees as inherent in each stage of the revolutionary process, Trotsky saw largely as its end result.

For Trotsky, genuine socialist ideology and a new socialist man can only arise after an advanced material base is developed. Like many other European Marxists, he believed that "the society in which he [socialist man] lives has to be so highly developed, so wealthy, educated, and civilized that there is no objective need or necessity for it to allow any recrudescence of inequality or oppression. This is what *all* Marxists before Stalin took for granted."[92] Socialism and proletarian values thus require a level of productivity that releases people from the tyrannies of work and the division of labor; a collective work force possessing the scientific and cultural prerequisites to achieve the fullest popular control of the production process; and a population capable of sustaining unprecedentedly dynamic and innovative forms of direct democracy. Such values had barely emerged in the highly concentrated factories of urban Russia. Russian capitalism was too underdeveloped, and Trotsky saw the peasants repelled by even these nascent proletarian ways.

A deepening of the revolution after the seizure of power, through a combined, intertwined process of revolutionary transformation of both the economic base and the superstructure, thus has no part in Trotsky's theory of uninterrupted revolution. The values and attitudes Mao sees as capable of transformation in the superstructure are for Trotsky only changeable through the prior transformation of the material base. "A socialist economy on the way to surpassing capitalism technically would be assured of a socialist development almost automatically."[93] While Trotsky saw socialist man emerging only after the fulfillment of socialism's prerequisites, Mao sees the need for conscious transformation at each and every step of a deepening revolutionary process. As organizations are retooled, motivation must be changed; it is in the transformed spirit of the collective that the material strength necessary to build a new society finds birth. Where Mao has sought to explain a process of remolding the small producer-peasant—for example, the contradictions in each stage and how to resolve them—Trotsky denies the very possibility of such ideological remolding through a step-by-step revolutionary process.

Part of Trotsky's aversion to ideological remolding lies in his conception of culture. By "culture" he meant either high culture, the artistic accomplishments of the bourgeoisie that everyone could gradually come to share and appreciate, or basic literacy. "The main task of the proletarian intelligentsia in the immediate future is not the abstract formation of a new culture regardless of the absence of a basis for it, but . . . a systematic, planful and, of course, critical imparting to the backward masses of the essential elements of the culture which already exists."[94]

Whereas Trotsky saw high culture as separate from the daily values and attitudes of people in the workplace, Mao sees culture and superstructure as practically synonymous and intricately interwoven with all aspects of life. The values and attitudes Trotsky usually saw mechanistically tied to the productive forces, Mao sees as part of the superstructure, developing in a dynamic dialectical relationship with the base. Herein is the basis for Mao speaking of cultural revolution in a way Trotsky could never envision.

In their bitter dispute after Lenin's death, neither Trotsky nor Stalin confronted the issue of continuing the revolution. Their arguments focused on the pivotal issues of the nature of the worker-peasant alliance and the possibilities of building socialism in one country. "Lenin fought the adherents of 'permanent' revolution," Stalin argued, "not over the question of its uninterruptedness, for he himself maintained the point of view of uninterrupted revolution, but because they underestimated the role of the peasantry" and the ability of the Russian proletariat to lead them. This "hampered the work of emancipating the peasantry from the influence of the bourgeoisie, the work of rallying the peasantry around the proletariat."[95]

Trotsky saw a dynamic role for the peasantry in the revolutionary struggle for power, but no unified front developing between the workers and the peasants that could lay the foundations for the building of socialism. Stalin argued that the peasants, given land and peace by the proletarian revolution, had become "the reserve of the proletariat" and could thus be drawn into the work of socialist construction. He confidently stated: "We possess, under the dictatorship of the proletariat, all the requisites for the building of a complete socialist society by overcoming all internal difficulties, for we can and must overcome them by our own efforts."[96]

Mao certainly agreed with Stalin's decision to build socialism in one country. But unlike both Trotsky and Stalin, Mao maintained that a new superstructure is not automatically generated from the economic base. New relations of production do not spontaneously arise from the forces of production. The lag in both requires conscious action. Being, Mao argues, is the overarching foundation of consciousness; a breakthrough development of new productive forces is the historical prerequisite for changes in the relations of production and the superstructure. But within this epochal context the superstructure can become dominant, allowing for changes in either the base or the superstructure, depending upon an analysis of the specific situation.[97]

Just as the superstructure is not spontaneously generated

from the base, Mao Tsetung Thought—so the Chinese argue—is not mechanically derived from the Chinese proletariat. While progressive and revolutionary qualities are labeled "proletarian," they are not simply implicit in the forces of production and the urban workers in large-scale modern industry. Mao's writings are imbued with a sense of the enormous diversity of attitudes and divisions among and within classes and the aspirations for change among the majority of people. Yet even as Mao Tsetung Thought drew upon a host of Chinese traditions and values, even as the peasants were the main force organized during the revolutionary seizure of power, the Chinese argue that this in no way entails an ideological pluralism of classes or a vanguard party outside a class base. The Communist party could emerge and lead the revolutionary struggle only on the basis of the historic potential of the modern proletariat. Its role as the vanguard takes on its full meaning only in the context of the dynamic and creative quality this implies for the superstructure. At each stage of the revolution, cultural struggles are intricately interwoven with the creation of new values, attitudes, and methods of struggle in all other parts of society.

Trotsky's and Mao's differing views on the superstructure underlie their understanding of the relationship between class, bureaucracy, and backwardness. Russian backwardness left a weak proletariat facing the awesome task of socialist construction. Though the foundation of a socialist society was laid through the substitution of state and cooperative ownership for private ownership of the means of production, Trotsky maintained that the edifice itself could not be built without a decisive increase in the productive forces, which would only become possible with the proletarian revolutions in Europe. Without that assistance, Russia's backwardness would wreak its revenge through the growth of bureaucracy and the privileged stratum Trotsky saw emerging under Stalin's leadership in the 1930s. This was not a new class, however. Private property, Trotsky insisted, had been abolished, and with it the traditional bourgeoisie.[98]

"Putting politics in command" emphasizes Mao's concern with the transformation of human beings and their relations to each other. When he renewed his call in 1962 to "never forget class struggle," Mao was raising the difficult theoretical problem of class and bureaucracy in a socialist society. If one understood the term "class" in its traditional way, the slogan would mean a call for continuous struggle against the old national bourgeoisie, bourgeois intellectuals, former rich and middle peasants, former landlords, etc. And Mao did indeed speak during the 1960s of the power of these overthrown classes, the force of old habits, the strength of small production.

Yet clearly these were not Mao's immediate concerns. His criticisms of the Soviet Union before the Cultural Revolution show his preoccupation with new bourgeois elements created in the process of building a socialist society and their power within the Communist party. Until the end of the Cultural Revolution, however, a certain ambiguity ran throughout discussions of this problem by Mao and his supporters. They often talked of the old classes when they were really discussing what they saw as new bourgeois elements in the party and their commitment to bureaucratic administration.

Many Communist party members who were criticized during the Cultural Revolution as supporters of Liu Shao-ch'i probably believed in the "traditional" economic conception of class. When Liu stated in 1956 that "the question of who will win in the struggle between socialism and capitalism in our country has now been decided," he was pointing to these traditional class forces. When Mao drafted his "Twenty-Three Articles" in 1964, he wrote repeatedly of class struggle, but the one issue mentioned as worthy of organizing the campaign around was the party organization. Landlords, rich peasants, even former counterrevolutionaries and bad elements need not be permanently condemned for their past class status. Their present political status should be reviewed and decided by the masses themselves. In mentioning his five requirements for being a revolutionary successor, Mao did not include class origin.

By contrast, Liu's "Later Ten Articles" stipulated that the class status of peasants should be determined on the basis of their economic status at the time of the land reform. Only in exceptional cases should the children of bourgeois parents have their status altered. Marriage across class lines was prohibited. Liu, in short, saw class in a way that did not raise the question of the unequal distribution of political power in Chinese society. Mao, however, was insisting that the divisions in Chinese society had to be understood through the dangers of bourgeois right in society and bureaucracy in the party. He feared the party was weakening its ties to the people as it became a ruling establishment, spreading its roots horizontally among the well educated and the powerful rather than vertically among the masses. Thus the influences on the party and the leadership could not be correctly understood and handled. In time, an increasingly bureaucratic leadership would seek to cope with change by resorting to domination, intimidation, and sometimes even terror.

Mao has not publicly systematized his criticism of the new class and bureaucracy in a way satisfactory to many Western mechanical Marxists. But what developed during and after the Cultural Revolution was a theory of new bourgeois class forces which thrive on the inequalities in Chinese society. These new bourgeois elements reflect the demands of the old class forces, the Maoist argue. They cluster around the party, finding their natural home in the bureaucracy. In this sense they pose a greater threat to the revolution than the old classes, for their control of the powerful bureaucratic apparatus or their influence in the superstructure would allow them to restore capitalism in China, Mao argues, much as has already happened in the Soviet Union. In short, they are viewed as "Communists in name but new bourgeois elements in reality." The great danger arises from those in positions of privilege and authority in the state apparatus and the economy (including the educational, cultural, and professional institutions) who desire to hold onto their positions and to find new ways of stabilizing, protecting, and perpetuating their status in society.

This is the context within which Mao warns of the perils of bureaucracy. It is far more than a sign of backwardness; it is the greatest threat to the revolutionary process. Left to its own device, the spread of bureaucratic organization will dominate the process of change, and in so doing create a privileged élite that thrives on the inequalities and the tendencies toward capitalism that will long remain a part of the building of a socialist society. Bureaucracy and questions of class are thus closely linked. "The bureaucratic class," Mao wrote in 1960, "is a class sharply opposed to the working class and the poor and middle peasant classes. These people have become or are in the process of becoming bourgeois elements sucking the blood of the workers."[99]

Trotsky raised few of these problems in his analysis of the revolutionary process. Uninterrupted revolution was primarily an idea that connected the liquidation of absolutism and feudalism with a socialist revolution. Mao's notion of class struggle throughout the socialist stage, the eternality of contradiction, the continuing of the revolution under the dictatorship of the proletariat and the dynamic and creative role of the superstructure were antithetical to Trotsky's quite specific and limited conception of a revolutionary process. Indeed, in rejecting the idea of an uninterrupted revolutionary process both Trotsky and Stalin essentially agreed with the modernization theorists.

The contrast between modernization and uninterrupted revolution can now be further explored by temporarily setting aside these Russian views and directly joining the debate between these two perspectives through the following comparisons.

The Death of the Revolution
Versus Continuous Revolution

Ever since the establishment of the People's Republic of China, American observers have portrayed Mao as administering artificial ideological stimulants to keep alive a terminally ill revolution. But death was inevitable. The revolutionary cadres became bureaucrats; the revolutionary élan gave way to self-interest; the simplicities of guerrilla warfare gave way to the imperatives of modern industrial ways and the privileged role for those who work with their minds instead of their hands.

For many American observers, Mao's mass line was a plausible way to fight a guerrilla war. After liberation, the "formula remained but the situation changed."[100] By the mid-1950s, mass campaigns required an enormous expenditure of time and effort, yet only momentarily achieved close ties between cadres and masses. The death of the revolution was occurring. The "natural" tendency of any society toward stabilization was settling in. An "obsessed" Maoist faction among China's leaders was forced, like pushers, to give the Chinese people bigger and bigger hits of their ideological fix to get the same effect of mass revolutionary "enthusiasm." Sooner or later they would O.D. fatally. By the late 1950s the "ghastly failure" of the Great Leap Forward, that "hyperbole of the mass line," clearly marked the "recurring conflict between theory and reality."[101] Of course, the Cultural Revolution was Mao's final doomed gamble to reverse the whole process.

If to American commentators revolution is a momentary upheaval which quickly dies away once political power is seized, to Chinese it is a long protracted process through which China has come to life. What Americans describe as a Maoist ride up the "ideological escalator" is for the Chinese a process of deepening the revolution through the mass campaigns since 1949. These campaigns, the Maoists argue, are not artifically prolonging the life of archaic ways.

As an example of uninterrupted revolution, Mao points to the social revolution in the rural areas since 1949. Moving quickly from private landholdings to mutual-aid teams, from lower to higher collectives, and finally to the communes involved a series of mass campaigns. Each sought to confront certain existing problems; each led to new problems to be resolved, new lessons to be learned. That these movements are not all spontaneous does not mean they are artificial. That they do not all succeed does not deny the effectiveness of the approach.

Americans, however, whether dealing with changes in the rural areas, the factories, the schools, or in methods of administration, reduce the process of social change to a question of the techniques of party leadership, control, and domination. The CCP alone emerges as an active agent, the external manipulator of a largely passive population. The party is torn out of a developing revolutionary process in which some classes and groups struggle vigorously to defend their traditional way of life, some hesitate because they fear the risks of further change or its uncharted course, and some demand even more rapid transformation. The struggles after 1949 between the Communist party and the bourgeoisie, the landlords, and the traditionally educated are analyzed apart from a process of deepening revolution in which these groups fought to hold onto their privileges and élite life-style.

It is not surprising that the conflicts between the party and newly emerging groups satisfied with their positions of privilege and authority in the bureaucracy and the economy after the mid-1950s are seen apart from the deepening socialist character of the revolution. Economic development for American observers rarely entails consideration of the equitable distribution of the products of economic growth, the creation of collective relationships, the elimination of exploitation, or the overcoming of the contradictions between mental and manual, urban and rural, agriculture and industry. The attack on those who thrive on what Americans see as justified inequalities is thus dismissed as ideological utopianism.

As Kung Chung-wu shows, however, an underlying pattern to these mass campaigns since 1949 is apparent in the way they extended the revolution step by step into more and more areas of Chinese life. Each campaign required and built on those preceding it. The Great Leap Forward would not have been possible without a decade of transformation in the rural areas and the cities; the Great Proletarian Cultural Revolution presupposed over fifteen years of socialist development. Tying these campaigns together is the undeviating Maoist determination to build a socialist economy and a new socialist man.

By tearing such struggles out of the context of the deepening of the revolutionary process, American observers have reduced the history of the great mass campaigns in China to a series of gyrations between chaos and order, revolutionary ways and pragmatism, a series of fitful starts and stops. The American attachment to a smooth, efficient, orderly process is indeed ironic. If one compares contemporary China to nineteenth-century England's business cycles or the recurring recessions and depressions in twentieth-century America, the "unevenness" of development in China seems less a consideration for American observers than its socialist direction.

The fact is, those "gyrations" are so judged because methods that radically challenge American capitalist ways are again and again judged as emotionalism. No theme is more persistent among American observers than this equation of revolutionary struggle with emotionalism. When the Chinese speak of "collective action" and developing "consciousness," this is usually translated as "emotional mobilization" and "voluntarism." Mao's conception of change is reduced to "an emotional storm, in which hatreds, resentment, and a sense of hopeless desperation burst through social restraints in an overwhelming surge." The emotions that fuel political involvement "rise to crests and then diminish through action." Such emotions mean that "hatred" is "the motive force behind political action."[102] Indeed, there is a "close relationship between activism and the cultivation of sentiments of hatred in the Party leadership's conception of political motivation. . . ."[103] In all activists, in short, there is "an association between political action and the emotion of hate."[104] No wonder that, in the language of the social scientist, "we must ask whether the Maoist notion of political activism based on indignation, rage, and hatred at exploitation is an appropriate motivational basis for a nation's social development."[105]

Thus, mass campaigns can only fail again and again. They don't teach people anything, except perhaps how to endure them. Consciousness has not been raised, only emotions frayed. After all, to speak of "raising emotions" and "relying on voluntarism" over a prolonged period of time hardly makes much sense. That is why Mao "has resorted to ever more strained and artifical methods of emotional manipulation."[106]

With the great mass campaigns reduced to something easily dismissed—emotional upheavals—and the human "emotions" separated from the real "tasks," American social scientists are ready to tackle the problem of understanding China. Theirs is a snapshot approach that breaks down any process into a host of nicely manageable "problems." Problems are plucked from their historic and revolutionary context, treated statically, and analyzed.

This intellectual approach characterizes not only the bureaucratic conception of Weberian thought and the rationality of modernization theory but the very values and assumptions of the government-academic world in which most China watchers live. Their world has no direct experience of revolution. It is a world built upon the hierarchy, status, competitiveness, and self-interest they see as endemic in China. An élite world predicated upon the division of theory and practice, mental and manual work, it quite naturally feels an ideological sympathy for the life-style, privileged claims, and rational role of élites in other nations. Almost all the notions of "individualism," "rationality," "bureaucracy," and "problem solving" China watchers project on China are embedded in their own way of living and thinking. Assuming such a world is ultimately the only rational one, they proceed to carry out the dissection of the Chinese revolutionary corpse.

The first requirement of this task is to destroy the revolutionary process by not seeing it as a process, and then to claim it doesn't work. Thus they dismiss the Maoist notion of contradictions and dialectical thinking. Above all, the possibilities of deepening the revolution through stages that combine a process of material development and social transformation in a collective context are discarded as revolutionary rhetoric.

The tradition of treating revolutions and revolutionary struggle as pathologies analogous to human diseases is an old one, yet rarely has it been pursued so feverishly or for so long as in American studies on China. This emphasis on Mao's faith in emotions, disorder, and even chaos is almost comical, for by any imaginable comparisons the last quarter-century has been the most orderly, efficient, and rational period in several centuries of Chinese history. The Maoist insists this has been possible precisely because of the emphasis on continuous revolution, which acknowledges the real conflicts existing in contemporary Chinese society and confronts them through the various mass movements American observers decry. The way to overcome violence, they argue, is to continuously learn to resolve the contradictions that arise, to use revolutionary ways to solve problems. Seeming stability and calm only mask the growth of vested interests. It is not emotionalism but consciousness that overcomes the dichotomies and dualities through which Americans structure their view of China and distort its revolutionary process.

Ideology

Since the lessening of cold-war tensions, American observers have come to insist that modernization theory is not an ideology. Ideology is something others have, something incompatible with the objective, detached perspective they insist their scholarly work enshrines.

From their "objective" perch, they discern two general views of ideology in China. On the one hand, ideology is an essentially emotional process that makes unpleasant objective conditions psychologically acceptable to the Chinese. It provides "legitimacy," helps resolve a Chinese "identity crisis," provides useful internal and external enemies to mobilize the population against, substitutes ideological for material incentives, even provides in the eyes of some observers a useful historic father figure ("a symbol at the center to fill the void left by the Son of Heaven"[107]). Ideology is thus an emotional crutch that distorts objective reality. It is portrayed as dangerous because the preoccupation with abstract values and utopian visions makes it prone to ignore the imperatives of rational development.

On the other hand, ideology is understood as an instrument of manipulation, often cynically utilized by members of the Chinese élite to enforce their objectives. From this perspective, it is primarily a way of penetrating the masses and forcing them to respond with little regard for their personal needs and interests. In time, as the initial revolutionary enthusiasm dies, "either the increasing disparity between words and actions will undermine the sense of relevance of Mao's concepts or—as in the Soviet pattern—subsequent generations of Party leaders will revise Mao's thought" by invoking his name while discarding his ideas.[108] Thus ideology becomes "a manipulative vehicle of communication and career advancement rather than an intellectual tool for evaluating the world."[109]

In neither perspective can ideology provide tools for "evaluating the world." It may temporarily galvanize people, often into a "frenzy" so that individual interests will momentarily be overcome, but materialistic self-interest is so universal, so rooted in human nature, it will reemerge when the mass campaign subsides. Peasants want private plots; workers want better wages; leaders and intellectuals want status, privilege, and power. In almost all China watchers' descriptions of the People's Republic of China, group activity is denigrated as "ideological" and judged negatively as a form of subordination of the individual's real interest. This pivotal assumption fosters a pervasive hostility toward any forms of collectivity.

Such hostility was graphically portrayed in Robert Lifton's widely applauded book, *The Psychology of Totalism*. In the 1950s Lifton warned that man's psychic state can be pushed just so far. The Maoist vision, "a totalistic vision of absolute subjugation of self to regime," was creating a "psychology of the pawn."[110] Social forces are manipulated by the leadership to appear so much more overpowering than the individual that his efforts are all geared toward adaptation. The individual becomes sensitive to all kinds of cues, "expert at anticipating environmental pressures, and skillful in riding them in such a way that his psychological energies move with the tide rather than turn painfully against himself."[111] The "thought-terminating cliche" characterizes the language of the totalist environment; the "most far reaching and complex human problems are compressed into brief, highly reductive definitive-sounding phrases, easily memorized and easily expressed. These become the start and finish of any ideological analysis."[112] All this strips the individual, robs him of part of himself, and makes him live an alien and artificial life to such an extent that he obeys impulses that are totally foreign to himself.

This vintage cold-war portrait of individuals caught in a highly menacing environmental spider web remains a widely held position among American China watchers. In it are rooted two perspectives—that of coercion and voluntarism. The latter stresses the subtle, less "threatening" and thus more "palatable" techniques of rule. In this perspective the problem for the "modern totalitarian regime" is to "minimize dissatisfaction while making its people do what they do not wish to do."[113] Obviously, it is argued, "when such a forcing process is carried out on a

society-wide, totalistic scale with the full pressures of government and an engineered public environment behind it,
both the dissonance and the willingness to change in order
to relieve it are at their maximum."[114] "Citizens are not
forced; they volunteer."[115] The "virtue of being 'active' in
dealing with a variety of harsh and manipulative social
authorities"[116] is self-evident. With various diffuse and de-
layed sanctions, the refusal to "volunteer" will in time
create such anxieties that sooner or later "complete obedience" will be obtained.[117]

To Benjamin Schwartz such techniques as "study,"
"thought reform," "confession, etc.," and the universal
application of mass-organization techniques were "proving
that totalitarian consolidation of a people could be carried
out effectively by relying on 'man' rather than technology."[118] He points to the Maoist vision's "emphasis on
the individual's total self-abnegation and total immersion
in the collectivity as ultimate goods"—"a kind of collective
mysticism."[119] Here again is that prevalent American assumption—that what is abnegated is the individual, not
individualism or privatism. Totalism and politicalization
blur these all together, leaving the stereotypes of "individual" on one side and "mass" on the other. The stage is thus
set for a variety of sweeping Orwellian conclusions about
life in China.

Group study sessions, the numerous meetings, and self-
criticism methods are widely judged as totally negative
developments. They are held instrumental in the creation
of the "mental monotone imposed upon the country." "All
thought, all ideas past, present, and future, not to mention
the historic record, are twisted, manipulated, rooted out,
and flattened into one, expressed in half a dozen slogans
dinned incessantly and insistently into the heads of the
public."[120] Or again: "the communists seem to believe that
the mind of the people can be wiped clean at any moment
. . . to make room for any new thoughts and ideas the
manipulators of 'public opinion' may choose to implant."[121]

Such views, pushed to their logical conclusion, suggest that China's human and social developments are paving the way for a *1984* (the coercive power of the state) or a *Brave New World* (voluntarist manipulation). Both perspectives argue that character and identity are reshaped, not in accordance with an individual's special nature or potential but with the contours of doctrinal models.

Fortunately, establishment writers conclude, like the routinization of revolution, there must inevitably be a retreat from this dehumanizing vision of collectivity—a consequence, in the language of Robert Lifton's *Revolutionary Immortality*, of the "mounting response of inner antagonism or 'hostility of suffocation'; the effective penetration of the 'idea-tight milieu control' by outside influences that undermine the closed communication system; and a 'law of diminishing conversions' operating among those subjected to repeated reform experiences, according to which inner enthusiasm is increasingly replaced by outward compliance."[122]

The alternative to totalism and "psychism" is once again portrayed as "pragmatism" and "liberalization." As this occurs, the conflict between "individual" and "collective" will reemerge. A few observers merely ask the question: "Will Mao's masses one day become aware of their individual existence? Will they become conscious of the contradiction between their individual interests and those of the collective when the more urgent collective interests such as the honor of the nation and the irrigation of a commune are satisfied and fade into the background?"[123] Here is the basis for views of the Chinese people today as beasts of burden, the vast majority barely conscious, with poorly developed individual personalities, easily swayed by the nearest loudspeakers broadcasting Peking's latest line, or stubbornly trying to pursue their own interests despite the ideological barrage and élite manipulation.

Opposing the American views is the Chinese understanding of Mao Tsetung Thought. To them it is the summation of Chinese revolutionary experience, a series of concepts, principles, and styles of problem solving embedded in the very history and practice of revolutionary struggle.

To most American observers, consciousness is not really raised unless there is a greater awareness of self-interest, and thus of the innate conflict between individual and group. The Chinese, on the other hand, insist that only through organized group activity, study sessions, and collective work can they gradually learn to analyze the world around them. Social conservatism is rooted in the unreflective way people go through life, accepting old habits, customs, and ideas. Through collective work and group study, through criticism and self-criticism, people learn how to analyze problems in all their varied dimensions, gradually creating a shared way of conceptualizing them in a spirit of cooperation. By asking what the results (for individuals, their organizations, the entire society) would be if one course of action is chosen over another, behavior is gradually supposed to move more toward the path of careful reflection, group analysis, and concern for others.

Herein lies a major distinction between modernization theorists and the Maoists. In dealing with the nature of group participation, the role of specialists, the meaning of culture and ideology, the Maoist insists that thinking about problems is a process that will gradually involve everyone. The Maoist does not criticize different types of work or question the need for trained specialists. But underlying these different tasks is a process of conceptualization that emphasizes a similarity of assumptions, goals, and methods of analysis. Though the level of conceptualization is often more sophisticated for intellectuals and specialists, they do not have a preeminent hold on the fundamental ways of thinking.

Mao's three-stage conception of cognition strikes at the heart of American views of the division of labor where some individuals are empirical observers, some theorists, some men of labor and action. For Mao, everyone is at once empirical observer, theorist, and man of action. It is on this epistemological basis that he advocates the integration of work and study, mental and manual work. It is why researchers are to pursue practical problems as well; why workers and peasants are encouraged to participate in the arts and philosophical thinking. If social man is to truly become master of his destiny, all must not only have a commitment to change but gradually acquire the shared tools to carry it out.

In part this is why cultural revolution and cultural transformation are seen as so crucial. Cultural and ideological questions are at the core of thinking of social relations. They entail both the categories of analysis and questions of motivation and collectivity. They are thus always inherent in thinking of specific problems as part of an ongoing, interrelated process of change, always a part of the slow, painful, exceedingly difficult creation of a common way of conceptualizing and problem solving. Such a theory of knowledge presupposes the Chinese notions of collectivity, mass consciousness, and the liberating nature of group participation.

This theory, however, is far less examined by China watchers than the Maoist notion of collectivity on which it is based. The integration of the personal and the social, the cultural and the political, the commitment to extend the principle of community control to almost all aspects of human life, is at the center of the Maoist approach. It is a radical alternative to intellectually articulated American values, and underlies the hostility of American observers to all forms of collectivity.

The activities of the individual are seen by the Maoists as the concern of the community in which he lives and works. A person's personal life, work performance, health are all understood as part of the public domain, for they all affect one's role in and contribution to the community. The community, therefore, is responsible for helping the individual, through criticism, through direct assistance, and, if necessary, by changing the environment. The growing acceptance of certain moral tenets of social behavior in the last quarter-century, the qualities of personality to value and cultivate, the nature of the good life means that people generally know what to expect from one another and from the groups in which they live and work. The process requires that individuals continuously struggle to translate social goals into individual and moral goals through a process of self-examination, self-criticism, and transformation. It is a lifelong task.

None of this denies the individual personality. As Nancy and David Milton write:

> Chinese are acute psychologists, but their sophisticated assessment of different personality traits is not, as in the West, to understand the individual for himself, but rather to mesh the individual, with all his expected idiosyncracies, harmoniously into the group. Thus, conscious and precise understanding of the individual is necessary to determine how he or she will relate in a group setting, how the group will have to adjust to each differing personality and what necessary adaptations might have to be made in order to guarantee group survival. In this way the group culture incorporates and tolerates a wide range of personality types, and through an atmosphere of intensive debate and lively discussion, seeks consensus through persuasion rather than command.[124]

Collectivity and Problem Solving

The American observer argues that the Maoist approach to community and collectivity destroys an essential barrier between citizen and state, individual and group. Americans see rights as defensive—to hold off outside forces, preserve a domain of privacy within which individuality and talent can flourish. Rather than integration, therefore, they favor

separation and compartmentalization. To the Maoist, however, rights are something positive, defined in terms of the
group and its purpose. Liberation requires increasing conscious integration into the community, thus ability to
control through the growth of community external manipulation and domination. But a society where the "restraint"
of power is through collective organization, where rights
are positive and defined in terms of groups rather than
defensive and defined in terms of the individual, remains
largely incomprehensible to most American China specialists.

Since almost all Maoist comments about mass participation, criticism, and collectivity are judged within the framework of American assumptions, it is essential to ask what
economic, political, and social policies are really discussed
in Chinese and American society, and by whom. Do people
believe they are raising essential issues that affect their
daily lives and livelihood? If a society is judged partly by
how much criticism can be voiced and what it is possible to
complain about, we must also ask: Do the complaints do any
good? Are individuals in each society acquiring a greater
understanding of how their society operates and a gradually
increasing confidence in their ability to control it?

Before turning to specific comparisons between China and
America, an essential difference must be kept in mind. In
America, community problems are the domain of special
occupations—social welfare is dealt with by welfare workers,
unemployment by unemployment agencies, marital problems by marriage counselors, emotional problems by thera-
pists, care for the elderly by homes for the aged, problems
of crime by an internal security system, and so on.

Such "specialization" has again and again served to cut
people off from working with each other. It assumes the
absence of community, just as much as modernization theory
does. As a result, isolated individuals are forced to turn to
various bureaucracies for help, only to find themselves
faced with seemingly alien, impersonal, uncontrollable

powers. When bureaucrats speak of helping people "individually," this might be far more accurately described as treating them in "isolation." In such isolation lies an often noted relationship between bureaucratic operations and mass incompetence. By "helping" isolated people, bureaucracy encourages passivity. Despite his outrage and anger, which may even be explosive at times, the individual is often passive in a most important sense—the situation is accepted as inevitable. The only escape is through making enough money to avoid its most painful aspects.

Such attitudes only reinforce a trend towards more state, federal, and local bureaucracies, more special services, which create further obstacles to community control. There remains no internal dynamic to allow for control from within. The liberals argue that more and more must be done because the people can do less and less for themselves. The conservatives reply that those who do less and less must be left alone so that they will be forced to do more and more on their own. It is a two-sided argument whose assumptions are mutually reinforcing. Neither side tackles the root problem—passivity embedded in isolation. Passivity alternating with passionate outbursts is not an unusual response to bureaucratic exploitation, as the long history of Chinese peasant uprisings suggests.

In analyzing China, American observers often agree that it is a "bureaucratic state." Yet if one takes the simplistic conceptions of "bureaucratization" underlying so much work on China and applies them to the United States, then the growth of bureaucracies over the last four decades, the expansion of bureaucracy into all areas of daily life, the extent to which conflicts among national leaders are largely "bureaucratic" politics would suggest some doubt as to which nation has a more acute case of spreading "bureaucratization." If one asks whether the institutions in each society seem formal, remote, with little or no relationship to the average individual's experience, will it be self-evident which society appears more bureaucratized to the people who live in it? If one examines whether (and which) bureaucrats are responsive to criticisms from below, whether their work-style can ever be seriously challenged, can it be concluded that China, rather than America, is becoming a "bureaucratic" society?

American viewers are remarkably unreflective on just these key questions. Yet any number of examples challenge American assumptions not only as they are projected onto China, but as they relate to American problems.

Police and the Community

American observers argue that the relation of police to the local community in China reflects a "single-minded pursuit of the maintenance of order since 1949."[125] The police "supervise" numerous community activities—health inspections, lost and found, fire inspections, neighborhood work, schooling, etc. Such "familiarity with all the details of the households on his beat . . . ensures the primacy of security considerations."[126] In other words, to be involved in the local neighborhood, from this perspective, is an important measure of domination and infiltration.

Yet in America numerous proposals for reforming the police express the need for breaking down their isolation from the community. Today, police patrol and enter large urban areas almost as intruders. In the last decade, and at a phenomenal rate, the police have become a sizable internal armed force, linked increasingly with other security forces through computerization. The use of "infiltrators" to "penetrate" the community seems to conform to the worst American visions of events in China. Genuine police involvement in the community, various reformers argue, is the only way to break this vicious cycle. The police will gain knowledge of the community and its needs while the community will obtain greater control over the police. Thus, the American lack of community is seen as reinforcing the paramilitary character of the police, while police involvement in community activities is judged an instrument of control and domination in China.

Having the community watch over politically or criminally suspect people is another Chinese "control mechanism" criticized by American observers. Yet unlike America, such community involvement also includes a responsibility for the community to provide work and assistance. To throw a convict back into society, accountable only to a parole system and the constant if arbitrary regulation it entails, would undoubtedly seem unrealistic to the Chinese. The convict would be without a job, largely isolated from the community. Not surprisingly, most attacks on the parole system and most ideas for its reform ultimately presuppose a radically different relationship of the convict to the community.

The lack of community is also at the center of the controversy over the U.S. public-welfare system. In their work on America's public-welfare system, Cloward and Piven tried, in their own words,

> to convey the sense of fear which this system generates in people, the degree to which they are intimidated by all manner of policy and procedure, the routine invasions of their households by caseworkers under the guise of rehabilitation when, in fact, they are there to perform the function of surveillance, and all of the other mechanisms by which people feel that big brother is watching them.[127]

Their description sounds much like an American China watcher's analysis of control techniques in the People's Republic.

Ideology and the Two-Line Struggle

The Chinese maintain that the "two-line struggle" is an essential part of the history of the Chinese Communist Party that indicates radically different ways in which China could be developed and governed. Ironically, the American

observers have frequently attacked the simplicity, muta-
bility, and self-serving nature of the Chinese depiction
of their two-line struggle; yet the American version of
the two-line struggle is far more deterministic and dogmatic.
For when China watchers speak of a two-line struggle, they
reduce it to one between those willing to adapt to the
universal imperatives of industrialization, of science and
technology, and those opposing them with essentially unrealistic emotional and ideological alternatives.

Ample evidence now suggests a prolonged struggle during
the 1950 between those Chinese who followed the Soviet
model and those seeking an independent Chinese path. The
role of modern industry and the course of the rural revolution, which eventually led to the communes, were just two
of the central issues that the participants debated with a
relatively clearly defined Soviet alternative in mind.

By the early 1960s, however, the situation is less clear.
The Cultural Revolution suggests profound differences of
principle between the Liuists and the Maoists, yet it is
hard for the outsider to really know whether there was an
articulate, fully elaborated alternative to Maoist policies.
The methods used to overcome the problems of the "three
difficult years" after the Great Leap Forward involved a
great deal of expediency, but where short-run stopgap
measures violated long-range principles is difficult to know.

The Cultural Revolution, of course, revealed both to
observers and the Chinese people profound policy disputes
within the party élite. Yet the accusations of Maoists during
the Cultural Revolution involve so much quotation out of
context, so much mudslinging, so much rhetoric that it is
hard to know where some major leaders really stood. It is
not likely that the two groups clashed at every point in the
spectrum of political, economic, social and cultural issues.
Thus, what is a line? When do disputes over issues and
policies become questions of line? And are these questions
ultimately decided by who sides with Chairman Mao?

That Mao has played a pivotal role in decision making

during decades of the history of the Chinese Communist Party does not make Mao Tsetung Thought subjective. What is important to understand is not whether a two-line struggle at the top was always a clear-cut, black-and-white struggle between two clearly defined groups of leaders, but the way the idea of two lines was used during the Cultural Revolution. Just as Mao decades before took the Leninist notion of democratic centralism within the Communist party and applied it to society as a whole, so now he took the concept of the two-line struggle, previously used largely to describe struggles at the highest levels of the party, and applied it to society as a whole.

One way of preventing the victory of privilege, Mao argued, was to make the masses more conscious of two opposing trends in all their social, economic, political, and cultural activities. Understanding social reality in terms of competing "lines" would encourage critical awareness. Thus, conflict between two highly generalized opposing alternatives, regardless of whether they are a direct reflection of high-level splits among the party leaders, is a first step in encouraging the masses to think in terms of the long-range implications of particular decisions, of relating them to the goals of the revolution. Analyzing the two alternatives will help people become conscious of the implications of their work; help them to evaluate their work against certain basic principles and methods of problem solving enshrined in the formal statements of the Mao–versus–Liu Shao-ch'i struggle; help them understand the resistance that is generated by each stage of the revolution both at the local level and in the top echelons of revolutionary leadership.

One way to understand the implications of party leadership conflicts for the masses is to explore the struggles of the 1960s over the use of such models of development as Tachai and Taching. Just as Mao Tsetung Thought is a model of thinking rooted in concrete historical reality, so are models rooted in actual social situations. They are based on real people and the actual experiences of communities.

They suggest a level of attainment that others can successfully strive for rather than an ideal incapable of realization. If the positive qualities of Tachai and Taching at times are exaggerated in Chinese publications, they are nonetheless real models and the struggle over them is testimony to the pivotal role of such models in China today.

Many American observers look at the average performance of the Chinese economy or the communes, when, given the short period of time in operation and the localized application of various models, it is not the average but the best performance that is important for analyzing long-term possibilities for change. The Chinese leadership argued over these advanced models. Did they or did they not contain the seeds of path-breaking methods of development suitable for other parts of China?

The documents that came to light during the Cultural Revolution show that Mao and other leaders read innumerable reports from basic-level units—productions brigades, communes, factories, and city governments—frequently distributing them throughout the party as negative or positive examples. In addition, leaders often took certain models under their wings. Thus Liu and his wife are portrayed as deeply involved in making Taoyuan a model community based on heavy financial aid from the state—special allocation for fertilizers, high-yield seeds, direct state subsidies for buying machinery and putting in electricity. T'ao-yüan was to be a one-crop community, and the entire process was to be closely watched over and controlled by party personnel outside the community.[128]

Tachai, with its emphasis on self-reliance, was a Maoist model. Planning was initiated from below with various goods and services purchased from internally generated resources. In this drought-ridden area in the mountains in Shansi, a brigade had quite literally organized itself and taken some remarkable steps forward under the leadership of a local former landless peasant.

But even within a model community the struggle could be intense. Taching, the oil town, became the center of various conflicts, with Chou En-lai intervening at various times in the struggles that erupted over the area's course of development. Central-leadership involvement in various models for development is among the least explored aspects of contemporary China's development. But it offers an insight into how the two-line struggle could be concretely understood by the masses.

Throughout the early 1960s in most parts of China there was little local-level discussion of major differences in policy. Many local cadres undoubtedly thought that any instructions from Peking must be implemented without question. One important aspect of the popular notion of the two-line struggle is that it has encouraged each local unit to consider the dangers in continuing to blindly implement policies. As Ch'ang Shih-chun, a Chinese trade union leader, commented, there is no substitute for the necessity

> to choose between two lines or even to recognize that such a choice is necessary. For many of the veteran workers, it was sufficient for someone to say: "This is party policy" for them to accept it because of their fundamental loyalty towards the party. But the rank-and-file must grasp the fundamentals of Marxism-Leninism to be able to challenge anyone using party authority to put across wrong policies. The aim of studying the classical works of Marxism-Leninism and of Chairman Mao is to arm the workers, veterans and young alike, with correct ideological standards and to prepare themselves for communism. They must be ideologically prepared to challege anyone at any level if they consider his views or policies are erroneous.[129]

One of the long-term legacies of the Cultural Revolution may be the right to question a "line" and the encouragement of the people to think in terms of alternative ways of developing Chinese society. This legacy is to be handed down amidst serious contradictions brought out by the Cultural Revolution.

The cult of personality at the height of the Cultural

Revolution raises questions about the short-term prospects of raising mass consciousness. One may sympathize with Mao's warnings against the dangers of bureaucracy, yet ask whether the aspiration to confront this problem in the Cultural Revolution was distorted because of the bitter intraparty conflicts that buffeted all local struggles, throwing them into intense political factionalization. One can understand the attack on Liu Shao-ch'i, yet question the way the methods used against him became a model for criticism against opponents in a local unit. One may question whether the campaign against Lin Piao after the Cultural Revolution has twisted the struggles at the top to conform to the immediate political needs of the current leadership in a way far greater than did the attack on Liu Shao-ch'i. Yet none of the answers to such questions precludes the concurrent development in China of a far more sophisticated understanding of ideology and the two-line struggle, a possibility simply dismissed in so much of current American research.

Intellectuals

Throughout the course of the Chinese Revolution, great debates over literature and the arts have directly challenged the role, status, and power of intellectuals. These debates have not just concerned the traditional role of China's mandarins, they have also questioned whether certain traits are or are not inherent in the role of intellectuals. Are detachment and aloofness, privatism and egoism an inherent part of an intellectual's role? If so, what are the implications for a society if it highlights the status, life-style, or "values" of intellectuals? Is intellectual criticism the model for all types of criticism? Or can it be in contradiction with mass criticism and mass creativity?

Such questions might be expected to spark serious reflection by American observers. After all, how do you describe a society that rejects the individualistic, competitive notions of intellectual life, that treats them as the very touchstone of everything negative and antisocial? How does one analyze freedom and the role of criticism in a society that denies the very role of the "independent" critic? How does one observe a society that challenges the existence of the detached intellectual observer? These questions pose some of the most difficult issues for any Western intellectuals trying to understand the Chinese Revolution, yet they are rarely, if ever, explored by observers. The questions are ignored in American intellectual circles because the answers are simply assumed.

A typical American inquiry into "literary dissent" in China probed the "critical-thinking" minority in China's literary world since the 1940s in order to "gain insight into the kind of totalitarianism that has evolved in Communist China. The clash between the revolutionary writers and the party dramatizes the moral dilemmas of means versus ends, ideal versus reality, consciousness versus authority which have faced thinking men in all civilizations."[130]

"Critical thinking," "thinking men," the "voice of conscience," that "special sort of person" involved in "a highly individual craft"—such terms suggest the domain assigned the intellectual. As presented, it is a universal domain, largely stripped of both its historic context and its class base. Artists, writers, and other higher intellectuals in China are thus portrayed as demanding what is inherent in their discipline—a rejection of ideology, nonliterary criteria, and political intrusion into their autonomy. Because "literary creativity in itself is a highly individualistic skill," Mao "appears to have concluded that it is not only writers but literature itself that is subversive. As in Huxley's *Brave New World*, Mao now finds that the Party's utopia cannot function with art."[131]

Before embracing too quickly this very attractive view of intellectuals as social critics and seekers of truth, a few preliminary questions about their role in both China and the West might be useful. More is involved here than questions about the historical tendency of Chinese intellectuals to see themselves as "special people" or "those best able to perceive the community's problems"—in a nation with a long history of the pious homily covering a privileged bureaucratic life. More is required than investigating the diverse loyalties, attitudes, and methods of problem solving created by the West's century-long invasion of China which produced intellectual groups inclined toward different nations (Russia, America, Japan). More is implied here than the tendency among American China watchers to portray people they conclude are their counterparts in another society as keeping "alive a sense of freedom" and "an appreciation for human and artistic values."

Underlying all such questions is a hostility toward a "politicized culture," the very basis of the Maoist theory of knowledge and the mass line. Even a quick perusal of various Western intellectual traditions suggests the extent to which "separation" is assumed in conceptions of freedom, power, criticism, and the role of the intellectual. The individual becomes free from the group and traditional social customs; reality is broken down into its component parts so that it can be analyzed by professionals and specialists; politics is separated from daily life, ethics from economics, culture from morality.

Is not this hostility to politicized life graphically evident in the traditional liberal credo "the less politics the more freedom"? Is it not true that the smaller the space occupied by the political, the larger what we normally speak of as the domain left to freedom? Do we not measure the extent of freedom in communities by the scope it grants to such "nonpolitical" activities as teaching, culture, the press, religion, and various intellectual pursuits? Is it not true that politics is compatible with freedom only because and insofar as it guarantees freedom from political action?[132]

It is striking how often social and political problems are separated in the West, how often the individual is proclaimed the end and society only a means. "Modern political discussion" is rooted in conceptions of individualism, liberty, and the state, not group or collectivity.[133] Freedom is individual (not primarily social or national), residing "in the preservation of an inner sphere exempt from state power" (Lord Acton). Liberty is popularly viewed as "the holding off of something or someone—of others who trespass on my field or assert their authority over me. . . ."[134] Freedom is not experienced primarily in acting and cooperating with others. It is to many a question of free will, independent from others, seeking eventually to prevail against them.[135] Freedom thus becomes closely linked with one's ability to help oneself; our talents and skills are our exclusive possessions.[136] Though one enters groups to work and obtain certain limited objectives, the group is always secondary.

The conception of society as a collection of self-interested, morally autonomous, and psychologically free individuals has long been criticized as unrealistic. Yet even as pluralist (and conservative) critics criticize traditional views of freedom, they resurrect them as a theory of leadership. The rules of the game remain the same, only vested-interest groups are now substituted for individuals. The "public realm" regulates the interplay of competing group interests, where once it was understood to regulate competing individual interests. In the pluralist perspective, group activity becomes a control device, restraining members' "anarchic" qualities and thus preventing the outbreak of mass emotional movements seeking abstract, moralistic, utopian goals. Only through the leadership of the various groups can economic and social objectives be attained. Here is where pluralist theorists bring together a theory of élite leadership with the traditional concept of freedom. With their multiple associations and exposure to competing group demands, leaders gain perspective. Learning the political rules of the game makes them responsible to the system as a whole. Their broader perspective, however, is predicated upon leadership autonomy, its "representative quality."

With such assumptions, it is quite natural to associate the dynamic forces of society more with individuals than with the people. That old, often-invoked folklore depicting the American Revolution as the act of outstanding, resourceful, and innovative individualists, the "Founding Fathers," reduces political participation to questions of leadership.

Politics is thus not a daily concern or responsibility of the citizen—and most people, it is often argued, prefer it that way. They are interested primarily in their private apolitical concerns, desiring only to be rid of all public cares and obligations, to have a mechanism of administration that restrains their leaders while they themselves enjoy the advantages of independence from time-consuming political involvement. Only those with the time or wealth (politics as a profession), those with the time to think and learn (specialists and intellectuals), or leaders of powerful organizations (labor unions, business executives) can deal with modern society's complexities.

Direct participation in government affairs is at best the prerogative of a small community like the New England town. In a more complex society, the most valuable aspect of the representative system becomes "the formation of a political élite in the competitive struggle for the votes of a mainly passive electorate."[137] This is not viewed as an oligarchy in the traditional sense of the word—the rule by the few in the interest of the few—but rather a form of government where the few rule in the interests of the many. Though Schumpeter, among other critics, warned that "without the initiative that comes from immediate responsibility, ignorance will persist in the face of masses of information however complete and correct,"[138] citizen passivity is the very cornerstone of the political process. For problem solving is a process that must move upward into the world of competitive élites, not downward into the community. This is as it must be, it is argued, because only within that competitive world can the interests of the system itself evolve. Consciousness of the totality is the preserve of leadership; passivity is the contribution of the electorate.

Many of these assumptions underlying the traditional theories of freedom and representative government are quite compatible with a privileged role for intellectuals. That élite role is often widely defended. The ideology of the major universities, for example, is rooted either in detachment, withdrawal, objectivity, or they are centers for "disinterested" advice for the U.S. government. Education only becomes possible with "some degree of separation from real life, some protection from immediate responsibility for thought and action."[139] That is why intellectuals have historically sought a midpath between the demands of "freedom and innovation" and the "requirements of social stability." It is also why thinkers have been led again and again "to wall themselves off from the rest of the social order, to obtain special dispensations and privileges within this order. . . . Universities, professional associations, and the artist's bohemia with its claim to artistic license and a special code to govern the artist's behavior, are the main manifestations of this tendency."[140]

Here privilege and special dispensations become an essential part of the intellectual's role. Withdrawal, not participation, is the avenue to truth and creativity. The separation of mental from manual labor is not only assumed, but desired.

Such detachment, while admittedly often rewarded with status, relative wealth, and free time, is nonetheless judged incidental to the results of intellectual and artistic work. For intellectuals, the question of whether their views are deeply conditioned by a class position is swept aside as they speak of their commitment to "universality." And if their influence on public issues and their freedom of expression are in reality often greater than the common man's, this only reinforces their special role with its unique intellectual responsibilities. Whether their intellect is used to seek the truth depends, of course, on each individual. But the role itself is beyond dispute. Without it, they insist, no serious criticism would exist in modern society.

The acceptance of intellectual inequality in society is so

pervasive among intellectuals that any radical alternatives to it are dismissed out of hand. Though a willingness to at least question their class base is a prerequisite for genuinely exploring Mao's perspective, almost no Western intellectuals have even seriously confronted the issues involved. One who did in the context of Western history, Karl Mannheim, is more famous for his defense of the intellectuals' traditional role. But his writings also convey a profound awareness of their class position and their role in the division of labor.

Intellectuals, Mannheim argues, dwell on a "level of abstraction on which one faces no consequences. Ideas which cannot misfire easily become ends in themselves and a source of solitary intoxication." The thinker is "prone to forget the principal purpose of thought: to know and to foresee in order to act." Ultimately, the very psychological makeup of the intellectual is understandable only in terms of the assets and liabilities inherent in his position in the division of labor. And this leads to certain specific traits.

First, the "intellectual's proneness to lose touch with reality has something to do with his tendency to stay in his study and to meet only individuals of his own kind." The assets of leisure are balanced by the temptations: Even leisure is a source of "estrangement from reality for it conceals the frictions and tensions of life and invites a sublimated and internalized perception of things."

Second, while books expose students to situations to which they have no direct access, "they also create a false sense of participation—the illusion of having shared the lives of people without knowing of their toils and stresses."

Third, intellectuals are drawn toward a retreat into privacy. Indeed, their very position depends on a sharp "polarity" between the public and private domain. Intellectuals obviously had little role in village life where privacy was limited, and historically intellectuals fought for the withdrawal of certain concerns from public exposure as the very prerequisite for their existence. The disappearance of the all-inclusive public domain in the city—

the breakup of neighborhood organizations, fewer common concerns that require the close cooperation of each individual, the isolation encouraged by the size of the cities— means the loss of interdependence among people and a major de-emphasis of social integration as the source of personal meaning. Even intellectuals who mourn the loss of community do so from their domain of privacy. More often, however, this modern privacy "creates an aspect of the ego in which the individual is and wants to be different from everybody else." The intellectual "tends to claim privacy for nearly everything he does, and where he succeeds the urban process of individuation reaches its apex." This forms the basis for the well-known tendency toward introversion and de-emphasis of more social and overt behavior. "That leisure-time interests have taken a characteristic direction towards the 'deepening' of experience is due to the paradigm set by urban intellectuals. Were it not for their example, all spare-time interests of our time might take an 'outer' course, since a mass society tends to favour such leisure-time activities as sports, contests, public debates, and public performances."

Finally, the introversion of the intellectual is a fertile ground for that "critical tension between the person's inner life and his outer world" which can often impair his capacity to maintain normal social contacts.[141]

Like Mannheim, Mao sees intellectuals gravitating toward a self-contained world, defined in terms of other intellectuals, and thus cut off from the real world. It is a world of competition and ego, grounded more in conflicts with other intellectuals over status, prestige, and power than in cooperation and collective effort with other segments of society. Thus Mao criticizes Chinese writers and intellectuals for the very traits applauded by American observers of China—their lack of ideological commitment, their belief in the individualistic nature of creativity. They are criticized for their "egoism," "individualism," for seeking to make a "name" among a small "sophisticated" audience. Translated into the university world, such attitudes are described as encouraging a spirit of individual competition, "championism," and "careerism," and discouraging cooperative learning.

Such a self-contained educational world, Mao argues, can only reinforce those strong tendencies in Chinese history to regard education as a career vehicle. Knowledge once again becomes a weapon of oppression rather than a tool for liberation. It becomes one's personal possession rather than a community resource. "Among intellectuals," Mao writes, "the question of world outlook often is symbolized by the way they look at knowledge. Some people consider knowledge as their own possession and wait to get a good price in the market."[142]

For Mao, study and knowledge are not the same thing. Education is not understood as a process that takes place largely within schools. Education has its formal aspects, Mao argues, but it is fundamentally a lifelong process to which all organizations and work can be made to contribute. After all, people acquire most of their knowledge outside of schools as a by-product of other activities. The community must be organized to encourage learning in all facets of one's work and life, to promote creativity, and inquisitiveness. But such learning comes faster when people are involved in a cooperative effort for a meaningful objective. A self-contained intellectual world breeding values of egoism and private ownership of one's skills can only intimidate the masses while isolating the intellectuals. Education requires the active participation of everyone, Mao states over and over again, and this requires that the gap between leaders and led, between those who think and those who do, be increasingly reduced.

The values underlying this educational process, however, are most vulnerable at their apex—among cultural workers, writers, artists, propagandists, and the bureaucrats associated with them. A good cultural trend, Mao repeatedly affirms, is required to consolidate the base. It can reinforce the revolution in the economic, political, and technical spheres or seriously erode it. Culture has to do with values, motivation, and unless it reflects a commitment to collective work and collective forms of organization, the entire socialist system will quickly be undercut.

"The intellectual remolding of writers should be more urgent than any other intellectuals," Yao Wen-yuan wrote.[143] Both historically and symbolically they are at the center of arguments over which values should influence Chinese society. Literature and art are to fit into the "revolutionary machine as a component part . . . as powerful weapons for uniting and educating the people."[144] Writers are not free to write as though their writing lacks political content. Their work must promote certain types of values, and it must be understandable to the workers and peasants.

"Take for example," writes Yao, "a person who had spent a long time teaching in school in the past but who never came in contact with the students' movement, had little intercourse with friends in other circles, and adopted the attitude of leading an isolated life for his own good. . . . After liberation, he wanted to take such 'life experience' as the 'source of creation.' "[145] A work of art might well emerge from this intellectual's portrayal of his experience, but it would not be valuable. "Bourgeois ideology is often most deeply rooted in sexual relations," and if "one should concentrate on the foundation of bourgeois love affairs—the personal hedonism, the description of women as a man's tool of enjoyment,"[146] a very accurate depiction of some individual's experience might result, but it would not be useful. The personal conflicts and vacillation, the doubts and waverings of a bourgeois in China might be material for art, but it would not be inspiring. To play up such experiences, the Maoists insist, is to make them publicly acceptable and can only undermine the values essential for deepening the revolution. The prime need is not for "more flowers on the brocade" but for "fuel in snowy weather."[147]

Such views are usually dismissed by American critics as

a hackneyed rendition of Stalin's socialist realism. While one of the greatest writers of this century, Lu Hsün, is lauded in China today as a model, it is hard not to agree that officially sanctioned culture sometimes appears dull and stiff to Western eyes. Yet a great deal has been done in terms of the popularization of art, its value orientation, and who participates in its creation.

While American observers believe that no valuable culture can grow out of mass participation, the Maoists insist that it must, and in a way that in the long run challenges the professionalization of art. The question for artists and intellectuals ultimately comes down to this: Is artistic creativity to be relegated to the artists as specialists or is it to become available to the entire society? Either art or truth can be limited to the work of specialized groups and privileged individuals and thus isolated from the general population, or everyone can be given the tools and the encouragement to participate.[148]

The task of socialist literature and art is closely tied to the entry of millions of people into cultural life. Increasing literacy is a major aspect of this cultural transformation. But so also, the Maoists argue, is the process of change in the artist's role if a collective society is to be built. Throughout the stage of building socialism, the professional will remain. But the artists are to participate, educate, and in turn be educated by the masses. Technical skills are to be put at the disposal of the workers and peasants, and as the literary and cultural level of the people is raised, so will the relation of the professional to the masses be transformed.

Such an approach simply cannot be seriously considered by most Western observers; almost no models exist for understanding culture and art other than as the product of the detached, isolated artist. Hence the Chinese challenge to the "universal imperatives" of art and the "innate requirements" of the creative, exceptional individual unleashes a storm of denunciation from most Western intellectuals. These attacks, however, almost always blur together two basic questions—the collective potential of art and the role of the Communist party in pursuing the goal of a collective society.

Rejecting the collective potential of art and mass participation in cultural life, observers depict the party's role largely as a weapon of control and domination which denies the freedom to speak and write as one pleases. By tearing art and culture from any process of revolutionary transformation, conflicts between artist and party become only another chapter in the intellectual's favorite portrayal of himself as eternally locked in a bitter dispute between truth and power.

The Maoists argue, however, that literature and art, like all other aspects of contemporary Chinese life, cannot be considered abstractly, apart from questions of class, or in isolation from the building of a socialist society. The consequences as well as the intention of a work must be considered. To demand artistic autonomy and personal privilege, to once again divide society into self-contained compartments, is a clear-cut political stand that denies the extent to which politics is integrated with culture, morality, and motivation. It would signal the death of the revolution.

None of this is to deny the problems involved in the party's control over cultural life. There are indeed great dangers and contradictions in its role. Yet, viewed in the context of the step-by-step, stage-by-stage deepening of the revolution, there is also great potential. If artists and intellectuals are to become more deeply involved in this process, the question is not whether the party should be involved, but how.

From this perspective, the sweeping judgments of Western observers only crudely distort an enormously complex process of cultural transformation. Changing the understanding of knowledge and who possesses it in a society is an immensely difficult and often painful task. Few models exist to point the way.

Moreover, while it is true that Western artists and writers

have great freedom to speak and write what they wish, such freedom is built on their separation from meaningful relations with other classes. Their contribution is rooted in detachment and aloofness. By comparison, Chinese artists and intellectuals appear "restrained." What they write and create must be relevant to the masses and part of a process that is transforming their very role. To the Chinese, however, the artists' deepening roots in society make their contributions more directly tied to its needs in a way that only regular involvement with other classes can ensure. In this context, who is alienated and who is meaningfully involved becomes a more open, far more complex question.

Such questions and issues are simply ignored in the American haste to dismiss the Maoist approach as a crude reduction of art and culture to a morality play at the beck and call of the Communist party. Yet even a brief comparison of the values in America and China embedded in the popular art and culture suggest a more useful and illuminating perspective.

Many of the forms so criticized in China are pervasive in America—the either/or, black-and-white moralizing, the various stereotypes of the good life, the acceptable ways of problem solving, the limits defining what is politically and socially acceptable. Instead of comparing the "high culture" and the "highbrow" writers of the West with popular Chinese writing and culture, a more appropriate method is to compare Chinese and American mass culture, including American television programs, commercials, comic strips, pop music, and pulp fiction.

If Chinese broadcasts stress frugality and dedication to the collective, American television incessantly promotes acquisitiveness as an individual's primary virtue. Being is having, the commercials and the shows state in myriad ways. Self-indulgence fuels the commercial process. Desires should be instantly gratified ("You only go around once, so you've got to grab for all the gusto you can get"). Objects symbolize values ("Freedom's just another name for Datsun"). And the economic flip side of buy, buy, buy is the quick obsolescence built into things (the car that lasts only a few years, the spare parts that soon disappear for older machines). Luxuries are defined as necessities, but they are soon traded in or tossed away.

While the Chinese speak of conflict and class struggle, American popular culture is dominated by violence. Whereas group cooperation and investigation are constantly stressed in China as the way to solve problems, American television often portrays "violence and death . . . as the most obvious, if not the only way to settle personal problems."[149] As one critic summarized a Saturday-morning schedule of television programs for children, it was almost "totally a matter of cartoon superheroes beating the brains out of supervillains."[150] Invariably absent "are the damage, pain, grief, mourning, destruction, and other consequences of violence in real life."[151] If American observers see the Chinese propagating models of simplified problem solving for their children, heroes on American children's shows are hardly paragons of problem-solving versatility. "You can use magic or cunning or even cheating," but "rarely do characters use thoughtfulness, cooperation, or reason to resolve them."[152]

American observers of the Chinese mass media condemn its emphasis on the "heroic cog" in the revolutionary machine, the man who does meager manual tasks without complaint, and bemoan the attacks on intellectual values. Yet one looks almost in vain in American popular culture for films about blue-collar work or challenges to the glamorized white-collar professions. Movies tend to degrade people, argues film critic Pauline Kael, if they don't have white-collar professions. "Movies set up these glamorized occupations. When people find they are waitresses, they feel degraded. No kid says I want to be a waiter, I want to run a cleaning establishment." Indeed, "work is rarely treated in films." You "get something about the Molly Maguires, which is set in the past, but you don't see how the working relationship is now." There are no films on Lordstown, none on what happens to workers when after twenty years of work the plant closes down and they lose their pensions. "To show accurate pictures, you're going to outrage industry."[153]

The Chinese set quite definite frameworks within which all analysis is made; and in some ways it is far more consciously explicit than in the United States. Revolution is good. Imperialism is bad. Socialism is good. Capitalism is bad. Collectivity is lauded. Competitiveness based on self-interest is denigrated. Yet American mass culture also operates within clearly definable assumptions. Commercial television rarely lauds the virtues of collectivity over individual self-interest. No anarchist or communist is favorably portrayed. Few pacifists stands out against the onslaught of American violence. No shows challenge the status quo by suggesting an insoluble class conflict. Giant corporations are portrayed as humane, strong supporters of high culture.

Perhaps, as E. H. Carr argues, certain "simplistic" and moralistic values are inherent in any process of industrialization. In comparing Victorian and Soviet literature, Carr pointed to the "same crude moralizing tendencies, the same inclination to paint human conduct in sheer black and white, the same simple, unsophisticated eagerness to reward energy with success and to punish sloth with disgrace."[154]

The Maoists, however, are not arguing that Chinese culture will stay at its present level, though China will remain for several decades a largely rural society. The culture that emerges out of the attempts to overcome the three great contradictions in Chinese society must, the Maoists insist, be one that all can share and contribute to. It may not be art as Western observers now define it, but it is culture, and one that already can be compared favorably with the simplistic values in popular American culture. The long-range potential for art, once itself understood in certain Western traditions as rooted among unknown people in pre-Renaissance Europe, is yet to be decided.

THE RUSSIAN VIEW
OF THE CHINESE REVOLUTION

With the rapid deterioration in Chinese-Russian foreign relations in the late 1950s, the Russians began to argue that the roots of Maoist hostility toward Moscow lay in the course of the Chinese Revolution and the nature of Chinese history. Over the last fifteen years, as relations worsened, the Russians have produced a fairly consistent perspective for evaluating the social and economic forces at work in the Chinese Revolution, the struggles between Mao Tsetung and his opponents, and the methods which should have been utilized to build a socialist China. Like any propaganda and ideological position, however, much is revealed about the values and assumptions of its formulators. Obviously, what is emphasized, what is ridiculed, and how it is done does not just come from thin air but from various historical, ideological and social traditions.

The following description of the Chinese Revolution draws upon a multitude of writings by Russian government spokesmen and officially published academics. Their privileged and official role obviously influences all their writings, but does not preclude a diversity of views; as they disagree both about developments in China and the appropriate Russian government response to them. Yet the consistency of certain themes is as noticeable among them as it is among American modernization theorists and China watchers.

The following picture of Russian views of the Chinese Revolution has been focused to reveal basic assumptions about the Soviet Union and its élite's understanding of the nature of revolution. In the process, those traits that the Maoist leadership regards as revisionist emerge. Much of what the Russians are proudest of in their own revolution the Chinese attack today as a betrayal of socialism. The methods the Russians see as essential in building a modern economy are condemned by the Chinese as capitalist ways that have led to a new privileged, bureaucratic, capitalist class in the Soviet Union. And what the Russians attack as a betrayal of Marxism is, the Chinese insist, proof of their own accusations of Russian revisionism.

Russian Criticisms of American Modernizationists

While America's "ideology of modernization" (or "industrialism") was a response to the needs of international capitalism and U.S. imperialism after World War II, some Russians argue it was really only the latest variant of "an ideology of industrialism" which has its "fullest conceptual expression" in the writings of Max Weber.[155] What Weber and his disciples did was to make capitalist methods appear universal; "the institutions and values of bourgeois society began to be regarded as something basically inherent in machine division of labor."[156]

By arguing that capitalist ways are universal, alternatives to them could be quickly dismissed as irrational, primitive, or uneconomical. Social development came to be analyzed "exclusively in terms of adaptation, of the passive adjustment of social institutions and values to the 'supra-social' and 'universal' demands of the 'industrial imperative.' " Having "limited social progress by bourgeois 'modernity,' [all] the ideologists of 'modernization' . . . had to do was wait for the embraces of their 'backward fellows.' " The history of imperialism and class struggle was ignored. The "so-called concept of social modernization" reduced "historical development to peculiar splashes of 'reason' by thrusting peoples out of the centuries of backwardness of 'traditional society' into the industrial 'modern age.' "[157]

The contrast between the "industrial-urban community" and the "traditional-rural unit" is for the Russians the lodestar of modernization theory. In speaking of a "rationalized" community of individuals that corresponds to the requirements of modern science and industry, these theorists conceal, the Russians argue, all questions of class struggle. When Frederic Le Play and Emile Durkheim, major theorists of industrial society, analyzed bourgeois society, they reached the conclusion that "the degradation of the collective spirit in bourgeois society, the isolation of the individual members, the loss of an effective bond between them and various social groups, was explained mainly by the distinctive features of the 'industrial community.' "[158] Such is the price of "modernity."

The Russians maintain that much the same is true for Max Weber. His notion of "formal rationalization," they claim, is nothing more than the transfer of the principle of "profit estimate" to the sphere of social relations ("social modernization"), the turning of capitalist business relations into an absolute principle for all relations within society. Individuals are reduced to means, consumed by self-interest, and caught up in an endless process of competition. For Weber as for Durkheim this was both the price and essence of modern society. It was what is "rational." Neither theorist, nor those who followed in their steps, the Russians argue, could distinguish between the rationality of technique and the rationality of domination. By blurring the two together, they precluded any serious appreciation of the potential of socialist solutions to capitalism's problems.

But these assumptions about "industrial society" are precisely what enable America's ideologists to conceal and distort the inevitable sharpening of internal contradictions in both advanced capitalist societies and backward nations. Herein lies a difference between Russian and American views of the Chinese Revolution: Unlike American modernization theorists, the Russians utilize the language of class struggle in China and speak of imperialism coming from the West. They ridicule those Western theorists who attribute socialist revolutions largely to external influences— wars, invasions, or foreign occupations leading to chaos that professional revolutionaries can "exploit."

The Russians also speak of the need for planning in a

young socialist society. They maintain that the market mechanism and the spontaneous market relations inherent in the capitalist mode of production operate against the requirements of productive forces and create extremely contradictory conditions for these forces' development. They laud the Russian form of urban-based centralized planning, arguing that it creates the essential conditions for the favorable development of productive forces. They support at least initial steps toward breaking up the traditional peasant ownership of the land and deplore the play of the market forces in the rural areas.

Yet what the Russians say and how they actually apply what they say in their analysis of the Chinese Revolution are two different things. The Russian emphasis on class struggle, imperialism, and centralized planning are the abstract touchstones for their ideological differences with American views. In practice, however, the distinctions between American and Russian attitudes toward the Chinese Revolution become so blurred as to suggest far greater agreement than disagreement.

The Russian View of the History of the Chinese Revolution

The Russians proudly claim that their revolution brought Marxism-Leninism to China.[159] But Marxist intellectual tools could only build a new China, the Russians argue, if the Chinese proletariat was the leading class in the revolution. Together with their natural allies, the critical wing of the urban intellectuals, they would provide recruits for the newly organized Chinese Communist party (CCP). Emerging out of highly organized work contexts, amenable to discipline and clear-cut chains of command, and familiar with aspects of modern technology, the Chinese workers through the Communist party could successfully struggle against the "commodity-anarchical" tendencies of the peasantry and thus lead the revolution to victory.

The history of the Chinese Revolution is for the Russians the story of the ultimate failure of the Chinese proletariat to overcome the attitudes and forces rooted among the peasants. Like the Maoists, the Russians see a two-line struggle throughout the course of the Chinese Revolution. One line, the "internationalists," pursued "genuine Marxism-Leninism," followed the experience of the Soviet Union, and understood the importance of a working-class party. The other line, the "petty bourgeoisie," sank its roots exclusively into the peasantry and was thus constantly tempted by great Han chauvinism, nationalism, and anti-Soviet attitudes. This line, of course, was the basis of Mao's rise to power.

In the 1920s, the Russians argue, the young and vigorous Chinese Communist Party found a receptive audience in China's cities. Though numerically weak, surrounded by a boundless ocean of peasants in the countryside and a strong petty bourgeoisie in the towns, the workers were the only powerful modernizing force in an extremely backward semicolonial, semifeudal nation. Not surprisingly, therefore, the Communist party reflected the weaknesses and immaturity of China's first working-class revolutionaries. The appeal of the Leninist theory of imperialism to large numbers of bourgeois nationalists, anarchists, revolutionary democrats, and supporters of peasant utopian socialism brought numerous competing tendencies into the very heart of the CCP. Such a party could expect many reverses.

With the CCP's brutal suppression by Chiang Kai-shek in 1927 in Shanghai and other urban areas, leftist "putschist" activities in the cities paralleled a gradual movement by various elements of the CCP to the most economically backward rural areas. Thus started a process of isolation from the modern, progressive tendencies of the cities. The Russians claim that in 1927 nearly fifty-eight percent of the CCP's members were workers; by 1949, only three percent. The shift of the class base explains for the Russians the emergence of Mao Tsetung and his "revolutionary strategy" of surrounding the town with the countryside.

For the Russians, class background is not an essential prerequisite for an individual to join the Communist party. But a party composed largely of peasants is another matter. Peasants and the small producers are incapable of "perseverance, organization, discipline, and steadfastness," say the Russians, quoting Lenin. In going to the peasants, the CCP became isolated from the Chinese workers as well as from the revolutionary heritage of the West. Deeply rooted reactionary Chinese traditions began to take hold. Unlike Russia, with its rich urban revolutionary traditions and its close assocation of Russian revolutionaries with other European movements, the CCP was sinking into the quicksand of peasant rebellion. By the late 1930s, cut off from the outside world and its toeholds along China's coasts, both Mao's leadership and the traditional chauvinist view of China as the center of the world flourished. In time, the Russians argue, the Maoists even came to regard the urban areas as bulwarks of reaction, entirely ignoring the tremendous revolutionary energy and political experience of the industrial proletariat. Thus there was little defense against the idea of the peasantry becoming the most consistent fighter for "socialism."

Both the Russians and the Americans see the years the CCP was centered in Yenan (1937–45) as being of pivotal significance. To the Russians this was the period when the negative impact of the Chinese tradition, the mentality of the peasantry, and the methods of guerrilla war against Japan blended into a potent ideology—Maoism. This was the time when, because of the protracted nature of the armed struggle, the Chinese Communist army became the main component of the state. Though the CCP spoke of the party controlling the gun, the Russians see in the Chinese leadership essentially a military élite. Formed in the crucible of peasant war, this militarized leadership came to see war and militarized situations as the essence of politics, the ideal context for mass mobilization. Years later, when the Maoists referred to the Yenan period as exemplary, it was this militarized mobilization of the population that they were idealizing.

"The tradition of all the dead generations weighs like a nightmare on the brain of the living." To the Russians, the truth of Marx's words is nowhere more evident then in China. Traditions formed for millennia, generated by a feudal way of living and by features of Asian despotism, would have bedeviled even the best efforts of the Chinese Communists. But Mao and his supporters, through their conception of "sinification," actively sought to incorporate the most negative traits of the Chinese tradition.

Ever since the late 1930s, Mao has insisted on "sinifying Marxism." Thus the ideological struggles throughout the Yenan period between chauvinism in the CCP and the genuine Marxist-Leninists took the form of a somewhat abstract discussion of the relation between the specific and the general, the Chinese and the foreign. The Maoist attack on the genuine Marxist-Leninist group culminated in a broad campaign for "correction of style," the *cheng-feng* movement. By 1945 Mao was so confident of his work that the seventh CCP Congress was informed that he had produced a "Sinified Marxism." This Congress also saw the emergence of Mao's personality cult and a marked strengthening of Sinocentrist attitudes throughout the party.

Mao's sinification, the Russians insist, led less to an application of Marxist principles to specific Chinese conditions than to the preservation of traditional Chinese social psychology—the understanding of the world through the aphorisms and rules formulated by the authorities, the repetition of approved wisdom in simplified and clichéd form, the inculcation among the peasantry of a dogmatic faith in the authorities. Mao's simplistic propositions, later to reach their apex in the Little Red Book, were given the appearance of sayings similar to the traditional maxims of the Confucian classics. This sort of simplification, the Russians point out, may be useful for increasing literacy, but it only reinforces the baneful impact of medieval Confucian educational ideals instead of the struggle against them. Such simplicities in ancient times had required a cult of Confucian wisdom to make them palatable. Mao's would require a similar cult.

Mao, the Russians argue, often relied on the pragmatic and eclectic use of Marxist quotations to justify his constantly changing policies. These random statements were linked more through the emotions generated by the cult of the leader than their scientific accuracy. The Russians point out that Lenin had eloquently warned that this lack of inner theoretical wholeness is a characteristic of the petty bourgeoisie. Yet these petty bourgois traits were precisely what Mao committed himself to—the emphasis on will, temporary outbursts of mass emotion followed by pessimism, a stress on primitive universal eqalitarianism, the reliance on leaps and their artificial speeding up of history.

Such ideas offered little protection against much of traditional Chinese philosophy. The belief that the transformation of society and the success of revolution begin and end with the transformation of man's subjective world, the Russians claim, is central to both Mao and the Confucian tradition. Such a belief favored the deprecation of economic forces in the development of a revolutionary party and in the building of a socialist society. The impact of modern science and the study of economics was thus neglected. The narrow range of Chinese philosophic interest, moreover, limited as it was mainly to ethics and society, offered little encouragement to the development of individual autonomy and creativity. Instead of conscious, purposeful activity of the masses according to the laws of social development, the Maoists advocated action that could only blindly seek to realize the subjectivist propositions of the leaders. Maoism to the Russians is thus an "apology of voluntarism and subjectivism."

With the victory of the revolution in 1949, the CCP moved into the urban areas. Confronted with the hostility of American imperialism, a blockade of coastal cities whose existence depended on foreign trade, and a rival government on Taiwan, even the Maoists, the Russians argue, sought to learn the lessons of the Soviet experience. Initially, they had to admit that guerrilla methods, once the revolution was over, were neither suitable nor applicable to China's urban population.

Thus the Soviet Union's great power at the end of World War II, the emergence of the socialist world system, and the friendly relations sought by Moscow with China are portrayed by the Russians as having a positive influence in fortifying the weakened Marxist-Leninist forces within the CCP. Kao Kang, the Chinese Communist leader in Northeast China, represented those forces of which the Russians approved. Kao quickly made China's traditional industrial base a "testing ground" for socialist changes throughout the country. Working closely with Soviet political, military, economic, and technical experts, he moved China "along the path of scientific socialism" by emphasizing the heavy industrial sector and the virtues of planning. "All this sealed his fate." His purge in 1954 during the period of the transition to socialism was the "first big clash" between the Maoists and the "healthy forces in the party."[160]

Kao Kang's purge, however, did not immediately allow Maoist policies to triumph. Instead, the period from 1949 to the Eighth Party Congress in 1956 was the high tide of socialist construction in China. The Russians vigorously support the extent to which key economic institutions were directly borrowed; the way the party was somewhat remodeled along Soviet lines with urban workers and intellectuals becoming increasingly important; the degree to which heavy industry was lionized; and the speed with which the armed forces were reorganized in Soviet fashion, especially after the outbreak of the Korean War.

With agrarian reform in the early 1950s eliminating feudal relations of production by destroying the landlord class and giving land to the peasants, and with the campaigns against the national bourgeoisie (the Three-Anti and the Five-Anti movements) successfully concluded, the Russians saw the rehabilitation of the national economy well under way. They applauded the CCP's general line to gradually carry out socialist industrialization and socialist change in agriculture, handicrafts, and trade. These tasks were to be fulfilled in roughly three five-year periods. By 1967 China was to become a "great socialist state."

As the Russians see it, the Eighth Party Congress in September 1956 was socialism at its best. Concrete plans were mapped out for a considerable growth in the working class (still only 2.3 percent of the population), improvements in its professional training, and for more effective use of intellectuals through efforts to raise their political and ideological levels. Science and technology were to be introduced gradually into agriculture. Mechanization was recognized as the prerequisite for further great changes in China's agriculture.

The Russians favored the resolutions of the Eighth Party Congress which stated that the class contradictions between the proletariat and the bourgeoisie were resolved in favor of socialism, thereby deciding the issue of "who wins" in the struggle between socialism and capitalism. Thus the principal contradiction in Chinese society was defined as being "between the advanced socialist system and the backward social productive forces."

Material production was the main task. The Russians approvingly quote the report of the CCP that the "period of storm and stress is past, new relations of production have been set up, and the aim of our struggle is changed into one of safeguarding the successful development of the productive forces of society." Such positions required that any mention of Mao's thought as the theoretical guide for the CCP be dropped, that the rules of collective leadership be reaffirmed, and that calls by such leaders as Teng Hsiao-p'ing for vigilance against the cult of personality be heeded.

Had it not been for the "voluntarist decisions" of Mao and his supporters, say the Russians, the Chinese would have "continued to advance along the socialist path after 1957." The return to methods symbolized by Yenan, however, was not just an act of will. The social changes carried out in China up to 1956 did not yet mean the complete establishment of socialist relations of production. These were still very immature and rested on an extremely backward material and technical basis. "The country was just making a start on all-round industrialization." China's immense problems and the years it would take to solve them put enormous pressure on the entire leadership to adopt policies to overcome all difficulties by relying only on the enthusiasm of the people. China's backwardness and enormous reserves of manpower were the prerequisites for Maoist subjectivism. Subjective activity would compensate for the absence of material prerequisites for progress. The development of man's physical and spiritual powers would replace a carefully planned system.

Even at the time of the Eighth Party Congress, the Maoists and their opponents were divided over the methods and pace of socialist construction. Mao sought to push the peasants into a stepped-up transformation of their individual property without providing any material and technical basis for such a changeover. His opponents, the Russians argue, "insisted that any changes in the social character of the peasantry should be tied in with changes in their economic life and their mentality."[161] Yet Mao pushed recklessly ahead. Instead of the fifteen to eighteen years initially envisaged, the cooperatives were set up in just two years.

Such Maoist policies, the attacks on the discipline of the still weak CCP, the criticisms of the Soviet model, and the crude appeals to nationalism led the turbulent peasantry and the petty-bourgeois forces to momentarily overflow their banks. Dissatisfied with the complexity of modern planning and the seeming slowness of industrial development, the Maoists sought to resolve China's problems by skipping vital stages, breaking into the realm of communism by a "great leap."

To the Russians the Great Leap Forward, which began in 1958, revealed the folly of the Maoist economic model. The Maoist "cavalry charge" approach rejected gradual, planned, proportional economic growth. The Maoist perception of the class struggle as a wave that rises and falls smacks of anarchism and demagoguery to the Russians. It reduces the class struggle "to the level of a tantrum thrown by the elemental forces of nature."[162] It rejects any laws of planning and conscious use of the laws of social development, leads to a vast underrating of the large modern-enterprise sector of the economy, and greatly overrates small-scale, primitive rural industry. It results in economic adventurism and "attempts to solve all the social and economic problems by means of incessant 'leaps' and 'uninterrupted revolutions.' "[163]

The Chinese rural communes formed during the Great Leap Forward draw especially caustic Russian comments. To imagine that the communes could move China from collective to public (the Russian term for state) ownership in agriculture and to the communist principle of distribution within a matter of years is to the Russians one of history's most ludicrous examples of peasant utopianism. It utterly denied that there were any material prerequisities for socialism, and it assumed that "the village commune is an embryo of socialism, that the peasantry is imbued with 'socialist instincts.' "[164]

Therefore, while the "speedup" in the cooperatives, the "rapid moving from lower to higher stages without consolidation," was bad enough, the amalgamation of some 700,000 of them into some 74,000 communes with populations ranging from 25,000 to 100,000 was sheer folly. The peasants lost what little influence they possessed, as teams and brigades became subject to commune boards that had the power to dispose of their labor and property. The Russians foresaw rigid administrative and ideological control as the inevitable result.

To the Russians, this was a "barbarous use of the available productive forces" based on the "perverted belief" that, by utilizing all available manpower, production could be quickly increased. This in turn assumed that labor was to be intensified while wages were reduced. Thus the Maoists "gave precedence to political consciousness and moral incentives over material incentives, proclaiming the former revolutionary and the latter backward, bourgeois manifestations of 'individualism' and 'selfishness.' "[165] In practice this meant disregarding the socialist principle of distribution according to work.

The Russians point to the CCP Central Committee's call on August 29, 1958, to "militarize organization, take combat action and carry out a collective way of life" as the epitome of the Maoist attitude toward organization in the communes. The "so-called collective way of life" was nothing more than an "extra-economic coercion of the working people." Army regulations were introduced everywhere: "Labor organization was militarized; the peasants were formed into companies, regiments, and divisions." Peasants were to become "faceless little screws doing the will of their senior." The communes thus served only to divert the peasants "from the natural socialist path of development onto a path of artifical egalitarianism and a barrack-room social system."[166]

The barrack-room atmosphere could not compensate for the peasants' loss of personal material incentive. Chaos spread as tens of millions of peasants were switched to industrial and building operations through the "labor armies," stripping agricultural production of essential manpower. As primitive, inefficient handicraft enterprises were stressed, the quantitative and qualitative growth of the working class was slowed. The relatively long period required for the transformation of state-private enterprises into socialist enterprises was ignored. Specialists who opposed modern science and technology were attacked as "conservatives" and "reactionaries." The spread of the "backyard steel furnaces" was only the most absurd and costly aspect of the Maoist fling into economic madness.

The Russians, moreover, ridiculed what they portray as

Mao's aspiration to make the communes, districts, and entire provinces economically self-sufficient. Instead of recognizing the need to set up an integrated "national economy with developed economic ties and rational specialization and cooperation of its units," Mao "set up for China the ideal of a semi-subsistence economy claiming that economic cells isolated from each other constitute a communist system."[167] Each commune was to contribute to the state without expecting any financial help in return. Such "self-reliance" partly explains the misshaped development of China's economy—"the atomic bomb and the rickshaw, the electronic equipment of missile systems and the conservation of backwardness."[168] The money drained from the rural areas goes to build up China's defense industry, proving, the Russians insist, the hostile nature of the Maoist leadership.

The practices at the Taching old fields and the Tachai production brigade are ridiculed. Taching is attacked as the symbol of Mao's desire to turn workers into peasants. "There is hardly any difference," the Russians quote *Hsinhua*, the official Chinese news service, "in the housing of the oil-workers and the peasants of the nearby villages. Besides, they are situated near fields where the members of the workers' families engage in agriculture." This for the Russians constitutes nothing less than a "flagrant violation of modern industry's demand for a specialized, highly trained machinery of management." It signifies a "regression, as Marx put it, 'to the *unnatural* simplicity of the *poor* and undemanding man,'" to the artificial cultivation of universal exhausting manual work, to closer day-to-day contact of workers, engineers, technicians and office employees with backward agricultural production."[169] If this is communism, the Russians conclude, it is the barracks communism Marx and Engels ridiculed years before.

Nor do the Russians see the model of Tachai in a better light. Creating isolated rural economic units can hardly hope to solve China's massive agrarian problems; it can only divorce them from the interests of the state and the improvement which planning can bring to especially backward areas. The slogan of "three never asks" (never ask the state for grain, money, or materials) will prevent mechanization of agriculture.

In addition, by rupturing cooperation among the different regions of China, the centrifugal tendencies that have long plagued the nation are set loose. Unity therefore increasingly requires involvement by the superstructure which is often ineffective. For example, it leads to the involvement of the party in specific technical details of management (Liu's stopgap approach after the Great Leap) or, worse, the creation of a "military-bureaucratic machinery of administration" (Mao's Cultural Revolution policy).

The "failure" of the Great Leap Forward, the Russians argue, led to the second sharp clash between the Maoists and the "healthy forces" in the party in the "case of P'eng Te-huai and his followers (Chang Wen-tien, Huang K'o-ch'eng)." The Russians laud P'eng, then China's defense minister, for his courageous denunciation of the Great Leap—his attack on the communes as "petty-bourgeois fanaticism," a foolish attempt to "enter communism at one stroke"; his insistence that politics and economics have separate and distinguishable laws (economic activities cannot be replaced by ideological crusades; political sloganeering is no substitute for day-to-day economic activity); his insistence that socialist laws require planned and proportionate development, not unbalanced, wavelike approaches.

The Russians accuse Mao of crushing P'eng's "principled criticisms" by intimidation and threats and by charging P'eng with "secret ties with foreign states"—i.e., the Soviet Union. But it was a costly victory, for P'eng "actually became the initiator of a wide opposition within the Party to Mao." The struggle at the Eighth Plenary Meeting of the Central Committee of the CCP "marked the beginning of a profound ideological, political and organizational crisis of Maoism which has been lasting for almost fifteen years."[170] One side supported "rational methods" of developing China and sought to overcome the calamities brought by the Great Leap Forward. They drew on the experience of other socialist nations, favored centralized planning and the development of a modern industrial sector through the education of needed technicians and experts, and the expansion of the party's urban base.

The Maoists, however, rejected the internationalist experience of the socialist movement, withdrew ever more deeply into Chinese chauvinism and its peasant base, turned to the largely conscript peasant army for political support, and clung vehemently to voluntarist methods for speeding up economic construction.

Though Liu Shao-ch'i actively promoted the Mao cult in the 1940s, in 1956 he sided with those who criticized the cult of personality. It was the disaster of Maoist methods in the Great Leap Forward, various Russian observers note, that taught him and his followers a profound lesson in the real consequences of Maoist adventurism. Mao's line thereafter was "opposed not by a 'miserable handful of traitors' but by the overwhelming majority of the CCP members, headed by the old Party guard, including such formerly convinced Maoists as Liu Shao-ch'i and P'eng Chen and many others." Indeed, Liu's "turning from a preacher of Maoism into the main political opponent of Mao Tse-tung" testified to a recognition among old party cadres that the rational course was to return to the line mapped out by the Eighth Party Congress. While Liu may not have articulated this position clearly, the Russians often portray him as a spokesman for a realistic policy of adjustment after the Great Leap.[171] At the Ninth Plenum of the CCP in 1961, Liu's role was portrayed as that of a critic of "subjectivist methods" and commune excesses, and a vigorous proponent of planned, orderly, gradual growth.

In short, the Russians see Liu's social base as being in the modern sector of Chinese society, among the working class in the highly organized, modern factories. Thus, as long as the CCP existed—even in its Liuist form—the Russians could foresee the Chinese returning to the socialist world system. At the Ninth Plenum in 1961, Liu mapped out a new economic course the Russians describe as based on planned guidance of the national economy and requiring the leading role of the working class. This meant, "to a certain extent, that the leading role played by the Central Committee of the CCP as the Party's collective organ was restored." When in 1965 Liu began to call for "industrial co-ordination both within the individual industries and between industries, and the need to develop specialization and co-operation under a single state plan," China was at last on the threshold of regaining the momentum lost after 1956.[172]

The Maoist counterattack to Liu's policies took a variety of forms, eventually culminating in the Cultural Revolution. The first and most important step for the Russians was Mao's insulation of the CCP from the world communist movement. Without a worsening of Sino-Soviet relations, they claim, Mao's Cultural Revolution could never have started; thus it is not surprising that the Maoists fired their first public shots at the Soviet Union shortly after the failure of the Great Leap Forward. According to the Russians, the more details that emerged concerning the scale of the setbacks in domestic policy, the more intense the anti-Soviet campaign became; the more obvious the foreign policy failures of the Maoist line in the early 1960s, the more vehement the denunciations of Moscow's foreign policy; the further the Maoist leadership deviated from the principles of scientific socialism, the louder and more insistent became Peking's propaganda that the Soviet Union was "betraying the interests of the revolution" and "restoring capitalism." In Mao's resort to territorial claims against the Soviet Union itself, accusing Moscow in July of 1964, of ruling an empire of conquered peoples, the Russians see the Maoist leadership publicly revealing its chauvinistic views.

Whereas the Russians once ridiculed the American notion that China needed an external enemy to ensure domestic order, they now espoused a variant of this "principle": "When things go from bad to worse, when one political action after another fails, such people believe the only way out is to shift the blame for all their troubles onto 'enemies'—'internal' and especially 'external.' It is on just this principle that the Peking leaders are operating today."[173]

The Russians describe the movement for socialist education, beginning in 1962, as a major purge of the CCP. The "Thought of Mao Tsetung" and the personality cult became increasingly important; Chiang Ch'ing's pernicious influence, reminiscent of the role of the empress dowager in traditional China, spread in the cultural world; and the People's Liberation Army, under Lin Piao's command, became Mao's new institutional base.

Lin Piao's reforms in the army and the use Mao made of them are further proof of Mao's militarist approach, say the Russians. The organization of the PLA's social life is so attractive to the Maoists, insist the Russians, because of a number of its specific features—a rigorous discipline that presupposes the execution of orders without discussion; the small role material incentives play in military duties; and the possibilities for cultivating passionate enthusiasm and devotion to a leader. It is the one organization where "extreme collectivity" and relatively equal salaries can be attempted with the least disruption to society.[174]

To carry out its attack on the "rational" policy of elements of the CCP, the Maoist leadership needed a theoretical alternative to the decisions of the 1956 Eighth Party Congress. The Russians argue that they found it in their antisocialist arguments that China "would degenerate" and "restoration occur" unless the class struggle was intensified and the revolution continued. This was Mao's justification for attacking "those inside the Party who follow the capitalist road" and for describing the Cultural Revolution as a "political revolution waged by the proletariat against the bourgeoisie and against all the other exploiter classes under the proletarian dictatorship." Such "theoretical contributions," the Russians note sarcastically, along with Mao's specious conception of the "two types of contradictions," are the sum total of his gift to Marxist-Leninist theory and practice.

Perhaps no position so outraged the Russians as Mao's argument that, if class struggle was denied, there would inevitably be a counterrevolutionary restoration "with the Marxist-Leninist party necessarily becoming a revisionist and fascist one and the whole of China changing color." The position that the Communist party could become fascist denied for the Russians the very class basis of fascism and socialism and demonstrated a blatant disregard for the nature of the proletariat and all Marxist categories of economic and political analysis. To the Russians, Mao's thesis proved his total theoretical bankruptcy and was a tacit admission that his policies were creating intense conflict in Chinese society.

Under the pretext of fighting a capitalist restoration, say the Russians, Mao attacked the party cadres who demanded a return to planned socialist methods of economic growth. He fought opponents of the cult of personality which had "frozen the life and creativity of the Party." He dismissed party leaders who insisted on better relations with the Soviet Union and greater assistance to the Vietnamese in their struggle against American imperialism. He opposed those who urged the use of "scientific socialist" methods. He heaped scathing sarcasm on spokesmen who asked that the "intelligentsia be given more freedom of initiative and allowed to pursue its own creative quest."

As the Russians see it, Mao's view of things forms "a pretty weird picture: it is not the bourgeois elements, but Party cadres who have visions of restoring capitalism in China," and yet, after years of ridiculing Liu and his supporters, the Maoists are unable to produce any evidence to support the "absurd assertion" that Liu was seeking to restore capitalism. "The fact is that, beginning from the mid-1950s, Liu (like other sober-minded Party leaders) increasingly differed with Mao and his followers on the various aspects of the content and pace of China's socio-political and economic development." This underlying difference was the basis of a "two-line struggle," but hardly an attempt at capitalist restoration.[175]

Mao's onslaught against all the "reasonable" elements in the CCP enabled him, the Russians conclude, to appeal to the young to spearhead the attack on the traditional party apparatus. Yet the Red Guards could hardly break the old social superstructure, let alone build a new one. The resulting chaos from this youthful "rampage" led to the direct involvement of the PLA. By August 1967, to prevent civil war, an open military dictatorship emerged. Drawing on feudal traditions of the deification of the country's supreme ruler, the age-old habits of peasant obedience to superiors, and the low cultural level of the population at large, the Maoists set up a "regime of personal power constituting the core of the hierarchal system of military-bureaucratic dictatorship."

The Russians paint a dismal picture of the chaos and terror wreaked upon China by the Cultural Revolution. They fail to see a single redeeming feature, only a shattered Communist party, a growing militarization of the nation, the breakdown of any checks on a large and still growing bureaucratic apparatus, and the collapse of the nation's economic development. "However hard the Maoist ideologists, donning a 'Marxist' mantle, strive to present the 'cultural revolution' as 'one of the most revolutionary stages' in the continual, 'uninterrupted revolution,'" the Russians conclude, "honest and sober-minded men will always regard it as one of the darkest periods of Chinese history."[176]

The Russian Evaluation of Mao

Underlying the entire Russian perspective on Mao and the Chinese Revolution is the conviction that "Maoism" radically distorts the fundamental conceptual framework of scientific Marxism, its class base, and its international validity. Lenin, they argue, never spoke of the "Russification" of Marxism because he knew that revolutionary theory was indivisible—"it grows out of the sum total of the revolutionary thinking of all countries of the world." His emphasis was on the common in the specific, the objective in the subjective, the international in the national. In order to correctly develop Marxist theory for the Russian Revolution, the Russians say Lenin insisted that the party study both the history of socialism and democracy in Western Europe and the history of the revolutionary movement and the labor movement in Russia, correctly applying the conclusions to the actual state of the Russian working-class movement. The international character of the working-class movement requires that the experience of all nations be assimilated. That is why Lenin *"did not remake* Marxism to fit it into national specifics and did not give it a Russian national form."[177]

This, the Russians insist, is the very opposite of Mao's "sinification" of Marxism. Throughout their analysis of the Chinese Revolution, they stress how it can only lead to nationalism and the destruction of Marxist theory. Is that not, they ask, where Mao's thought leads when he writes that, "there is no such thing as abstract Marxism, but only concrete Marxism. What we call concrete Marxism is Marxism that has taken on a national form . . . talk of Marxism apart from Chinese peculiarities, this Marxism is merely an empty abstraction."[178]

Such a perspective, the Russians argue, denies the integral teachings of Marxism in which all aspects are necessarily interrelated and supplement one another. By definition, theoretical analysis must stand above the various national experiences of revolution and provide a worldwide doctrinal framework within which the various national experiences can be understood. So too can the individual theorist move beyond his national and particular experience. It is not a question of Russian or Chinese models, the Russians insist, but of a body of international doctrine.

Mao denies this when he writes as though Marxism-Leninism exists as an "international" teaching only as the sum of its national forms—as German, Japanese, Russian, Chinese, and so on. The extreme consequences of Mao's position, the Russians argue, is illustrated by the use of the Little Red Book during the Cultural Revolution. In it, theory is reduced to a collection of individual generalizations of narrow empirical experience, "rendering impossible the development and enrichment of theory." Theory is reduced to a few elemental concepts, then twisted to fit the immediate "practice" demanded by the leader.[179]

Such theoretical bankruptcy is evident even in Mao's most "advanced" writings. "Mao contrasts sensual and rational knowledge, and theory and practice, and connects practice only with purely sensual knowledge, with 'experience,' thereby depriving practice of its rational character, and refusing to recognize it as rational activity in the process of cognition."[180] By breaking up the process of cognition into independent, discrete processes alternating with each other, by making knowledge the result of a series of "leaps," Mao rejects all mediated experience. Thus he concludes that theories, directives, plans, measures have to be taken afresh through all the stages of knowledge. Mao's own views on intellectuals, the Russians argue, graphically portray the dichotomy he posits between theory and practice. In what position do students find themselves, Mao writes,

> who graduate and leave their school where they have been completely isolated from the practical activities of society? A man studies from grade school to university, graduates, and is then considered learned. Yet . . . what he possesses is merely book knowledge. Would it be possible to regard such a man as a complete intellectual? It would be very difficult; at the most I would consider him a half-intellectual, because his knowledge is still incomplete.[181]

How, asks Mao, does a "half-intellectual become an intellectual"? There is "only one way: to see that those with only book knowledge become practical workers engaged in practical research."[182] Confined to their intellectual life, intellectuals engage only in mental, theoretical activity which yields only "rational"—i.e., partial, incomplete, or dogmatic—knowledge. The intellectual is only "half complete" because the mental phase by itself is incomplete.

Such a dichotomy, the Russians insist, leads to the dangerous equation of ideal practice (and its inherent semi-autonomy) and idealism. They point to Mao's "Dialectical Materialism" where he argues that the basic social cause of idealism is the division between mental and manual labor.[183] "With the development of production," they quote "the separation between manual labor and intellectual labor was responsible for ranking idealism first among currents of philosophic thought."[184] Rulers and intellectuals develop idealist conceptions because "they despise manual labor." Idealism is the easy way out, a luxury of the aloof and separate person. As the Little Red Book states, "unless one makes the effort, one is liable to slip into idealism and metaphysics. . . . People can talk as much nonsense as they like without basing it on objective reality or having it tested against reality."[185]

Russians writers do agree with Mao that in the earliest stage of history ideal and material practice were not separate from each other. Only with the division of practice into material and ideal spheres do intellectuals slowly develop as a special "substratum" with ideal practice as their prerogative. Under capitalism this division is manifest in the contrast between ordinary people and the intelligentsia. But while such a division is demoralizing, forcing men into special social functions, it also provides a strong impulse for the development of the productive forces, science, technology, and the arts. Most important, the Russians insist, the social roots of idealism should not be seen in this division between manual and mental labor but in the division of society into classes.

Locating the roots of idealism in the division of society

into classes rather than in the division between mental and manual work is essential, they say, for understanding the role of intellectuals in socialist society. The increasing importance of science and technology enhances intellectual work. The "activity of those who engage in brainwork turns out to be the most important factor without which it is impossible for society to function normally."[186] To accelerate the integration of ideal and material practice by seeing class differences involved in their division as Mao does, the Russians conclude, can only halt development, leading to the frequent disruption of economic process as in China.

The Russians certainly agree with Mao that "many who have read Marxist books have become renegades from the revolution." But they denounce Mao's insistence that "illiterate workers often grasp Marxism very well."[187] They maintain that such slogans as "The masses study history, the masses develop theory" and "Draw from the masses and take to the masses" blatantly disregard Lenin's warning that the working class was only capable of developing an awareness of its immediate economic requirements.[188]

Thus, to the Russians, Mao's calls for intellectuals to learn from the masses, to view them as "revolutionary" or "advanced," ends up "denying the sphere of ideal practice to the intelligentsia."[189] Philosophy, they insist, "is the science of sciences. Its elaboration requires extensive knowledge and, therefore, remains the prerogative of scholars and those political leaders who were trained in the field."[190] The very idea of intellectuals going to the rural areas to perform manual labor is "neither 'reeducation' nor required by 'economic necessity.' "[191] This is by no means "throwing a bridge between town and countryside." "It is leading to alienation, to a rift between urban dwellers and the peasants, to surplus and unproductive migration."[192] Indeed, forcing intellectuals to do manual work is only a crude form of punishment. What, ask the Russians, could be more wasteful than having the president of Peking University "forced to work as a garbage collector?"[193] After all, "the people have not so much to enlighten as to be enlightened by this same intelligentsia."[194] Only if it is allowed to fulfill its role can this be accomplished. The intellectual should not be dragged down to the peasants' level—the task is to "raise the peasant to the level of the intellectual."[195]

Nowhere are the Russians more vehement in their denunciation of Mao than in their attacks on his approach to "art" and "culture." Lenin's injunction to revolutionary workers in culture was not to go down to the cultural level of the masses but to raise it. To make the development of art and literature dependent on the ability of the Chinese peasants to understand it is to "deliberately doom Chinese culture to prolonged stagnation."[196] While peasant illiteracy must be overcome, this effort should not be equated with the development of art or culture.

The emphasis during the Great Leap Forward and the Cultural Revolution on the promotion of amateur instead of professional artists and the reforms associated with Chiang Ch'ing are the symbols of Maoist refusal to accept the professional autonomy of cultural workers. The "idea that 'the proletarian artists will be both artists and workers,' " the Russians argue, had been "described by Lenin as 'nonsense.' "[197] For the Russians,

> even in an advanced communist society, differentiation of labor will remain. There will be then, as there are today, professional writers, poets, artists, musicians, film directors, etc. Otherwise, cultural standards would become much lower. New trails in art will inevitably be blazed mainly by gifted professionals devoting all their energy and talent to their favorite work. The task, therefore, is to provide them with the best conditions for creative work.[198]

As the Russians see it, it is not really art the Maoist advocates but material for "didactic agitation and propaganda." Its function is simply to illustrate ready-made themes and formulas with "examples for life"—ideal men, endowed like Lei Feng with "all possible merits except one—the ability to reflect."[199] Reflection is lost in the passion for obedience, the implementation of simplistic formula, and the "value" of asceticism. All this was brought together during the Cultural Revolution in the campaign to "revolutionize thinking"—i.e., to reduce individuals to the level of a simple mechanism, "disinherited pawns on the political chessboard." The Russians conclude that the new moral criterion of heroes—"I want to become an individual cog"—is the very essence of Maoism.

Russian and Chinese Views: Comparisons

Though they speak of a "scientific" path to development rather than modernization, the Russian understanding of the role of experts and technicians seems far closer to the American than the Chinese view. Both Russians and Americans often equate mass movement and mass participation with mob rule and as inherently inimical to expert knowledge and efficient organization. Neither see any value in growing mass consciousness, nor sees it even as plausible. Both usually associate the dynamic qualities of their own societies with science and technology, to which the people essentially only "respond." Both frequently assume a near total separation between knowing and doing, believing that those who know are socially more valuable than those who do. Both see politics as a narrow slice of life.

Soviet criticisms of Mao and their perspective on the course of the Chinese Revolution signal their abiding confidence in "scientific" analysis and in blueprints for building the new society; carefully drawn-up plans implemented through skilled (and necessarily privileged) technicians, engineers, and party officials. Experts draw up the general plan; nonexperts are provided with the limited knowledge they need in order to fulfill their specific tasks. The pieces are assembled in a way similar to that of a contractor following a blueprint. Only the contractor needs to know how the pieces fit together. What is to be achieved is decided by those who command the resources, power, and organization to obtain the preordained result. Since the plan is theoretically a scientific and objective understanding of reality, the assumption is that nature and men can be molded to fit it.

It is thus not surprising that the engineer had such a prominent place in the early stages of building Russian socialism after 1917. Like the bulldozer overcoming obstacles through brute strength, everything can ultimately be overcome with sufficient power and force to implement the blueprint. Nor is it startling to observe that cybernetics has been more and more lauded in Soviet writings. Replacing the bulldozer in a now more sophisticated society, cybernetics will allow a more efficient, rational yet still fundamentally similar process to work.[200]

Unlike the Russians, the Maoists speak of constant experimentation, of models that succeed and fail. In contrast to a blueprint, a model is not to be strictly followed. It is rather to be studied as a way in which others have sought solutions. It is a way of learning to think about various aspects of a situation, a way of gaining perspective and broadening the range of the possible. There is no master plan or blueprint for all levels of society, setting forth preordained solutions. "Application" requires constant study, practice, and summarizing, and gradually this process draws in greater numbers of people. Such decentralization, however, is only possible if people are organized to meet common needs themselves, if they share certain moral tenets of social behavior, and if there is a common approach to solving problems. To speak of models in a Chinese context is thus to return to those assumptions about how groups and society operate that were explored in the section on American-Chinese comparisons.

This distinction between Russian blueprints and Chinese models is also evident in the Soviet emphasis on universal doctrine and the Maoist reliance on thought. The Russian attack on Mao Tsetung Thought reflects the Russians' belief that sinification has obliterated the traditional conception of Marxist theory and the semiautonomous role of intellectuals and experts. Mao's major writings on sinification do indeed have a close connection with his views on intellectuals and practice. His is a notion of "adapting" the classic truths of Marxism-Leninism in a way that promotes self-reliance, just as his emphasis on centralism is a way of promoting local initiative.

The Chinese speak of Mao Tsetung Thought, not Maoism. Thought emerges from the application of "fundamental theory," generally unchanging theoretical concepts. Only through highly flexible and experimental applications of certain laws does a practical ideology like Mao Tsetung Thought develop.

In 1956, while criticizing "complete Westernization" as "impractical" and unacceptable to the Chinese people, Mao stressed the need to learn fundamental theory.

> Some people advocate "Chinese learning as the substance, Western learning for practical application."
> Is this idea right or wrong? It is wrong. The word "learning" in fact refers to fundamental theory. Fundamental theory should be the same in China as in foreign countries. . . . Marxism is fundamental theory which was produced in the West.[201]

While Marxism was produced in the West, its fundamental principles, Mao says, are "the same in China," useful as a tool only in a specific context or concrete situation.

The Russians argue that when Mao speaks of Marxism-Leninism losing its "foreignness," he ends up denying universal doctrine, reducing it to a grab bag of potential techniques. Mao insists that only revolution from within the Chinese tradition and the specific circumstances of China in a form the masses can understand is an appropriate basis of fundamental theory. Elaborate theoretical constructions, he suggests, are not transferred from society to society, only fundamental principles out of which each struggle develops its own specifics. The basic principles or laws can become increasingly understandable to all and gradually, through struggle, become a base for common ways of analyzing problems. In Mao's view, to insist, as the Russians do, that elaborate doctrines evolving out of one nation's revolution or even the European experience must be accepted in their totality—e.g., that the Russian Revolution can be a blueprint for others—is to tear fundamental theory from its specific context and to succumb to national chauvinism. He sees it as an attempt by the Russians to hide their intense nationalism under the thin veil of universal doctrine.

Herein lies the basis for the emphasis on Mao Tsetung Thought, rather than Maoism, as a doctrine for others to apply. Mao Tsetung Thought offers foreigners not a body of doctrine or a blueprint for their own societies but a model for thinking. People can use the Chinese revolutionary experience to try to understand, say, the contradictions within a given situation in their own society (the nature of the class conflict, the balance of forces, the organizational conflicts and possibilities, and so on) and on the basis of such an analysis make a "principled" choice of action. In doing this, they can read at length exactly how it was done in the Chinese Revolution. Despite the strident calls at certain times by some Chinese to make Mao's thought into a doctrine or a "recipe for revolution" throughout the world, the primary emphasis in Mao Tsetung Thought is on fundamental theory which is always rooted in specific situations. Understanding its implications requires experimentation and the initiative of the observer or nation involved. Neither abstract theory nor another movement's practical ideology provides detailed, concrete strategies or tactics, only guidelines for the investigation of problems. While the borderline between these and principled methods can never become entirely clear, the fundamental assumption remains that only specific "application" of principles leads to thought. What initially appears to be "foreign," however, will gradually be understood as always implicit in the local situation. The principles are the summation of experience into laws, but their implications and meaning are only understandable through practice.

The Russian argument that all this is utterly preposterous is succinctly captured in their denial that "illiterate workers often grasp Marxism quite well." For the Russians, to grasp Marxism "quite well" is to know Marxism in all its theoretical flowering rather than pointing to its roots in the earth. It is to dwell on theory in all its complexity instead of the basic principles from which it grows. It is to make Marxism an instrument translated by knowing experts to the unknowing masses rather than, as the Maoists insist, a means of shaping reality through mass practice.

Such Russian attitudes permeate and structure their entire view of the Chinese Revolution. They reflect both a vehement denunciation of ways of building a society from the "bottom up" and a strong defense against accusations that a new class has emerged in the Soviet Union. Yet from the perspective of uninterrupted revolution, Soviet criticisms of Mao reveal an overriding commitment to that same new class they so often deny. Their attacks on Mao and his policies reflect their confidence in a privileged leadership as the most active element in political and social life. The vanguard party is reduced to a scientific-technological élite or a meritocracy. Change is constantly depicted as flowing from the top, and this is evident again and again in their theory of knowledge. Knowledge is tightly compartmentalized; fields develop a special language hostile to contributions of the nonexpert. Scientific-technical knowledge is thus the preserve of specialists, and general knowledge is the preserve of the political élite. The interrelationships in society are understandable only by those at the top, those trained to know. Scientific leadership brings together technological knowledge through planning in a way that reduces politics to coordinating diverse positions among the educated élites.

All this is justified by the Russian conception of the vanguard party. The limitation of trade-union consciousness is overcome by the party leaders. The party becomes the sole initiator of change because it is the sole judge of "objective conditions." The Russians admit that serious deviations may occur, as they did under Stalin, but the party organization has all the resources to provide correct, scientific leadership.

In their attack on China, the Russians weave together the "rational imperatives" of science and the division of labor, with the privileges of power. Knowledge "liberates" by showing the correct path, by preventing people from attempting the impossible or the foolish. To refuse to accept what is "rational," to dispute those in a position to know, is emotionalism and indicates a lack of consciousness. Thus in a major current of Soviet psychology there emerges the image of the dichotomized individual, torn between basically rational inclinations (objective reality) and his emotions. Consequently, the task of motivational research is to subordinate emotionalism to "reason" by convincing the person of his greater role in applying a directive or performing a task assigned from above. Action at the base is portrayed as technical, operational, effectively applying directives from above and efficiently communicating results from below.

Thus the Russians argue that Marxism-Leninism provides the theoretical base for the strategic, global scientific conception of social development, as well as the operational, tactical conception. The Russians cite Lenin in arguing that it becomes a question of "the transformation of the whole of the state economic mechanism into a single huge machine, into an economic organism that will work in such a way as to enable hundreds of millions of people to be guided by a single plan. . . ."[202] Modern industry, they insist, demands such strict unity. The democratic force of the people must be "combined with *iron* discipline while at work, with unquestioning obedience to the will of a single person, the Soviet leader, while at work."[203]

The factory, in short, is a microcosm of work at the national level where rational planning, calculation, and the quantification of all relevant factors are fed into the plan. Factory management unifies all activities within its domain into a coherent whole, utilizing appropriate "socio-psychological" factors to encourage morale among the workers. There is no questioning here of the position of knowledge or of the monopoly of the means of intellectual production. It remains throughout the Russian critique the property of those who know and thus lead—of those who lead and thus know. Only the manager can bring the various parts together; only he has a consciousness of the totality. Thus intellectual powers are kept separate from the workers; they are useful only at the level of the whole. There is little communication among those at the lowest levels; connections are primarily vertical or at least controlled tightly by hierarchy. Thus, unifying the work of the proletariat can only be the task of a central, coordinating will. In a sense, control and value consensus become the same thing, for the worker will "realize" the objective and rational part he is fulfilling in the total scheme of building the new society. Just as the professional revolutionary brings consciousness to the workers from outside, just as theory is engendered from without, so in the building of Russian society is general consciousness and theory professionalized.

None of this is possible, the Russians maintain, if antagonistic contradictions are as prevalent in socialist transformation as in bourgeois society. Such contradictions deny the very idea of scientific management rooted in "a social, political, and ideological unity. Indeed, what antagonisms can there be in a society where all members of the intelligentsia come from working-class and peasant families?"[204] Scientific administration and consensus, in short, are inherently tied together. For the first time, progress "is achieved in a way that does not involve the division of society into two hostile, conflicting classes, but on the contrary, is based on the unity of interests of all classes and social groups, a unity that grows and becomes stronger as time goes on."[205]

Thus for the Russians Mao's argument that new social classes develop or old ones reemerge denies the very meaning of the socialist ownership of the means of production. It implies a multicausal explanation of social forces whose subjectivism is evident in the Maoists' changing stress on ideological, economic, or cultural factors, depending on the needs of the leadership. What happens, the Russians ask, to scientific planning in this miasma of contending forces? On what basis can there be any objective analysis?[206] Objectivity, after all, is rooted in the party's ability to ensure the dynamic operation of a modern socialist system, and this it cannot do, they argue, if qualities associated with a new class or privileged stratum are seen as part of an emerging new society rather than as relics of the old.

Mao and the Russian Revolution

To Mao these Russian arguments add up only to a defense of privileged bureaucratic power. Universal doctrine, "scientific" analysis predicated upon a uniformity of interests in socialist society, the denial of struggle and antagonistic contradictions, the semiautonomous role held essential for political and intellectual élites, the separation of mental and manual work, and the justification for large salary differences—these are just a few of the ideological accountrements Mao foresees from a new bureaucratic class.

Over the last fifteen years, Mao has spoken of learning from the Soviet Union, treating its revolutionary experience as a "negative example." Viewing the Soviet Union as a "model" to think through the problems of the Chinese Revolution, Mao has sought explanations for the course of both revolutions. If, for reasons of political expediency and foreign policy, public Chinese comments about the restoration of capitalism and bureaucratic power are directed at Stalin's successors, Mao's writings go to the very heart of the Stalinist model of industrialization and the widespread Bolshevik hostility to any conception of uninterrupted revolution.

In his speech of May 17, 1958, Mao criticized two of Stalin's key slogans: "We do not put forward the slogans 'Cadres decide everything' and 'Technology decides everything.' . . . The first two slogans were formulated by Stalin; they are one-sided. If you say 'Technology decides everything'—what about politics? If you say 'Cadres decide everything'—what about the masses?"[207]

Slogans that cadres and technology "decide everything" indicate to Mao Stalin's near total subordination of the transformation of social relations to the development of productive forces. Change man's material conditions, Stalin often suggested, and everything else will change. Bend all aspects of society to the demands of the productive forces, and the desired changes will continually sweep through the rest of society. "First the productive forces of society change and develop," wrote Stalin, "and then, *depending* on these changes and *in conformity with them*, men's relations of production, their economic relations change.[208] The anachronistic and backward elements in the superstructure will be swept away as the economy is liberated from its fetters.

Thus for Stalin, as for his successors, bureaucracy was not a question of class in a socialist society. Rather it resulted from the cultural and educational backwardness of the masses. Though a serious problem, bureaucracy would gradually be overcome through education, especially as the workers learned to understand the rationality inherent in the material base under socialist conditions.

Mao sees Stalin's preoccupation with the productive forces as parallel to his disregard for the superstructure and thus for the masses. As he commented on Stalin's last work, *Economic Problems of Socialism in the USSR*: "From the beginning to the end of this book, Stalin says nothing about the superstructure, he does not take man into consideration, he sees things but not people."[209]

Once social ownership of the means of production was accomplished, Stalin argued, the job of the planned, orderly building of socialism could begin. When Stalin confidently concluded in 1938 that "here there are no longer exploiters and exploited. . . . Here the relations of production fully correspond to the state of productive forces,"[210] he was suggesting that the productive forces, carefully promoted by technicians and the "scientific" party vanguard, would bring about the inevitable social transformation. Mass participation and revolutionary struggle had become historically irrelevant.

Though during the Cultural Revolution Liu Shao-ch'i was called China's Khrushchev rather than China's Stalin, the attack against him as the purveyor of the "theory of productive forces" can be read as a summation of the Maoist attack on Stalin's views as well.

> The "theory of productive forces" hawked by Liu Shao-ch'i one-sidedly describes the progress of society as the natural outcome of the development of the productive forces, chiefly the instruments of production. It completely denies that, under certain conditions, the superstructure and the relations of production play the principal and decisive role in relation to the economic base and the productive forces; it also denies that the proletariat's consciously making revolution under the guidance of revolutionary theory, seizing political power and changing the relations of production play the decisive role in greatly developing the productive forces and pushing social developments ahead. It categorically denies that "*the people and the people alone are the motive force in the making of world history*" and that "*revolutions are the locomotives of history*." It uses mechanical materialism to replace dialectical materialism, and vulgar evolutionism to oppose revolutionary dialectics. The "theory of productive forces" is an out-and-out counterrevolutionary fallacy.[211]

Underlying this Maoist position is one of the most controversial questions in the Marxist tradition: Does the superstructure serve only to uncover the inherent rationality of the productive forces, making manifest the social forms latent in them? Or does the superstructure, interacting with the base, bring new elements and new ways of developing social relations which are only possible through revolutionary struggles and mass participation? Ideologically, Stalin agreed with the former, Mao with the latter.

To the Maoists, the mere development of the productive forces can never make exploitative social relations and the ideologies rooted in them disappear. The socialist ownership of the means of production "is insufficient by itself and cannot be consolidated" without "socialist revolution on the political and ideological fronts."[212] Revolution in its fullest and most profound sense, therefore, must be continuous. New ideas, new social forms, breakthroughs of various kinds require mass participation. The goal is not to reach a point where someday this may end but to liberate the process as much as possible from the forces that fetter it.

Mao argues, moreover, that, historically, superstructural questions have played a far more important role than is usually understood.

> Of course, the change in the relations of production is caused by the definite development of productive forces. But enormous development of productive forces always takes place in the wake of a change in the relations of production. Historical experience has proved that only by first creating revolutionary public opinion and seizing political power, and then changing relations of production, is it possible to greatly develop the productive forces. This is the general law of social development.[213]

Mao is even blunter when he says: "First and foremost, create public opinion and seize power. Then resolve the question of ownership. Later, develop productive forces to a large extent. This in general is the rule."[214] Indeed, although bourgeois relations of production grew up in a preliminary way under feudal society while socialist relations of production did not exist prior to a proletarian revolution, Mao argues there is a "fundamentally identical" process in both revolutions. The bourgeoisie did not launch their revolution "after the industrial revolution, but before it. They also brought about a change in the superstructure and acquired the state apparatus first and then conducted propaganda, gained strength and pressed vigorously for a change in relations of production."[215]

Indeed, says Mao, this is the pattern throughout the history of capitalism. At first, there were simple forms of coordination and cooperation which gradually developed into handicraft workshops. Though production was still not by machine, by this time capitalist relations of production had been formed. Such capitalist relations of production gave rise to a need for improved technology, thus creating the conditions for the growing use of machinery.

> In England it was after the bourgeois revolution (post–17th century) that the industrial revolution (from the closing days of the 18th century to the early stage of the 19th century) got under way. Germany, France, the United States, and Japan also went through different forms of transformation of the superstructure and production relations before their capitalist industries were developed on a large scale.[216]

Mao's emphasis on the superstructure and the production relations underlies much of his criticism of the Soviet Union and much of their criticisms of him. Those very forces that both the Russians and the Americans describe as "rational," "inevitable," or "universal," forces that only well-educated élites can hope to master, for Mao must themselves be controlled through the continuous transformation of the superstructure, a process that can only be rooted in revolutionary struggle and mass participation.

The reasons why the Russians failed in this, Mao suggests, are many and diverse. They walked "only on one leg." They relied too much on technology and cadre leadership. "They emphasized specialization but not redness, cadres but not the masses."[217] All this becomes graphically evident in their approach to planning and heavy industry. While the Russians laud heavy industry as almost the basis for all other changes in society and sharply criticize Mao for denying this, Mao argues that "the experience of the Soviet Union . . . shows that if agriculture and light industry are not developed, it will be harmful to the development of heavy industry."[218] The needs of the country will be subordinated to just one sector of the economy. In the short run this leads to the domination of the rural areas. In the long run, the dislocations will undermine even the process of heavy industrialization.

What Stalin and the Russians cannot accept, Mao argues, is the long process of work required to build socialist relations among the people. Employing compulsory administrative methods in organizing production, like relying upon administrative decree to carry out land reform, in the long run can only result in decreased production. The masses are not mobilized; the essential changes in attitudes and work relations upon which the process ultimately depends will not develop. This is just as true in industry as in agricultural production. Says Mao: "We cannot presume that under the socialist system, without any work being done, the creative cooperation between the workers and the leading personnel of enterprises will emerge naturally."[219]

If the Russians thought such socialist relations would emerge relatively easily in the urban industrial areas, they were far too pessimistic about the peasants. Stalin's "basic error is his distrust of the peasants," Mao wrote about Stalin's *Economic Problems of Socialism in the Soviet Union*. They could only be made into workers, regarded as second-class citizens and reliant on external powers to direct their fate. Yet, in their attacks on Mao, the Russian argument that mechanization must precede collectivization does not even fit the Russian example. That socialist industrialization is a prerequisite for collectivization, Mao points out, "does not correspond with the Soviet Union's own conditions. The Soviet Union by and large achieved collectivization in the years 1930 to 1932. At that time, although their tractors were greater in number than ours, the area under mechanized farming in 1932 constituted less than 20.3 percent of the total cultivated acreage."[220] The issue, therefore, was not mechanization versus collectivization, but the way collectivization was accomplished. Unable to trust the peasants, totally confident of his policy of heavy urban-based industrialization, Stalin inaugurated a "revolution from above" to brutally solve the agrarian problem. Once again, Stalin chose a method of bureaucratic and administrative decree to solve a serious problem in the Russian Revolution. Like his other decisions, it was to leave an important legacy to his successors.

Domestic Roots of the Russian Views of the Chinese Revolution

Chinese public statements praise Stalin's achievements while acknowledging his "mistakes" and blasting the revisionism of his successors. In the long run, however, it is hard to imagine that the Chinese public understanding of Russian revisionism will remain at this level. Indeed, in looking at the Russian Revolution with Chinese revolutionary experience in mind, it is possible to suggest some of the factors that account for Russian revisionism. To do this requires an examination of both the leadership and class makeup of the Russian Revolution.

Three great forces shaped the Russian Revolution: the peasant demand for land; the non-Russian minorities' desire for independence or autonomy; and the uprising of the workers in the cities for socialism. All wanted peace in 1917, and together they swept away the aristocracy and the great landowners clustered around the czar.

But no unifying center could emerge to quickly replace

the feudal autocracy. The bourgeoisie, lacking the independence of their Western counterparts and indebted to international creditors, could not even fill the vacuum in the cities. It was the workers of Russia who were the really dynamic and powerful urban force, and these the Bolsheviks led with increasing success. The role of the proletariat has often been underestimated, even as to their numbers. In 1909, workers in large industry numbered more in Moscow than in Paris. In Moscow there were 130,000; in Paris only 110,000—though Moscow had only 1.3 million inhabitants while Paris had 2.8 million.[221] Unlike France, this was truly a modern workers' uprising in the cities.

This urban uprising, however, was quite cut off from the rural struggle, and unlike the French Revolution, the dynamic heart of the nation could not be obtained merely by seizing a few key cities. Lenin persuaded reluctant colleagues to accept the rural upsurge; but without rural roots, the Bolsheviks had few ways to lead this enormous revolutionary movement.

Their isolation in the urban areas reinforced the Bolsheviks' organizational and ideological predilections, shaped by fifteen years of illegal, clandestine activity. Operating under the terror of autocracy, cut off from the peasants, and with their rear social base and models shaped by the socialist traditions of Western Europe, it is hardly surprising that the Bolsheviks regarded themselves as an urban-based, civilizing vanguard. Nor is it remarkable that such a party came to see an enormous abyss between action and consciousness, a gap as great as that between the urban and rural worlds in the Russian Revolution. Revolutionaries should be professionals, Lenin argued, and if the working class could not cultivate its own intellectual élite in the womb of capitalism, then initially some of its ranking members should come from the bourgeois intelligentsia. Their base, however, could only be the urban proletariat.

Confronted with this limited social base and its organizational history, the Bolsheviks faced the onslaught of ferocious civil war, international intervention, blockade and isolation from the capitalist world. It has been argued that the Stalinist road might never have been traveled if the revolutionary proletariat in the West had obtained power, if the capitalist powers had not intervened to destroy the revolution, if the threatening capitalist encirclement had not occurred. But this would be to take the Russian Revolution out of its historical context.

Instead of emerging with a powerful, experienced party deeply rooted in diverse segments of the population as in China, Russia of 1921 found the Bolsheviks faced with a savagely depleted working class, an élite vanguard transformed into an officialdom cut off from its class base, the rapid spread of governmental centralization, and proliferating inequality.

Still weak in the cities, the party was only a "drop of water in the ocean" of peasants. During the Civil War a decisive part of the peasantry, confronted with extremes of left and right, probably accepted the political direction (especially military) of the Bolsheviks. Yet accepting party direction hardly signified peasant adherence to Bolshevik ideas in either the domain of revolutionary Marxism or even the immediate measures thought necessary by the party. Indeed, the rural upheaval probably reinforced a unity of the villages against the city, a process beneficial to the middle and wealthy peasants who fought to defend their gains. Even though various ways may have been possible of defining the relationship between urban and rural areas during and after the Russian Revolution, what is essential to emphasize is that the Russian situation offered few alternatives to the course that was eventually chosen.

The contradictions between rural and urban areas, workers and peasants, Russian and non-Russian minorities all had to be confronted by a government and a party radically changed by the bitter years of civil war. The state apparatus became more autonomous and powerful—in the army, in the secret police, in the various bureaucracies.

Historic reasons for the power of the bureaucracy now joined with the needs of survival. Lenin himself justified such centralization in his support of state capitalism, arguing that the horror and misery of the war, the near-famine conditions, the pervasiveness of bourgeois and petty-bourgeois ideas temporarily required strict discipline and centralization just to keep the gains already achieved.

In these early years of the Russian Revolution, from 1918 to the mid-1920s, initiative among the workers all but disappeared. In its place came centralized administration, the rapid multiplication of rules and regulations and other state constraints. All these tendencies were evident in the suppression and collapse of the workers' committees—and in many other ways as well. As the private activities of the bourgeoisie were eliminated at the heights of the economy, they became to a sizable extent, along with members of the old intelligentsia, the technicians and administrators for the Bolsheviks. Their privileged role and the restoration of various traditional work methods in the factories, often against strong opposition and various local experiments, was a further step in the cycle of repression. Lenin could not envision sufficient unity and initiative among the war-shattered masses to provide control over these temporarily useful bourgeois specialists.

Much to their surprise, members of this old intelligentsia found many Bolsheviks quite willing to retain many of the traditional forms of the capitalist division of labor, the old social relations, the old forms of privilege and élitism in administration. Later Stalin was to purge many of these people and replace them with technicians from workers' backgrounds, but he would leave management and administrative operations relatively untouched. Indeed, many Bolsheviks remained confident both of their organizing abilities and the organizational achievement of modern capitalism. Just as the czars turned to the largest modern factories to industrialize, so the Bolsheviks turned to the most advanced forms of capitalist organization. Thus Lenin turned to theorists like Taylor and to the assembly line epitomized by Ford—to capitalist organization without capitalists, to modern factories without bourgeois managers. With mass initiative and experimentation in the factories crushed, many placed their hopes in the organizing ability of modern techniques and party control.

Nowhere were the consequences of such views and the implications of Stalin's leadership to become clearer than in the policies of collectivization and industrialization adopted in the late 1920s. The organizing power of the state, exercised through coercion, education, and sheer terror, substituted for the type of mass action associated with the Chinese Revolution. The peasants bore the full brunt of its brutality.

Even the most widely simplified views of the debates in Russia during the 1920s about collectivization and its relation to industrialization reveal the Bolshevik dilemma. There were two ways, it was argued, to approach the fragmentation of land that resulted from the Russian Revolution: by emphasizing the "strong" peasant drive to acquire more land and more control of the tools of production, or by collective organization of agriculture. In turn, collectivization implied two choices about the rate and type of industrialization: to emphasize the production of capital goods as a prelude to more intensive industrialization through planning and through abandoning reliance on the market, or to reduce the tempo of industrialization and emphasize the production of consumer goods for the market.[222] During the New Economic Policy (NEP) period, debates tended toward one position or the other. As E. H. Carr argues, the NEP "represented a balance of forces in which the revolution had carried the towns and factories and the urban proletariat, and had failed to carry the peasant countryside."[223]

Underlying these two alternatives was the belief shared by practically all the Bolsheviks that the peasants could not be organized from the bottom up as was just then beginning to take place in parts of rural China. Most Bolsheviks showed little confidence in the peasants, or in any new forms of social organization in the villages which could provide a basis for both mechanization and obtaining market surplus. Deeply influenced by European Marxist traditions, most of them saw the peasants as the Russians describe them in their analysis of the Chinese Revolution—inherently petty bourgeois, prone to sporadic outbursts of violence and anarchism, and preoccupied with their limited self-interest. Such people must be liberated by the workers, becoming more like them in the process. The cities must pull the peasant into the modern world by migration from the rural areas (Russia's urban population would grow by 100 million in the next forty years) and by a program of mechanization based on the model of discipline and organization usually associated with modern factories.

Within the Bolsheviks the major criticism of such views came from men on the right like Bukharin. Primitive accumulation to support heavy industry, he warned, would exacerbate all the problems resulting from Russia's backwardness, the bureaucratic overcentralization of government, and Bolshevik isolation from the peasants. The city would end up ruthlessly exploiting the rural areas. Alienated from the masses and facing a proliferation of administrative élites, the party would become a "monopolistic caste" and "turn into the embryo of a new ruling class." The alternative was the growth of voluntary organizations and "mass initiative at the lower levels" as opposed to "statization."[224]

Yet this posed an insoluble dilemma for Bukharin. Emphasis on "mass initiative" in the rural areas, he concluded, meant reliance on the middle (and his critics charged uppermiddle and kulak) peasant classes. Bukharin himself argued that it was "scarcely possible to think that the collective farm movement will capture the whole wide mass of poor peasants"[225] and probably hoped for the growth of a "uniformly prosperous middle-peasant countryside" instead of kulak power. Such an approach was easily challenged by his critics, for it seemed to ignore the inherent backwardness and low productivity of Russian agriculture. Foreign crises increased demands for a heavy industrial base for military preparedness, which Bukharin's program could not easily encompass. It left the initiative for industrialization in the hands of the peasants and ultimately the world market. And it had no answer to the problem of absorbing the millions of peasants who were in the process of migrating to the cities.

Looking at these debates among the Bolsheviks over collectivization and industrialization, it becomes clear why the Chinese conception of the mass line was so utterly anathema, so inconceivable. For those who spoke with conviction of mass initiative in the rural areas were largely on the right. The left was quick to argue that such initiative was largely from the middle and the most prosperous peasants. The left equated rural initiative with rightist forces. The right saw leftist urban domination as leading to a new privileged class that would reinforce the bureaucratic and statist aspects of traditional Russia. Neither could envision a way out of this contradiction as the Chinese did. The alternatives were defined by their organizational history and ideology, and deeply conditioned by the history and class makeup of the revolution. Yet the way these alternatives became defined points to the historical roots of what the Chinese today call Russian revisionism. Whether there were genuine alternatives is an open question, but that the history of the Bolshevik party precluded them seems quite likely.

Any campaign of collectivization would have involved a certain amount of violence. "The weakness of the regime in the countryside and the alienation of the peasant from it" assured it would be violent.[226] The extraordinary brutality of Stalin's approach, however, illustrates the consequences of the failure to organize the poorer peasants or train either urban or rural cadres to lead them. By April 1929 a large number of the party's "practical politicians" backed Stalin.[227] They may have underestimated the degree of solidarity among the different strata of peasants, but they generally agreed that the city-based transformer would simply have to dominate the peasants from above. Progressive influence was a one-way street. "To get the small peasant village to follow the socialist city," Stalin said in December 1929,

> it is necessary . . . to *implant* in the village large socialist farms, collective and state farms, as bases of socialism, which, with the socialist city in the vanguard, can drag along the masses of the peasants. . . . The socialist city can drag along the small peasant village in no other way than by *implanting* in the village collective and state farms and by reshaping the village on new socialist lines.[228]

The party mobilized some 25,000 of its urban members to act as shock detachments in the countryside. Largely Civil War veterans and industrial workers, they were not just propagandists, for they were put into positions of rural authority, often as chairman of the kolkohoz-to-be. Often ignorant of rural conditions, they dealt brutally and often fanatically with the peasants, as Sholokov's *Upturned Virgin Soil* sometimes graphically portrays. Even today, Russian publications continue their derogatory depiction of the peasants, as they do throughout their perspective on the Chinese Revolution. Collective farms are to be replicas of industrial organization. Workers who remained as farm-machinery operators were idealized as the leading contingent in the rural areas. Others, associated with mechanization and the machine-and-tractor stations, joined the "honored" workers list.[229] Organization came entirely from above, and from urban ways to rural backwardness. Russia became almost two countries: one was increasingly urban, industrialized, firmly disciplined and harsh, yet provided some social services and some material improvements. The other, rural Russia, was ruthlessly exploited, embittered, with few fruits for the peasants from the revolution.

All the contradictions between manual and mental labor, between privileged élites and hierarchies of work, between the atomization of human relationships and the promotion of material self-interest among the workers in the Stalin years were greatly exacerbated by the way the gulf between urban and rural worlds was handled by the state. When Stalin described collectivization as a revolution "accomplished from above, on the initiative of the State power, and directly supported from below,"[230] he was accurate. But the "direct" support came almost exclusively from the urban areas and was used to dominate the peasantry. When in their analysis of the Chinese Revolution the Russians argue for necessary divisions between manual and mental labor, urban and rural areas, privileged élites and the masses, it is useful to recall these roots in their own revolution.

By the early 1930s, collectivization and the first Five-Year Plan had brought together the essential Stalinist vision of the industrial society. As heavy industry developed at the expense of consumer goods, "every political decision seemed to be shaped by a single end—more production, and still more." Not "politics in command" but "accumulation in command" summarizes the Stalinist position.

> Precisely those features which Marx had character-
> ized as typical of "high" capitalism, and which he had
> condemned accordingly, reached their official apoth-
> eosis in the Soviet Union, legitimized only by the
> destruction of the private capitalist as a class and
> his replacement by "the workers" state.[231]

This "second revolution" wove together the growth of modern industry and the enormous extremes of inequality that the Chinese would later so vehemently criticize. A master of bureaucratic psychology, "Stalin systematically inculcated respect for rank in every field of life. All sorts of tables of ranks were worked out, and promotion was accompanied by privileges rigorously defined for each rank, as well as by increased responsibility and pay."[232]

Several groups of Russians strongly supported this bureaucratized world, and out of these groups came the social basis for Stalin's cult of personality. In the 1930s the cult had its social base among workers in the party stratum of the working class and among the new young intelligentsia of worker origin. The enormous scale of the purges resulted in great shortages of cadres. Hundreds of thousands of officials were pushed up from below. Tens of thousands of Stakhanovite workers became factory directors. Ordinary soldiers became platoon and company commanders, regimental commanders rose to command entire armies, and so on. Many rank-and-file scientists took over laboratories, research projects, and major institutes.[233] These people had attained an undreamed-of life which many attributed to Stalin's leadership and his policies. Centralization of power and the lack of any control from below came naturally to them. Privileges eased any consciousness of crimes committed to obtain their positions. Their very life was structured to command and administer those below them, while themselves accepting direction from above. From this group came the "new experienced managers" who flourished during and after World War II and were Stalin's real successors by the late 1950s. To the Maoists they were full-blown revisionists, yet they were the products of the Stalinist pattern of development.

The extraordinary differences between the Russian and Chinese revolutions are particularly evident in the Communist party's relation to the social and class forces in each society. The Bolshevik leadership's alternatives were always limited by their profound alienation from the peasantry and their acceptance of state power to control and quickly dominate independent forces. Mass initiative was thus a much more difficult alternative even in the best of times for the Bolsheviks to accept. The resort to bureaucratic power to control from the top down—to lead a second revolution through administrative decree—was the result.

The Chinese Communist Party, on the other hand, had developed deep roots among many diverse groups in Chinese

society. Though the Chinese Revolution is sometimes portrayed as the opposite of the Russian (the former isolated
from the urban areas, the latter isolated from the rural
areas), the gap between these two worlds was actually nar-
rower in the Chinese Revolution than in the Russian. After
1927, people from the urban areas and those inspired by
modern revolutionary ideas gradually learned how to merge
with and organize the peasants in a way that made the
Chinese Communist Party a modern revolutionary force.
The young, the disaffected intellectuals, the peasants, the
workers—all came together in a context pregnant with possibilities quite different from those of their Russian counterparts.

By 1949 the CCP was confident and experienced. Their
hopes were not dashed by the travail of civil war as in
post-1917 Russia. They had learned to organize from the
bottom up, to develop methods of amazing flexibility and
of sensitivity to the peasants. Though these methods took a
back seat to attempts to adapt the Soviet model in the
early 1950s, implicit in them were alternatives to the way
Stalin dealt with the contradictions between urban and
rural areas, workers and peasants, mental and manual labor.
In time, as the Maoist leadership struggled to find ways to
industrialize China that would benefit the vast majority,
especially the peasants, this would lead to a direct clash with
the methods so deeply associated by the Russians with the
very essence of their revolution. In retrospect, it is far
easier to see the alternatives open to the Chinese leadership
after 1949 than to the Russian Bolshevik leaders after 1917.
That this appears largely in retrospect may also constitute
the strongest possible testimonial to the quality of Mao's
leadership.

Even in his unofficial comments, Mao does not dwell on
the class forces that led to Russian revisionism. As he wrote
in 1949, "the salvoes of the October Revolution brought us
Marxism-Leninism"—an alternative way to build China. In
the broadest historical context, the Chinese do not see the

Russian Revolution as a tragedy which threw European Marxism off the track. To view it as "premature" for them is to see history only in a European setting. What the October Revolution drove home to Chinese intellectuals was that the historical stage of capitalism could be skipped. In China, where all the alternatives up to then were breaking down or becoming badly tarnished, this was a message of incalculable import. Whatever his faults, the Maoists seem to say, Stalin industrialized and collectivized, built an alternative to Western capitalism, and survived. Socialism in one country was the necessary recipe for this process. The victory over the Nazis was proof of its success. Whatever the costs, without this alternative to the world capitalist system, "the international reactionary forces bearing down on us would certainly be many times greater than now," Mao wrote in 1949. The world China faced in 1949 was harsh and hostile, but far less so than the one Russia faced in 1917. To discredit Stalin and thus the Russian revolutionary tradition is to deny the historic context within which the Chinese revolution developed.

The Chinese, moreover, see many social forces that were once revolutionary falling behind, failing to develop further, and thus becoming reactionary or revisionist. What was revolutionary in the 1930s, what were once appropriate methods, in a radically altered world thirty years later could be judged revisionist. This has been the case again and again throughout the century-long Chinese revolutionary experience. To show where once progressive forces fell behind, however, is not to deny either their contribution or the revolutionary tradition.

Revolutionaries, the Chinese argue, build indirectly on the experience of others. The Russians themselves learned from Western revolutionary experience, but they were also often without models to think about, without alternatives for building socialism that come from others' experience. The Chinese revolutionaries had to learn to study both the positive and negative accomplishments of the Russian Revolution, thinking through the Russian experience as a model in order to avoid its mistakes. By taking Russia as a blueprint to be implemented in China in the early 1950s, this process of understanding was weakened. But Mao's own understanding of Russia has been involved in his efforts since the mid-1950s to find answers to the problems of building a socialist society revealed by Russia. In both the Great Leap Forward and the Cultural Revolution, the Chinese probed the limits of new paths that the Russians had not traveled. If this historical perspective is not shared, much of the Maoist view of revisionism at home and abroad cannot be appreciated.

NOTES

I am grateful to Herbert Bix, Kung Chung-wu, David and Nancy Milton, Victor and Brett Nee, Sam Noumoff, Marilyn and Ernest Young, Moss Roberts, and especially Tom Engelhardt and Susan Gyarmati for their criticism, suggestions, and editorial advice.

1. Richard H. Pells, *Radical Visions and American Dreams: Culture and Social Thought in the Depression Years* (New York, 1973), p. 139.
2. John K. Fairbank, Transcript of Round Table Discussion on American Policy Toward China Held in the Department of State, October 6, 7, and 8, 1949 (Unpublished Mimeograph), p. 246.
3. John K. Fairbank, "Communist China and Taiwan in U.S. Foreign Policy," in *China: The People's Middle Kingdom and the U.S.A.* (Cambridge, Mass., 1967), p. 95.
4. George Taylor, "An Effective Approach in Asia," *Virginia Quarterly Review* (Winter 1950), p. 37.
5. Edwin O. Reischauer, *Wanted: An Asian Policy* (New York, 1955), p. 186.
6. John K. Fairbank, Transcript of Round Table Discussion, p. 136.
7. John K. Fairbank, "In Search of a China Policy," *The Reporter* (January 3, 1950).
8. John K. Fairbank, "America and the Chinese Revolution," *New Republic* (August 22, 1949), p. 13.
9. Marion J. Levy, Jr., "The Problems of Our Policy in China," *Virginia Quarterly Review* (Summer 1949), p. 364.

10. John K. Fairbank, "Our Chances in China," *Atlantic Monthly* (September 1946), p. 38.
11. John K. Fairbank, "Toward a Dynamic Far Eastern Policy," *Far Eastern Survey* (September 7, 1949), p. 212.
12. George Taylor, "An Effective Approach in Asia," p. 35.
13. John K. Fairbank, "Toward a Dynamic Far Eastern Policy," p. 210.
14. John K. Fairbank, "The Great Wall," *New York Review of Books* (March 28, 1968), p. 28.
15. Mary Wright, *The Last Stand of Chinese Conservatism* (New York, 1966), p. 9.
16. John K. Fairbank, Edwin O. Reischauer, and Albert Craig, *East Asia: The Modern Transformation* (Boston, 1965), p. 404.
17. John K. Fairbank, *United States Policy with Respect to Mainland China*, Hearings before the Committee on Foreign Relations, Senate, March 1966 (Washington, D.C., 1966), p. 109.
18. John K. Fairbank, "New Thinking about China," in *China: The People's Middle Kingdom and the U.S.A.*, p. 95.
19. Conrad Brandt, *Stalin's Failure in China* (Cambridge, Mass., 1958), p. vii.
20. John K. Fairbank, "An American View of China's Modernization," in *China: The People's Middle Kingdom and the U.S.A.*, p. 23.
21. John K. Fairbank, "Why Peking Casts Us as the Villain," in *ibid.*, p. 17.
22. John K. Fairbank, *United States Policy with Respect to Mainland China*, p. 102.
23. Stanley Karnow, *Mao and China: From Revolution to Revolution* (New York, 1972), p. x.
24. A. Doak Barnett, "China and U.S. Policy: A Time of Transition," *Current Scene* (May 15, 1970), p. 2.
25. John Israel, "The Red Guards in Historical Perspective: Continuity and Change in the Chinese Youth Movement," *China Quarterly* (April–June 1967), p. 32.
26. Stanley Karnow, "Letter from Hong Kong," *Encounter* (April 1969), p. 91.
27. Edwin O. Reischauer, *Beyond Vietnam: The United States and Asia* (New York, 1967), p. 151.
28. John W. Lewis, "Leader, Commissar, and Bureaucrat: The Chinese Political System in the Last Days of the Revolution," in *China in Crisis*, eds, Ping-ti Ho and Tang Tsou (Chicago, 1969), pp. 459–460.
29. Richard Baum, "Ideology Redivivus," in *China in Ferment: Perspectives on the Cultural Revolution*, eds. Richard Baum and Louise B. Bennett (Englewood Cliffs, N.J., 1971), p. 69.
30. Benjamin Schwartz, "Modernization and the Maoist Vision— Some Reflections on Chinese Communist Goals," in *China under Mao: Politics Takes Command*, ed. Roderick MacFarquhar (Cambridge, Mass., 1966), p. 6.

31. *Ibid.*, p. 7.
32. Richard Baum, "Ideology Redivivus," p. 70.
33. Max Weber, *Wirtschaft und Gesellschaft* (Tubingen, 1922), p. 49.
34. *Ibid.*, p. 128.
35. E. J. Hobsbawm, *Industry and Empire: The Making of Modern English Society* (New York, 1968), p. 74.
36. E. P. Thompson, *The Making of the English Working Class* (New York, 1964), p. 445.
37. Friedrich Engels, *The Condition of the Working-Class in England* (Moscow, 1973), p. 144.
38. D. H. Lawrence, quoted by Thompson, *op. cit.*, p. 447.
39. Max Weber, *Gesammelte Aufsätze zur Religionssoziologie* (Tubingen, 1922), 1:544–45.
40. Max Weber, quoted by Arthur Mitzman, *The Iron Cage: An Historical Interpretation of Max Weber* (New York, 1970), p. 184.
41. Thompson, *op. cit.*, p. 362.
42. Etienne Balazs, *Chinese Civilization and Bureaucracy* (New Haven, 1964), p. 157.
43. Jean Chesneaux, *Peasant Revolts in China: 1840–1949* (New York, 1973), p. 7.
44. Balazs, *op. cit.*, p. 135.
45. *Ibid.*, p. 159.
46. Chesneaux, *op. cit.*, p. 75.
47. Louis Hartz, Introduction to Benjamin Schwartz, *In Search of Wealth and Power: Yen Fu and the West* (Cambridge, Mass., 1964), p. xv.
48. Yu-sheng Lin, "Radical Iconoclasm in the May Fourth Period and the Future of Chinese Liberalism," in *Reflections on the May Fourth Movement*, ed. Benjamin Schwartz (Cambridge, Mass., 1972), pp. 48–49.
49. References and quotes in this essay are taken from Chairman Mao's "Reading Notes on the Soviet Union's 'Political Economy,'" from the Chinese version reprinted in Taiwan, *Mao Tse-tung ssu-hsiang wan sui* (n.p., August 1969), and the American government translation in *Miscellany of Mao Tse-tung Thought*, Part II (Arlington, Va.: Joint Publications Research Service, 1974), No. 61269–2. Though the documents are almost certainly authentic, care has been taken to draw on them only when they corroborate or deepen implications in Mao's officially published writings. Hereafter referred to as *Reading Notes*.
50. Mao Tsetung, *Reading Notes*, p. 279.
51. Mao Tsetung, "Talk at the Chengtu Conference," in *Chairman Mao Talks to the People: Talks and Letters, 1956–1971*, ed. Stuart Schram (New York, 1974), p. 108.
52. Mao Tsetung, "On Practice," in *Selected Works of Mao Tse-tung* (Peking, 1964), 1:308.
53. Mao Tsetung, "Where Do Correct Ideas Come From?", in *Selected Readings from the Works of Mao Tsetung* (Peking, 1971), p. 503.

54. Mao Tsetung, "Speech at the Supreme State Council," in Schram, p. 94.
55. Mao Tsetung, *Reading Notes*, p. 278.
56. *Ibid.*, p. 306.
57. Mao Tsetung, "Talks at the Chengtu Conference," in Schram, pp. 118–20.
58. Mao Tsetung, "Get Organized!", in *Selected Works of Mao Tse-tung* (Peking, 1967), 3:158.
59. Mao Tsetung, "Some Questions Concerning Methods of Leadership," in *Selected Works of Mao Tse-tung*, 3:118.
60. Mao Tsetung, "Speech at the Lushan Conference," in Schram, p. 134.
61. Mao Tsetung, "On Contradiction," in *Selected Works of Mao Tse-tung*, 1:332.
62. Mao Tsetung, "On the Ten Great Relationships," in Schram, p. 75.
63. Mao Tsetung, "Talk at an Enlarged Central Work Conference: On Democratic Centralism," in Schram, p. 163.
64. Mao Tsetung, "Oppose Book Worship," in *Selected Readings from the Works of Mao Tsetung*, p. 42.
65. Mao Tsetung, "Speech at the Lushan Conference," in Schram, p. 133.
66. Mao Tsetung, "Talks at Chengtu: The Pattern of Development," in Schram, p. 113.
67. Mao Tsetung, quoted in *People's Daily* editorial, "Make a Class Analysis of Factionalism," April 27, 1967.
68. Mao Tsetung, *Reading Notes*, p. 272.
69. *Ibid.*, p. 300.
70. *Ibid.*, p. 275.
71. Mao Tsetung, "Talks at Chengtu: Against Blind Faith in Learning," in Schram, p. 122.
72. *Ibid.*
73. Mao Tsetung, "Speech at the Tenth Plenum of the Eighth Central Committee," in Schram, p. 189.
74. Mao Tsetung, *Reading Notes*, p. 275.
75. *Ibid.*, p. 273.
76. *Ibid.*, p. 267.
77. *Ibid.*, p. 307.
78. Mao Tsetung quoted by André Malraux, " 'I am Alone with the Masses—Waiting': Forty Years of Mao and Communism," *Atlantic Monthly* (October 1968), p. 119.
79. Mao Tsetung, *Reading Notes,* p. 275.
80. Mao Tsetung, "Talks at Chengtu: Against Blind Faith in Learning," in Schram, p. 117.
81. Jack Belden, *China Shakes the World* (New York, 1970), pp. 169–170.
82. Mao Tsetung, "Speech at the Supreme State Conference," in Schram, p. 94.

83. Mao Tsetung, "Talks at Chengtu: The Pattern of Development," in Schram, p. 110.
84. Mao Tsetung, "Sixty Points on Working Methods—A Draft Resolution from the Office of the Centre of the CCP," in Jerome Ch'en, ed., *Mao Papers: Anthology and Bibliography* (London, 1970), p. 65.
85. Mao Tsetung, "Speech at the Supreme State Conference," in Schram, p. 94. The Chinese word is the same for both translated as either permanent or uninterrupted revolution.
86. Leon Trotsky, quoted by Brian Knapheis, "The Social and Political Thought of Leon Trotsky," (ph.D. diss., Oxford University, 1973), p. 172.
87. Leon Trotsky, *The Permanent Revolution and Results and Prospects* (New York, 1974), p. 71.
88. *Ibid.*
89. Leon Trotsky, *The Revolution Betrayed* (New York, 1937).
90. V. I. Lenin, *Collected Works* (Moscow, 1958–65), 9:237.
91. V. I. Lenin, "Fourth Anniversary of the October Revolution," in *On Culture and Cultural Revolution* (Moscow, 1970), pp. 170–71.
92. Isaac Deutscher, *On Socialist Man* (New York, 1967), p. 18.
93. Leon Trotsky, quoted by Charles Bettelheim, *Les Luttes de Classes en URSS* (Paris, 1974), p. 27.
94. Leon Trotsky, *Literature and Revolution* (New York, n.d.), p. 193.
95. Joseph Stalin, *Foundations of Leninism* (New York, 1974), pp. 41–42.
96. Joseph Stalin, *Problems of Leninism* (San Francisco, n.d.), p. 64.
97. Samuel J. Noumoff, "The Philosophical Basis of the Theory of Social Transformation in China" (Ph.D. diss., New York University, 1975), p. 275.
98. Leon Trotsky, *The Revolution Betrayed* (New York, 1937).
99. Mao Tsetung, "Notes on Comrade Ch'en Cheng-jen's Report on his 'Squatting Point' " (January 29, 1965) in *JCMP*, p. 100.
100. James R. Townsend, *Political Participation in Communist China* (Berkeley and Los Angeles, 1972), p. 199, is a study predicated upon this fundamental assumption.
101. *Ibid.*, pp. 199, 200.
102. Richard H. Solomon, *Mao's Revolution and the Chinese Political Culture* (Berkeley and Los Angeles, 1971), pp. 166, 167.
103. Richard H. Solomon, "On Activism and Activists: Maoist Conceptions of Motivation and Political Role Linking State to Society," *China Quarterly* (July–September 1969), p. 98.
104. Lucien Pye, "Hostility and Authority in Chinese Politics," *Problems of Communism* (May–June 1968), p, 11.
105. Solomon, "On Activism and Activists," p. 108.
106. *Ibid.*, p. 113.
107. John Israel, "Continuities and Discontinuities in the Ideology of the Great Proletarian Cultural Revolution," in *Ideology and*

    Politics in Contemporary China, ed. Chalmers Johnson (Seattle, 1973), p. 37.

108. Richard H. Solomon, "From Commitment to Cant: The Evolving Functions of Ideology in the Revolutionary Process," in *Ideology and Politics in Contemporary China,* p. 76.

109. *Ibid.,* p. 72.

110. Robert Jay Lifton, *Thought Reform and the Psychology of Totalism* (New York, 1963), p. 423.

111. *Ibid.*

112. *Ibid.,* p. 429.

113. Ezra F. Vogel, "Voluntarism and Social Control," in *Soviet and Chinese Communism: Similarities and Differences,* ed. Donald W. Treadgold (Seattle, 1967), p. 169.

114. Chalmers Johnson, "The Two Chinese Revolutions," *China Quarterly* (July–September 1969), p. 19.

115. Vogel, *op. cit.,* p. 169.

116. Solomon, "On Activism and Activists," p. 77.

117. Vogel, *op. cit.,* p. 184.

118. Schwartz, "Modernization and the Maoist Vision," p. 15.

119. *Ibid.,* p. 11.

120. Barbara Tuchman, *Notes from China* (New York, 1972), pp. 3–4.

121. Theodore Hsi-en Chen, "Education in Communist China: Aims, Trends, and Problems," in *Contemporary China,* ed. Ruth Adams (New York, 1966), p. 278.

122. Robert Jay Lifton, *Revolutionary Immortality: Mao Tse-tung and the Chinese Cultural Revolution* (New York, 1968), p. 129.

123. Jerome Ch'en, "The Development and Logic of Mao Tse-tung's Thought, 1928–1949," in *Ideology and Politics in Contemporary China,* p. 114.

124. David and Nancy Milton, *The Wind Will Not Subside: Years in Revolutionary China* (New York, forthcoming).

125. Ezra F. Vogel, "Preserving Order in the Cities," in *The City in Communist China,* ed. John W. Lewis (Stanford, 1971), p. 90.

126. *Ibid.,* p. 87.

127. Richard A. Cloward and Frances Fox Piven, *The Politics of Turmoil: Essays on Poverty, Race, and the Urban Crisis* (New York, 1974), p. 119.

128. A very useful comparison of the experiences at Taoyuan and Tachai is in Wilfred Burchett (in collaboration with Rewi Alley), *China: The Quality of Life* (London, forthcoming).

129. *Ibid.*

130. Merle Goldman, *Literary Dissent in Communist China* (New York, 1971), p. 5.

131. Merle Goldman, "The Fall of Chou Yang," *China Quarterly,* (July–September, 1966), p. 143.

132. Hannah Arendt, *Between Past and Future: Eight Exercises in Political Thought* (New York, 1968), p. 149.

133. Robert A. Nisbet, *The Quest for Community* (New York, 1970), p. 112.

134. Isaiah Berlin argues that this belief underlies the essence of the conception of liberty in both its "negative" and "positive" senses, *Four Essays on Liberty* (London, 1969), p. 158.

135. Arendt, *op. cit.*, p. 163.

136. C. B. Macpherson, *The Political Theory of Possessive Individualism: Hobbes to Locke* (London, 1962).

137. Seymour Martin Lipset, *The First New Nation* (New York, 1963), p. 208.

138. Joseph A. Schumpeter, *Capitalism, Socialism, and Democracy* (New York, 1947), p. 262.

139. Barrington Moore, Jr., *Reflections on the Causes of Human Misery and upon Certain Proposals to Eliminate Them* (Boston, 1972), p. 94.

140. *Ibid.*, p. 91.

141. Karl Mannheim, *Essays on the Sociology of Culture* (London, 1956), pp. 159–62.

142. Mao Tsetung, *Reading Notes*, p. 257.

143. Yao Wen-yuan, *Polemic on Literary and Art Thought* (Arlington, Va., 1970), p. 45.

144. Mao Tsetung, *Selected Works of Mao Tse-tung*, 3:70.

145. Yao Wen Yuan, p. 11.

146. *Ibid.*, p. 18.

147. Mao Tsetung, *Selected Works of Mao Tse-tung*, 3:82.

148. Noumoff, *op. cit.*

149. Dr. Schowalter, quoted by Evelyn Kaye, *The Family Guide to Children's Television* (New York, 1974), p. 65.

150. Sam Blum, quoted by Muriel G. Cantor, "Producing Television for Children," in *The TV Establishment: Programming for Power and Profit*, ed. Gaye Tuchman (Englewood Cliffs, N.J., 1974), p. 105.

151. Schowalter, *op. cit.*, p. 65.

152. Kaye, *op. cit.*, pp. 51–52.

153. Pauline Kael, interview with Studs Terkel, *Working: People Talk about What They Do All Day and How They Feel about What They Do* (New York, 1974), pp. 155–56.

154. E. H. Carr, *The October Revolution: Before and After* (New York, 1969), pp. 87–88.

155. Institute of Philosophy of the USSR Academy of Sciences, *The Future of Society: A Critique of Modern Bourgeois Philosophical and Socio-Political Conceptions* (Moscow, 1973), p. 149.

156. *Ibid.*, p. 146.

157. *Ibid.*, p. 149.

158. *Ibid.*, p. 146.

159. This Russian view of the Chinese Revolution draws upon numerous books and hundreds of magazine and newspaper articles published by the Soviet Union over the last fifteen years. The result is a composite picture. Russian authors do disagree at times on their interpretations of events and the meaning of Mao Tsetung Thought. Yet beneath these disagreements is a shared per-

spective which is more important here than the differences. Only sources directly quoted from among the large public materials available will be footnoted. The following books, however, are among the most accessible of the Russian position in English: the Institute of Philosophy and the Institute of the Far East of the USSR Academy of Science, *A Critique of Mao Tse-tung's Theoretical Conceptions* (Moscow, 1972); M. Altaisky and V. Georgiyev, *The Philosophical Views of Mao Tse-tung: A Critical Analysis* (Moscow, 1971); Institute for the Far East of the Academy of Sciences of the USSR, *Leninism and Modern China's Problems* (Moscow, 1972); E. Korbash, *The Economic "Theories" of Maoism* (Moscow, 1974); *Maoism Unmasked: Collection of Soviet Press Articles* (Moscow, 1972). For a Russian overview of China's foreign policy, see G. V. Astafyev and A. M. Dubinsky, *From Anti-Imperialism to Anti-Socialism: The Evolution of Peking's Foreign Policy* (Moscow, 1974).

Among the books most useful on Russian history and politics for this section are the following: Charles Bettelheim's first volume on the history of modern Russia, *Les Luttes de elasses en URSS: l'ère période 1917–1923* (Paris, 1974); Stephen Cohen, *Bukharin and the Bolshevik Revolution: A Political Biography, 1888–1938* (New York, 1973); Brian Knapheis, *The Social and Political Thought of Leon Trotsky*, (Ph.D. diss., Oxford, 1973); Roy A. Medvedev, *Let History Judge: The Origins and Consequences of Stalinism* (New York, 1972); J. P. Nettl, *The Soviet Achievement* (New York, 1970); M. N. Pokrovskii, *Russia in World History: Selected Essays* (Ann Arbor, 1970).

160. V. Glunin, "Concerning the History of the 4th Plenary Meeting of the CPC Central Committee of the 7th Convocation," Information Bulletin, Novosti Press Agency, no. 4 (222), January 1974, pp. 3–4.

161. Institute of Philosophy and the Institute of the Far East of the USSR Academy of Sciences, *A Critique of Mao Tse-tung's Theoretical Conceptions* (Moscow, 1972), p. 171.

162. *Ibid.*, p. 187.

163. E. Korbash, *The Economic "Theories" of Maoism* (Moscow, 1974), p. 43.

164. *Ibid.*, p. 285.

165. *Ibid.*

166. *Ibid.*, pp. 219–20.

167. *Ibid.*, p. 220.

168. V. Vyatsky, "Militarisation of China's Economy," in *Maoism Unmasked: Collection of Soviet Press Articles* (Moscow, 1972), p. 177.

169. V. Gelbras, "Anti-Marxist Essence of the Mao Group's Socio-Economic Policy, in *Maoism Unmasked*, p. 203.

170. V. Glunin, "The Struggle of Two Lines in the CPC," Information Bulletin, Novosti Press Agency, no. 20 (238), June 1974, pp. 2–4.

171. *Ibid.*, p. 3. In their attacks on China in the early days of the Cultural Revolution, the Russians seldom referred to Liu Shao-ch'i as a spokesman for a "realistic policy" or an advocate of the "Leninist party." But since the late 1960s they have often interpreted Liu as representing or supporting such positions.

172. *A Critique of Mao Tse-tung's Theoretical Conceptions*, p. 231.

173. "On the Anti-Soviet Policy of Mao Tse-tung and His Group," *Pravda* (February 16, 1967), translated in the *Current Digest of the Soviet Press*, 19 (1967), p. 7.

174. I. Yelenin and A. Pamor, "The Militarization of Social Life in China," *Krasnaya zvezda* (February 25, 1972), translated in the *Current Digest of the Soviet Press*, 24 (1972), p. 1.

175. *A Critique of Mao Tse-tung's Theoretical Conceptions*, 197–200.

176. *The Economic "Theories" of Maoism*, p. 48.

177. A. Rumyantsev, "Maoism and Its Anti-Marxist Philosophy," in *Maoism Unmasked*, p. 46.

178. Stuart Schram's translation of this passage is used here. *The Political Thought of Mao Tse-tung* (New York, 1974), p. 172. The Russian translation reads somewhat differently and less accurately in *Maoism Unmasked*, pp. 44–45.

179. M. Altaisky and V. Georgiyev, *The Philosophical Views of Mao Tse-tung: A Critical Analysis* (Moscow, 1971), p. 153.

180. *A Critique of Mao Tse-tung's Theoretical Conceptions*, p. 61.

181. Mao Tsetung, quoted in *The Political Thought of Mao Tse-tung*, p. 176.

182. *Ibid.*, p. 177.

183. "On Dialectical Materialism" has not been officially released in China or ever stated by the Chinese to be one's of Mao's writings. In 1965 Edgar Snow asked Mao whether he had written it. "He replied that he had never written an essay entitled 'Dialectical Materialism.' He thought that he would remember it if he had." Edgar Snow, *The Long Revolution* (New York, 1972), p. 207.

184. Mao Tsetung, quoted in *The Political Thought of Mao Tse-tung*, p. 182. For the Russian translation, see *Philosophical Views of Mao Tse-tung*, p. 61.

185. *Quotations from Chairman Mao Tse-tung* (Peking, 1967), p. 212. Quoted by the Russians in *The Philosophical Views of Mao Tse-tung*, p. 63.

186. *A Critique of Mao Tse-tung's Theoretical Conceptions*, p. 269.

187. Mao Tsetung, "Oppose Book Worship," in *Selected Readings from the Works of Mao Tsetung*, p. 42.

188. *The Philosophical Views of Mao Tse-tung*, p. 147.

189. E. Batalov, "Destruction of Practice," in *Maoism Unmasked*, p. 91.

190. B. Bulatov, *Maoism Versus Culture* (Moscow, 1970), p. 32.

191. *Ibid.*, p. 13.

192. A. Vladimirov, "The 'Big Leap' and Its Consequences," in *Maoism Unmasked*, p. 166.

193. *Maoism Versus Culture*, p. 31.
194. E. Butalov, "Destruction of Practice," in *Maoism Unmasked*, p. 93.
195. *Ibid.*
196. V. Volzhanin, "Leninism and the Problems of Chinese Culture," in *Leninism and Modern China's Problems*, ed. M. I. Sladkovsky (Moscow, 1972), p. 180.
197. *Maoism Versus Culture*, pp. 57–58.
198. *Ibid.*, p. 56.
199. *Joint Publications Research Service*, pp. 41, 735.
200. Useful illustrations of such Soviet attitudes are D. Gvishiana, *Organization and Management: A Sociological Analysis of Western Theories* (Moscow, 1972), and V. G. Afanasyev, *The Scientific Management of Society* (Moscow, 1971).
201. Mao Tsetung, "Chairman Mao's Talk to Music Workers," in *Chairman Mao Talks to the People*, pp. 85–86.
202. Lenin, quoted by D. Gvishiana, *Organisation and Management*, pp. 87–88.
203. *Ibid.*, p. 94.
204. A. Arnoldov, *On the Path of Cultural Progress* (Moscow, 1974), p. 105.
205. *The Philosophical Views of Mao Tse-tung*, p. 123.
206. *The Scientific Management of Society*, pp. 199–202.
207. Mao Tsetung quoted by Stuart Schram. "Mao Tse-tung: A Self-Portrait," *China Quarterly* (January–March, 1974), p. 160.
208. Joseph Stalin, *Dialectical and Historical Materialism* (New York, 1973), p. 31. As F. V. Konstantinov argues in *The Role of Socialist Consciousness in the Development of Socialist Society* (Moscow, 1951), p. 52, "the development of the consciousness of the masses always lags behind the changes in society's material conditions of existence."
209. Mao Tsetung, "Critique of Stalin's 'Economic Problems of Socialism in the Soviet Union," translated in *Miscellany of Mao Tse-tung Thought*, part II (Arlington, Va., 1974), No. 61269–2, p. 191.
210. Stalin, *Dialectical and Historical Materialism*, p. 38. Konstatinov, *op. cit.*, p. 59, took this position one step further, as did many writers during the 1940s in Russia, when he argued that "Soviet socialist ideology has become the ideology of the entire people." The roots of the Russian position today on the "state of the whole people" and "the party of the entire people" are clearly revealed in such writings.
211. Hung Hsueh-ping, "The Essence of the 'Theory of Productive Forces' Is to Oppose Proletarian Revolution," *Peking Review*, no. 38 (September 19, 1969), p. 6.
212. "On Khrushchev's Phoney Communism and Its Historical Lessons for the World: Comment on the Open Letter of the Central Committee of the CPSU," in William E. Griffith, *Sino-Soviet Relations, 1964–1965* (Cambridge, Mass., 1967), p. 346.

213. Hung Hsueh-ping, *op. cit.*, p. 5.
214. Mao Tsetung, *Reading Notes*, p. 269.
215. *Ibid.*
216. *Ibid.*
217. Mao Tsetung, "Critique of Stalin's 'Economic Problems of Socialism in the Soviet Union,'" p. 191.
218. Mao Tsetung, *Reading Notes*, p. 277.
219. *Ibid.*, p. 283.
220. *Ibid.*, p. 257.
221. M. N. Pokrovskii, *Russia in World History: Selected Essays* (Ann Arbor, 1970), p. 144.
222. E. H. Carr, *The October Revolution*, p. 120.
223. *Ibid.*, pp. 99–100.
224. Stephen F. Cohen, *Bukharin and the Bolshevik Revolution: A Political Biography 1888–1938* (New York, 1973), p. 143. In this paragraph, Cohen is quoting Bukharin.
225. Bukharin, quoted by Cohen, *ibid.*, p. 194.
226. E. H. Carr, *The October Revolution.*
227. Cohen, *Bukharin and the Bolshevik Revolution*, pp. 327–28.
228. Joseph Stalin, quoted by Roy A. Medvedev, *Let History Judge: The Origins and Consequences of Stalinism* (New York, 1972), p. 87.
229. An example of this Russian approach to the peasants and the workers is in the *Outline History of the Soviet Working Class*, ed. Y. S. Borisova et al. (Moscow, 1973).
230. *History of the Communist Party of the Soviet Union*, ed. by a Commission of the Central Committee of the C. P. S. U. (San Francisco, n.d.), p. 305.
231. J. P. Nettl, *The Soviet Achievement* (New York, 1970), p. 126.
232. Medvedev, *Let History Judge*, pp. 547–48.
233. *Ibid.*, p. 315.

CULTURAL REVOLUTION IN MODERN CHINESE HISTORY

Kung Chung-wu

China in modern times was poor and weak. In spite of its once lauded governmental stability, cultural durability, and its size and population, China fell prey to all kinds of aggression by imperialist powers, from Great Britain to Portugal, Russia to Japan. China's long-established cultural independence and confidence were replaced by humiliation. Once a giant in Asia, China became a "colony of all powers in the world."

Faced with the onslaught of Western power in the middle of the nineteenth century, questions of national wealth and power, national survival, and cultural identity became central concerns for all Chinese. Each of China's classes—peasantry, landlords, bourgeoisie, and proletariat—confronted several basic questions. As China sought wealth and power in order to ensure its existence as a political entity, what changes were necessary to create a viable culture capable of combining the best of the old with the new, the indigenous and the foreign, and thus overcome the threat of Western bourgeois culture? How could China integrate the modern economic, scientific, and technological methods of the Western capitalist world into Chinese society? And toward what objective should all this be directed?

At every stage of the Western onslaught and deepening domestic turmoil, the Chinese intensely debated these questions. Confronted with this disintegration of the ancient regime in the middle of the nineteenth century, the Chinese people began an agonizing and traumatic transformation that eventually resulted in the all but total destruction of China's feudal past and the development of a new society. While conservatives clung to traditional methods and largely accepted the status quo, reformers and revolutionaries struggled to open the way to China's transformation. Yet again and again they found their attempts to build a new China brushed aside as inadequate to the enormous challenges facing the nation. Changes regarded as progressive by one generation were discarded as insufficient by the next; one generation after another saw their ways becoming a new orthodoxy challenged by new radical forces.

The challenge was indeed extraordinary. China not only had to build a modern economy but also create the values and culture to shape its development and direction. This demand for a new culture became a touchstone for generations of Chinese reformers and revolutionaries. New values and attitudes were necessary for the transformation of both individuals and the material base of society. Economic methods and the values guiding them were intricately interconnected.

For the conservatives, culture was something to be preserved, the old landlord culture that for millennia was inseparable from Confucianism. For the radicals and the revolutionaries, however, culture in its bourgeois or proletarian form was something potential, something that had to be built over a long period of time. For the Communists this was even more true, for the Soviet model was less established historically than the bourgeois culture of the West that Chinese liberals turned to for guidance and support. Anglo-American culture reflected the values of contemporary capitalism, particularly its association with liberalism and bourgeois-democratic forms of government. After 1917, the Russian Revolution brought Marxism-Leninism to China, along with some of the European socialist traditions. To the Chinese the Anglo-American and Euro-Russian models constituted two great social-economic-cultural alternatives and thus they were often treated as distinctive cultures. The first was the model for bourgeois culture; the second the model for proletarian culture.

Thus, for well over a century, "sinification" of foreign ideas and methods characterized all those who fought to build a new China. Each stage in the revolutionary process always involved a dialectic of internal and external influence, of debates over external models and domestic conditions.

When Mao Tsetung spoke during the late 1960s of the need for the Great Proletarian Cultural Revolution and foresaw the need for other cultural revolutions, he drew upon ideas deeply embedded in modern China's revolutionary traditions. "Cultural revolutions" have been an intricate part of China's historic transformation since the 1840s, marking the stages of China's rapid movement from feudalism to republicanism to socialism and today toward communism. Each stage reveals the bitter conflict over values and attitudes among and within China's classes, with Western imperialist powers, and, later, with Russia. The ideas of relatively tiny groups of intellectuals and political leaders are emphasized here only to show how they expressed various class interests. When Chinese intellectuals addressed current issues, they did so with a view to defending the interests of their own class or the classes they were committed to. They did not exist in a social or class vacuum and most of them quite consciously understood this.

The notion of stages in a revolutionary process and cultural revolution provide an essential way for understanding Chinese history since 1840. Four great cultural revolutions, each with its appropriate subdivisions, are analyzed in this essay to provide an introduction to China's revolutionary transformation and to suggest why the Maoists came to speak of their process as one uninterrupted revolution.

The Old Democratic Cultural Revolution (1840–1916) marked the end of the traditional form of peasant rebellion, even though the Taiping revolutionary's culture was in several ways quite progressive. Bourgeois culture also grew in this period, and together with the peasant revolutionary ideology engaged in bitter struggle against the traditional Confucian culture of the landlords. The New Democratic Cultural Revolution (1916–49) was marked by the struggle between bourgeois and proletarian cultures, two still largely potential cultures struggling for supremacy over the values and ideas that would lead the building of a new modern industrial China. After liberation, the Socialist Cultural Revolution (1949–58) saw the conflict between the growing power of a new proletarian culture and the still powerful culture of the defeated bourgeois, reinforced by the attraction of many Western capitalist methods. Finally, the Proletarian Cultural Revolution—marked by the struggle against revisionism, with its links to the Soviet approach to socialism—climaxed in the Great Proletarian Cultural Revolution.

Underlying this progression of cultural revolutions was a common concern for certain values which are embodied in the traditional notion of the public-oriented *ta-t'ung* (Great Unity) society. Rooted in China's historic material conditions, *ta-t'ung* refers to a society based on public ownership and free from class exploitation and oppression. It was a lofty ideal long cherished by the Chinese people. All classes in modern China shared this hope, in their own way. But the traditional peasant conception became utterly anachronistic at a time of Western imperialist aggression and the disintegration of China's feudal society. The Anglo-American-oriented Chinese bourgeoisie, and later the Russian-oriented Chinese revisionists, both failed in their attempts to reach this objective. The *ta-t'ung* ideal required the creation of a new culture in a way that would restore cultural identity, not a foreign substitute or a crudely adopted external culture. Why Mao Tsetung Thought was successful where other failed will become clearer as we follow the history of China's cultural revolutions since 1840.

THE OLD DEMOCRATIC CULTURAL REVOLUTION

The seven decades of cultural upheaval which shook the foundations of traditional Chinese society from 1840 to 1916 have been spoken of by Mao Tsetung as the Old Democratic Cultural Revolution.[1] A fierce attack on China's ruling class culture, its ultimate collapse, and the establishment of a short-lived republic modeled after the Western bourgeois democratic states defined the contours of this historical process. By contrast to the West, however, where the attack on the culture of the traditional landed ruling class was borne to victory by the young and dynamic culture of the native bourgeoisie, in nineteenth-century China there existed no highly developed bourgeoisie to speak of. Beneath the torturous cultural struggles of early modern China, therefore, was the relentless driving force not of a newly risen native social class but of the seemingly inexorable penetration of foreign imperialism. The Old Democratic Cultural Revolution, accordingly, became a protracted clash not of traditional ruling class culture with an indigenous challenging culture but with imported elements of European and American bourgeois culture. So ineluctable was this impact of the foreign powers on China, in fact, that the outcome of each successive struggle over these seven decades was ultimately decided by their overwhelming pressure. In retrospect we may see the unfolding course of the Old Democratic Cultural Revolution as punctuated by five phases, each marked by a fierce internal ideological clash, each paralleling a major war between China and Western or Japanese imperialist power: from the Opium War in 1840 to the defeat of the Taipings in 1864; from 1864 to the first Sino-Japanese War in 1895; from 1895 to the Russo-Japanese War in 1905; and from 1905 to Japan's Twenty-One Demands in 1915. In each of these phases foreign bourgeois culture made deeper and deeper inroads into feudal Chinese society, finally discrediting it almost totally. While Confucian and other traditional ideologies persisted as an underlying influence in China's modern development, after 1916 the ancient traditions in and of themselves were never again looked to as the source of ultimate strength and vision for Chinese society.

FIRST PHASE: 1840–64

The Old Democratic Cultural Revolution began with the First Opium War in 1840. During this period, in which the European and American bourgeoise first gained a legal basis for their presence through the "unequal treaties," large-scale domestic uprisings erupted among the peasants and minorities in China's hinterlands and frontier provinces—the Taiping and Nien rebellions, revolts by the Mao tribes and Moslems of the Southwest, and by Moslems of the Northwest. The largest and most significant of these was the Taiping Rebellion of the 1850s and early 1860s. The social and political upheaval of these years was accompanied, as well, by a violent clash of two cultures: that of the revolutionary peasants led by Hung Hsiu-ch'üan and Hung Jen-kan, and that of the landlord class, represented by Tseng Kuo-fan, Hu Lin-i, Li Hung-chang, and Tso Tsung-t'ang.

While the Taiping Revolution appeared similar to other Chinese peasant revolutions on the surface, it departed from them significantly in its ideology. In addition to its expression of fervent anti-Manchu and anti-Western nationalism, the ideology of the revolutionary peasants contained such unconventional ideas as equality between men and women, equal distribution of economic wealth, and international equality. The Taipings burned some of the Confucian classics, revised others to fit their own needs and tastes, and destroyed Confucian temples and those of the popular deities. They overthrew landlords by abolishing private ownership of land, encouraged industrialization, and discarded cruel criminal laws, slavery, and the concubine system. Through such heretical ideas, derived from a variety of sources ranging from the codes of Chinese secret societies to Confucianism and Christianity, the Taipings not only challenged the political power of the Manchu dynasty but fiercely attacked the very basis of the landlord class and its culture. For the first time in Chinese history, the feudal order was radically challenged.[2]

The Taiping revolutionaries rested the fundamental concept of their ideology on the ideal of *kung*, the public. Hung Hsiu-ch'üan, leader of the Taipings and a student of the Confucian classics before committing himself to the peasants' cause, drew this concept from the Confucian *Book of Rites*, where the ideal society was described as one oriented to *kung*, the public good. The name Hung gave to his revolutionary regime, "Heavenly Kingdom of Universal Peace," apparently referred, moreover, to the famous *Kung-yang Commentary*, which speaks of a third stage of history, the Age of Taiping (universal peace). When a society reaches this stage, according to the commentary, it will become a society of *ta-t'ung*, or great unity, in which the virtue of *kung* will prevail.[3] The "Heavenly Kingdom" in the Hung regime's title has a similar connotation derived from the Christian Bible. In Hung's vision we thus find the first attempt in modern Chinese history made by intellectuals rooted in the peasant class to reconcile the values of Western and Chinese culture.[4]

So modern was the Taipings' ideology, in fact, that Chinese Communist historians later asserted that it contained elements conducive to the development of bourgeois culture and thus inaugurated the Old Democratic Cultural Revolution of the bourgeois class. Sun Yat-sen, the founder of the Republic of China, was directly inspired by the Taiping Revolution. Others, including Communist historian Fan Wen-lan, claim that the Chinese Communist Revolution, as well, developed within this tradition of "people's revolution," completing the tasks left unfinished by the Taipings.[5]

Paralleling the evolution of the radical Taiping ideology among intellectuals rooted in China's peasant class was the emergence, among official scholars of the landlord class, of a number of new schools of thought challenging the prevalent school of Han Learning (also known as the School of Empirical Research). The penetration of Western capitalism, the introduction of the modern mode of production, and the emergence in the treaty ports of both modern industrial workers and a comprador class were radically changing traditional Chinese society, and the consciousness of various social classes was inevitably affected by this. Beset by a host of domestic and external problems, ruling Confucian statesmen in the Tao-kuan and Hsien-feng reigns of the Ch'ing dynasty (1821–62) became critical of the trivial pedantry of the orthodox Han Learning of the eighteenth century. Interest shifted dramatically from scholastic annotation to a groping for new values and ideas.[6]

As was characteristic of the second half of every major dynasty, the general political decline of the Ch'ing ruling class was accompanied by a burst of intellectual activity, reexamining and reinterpreting the complex traditions accumulated over thousands of years. Much of this intellectual ferment drew on the Confucian *ching-shih* (practical statesmanship) tradition. Originally, Confucian moral philosophy had been committed to upholding the external social, political, and economic world of China's early slave society. The moral values of these early Confucianists had never been simply ends; they were also means to preserve a "harmony and peace" which served the interests of the slave lords. With the adoption of Confucianism as the state philosophy of the landlord class during the Western Han dynasty (206 B.C. to A.D. 23), the original *ching-shih* tradition split into two schools, conservative and reformist.[7] Conservative officials represented the interests of the big landlords, while reformists defended the petty landlords. At times the latter were also sympathetic to the interests of the peasants, the handicraft workers, the merchants, and other toiling people.

The difference between the conservative and reformist

Confucian traditions is strikingly evident in their ways of dealing with the "inner" (spiritual) and "outer" (social, political, economic) realms of human existence. Conservative thinkers gave such precedence to maintaining the existing order of things that they virtually denied the necessity for change in either realm, inner or outer. If change was necessary at all, it was only to restore the old order of things. Reformists, however, recognizing the inevitability of change and drawing inspiration from Legalism, espoused drastic administrative and sometimes institutional reforms in the outer realm in order to safeguard threatened values of the inner.

The new schools of Confucianism arising in the late Ch'ing were marked by a great diversity of opinions. All, nevertheless, assumed that China's increasing problems resulted from a misunderstanding or distortion of traditional Confucian principles which were universally true. Thus in various ways they sought to revive the original Confucian ideal of *ching-shih* with its commitment to action, looking to the Confucian classics for the textual basis of this notion. By doing so, however, Confucian statesmen and scholars found themselves in a paradoxical position. As the landlord class faced unprecedented challenges from both within and without China, they continued to search for solutions almost solely within the archaic Confucian tradition. What had once been a wellspring of cultural and intellectual strength was becoming no more than a source of intellectual exhaustion. The landlord culture, embedded in the Confucian tradition, faced problems it could no longer explain or solve. Despite its great enduring power and several attempts by the Confucianists to reinterpret it, the landlord culture had passed its highest point of development.

In this context, the antagonism of the landlord culture to the revolutionary peasants of the Taipings was especially ferocious. The fundamental nature of the threat posed to the ruling class by the Taiping rebels was eloquently expressed in 1854 by Tseng Kuo-fan.

> Is this merely a crisis for the Ch'ing dynasty? It is
> indeed a crisis for ming-chiao [Confucian moral
> teaching] unprecedented since the beginning of
> Chinese civilization. For this Confucius and Men-
> cius must be weeping bitterly in Hades. How can
> the educated fold their hands in their sleeves and sit
> in peace without thinking of doing something about
> it?[8]

Tseng's call for waging a "sacred war" to defend the Confucian faith received an enthusiastic response from Confucian scholars throughout the empire. This was especially
so in Hunan, Tseng's native province, where he recruited
most of the soldiers and leaders for his Hunan Army of
Confucian scholars. By bringing about a temporary revital-
ization of the landlord culture, Tseng Kuo-fan was able to
overwhelm the Taipings. His alliance with the rising
Chinese comprador class and the foreign bourgeoisie in the
treaty ports brought military success: Tseng crushed the
Taipings in 1864.

In several senses the defeat of the Taipings ended an era.
The Taiping espousal of a popular protomodern ideology
exposed for the first time in modern Chinese history the
inadequacy of Confucianism by itself to solve China's
growing problems. At the same time, the savage confrontation between the Taipings and Tseng's Hunan Army
marked once and for all the end of the traditional form of
peasant revolution against the landlord class. Traditionally,
Chinese peasant revolutionaries, inspired by the vision of
Ta-t'ung, sought to implement a public *(kung)*-oriented
society which would remove all sources of peasant misery by
solving the land problem. The Taiping revolutionaries
carried on the *Ta-t'ung* ideal, while making radical innovations in its content. The ultimate defeat of the Taipings
despite their strong social base, however, revealed that deep-
seated social and economic changes in nineteenth-century
Chinese society would preclude a successful traditional
peasant revolution. Their program of agrarian socialism was

too anachronistic, their agricultural mode of production too backward, and their alienation from the intelligentsia too great. The weakness of the industrial class in the cities, moreover, prohibited this potential source of revolutionary support from supplementing the forces of the peasant rebels. The protomodern culture of the Taipings was much too crude compared to the dynamic Western bourgeois culture they would ultimately have had to face.

In the Taiping Revolution, the traditional struggle between landlords and peasants took on another new dimension. While Tseng recruited most of his fighters from his native Hunan, the Taipings came largely from Kwangtung and Kwangsi provinces. For the first time in modern history, domestic political struggle shifted from the old pattern of North China versus South China to that of the interior land versus the coastal land. This unprecedented phenomenon fully manifested the depth of Western imperialism's influence on the course of modern Chinese history. The role once played by Inner Asia and India as the source of political and cultural challenges to Chinese civilization was slowly but surely being taken over by the West. From 1850 on, South China was to assume an increasingly active role in the process of China's transformation, while North China, for centuries the political center of the Chinese Empire, would recede into the background until the Red Army retreated to Yenan after the Long March of 1935.

SECOND PHASE: 1864–95

The second phase of China's Old Cultural Revolution, the period from the late 1860s to the early 1890s, was outwardly tranquil. Both the ruling class and the people were exhausted after two decades of civil war. In the international arena, the "cooperative policy"[9] of the Western imperialist powers reflected their need to consolidate the privileges seized through the two wars jointly fought by Britain and France against China in 1858 and 1860. Domestically, one of the most important developments during these thirty years was the series of intense debates that erupted between the orthodox Confucianists—represented by Wo-jen and Sung Chin in the 1860s, and Chang Chih-tung and Chang P'ei-lun in the late 1870s and early 1880s—and the revisionist Confucianists—represented by the scholar-generals like Tseng Kuo-fan, Li Hung-chang, Tso Tsung-t'ang, and the statecraft thinkers like Feng Kuei-fen, Hsüeh Fu-ch'eng, and Wang T'ao.

Unlike the orthodox Confucianists, the revisionist Confucianists had a positive attitude toward aspects of Western bourgeois culture. Wei Yüan, one of the most articulate forerunners of the revisionist Confucianists, was motivated by the agonizing defeat suffered by China in the Opium War. In his book *Geography of the Maritime Countries*,[10] Wei argued that the superiority of the "barbarians" lay solely in the area of technology, particularly their manufacture of such modern armaments as "steamships and guns." To control these barbarians, China should learn and adapt their "superior skills." Wei was joined by Kung Tzu-chen and Lin Tse-hsü in putting forth the argument that Western bourgeois culture in the form of military technology could be incorporated into the Confucian framework. But this would only be incorporated into the outer realm of the *ching-shih* ideal under the traditional category of "barbarian affairs."

Feng Kuei-fen, another prominent statecraft thinker, basically followed Wei's approach in the 1860s. In his book *Personal Protests from the Study of Chiao-pin*, written in 1860 after China's defeats in 1858 and 1860, Feng included Western bourgeois culture in the outer realm of the *ching-shih* ideal as auxiliary to the inner realm.

> If we let Chinese human relationships and moral faith serve as the ultimate source, and let them be supplemented by the methods used by the various nations for the attainment of prosperity and power, would it not be the best of all procedures?[11]

To Feng, however, the "method" no longer simply meant technology. Now it included science and Western methods. Technology derived from science, especially mathematics. The adoption of Western science was thus the only way to lead China toward self-strengthening.

Acutely conscious that "barbarian affairs" were of utmost importance, the Ch'ing ruling class, led by Tseng Kuo-fan, Li Hung-chang, and Tso Tsung-t'ang, inaugurated in the early 1860s a vigorous and ambitious campaign for industrialization. Known as the "Self-Strengthening movement" or the "movement of Foreign Matters," its aim was to "enrich the nation and increase its military strength" and thus stave off the Western powers. Following the ideas of Wei Yuan and Feng Kuei-fen, they built military industries, set up language schools, translated Western books on science and technology, and sent students to Europe and America. Yet even though their strenuous undertakings were strictly within the outer realm, their actions unleashed a storm of bitter criticism from the orthodox Confucianists.

No critic was more prominent or articulate than Wo-jen. As the chief grand secretary, a tutor to the emperor, head of the Hanlin Academy and president of several of the six boards in succession, he commanded vast influence among the intelligentsia. On the occasion of the establishment of Western studies in the *T'ung-wen Kuan* (Foreign Language Institute) in 1867, he sent a memorial to the emperor which employed many of the arguments orthodox Confucianists used to oppose the adoption of Western science and technology.

> Your slave has learned that the way to establish a nation is to lay emphasis on propriety and righteousness, not on power and plotting. The fundamental effort lies in the minds of people, not in techniques. . . . From ancient down to modern times, your slave has never heard of anyone who could use mathematics to raise the nation from a state of decline or to strengthen it in time of weakness.[12]

Wo-jen so emphasized the inner ethical realm that the outer rational realm became completely passive and inactive. To him, science and technology were irrelevant or even harmful for the ordering of the Confucian society.

His moralistic and idealist approach was bluntly attacked as "empty talk" by the practical-minded Prince Kung, the court architect of the policy of self-strengthening.

> If he [Wo-jen] really has some marvelous plan which can control foreign countries and not let us be controlled by them, our ministers should certainly follow the footsteps of the grand secretary. . . . If he has no other plan than to use loyalty and sincerity as armor, and propriety and righteousness as a shield, and such similar phrases, and if he says that these words could accomplish diplomatic negotiation and be sufficient to control the life of our enemies, your ministers indeed do not presume to believe it.[13]

In this debate, Prince Kung clearly compromised his ideological convictions. The danger of the West was too great for orthodox Confucian ways.

Throughout Chinese history, the persistent tension between the inner and outer realms of the Confucian *ching-shih* ideal was evident in the historic two-line debates within the landlord class between the Legalists and the Confucianists in the western Han, between the Confucianists and the Legalist-inclined in the late northern Sung (960–1126), the early southern Sung (1127–1278), and the late Ming (1368–1644).[14] But in the debates between Prince Kung and Wo-jen there was a significant departure. In the past, the relatively unchanging agrarian mode of production usually assured victory to those who emphasized the inner realm. The Western imperialists, however, by the threat they posed and their economic might, strengthened the position of promoters of the outer realm. This profound split in the landlord culture was one directly caused by Western bourgeois culture and the military and economic power of the imperialists. An emphasis on man's moral forces based on a feudal mode of production was now extremely vulnerable. This was what Prince Kung really meant by the term "empty talk."

The second round of the debate, from the late 1860s to the early 1880s, was between a new generation of orthodox Confucianists and revisionists. The former, known as the Pure Current group (ch'ing-liu), was represented by Chang Chih-tung and Chang P'ei-lun; the latter by Hsüeh Fu-ch'-eng, Wang T'ao, and Ma Chien-chung under the leadership of Li Hung-chang, the successor to Tseng Kuo-fan. The pivotal point in the dispute revolved around the notions of righteousness (i) and profit (li).

Seeing the massive drainage of national wealth caused by the dumping of foreign goods on the domestic market and the serious shortage of urgently needed capital for the construction of defense industries, the revisionists argued for economic growth through the building of light industries.[15] By doing so, they argued, China would not only recover her lost rights but accumulate needed capital as well. The power and wealth of the Western nations, after all, were derived from commerce and industry rather than steamships and guns alone. Therefore, if China wanted wealth and power, the country should be enriched first by promoting trade and industry, then the nation could be strengthened militarily. Thus, these revisionist Confucianists departed significantly from Wei and Feng who paid exclusive attention to military power. This type of thinking guided the Self-Strengthening movement under the aegis of Li Hung-chang after 1870.

To stress profits from trade and commerce, however, was to diametrically oppose the Confucian moral principle which placed righteousness above everything else. This was why the Pure Current members, composed of young and ethically minded censors and the Hanlin academicians, were so angry and uneasy about Self-Strengthening; they feared that China would become a society characterized by meanness, vulgarity, and hideousness.[16] They focused their attack on Li Hung-chang, the "Lord Palmerston of Chinese middle-class liberalism."[17] But if on the surface they appeared to be blindly opposing those Western methods and ideas endorsed by Li Hung-chang and his followers, in reality their avowed aim was "to purify the currents of national life by calling upon the nation to live more strictly according to the Confucian principles."[18]

Though the Pure Current group was supported by the empress dowager and other powerful orthodox Confucian statesmen, their opposition to the Euro-American-oriented self-strengthening movement could not last long. The repeated humiliation the orthodox Confucianists suffered at the hands of Western powers doomed their cause far more than the power of their domestic political opponents.

In 1884 China fought against French aggression. Though China won the land battle, its southern naval squadron was virtually wiped out. During the war the leaders of the Pure Current group commanded the sea battle in Fukien Province (Chang Pei-lun) and the land battle in Yunnan Province and today's Democratic Republic of Vietnam (Chang Chih-tung). Both were profoundly impressed by the formidable power of modern weapons, against which strict Confucian principles alone were useless, and finding no escape from the necessity of adopting Western weapons, they began compromising their ideological convictions.

Chang Pei-lun became the son-in-law of Li Hung-chang and was converted to the latter's revisionist Confucianism. After the war he actively promoted the Self-Strengthening movement. His increasingly skeptical attitude toward Confucian moral principles is clearly betrayed in his growing interest in various non-Confucian schools of thought long synthesized into the Confucian framework. The decline of Confucianism among a growing number of literati is evident in these changes in Chang's beliefs.

Chang Chih-tung's change of attitudes toward Western things and Confucianism was more complex and traumatic. Like Chang Pei-lun, he had after the war actively promoted large-scale projects of industrialization in Kwangtung and Hupeh provinces where he served as governor-general.[19] Unlike Chang Pei-lun, however, his faith in Confucian moral principles remained firm. Thus he confronted a dilemma: how to justify the seeking of profits on the basis of Confucian moral principles. To reconcile the contradiction between these two values, Chang used the paired notions of *kung* (public) and *ssu* (selfish).

> Who says I am a man who only understands interests and doesn't care for right and wrong? . . . My anxiety and concern have not been for the individual and selfish interests, but for those of the public. Individual and selfish interests should not be regarded but public interests must be considered.[20]

To seek profits was justifiable, therefore, if it was public-oriented; otherwise, it would be frowned upon. While the notion of *kung-ssu* had often been used as a rationale for administrative adjustment and institutional reform, Chang Chih-tung was probably the first person in modern China to use it to justify the adoption of the modern mode of production.

Under Li Hung-chang's leadership, the Self-Strengthening movement flourished after 1885. Learning from the defeat in the Sino-French War, he promoted steel factories and ship building. Yet ten years later an even greater military disaster sent shock waves throughout the Chinese Empire. This time China was humiliated not by the Westerners with their "superior skills" but by the Japanese, a people traditionally regarded as culturally dependent on China. The defeat harshly unveiled the depth of the weakness of the Confucian state, utterly discrediting the self-strengthening approaches to China's problems that had developed over the preceding thirty years.

THIRD PHASE: 1895–1905

Chinese bourgeois culture did not really begin to emerge as a distinctive class culture until the 1870s. The cultural activities of the missionaries, the establishment of modern schools, the philanthropic institutions, the translations of Western books on science and technology, and the publication of various newspapers and magazines all greatly contributed to the growth of this new dynamic culture. In the late nineteenth century this new culture mainly reflected the consciousness of the compradors in the coastal provinces south of the Yangtze River,[21] from Kiangsu Province in Central China to Kwangtung Province, and Hong Kong in South China. Foreign-educated intellectuals like Hu Liyüan, Ho Ch'i, and Yen Fu further reinforced the impact of bourgeois culture, though until 1895 this culture was unable to play an independent role and thus was generally a side current of revisionist Confucianism. Only after the first Sino-Japanese War in 1895 did their economic and political ideas draw attention from the revisionist Confucianists.

While some of the early bourgeois intellectuals had supported self-strengthening in the 1870s and 1880s, by the 1890s others were criticizing the guiding principles of the Self-Strengthening movement. Many did collaborate with the revisionist Confucianists. Some became independent critics of both the moderate and radical Confucian revisionists. Some even became bourgeois revolutionaries following Sun Yat-sen.

The content and intensity of the debates during this third phase of the Old Democratic Revolution were conditioned by the changing impact of Western penetration. During the period from 1850 to the 1870s, Western capitalism was in a stage of free competition, seeking markets around the globe for its surplus commodities. The Western impact at this time took the form of profit seeking through trade, to which the Chinese landlord class could respond by promoting economic growth, the central goal of the Self-Strengthening movement. By the 1880s, however, Western capitalism had developed to the stage of imperialism, establishing spheres of influence in the noncapitalist countries to ensure access to needed raw materials and to facilitate the export of surplus capital. This new development greatly heightened the contradictions within the East Asian community. Japan entered the ranks of the imperialists. More important, up through the partition movement imperialism had cost China her traditional vassal states along the vast coastline (Korea, Vietnam, Burma, Okinawa); part of her territory (Taiwan); and the vast area bordering Russia. As the partitioning process reached its peak around 1898, the Chinese people, regardless of class, feared that their country and their civilization was on the verge of extinction. It was in response to this threat that modern Chinese nationalism arose. National survival was now placed above everything else, even above the concern for cultural identity. Anything necessary for achieving power and preservation as a nation became justifiable.

The repeated failures of the Confucian state to defend Chinese society from foreign invasion thus brought the inherent tension between state and society to the breaking point. From this point on, the leading role in guiding the changes in the cultural sphere began to shift from those Confucianists in power who were committed to the preservation of the Confucian state, to those in society who were not so obliged to defend the existing order. Radical Confucian revisionism thus sprang up outside the bureaucracy rather than within it.

The major struggle that broke out in the 1890s was between the radical and moderate revisionist Confucianists, led by K'ang Yu-wei and Chang Chih-tung. China's humiliation at the hands of the Japanese greatly radicalized K'ang, who along with his student Liang Ch'i-ch'ao and hundreds of *ching-shih* candidates began what might be called the first modern Chinese student movement. It started in Peking during the negotiations of the Shimonoseki Treaty in Tokyo in 1895 and greatly enhanced the climate for the swift spread throughout the empire of radical Confucian revisionism among young Confucianists. Assisted by his students and followers, K'ang actively promoted Western bourgeois values and ideas. Papers were started; books and pamphlets were published in Shanghai, Hunan, and Canton. These writings expressed a diversity of ideas, all rooted in the ideology of bourgeois democracy: concepts of a constitutional monarchy, people's rights, and the parliamentarianism espoused earlier by bourgeois intellectuals like Cheng Kuan-ying, Hu Li-yüan, and Ho Ch'i. Sweeping administrative, institutional, educational, and social reforms were demanded. These reformers looked to England, Japan, Russia, and Germany, seeing in these nations the framework of a constitutional government in which the old landlord class and the new bourgeoisie could coexist.[22]

Yet how could these radical ideas and reforms, so heretical to orthodox and moderate revisionist Confucianists, be justified in the Confucian framework? K'ang, a devout Confucianist, could see no other solution but to try to legitimize his radical cause within the Confucian tradition. Like Hung Hsiu-ch'üan, K'ang resorted to the *Kung-yang Commentary* and the *Book of Rites*.

The theoretical basis of K'ang's reforms lay mainly in two of his books, *An Inquiry into the Classics Forged During the Hsin Period* (1891) and *Confucius as Reformer* (1897). To adapt Confucianism to his time, K'ang depicted Confucius as a great sage, an uncrowned king intent on institutional reform, rather than as the great preserver and transmitter of ancient traditions. He energetically ferreted out those ideas in the Confucian classics that stressed the role of the people's rights and weakened the authority of the autocratic ruler. Drawing upon the Kung-yang doctrine of the "three ages" (disorder, approaching peace, and universal peace), and probably influenced by Darwin's theory of evolution, K'ang argued that China was now in the age of approaching peace, a time when the correct political order was constitutional government.

K'ang's other well-known work, *On Great Unity (Ta-t'ung shu)*, made him one of the most significant modern Chinese thinkers to "carry on the past heritage and open up the future." This book expressed K'ang's concept of public (*kung*). He advocated the abolition of private property and the family, and argued for socialized education, equality between men and women, the abolition of states, classes, and racism. Though traces of Western socialism are evident in these utopian ideas of the landlord class, they were derived largely from the *li-yun* of the *Book of Rites*.

Like Hung Hsiu-ch'üan's ideal of *kung*, K'ang's ideal expressed the vision of a better society for China's increasing masses of poverty-stricken peasants. As stepped-up economic aggression by the imperialist powers further undercut the agrarian economy, these rural masses were beginning to suffer acutely. The breakdown of the central bureaucracy and frequent natural calamities increased their problems. However, unlike Hung who identified with the propertyless masses by rebelling against his own landlord class, K'ang was motivated largely by the patronizing humanism (*jen*) of the ruling class. Confined by his class background and his idealism, K'ang was unable to understand either the nature of class struggle or the modern mode of production. His ideal of *kung* was only empty talk.

K'ang Yu-wei's doctrines were developed in a more radical direction by his disciple, T'an Ssu-t'ung. T'an's thought, in fact, was in many ways closer to the republicanism of his contemporary, Sun Yat-sen. In his book, *The Study of Jen*, T'an charged that the feudal monarchy was despotic and a public enemy, and that Confucian human relationships were artificial bondage. Yet he attributed these abuses not so much to Confucius himself as to the misunderstanding and incorrect application of the spirit of his thought. T'an championed an "authentic" Confucianism, and implicit in his work is the call for a "return to genuine Confucianism." T'an still found his spiritual home in the Confucian tradition, no matter how radical he appeared on the surface. The significance of his contribution lies in his role as a transitional intellectual figure, bridging the gap between radical revisionist Confucianism, with its espousal of constitutional monarchy, and republicanism.

Liang Ch'i-ch'ao, another brilliant student of K'ang's, made an important theoretical contribution to the collective effort to redefine Confucianism in a modern context. In his essay "New Citizens," he sought to create a modern ideal personality that could replace the old Confucian one. Liang saw the "new citizen" inhabiting a "collectivist" society where public morality (*kung-te*) and private morality (*ssu-te*), public interest and private interest, were organically balanced. To attack the burdensome moral responsibilities imposed on the individual by Confucianism, Liang's schema incorporated the concepts of civil liberties and individualism developed in the Western bourgeois democratic tradition. To dilute the adverse influence of the disdain for profits on traditional society, he stressed the value of profit seeking.[23] The appeal of Liang's highly sentimental writings, as well as his moderate intellectual stance, made him one of the great proselytizers of progressive ideas in modern China.

Before 1898, both K'ang and Liang tended to envision the realization of the Confucian *ta-t'ung* society in terms of a capitalist society along republican lines. There existed, it seemed to them, no basic contradiction between Confucianism and Western bourgeois culture.

In the writings of the radical revisionists, the Confucian *ching-shih* tradition was pushed to its extreme limit. Constitutionalism, with its skeptical attitude toward the virtue and divinity traditionally attributed to the monarchy, was able in this Confucian guise to deeply influence Chinese conceptions of the "kingly outer realm." At the same time, T'an's ferocious attack on the contemporary structure of human relations, K'ang's advocacy of social and economic equality, and Liang's definition of the new citizen made their mark on the "sagely inner realm" long considered the *terra sancta* of Confucianism. This penetration of Western bourgeois ideas into both the outer and inner realms of traditional Confucian thinking was particularly evident in the radical revisionists' acceptance of a lineal concept of history which radically undercut the traditional cyclical notion of Chinese history. No longer was Chinese history interpreted as a series of cycles, developing in a spiral course. No longer was it interpreted in terms of an inner-outer dualism, where the ethical, inner sphere was regarded as primary. Now Chinese history was portrayed as moving along a straight line, with science taking precedence in a science-democracy duality. Simply put, the Confucian inner-outer dualistic thought was being replaced by the liberal dualism of science and democracy.

Not surprisingly, these *Kung-yang* proposals for change, which resembled the ideology of Meiji Japan or Russia's Peter the Great, provoked a fierce counterattack by orthodox and moderate revisionist Confucianists. Su Yü, an orthodox scholar, vehemently charged that *Kung-yang* doctrines developed by K'ang "destroy the sacred classics; the notion of Confucius being a reformer confuses the established laws; the promotion of equality undermines the human relationships; and the enhancement of people's rights belittles the emperor."[24] Such arguments contained nothing new, but merely repeated in a more subtle manner the position formulated by Wo-jen in the 1860s.

Ideologically, the most effective blow to K'ang's school was dealt by Chang Chih-tung, the leader of the moderate revisionists. The strength of Chang's attack derived not only from his position as a powerful and prestigious local official but from his profound mastery of the Confucian tradition as well. The essentials of Chang's moderate revisionist viewpoint were well expressed in his polemical treatise "Exhortation to Study,"[25] first published in March 1898. Acutely aware of the inadequacy of the traditional righteousness-versus-profits (*i-li*) outlook, Chang proposed in its stead the paired notion of *t'i-yung* (essence-utility). Making the traditional distinction between the inner and outer realms, he divided his treatise into two parts. To the inner realm, Chang ascribed the pursuit of *jen* (humanism), the source of morality, and to the outer the pursuit of *chih* (knowledge or wisdom), the source of power and wealth. In a striking departure from Wo-jen, however, Chang assigned active roles to both the inner and outer realms. By replacing *i-li* with *t'i-yung*, Chang was able explicitly to accept the value of utility or profit making.

Yet how was the outer realm to be activated without putting the inner realm in jeopardy? How could modern means of production be adopted without discarding the long-established moral values of the landlord class? If the outer realm, now revitalized by Western learning, could not be guided by the inner realm, if Western science and technology could not be placed under the control of moral values, Chang warned, China would be like "a riding horse without a bridle, or a sailing boat without a rudder."

To overcome this dilemma, Chang formulated his famous slogan "Chinese learning for the base and Western learning for application."[26] He saw the strength of Chinese learning as embodied in the Confucian classics, which sought to develop man's moral potential and order human relationships ethically. On the other hand, Western learning, especially the natural sciences and technology, sought the rational laws of nature and held the key to man's rational potential.

> Chinese learning is inner learning, Western learning is outer learning. Chinese learning is for regulating the body and mind. Western learning is for managing the affairs of the world. It is not necessary to seek exhaustively for the corollaries of Western learning in the classics; nevertheless, we must make sure that it is not contrary to the principles of the classics.[27]

Chang argued that Western learning, stripped of its social and political values, could be used to generate power and wealth in the task of maintaining a hierarchical feudal social order consisting of the Manchu nobility and Chinese landlord class, the rising bourgeoisie, the traditional merchants, and, at the bottom, handicraft workers, modern industrial workers, and peasants.

To Chang, the points in dispute among his fellow Confucianists were not the ends (defending the nation, the Confucian teachings, and the Chinese race) but the means to attain them. Rigidly clinging to the tradition of Chu Hsi Neo-Confucianism, orthodox scholars argued that the current national ordeal could be overcome simply by restoring Confucian institutions to their traditional functions and by a correct application of Confucian principles. With the maxim "Chinese learning for the base and Western learning for application," however, Chang was able to ridicule the orthodox as "fossilized scholars," walking in the dark like blind men. He sternly warned that the political reality of a partitioned China would bring the extinction of their cherished Confucian teachings and the destruction of the Chinese race.

Still, Chang agreed with the orthodox Confucianists that the ethical principles of the inner realm were like natural laws, universal and everlasting. Thus it is not surprising that he vehemently attacked as "heterodox doctrines" the notions of people's rights, social equality, and other radical ideas espoused by K'ang and his followers. If K'ang had his way, Chang warned, "foolish people will assuredly be delighted; unruly people will naturally rise up; the laws will not be obeyed; and general disorder will arise on all sides."[28]

The outcome of the debate between the schools of K'ang Yu-wei and Chang Chih-tung was ultimately determined—like those of earlier political struggles—by the pressure of imperialism. By 1898 the division of China's entire coastal area among the imperialist powers, and the establishment of their spheres of influence even in the vast inland areas, had aroused the entire nation and greatly sharpened contradictions within the ruling class. It was amidst this mood of national crisis that the power struggle raging between the aging empress dowager and her stepson reached a crisis, causing the young emperor to turn to radical revisionist Confucianism as a weapon. Deeply upset by the crisis in his empire, Kuang-hsü, a conscientious but weak young ruler, sought to seize power from his stepmother, who still held the empire firmly in her grasp nine years after formally relinquishing it to her stepson. Determined to do whatever he could to save the empire from destruction, Kuang-hsü, assisted by his tutor, Weng T'ung-ho, turned to the doctrines of K'ang Yu-wei, Liang Ch'i-ch'ao, and T'an Ssu-t'ung. Thus the long-ignored work of the radical revisionist Confucianists finally found support in the highest realm of political power.

Despite strong opposition from orthodox Confucianists and conservative officials, Emperor Kuang-hsü on June 11, 1898, proclaimed sweeping reforms, which were masterminded by K'ang Yu-wei, Liang Ch'i-ch'ao, and T'an Ssu-t'ung. Among other things, the reforms called for the convening of an elected congress and the abolition of the imperial examination system and many outmoded departments in the central government. The radical nature of these demands, which would have seriously affected the vested interests of a great number of people, provoked a swift and furious response. Particularly alarmed were the ruling Manchu nobility, whose lack of a broad and solid social base in Chinese society made them especially fearful of any changes in the Confucian institutions and principles. In addition, the resistance to the reforms from orthodox and moderate Confucianists in the local and central governments was formidable. Though weakened ideologically, they were strong politically and the entire bureaucracy still remained firmly in their hands.

In September 1898 the empress dowager, backed by the conservatives in the central government, staged a coup d'état through which the Reform movement came to a sudden end only three months after it had been initiated. Two years later, reformers led by T'ang Ts'ai-ch'ang attempted to launch an armed uprising in the Yangtse valley. But this plot was discovered by Chang Chih-tung in Hupeh even before it could get started, and T'ang and hundreds of his followers were executed. K'ang and his followers were

now formally excommunicated from the Confucianist camp
as traitors, and their cause of radical revisionism banned as
heterodox doctrine.

K'ang's disastrous failure clearly betrayed his weaknesses.
The cultural and political movement he tried to lead commanded only the meager support of a few young and conscientious Confucianists, some compradors and intellectuals
from among the bourgeoisie, and an impotent emperor.
While Hung Hsiu-ch'üan had become alienated from Confucian scholars, K'ang became isolated from the Chinese
masses. For one thing, his ideas were too pedantic and
abstractly philosophical to appeal to the peasants or to the
traditional and modern workers. For another, his platform,
however radical in appearance, basically sought the preservation of the landlord class and the Manchu rulers and thus
could hardly assuage the miseries of the masses. As a result,
the opportunity for a traditional-style political alliance between discontented intellectuals and peasant revolutionaries, crucial to the success of any far-reaching political and
social change, was lost and was not to be restored until Mao
Tsetung returned to the rural areas in the late 1920s.

With the crushing of K'ang's Reform movement, the
moderate line of Chang Chih-tung became dominant. The
Boxer Uprising of 1900, when the Ch'ing ruling class's
will to resist was finally broken and China's status as a
semicolonial country formalized, lent further credence to
Chang's *t'i-yung* outlook. After 1900 the archconservative
empress dowager and her staunch followers implemented
some of the reforms suggested by Chang, including certain
administrative and institutional changes, especially in education. Yet within a few years the Russo-Japanese War of
1904 threw into relief the inadequacy of these moderate
approaches. The occurrence of a foreign war fought in
China's Manchurian territory rather than the territory of
the belligerent parties deeply humiliated Chinese intellectuals. Japan's victory over Russia not only caused deep

alarm among Chinese people at the possibility of similar military successes against China, it seemed to reveal more dramatically than ever before the path to power and wealth: constitutional government.

By 1905 the Confucian *ching-shih* philosophy had reached its demise as a guiding framework for coping with Western bourgeois culture. The moderate reforms of Chang Chih-tung had proved no more successful than the vision of K'ang Yu-wei in saving China from destruction. For Chang's essence-utility scheme presupposed the existence of an able and enlightened ruling clique, the embodiment of his infallible inner realm, which identified its own interests with the interests of the entire nation. Yet how could such a role be played by the tiny ruling Manchu clique which was now so intent on its own self-preservation that it prefered a China conquered by the imperialists to a China ruled by Han Chinese? The contradiction between the inner and outer realms—which Chang, in his writings, had done his best to mitigate—seemed irresolvable in the framework of the narrow, self-centered mentality of the Manchu nobility. Increasingly, bourgeois intellectuals and compradors, excluded by the parochial Manchu ruling class from sharing political power, began to arrive at the conclusion drawn by the Western-trained doctor, Sun Yat-sen, who as early as 1896 had decided that the only path to China's national salvation was revolution along Western bourgeois lines. For the first time the Chinese bourgeois class began to assume leadership in the cultural sphere. The shift of the intellectual climate from reformism to revolution marked the beginning of a new phase of the Old Democratic Cultural Revolution.

FOURTH PHASE: 1905–11

By the end of the Russo-Japanese War the voices of orthodox and even moderate Confucian reformers had ceased to be heard in the arena of China's intellectual debate, the role of protagonists in the intensifying ideological struggle passing to K'ang Yu-wei and his followers, and to the new bourgeois democratic revolutionaries led by Sun Yat-sen. Since both Sun and K'ang and their followers had been branded as traitors, the ideological struggle took place in the overseas Chinese communities in America, Canada, Southeast Asia, and particularly in Japan. With China's coastal provinces—Kwangtung, Chekiang, Kiangsu—including Hong Kong and Macao as a peripheral area, the Pacific Chinese communities, long onlookers of the political struggles on continental China, became the staging base for the young revolutionaries to spread the ideas of bourgeois democracy and Western bourgeois culture. This was in sharp contrast to the later communist movement which relied on the vast inland area as its staging base.

The most significant and decisive debates took place in Tokyo from 1905 to 1906. The focus of the polemics was the Three People's Principles formulated by Sun Yat-sen: nationalism, democracy, and people's livelihood. The revolutionaries argued for anti-Manchu nationalism and republicanism, while Liang Ch'i-ch'ao supported monarchy and a pan-nationalism which included the Manchus as Chinese.

A distinctive mark of Sun Yat-sen and his emerging band of followers was their limited familiarity with the Chinese intellectual tradition, a difficulty in identifying with the culture of any of the then existing classes in Chinese society, with the exception of the emerging bourgeois class. Sun had received a Western education in Hong Kong and Hawaii and spent most of his adult life abroad, thus his knowledge of the Chinese cultural tradition was shallow. Moreover, traditional Chinese culture lacked a distinctive urban culture of the merchant class to which Sun might have been drawn. Both factors enabled Sun and many of his foreign-educated followers to work with a much freer hand as they attempted to develop a Chinese bourgeois culture. Sun simply integrated whatever elements he deemed appropriate from both Chinese and Western culture into what was essentially an Anglo-Saxon political framework of republicanism. In the preface to the founding issue of his party journal, *The People*, Sun expounded a philosophy which was a hybrid of Chinese and Western ideas. Envisioning a simultaneous social and political revolution, he drew on Henry George's theory of state socialism, proposing a nationalization of land, the regulation of capital, and the abolition of taxation as crucial steps toward the creation of the *ta-t'ung* society.

The socialist features in Sun's program drew strong fire from Liang Ch'i-ch'ao. Socialism, he argued, had evolved in an advanced European society where the Industrial Revolution had turned the disparities between rich and poor into an extreme polarization. Since Chinese society was merely at the precapitalist stage, it lacked the conditions for a social revolution. Furthermore, to attempt to carry out a social revolution within a political revolution would only give free reign to the lawless instincts of beggars and rascals. Liang shared the deep distrust of the masses characteristic of the Confucian mentality, and opposed any drastic change which would undermine the vested interests of the landlord class and the Manchu nobility.

In response to Liang's critique, Chu Chih-hsin, a broad-visioned revolutionary who translated the *Communist Manifesto* into Chinese under the inspiration of the Russian Revolution of 1905, described what Liang regarded as the insuperable barrier to social revolution as a strategic advantage:

> A social revolution carried out when the inequality between the rich and the poor is not very great, would be quite easy to realize, although the ordinary people might not readily understand its necessity. When the inequality becomes very great, while it is easy [for the people to know] the necessity of social revolution, it is hard [for them] to act.[29]

Chu felt that social revolution could and should be implemented in China, despite its precapitalist conditions, as a way to prevent the social evils that plagued European societies, but he saw such a revolution as carried out through class competition rather than class struggle. The target would be the imperfect social institutions which were the ultimate source of all social evils. Since all men dream of a happy life, and this can be guaranteed only by the perfecting of social institutions, all men, regardless of their class origins, should work together to attain them. This class position, so naïve and often so ambiguous, was characteristic of Sun Yat-sen and his followers. Their beliefs revealed the influence both of a Confucian faith in man's essential goodness and their own bourgeois backgrounds. The socialist strains in Chu's thought, however, make him an important transitional intellectual figure standing between the early Kuomintang (KMT) and the Chinese Communist Party (CCP), analogous to T'an Ssu-t'ung who bridged the ideological gap between radical revisionist Confucianism and Sun's republicanism.

Sun and his followers attempted to "sinicize" Anglo-Saxon bourgeois culture, not only as the culture of their own class but of the nation as well. Yet, like K'ang Yu-wei and Liang Ch'i-ch'ao, their inability to resolve the fundamental contradiction between the demand for national survival and the demand for cultural identity doomed their efforts to ultimate frustration. As it had for generations of Confucian reformers before them, this contradiction stood in the path of the republican revolutionaries as an insurmountable obstacle. On the one hand, the task of developing the power and strength essential for saving China from extinction seemed to demand the adoption of the alien culture. On the other hand, Sun's program seemed marked with such a conspicuous foreign stamp that not only Confucianists and peasant masses but even merchants and the generally neglected industrial workers turned away from it. Sun's program lacked a broad social base.

The ideology of the bourgeois revolutionaries itself, moreover, was replete with weaknesses and contradictions. Lacking any profound, logical, consistent theoretical foundation, it was essentially an eclectic mixture of socialist, Confucian, and liberal ideas. Built into the very heart of Sun's program was an irreconcilable conflict between the political power of the bourgeoisie and the intended social and economic reforms for the masses. Private ownership in agriculture was to be abolished, for example, but there was to be no public ownership in industry and commerce. In addition, while the strength of China's bourgeoisie had grown rapidly since 1895, it was hardly strong enough to act as an independent political force. After obtaining political power, it would find itself forced to collaborate with the landlords in a way that would make any sweeping land reform impracticable. Nor could the workers in the cities expect much from a government that denounced public ownership. The persisting influence on Sun and his followers of their bicultural background powerfully reinforced these contradictory tendencies. By making it impossible for them to break out of a conciliatory stance toward imperialism, the ultimate source of the nation's troubles, this influence rendered Sun's philosophy unworkable as an official ideology and a leading national culture. It could hardly replace the role so dynamically played in centuries past by Confucianism.

Thus it came as a surprise to most Chinese that a political force far weaker than the Taipings succeeded in 1911 in bringing down the Manchu dynasty. Sun Yat-sen's presence in the United States at the time indicated his own unawareness of the imminence of the revolution. Despite the fundamental weaknesses in his program, however, the 1911 Revolution broke out in Wuchang at a time when Chinese society seemed unable to find any way out of its impasse except by following the path of the bourgeois revolutionaries. Indeed, underlying all the complexities in the political arena after the successful Wuchang uprisings was the impact of Western capitalism. This was the ultimate factor responsible for Sun's success. For the 1911 Revolution revealed the deepening roots of China's nascent bourgeoisie within the world economy, especially in the Pacific community which provided its economic and cultural world. The emergence of a republican government was eminently suited to the interests of both international capitalism and the Chinese bourgeoisie. Sun's political philosophy and the culture of the new Chinese bourgeoisie fully reflected the realities of China's semicolonial status.

The overthrow of the Manchu ruling house spelled the final destruction of the deeply entrenched institution of the Chinese monarchy, the mystical embodiment of wisdom and virtue in the outer realm of the Confucian *ching-shih* ideal. The establishment of a republican government brought the end of the Confucian state which had protected Confucianism as its official philosophy for over 2000 years. The process of seeking power and wealth to stave off the imperialist powers and guarantee national survival had ended up destroying the cultural identity of the landlord class for the first time in China's history. The inner realm of the Confucian *ching-shih* ideal was now fully exposed to the ruthless onslaught of bourgeois culture. The collapse of the feudal regime and the founding of the republic marked the beginning of the last phase of the Old Democratic Cultural Revolution.

FIFTH PHASE: 1912–16

For a few brief years the "heavenly mandate" appeared to have passed, for the first time in history, into the hands of the Chinese bourgeoisie. Yet Sun's party was only barely able to maintain nominal rule in the provinces of Chekiang and Kiangsu and in the cities of Nanking and Shanghai, citadels of the comprador class. Too weak politically to penetrate the base of China's immense society, Sun's government merely floated on the surface. Bending to pressure from the landlord class, represented by Yüan Shih-k'ai in Peking, the republican government permitted China to be divided politically and culturally between the landlord class, led by Yüan in the North, and the bourgeoisie, led by Sun in the South. Yüan, however, backed by superior military power, quickly moved to wipe out the influence of Sun's party through terrorism, assassination, and military actions, finally forcing Sun and his followers to flee to Japan. The constitutional monarchy presided over by Yüan from 1913 until his death in 1916 revived Confucianism as the ruling ideology. There were movements to make Confucius a pope and Confucianism the national faith, both led by K'ang Yu-wei and his supporters, but such revivalist attempts proved short-lived.

Looking back on the early years of the Republic, we find that the experiment resulted not in peace and harmony but in terrorism, chaos, and identity crisis; despair instead of hope. Power and wealth seemed even more remote than before. Worse still, when the European War broke out in 1914, the true face of the Japanese "monster" was unmasked in the notorious Twenty-One Demands of 1915. At the same time, the decline of Western bourgeois culture was dramatically manifested in the internecine strife of the First World War, where the imperialist powers were pitted against each other. Chinese intellectuals' admiration for Japan and the West was gradually replaced by disillusionment and disappointment. A whole new series of questions confronted them. If both constitutional monarchy and republicanism had failed to save China, what kind of society should be developed? If there were serious weaknesses inherent in Japanese militarist culture and Western bourgeois culture, in which countries could China find an example? If neither the landlord class nor the bourgeoisie could lead China out of its impasse, what social force could lead the struggle? Was it possible for a new culture and new leadership to emerge in the struggle for national salvation?

THE NEW DEMOCRATIC CULTURAL REVOLUTION

The collapse of the Confucian state marked the beginning of one of China's great transitional epochs. Like every transitional period in the preceding centuries, it was characterized by constant civil and foreign war, a seemingly irreversible process of decentralization, and the general disintegration of the social fabric. Unlike earlier years, however, there was no attempt in this period to restore the functions of the Confucian state. Chinese society had embarked on the construction of a new order.

In the three decades of momentous change, it was the nascent proletarian culture of China that emerged as the source of new life. China's modern working class had been in existence since the latter part of the nineteenth century, yet it required the stimulus of the May Fourth movement and the victorious Russian Revolution of 1917 to burst into self-awareness. From this time, Chinese leftist intellectuals, though often of upper-class background, began to turn to the urban proletariat, often living and working closely in their midst to give cultural expression to the experience of this new social class. But it was only through a protracted process of cultural transformation, led by the Chinese Communist Party, that a new and vigorous national culture was forged. This process led to a broadening of the notion of proletarian culture to include the experiences of the Chinese peasantry and the petty bourgeoisie as well. The emergence of China's new national culture can be seen in five phases: first, the May Fourth period (1916–21); second, the first civil war (1921–27); third, the second civil war (1927–37); fourth, the second Sino-Japanese war (1937–45); and last, the third civil war (1945–49).

FIRST PHASE

The May Fourth Period: 1916–21

With the collapse of central authority, the landlord class, now represented by numerous warlords, became locked in internecine strife which led to its defeat in 1927. The development of wars within the landlord class was linked with the threatening advance of the Japanese imperialists. With World War I, the "European wind and American rain" had subsided considerably, but alarm at the threat from Japan, manifested in the Twenty-One Demands of 1915 and the Shantung Question of 1919, burst forth in the historic May Fourth movement of 1919. The fervent anti-foreign nationalism of modern China now directed its force at Japan rather than the Western imperialist nations. As Japan's designs on China increased, national survival continued to be the overriding concern of the Chinese people. The Japanese threat emanating from Manchuria and Shantung made North China, long dominated by conservatives, a center of radical ideas for the first time in the modern era. With Peking University as its breeding ground, and carefully fostered by university president Ts'ai Yüan-p'ai, the radical movement in North China paved the way for a reassertion of the region's traditional political leadership.

The years of the May Fourth movement in China saw a blooming and flourishing of cultural activity comparable perhaps only to that of the Spring and Autumn and Warring States periods of Chinese history. Many foreign-inspired schools of thought bloomed and contended—socialism, liberalism, pragmatism, Darwinism. Anticipating the imminent birth of a proletarian culture, leftist intellectuals like Li Ta-chao, Ch'en Tu-hsiu, and Lu Hsün first tried to ally with liberal intellectuals led by Hu Shih and Wu Yü in the cultural sphere. Their main target was the tenacious Confucian concept of the inner realm as defined by the *ching-shih* tradition upheld by the twin pillars of moral teachings (*li-chiao*) and the classic literary style (*wen-t'i*). For both liberals and socialist intellectuals alike, these two traditions had to go if China was to be powerful, prosperous, and immune from the danger of national extinction.

But despite these common targets, the outlook of the liberals and the socialist intellectuals was radically different. The former, drawing mainly upon the Anglo-Saxon liberal tradition, wanted to substitute the notions of *te* (democracy) and *sai* (science), the theoretical bases of modern bourgeois culture, for the *i-li* and *t'i-yung* outlooks and the inner-outer dualistic mode of thought. They attributed the failure of republicanism in the early 1910s and the intensifying national crisis to the barbaric, backward Confucian ethical and literary traditions which were unscientific and undemocratic.

By contrast, Li Ta-chao's critique of these two Confucian traditions was presented in terms of the Marxian dialectical relations between the "upper" structure of consciousness and the "lower" economic base. Emphasizing the economic factor, Li argued that since the economic base had undergone such fundamental change since the 1840s, the destruction of Confucianism had been inevitable.[30] His dialectic mode of thinking, moreover, was tinged with a strong ethical flavor which was to remain characteristic of the sinification of Marxism-Leninism. By working out a theoretical framework that reconciled both the economic and ethical demands of industrial development, Li used Marxism-Leninism to theoretically resolve the contradiction between liberalism and the earlier Chinese traditions, a task which the Confucianists and the bourgeois intellectuals had never been able to accomplish. In short, Li proposed Marxist dialectics and a proletarian world view based on the contrasting concepts of *kung* (collective) and *ssu* (selfish) in place of the Confucian *i-li* (righteousness-profit) or *t'i-yung* (essence-utility) world outlooks and their inner-outer dualism.* For this contribution, Li is honored as the pioneer architect of Chinese Communist ideology.

The divergent perspectives of the liberals and the leftist intellectuals did not dampen the intensity and enthusiasm with which they attacked Confucian moral teachings. The scope and depth of their criticisms is well illustrated by their three slogans: "Mr. *Te* and Mr. *Sai*"; "Down with the Confucian shop"; and "Down with man-eating moral teachings." Under these slogans such iconoclasts as Ch'en Tu-hsiu, Hu Shih, Li Ta-chao and Lu Hsün bitterly criticized the

---

* For Li Ta-chao, *kung* meant "collective" rather than public, an indication of the impact of the introduction of socialism into China.

irrationality and class basis of such Confucian ethical values as benevolence, righteousness, loyalty, filial piety, and reciprocity. The liberals championed freedom, individualism, equality, rationality, utility. The leftists began to stress class struggle, materialism, social justice, and collectivity on a proletarian basis. All these ideas had been introduced before, but never had they had such great appeal as in this period. It was Lu Hsün who dealt the most effective blow to Confucian moral teachings. In his famous short story "Diary of a Madman" (1918), he characterized Chinese history as a "record of cannibalism" which had still not been brought to an end.

> In ancient times, as I recollect, people often ate human beings, but I am rather hazy about it. I tried to look this up but my history book has no chronology, and scrawled all over each page are the words "virtue" and "morality." Since I could not sleep anyway, I read hard half the night, until I began to see words between the lines, the whole book being filled with the two words—"Eat people."[31]

Lu Hsün's prescription for curing the disease of modern China differed fundamentally from those given by earlier Confucian thinkers. He argued that every vestige of Chinese landlord culture based on Confucian moral teachings had to be removed by its roots and destroyed. The Chinese people's entire basis of thinking had to be completely remolded. An ethical cultural revolution was necessary.

> You should change, change from the bottom of your heart. You must know that in the future there will be no place for flesh eaters in the world. If you don't change, you may all be eating each other.[32]

In this future world neither landlord nor capitalist "cannibals" would have any place. Lu's call is strikingly similar to the Maoist's characterization of the Great Proletarian Cultural Revolution as an ethical revolution "touching the very depth of the soul."

The passionate efforts of iconoclasts like Lu Hsün

dramatically discredited the authority of the "uncrowned king," Confucius, within a few years after the crowned emperor had been overthrown. The *i-li* and the *t'i-yung* outlooks were finally discarded as analytical schemas. The Confucian ethical and political traditions were clearly demonstrated to have lost their viability, while the Confucian social system, rooted in the feudal family system, was greatly undermined. The attack on *li-chiao* shook the very philosophical foundation of Confucian ethics, the concept of *jen,* from which all other Confucian virtues were seen as emanating.

This attack on the ethical tradition was accompanied by an equally ferocious assault on the Confucian literary tradition. Traditional Confucian scholars had long employed this literary tradition as the vehicle to contain and convey moral Confucian principles. During the May Fourth period, intellectuals from right and left challenged both its classical form and moribund content, seeking to replace them with a more popular and accessible language. The literary revolution became, in combination with the ethical revolution, the most effective movement for disseminating the new bourgeois and proletarian cultures.

The discrediting of Confucian moral teachings left Chinese intellectuals face-to-face with two crucial questions. First, toward what goal should China now move, capitalism or socialism? Second, how could that goal be reached, through gradual reform or radical revolution? Although similar questions had been debated in 1906 between the bourgeois revolutionaries Hu Han-min, Wang Ching-wei, and Chu Chih-hsin, and the constitutionalists led by Liang Ch'i-ch'ao, they were now raised by younger intellectuals in a new political and cultural context characterized by the failure of republicanism, the discrediting of the Confucian value system, and the introduction of socialism and other foreign "isms."

No sooner had the liberals and leftist intellectuals succeeded in toppling the Confucian ethical and literary traditions than they were engaged in a debate among themselves. Keenly aware of the rising tide of Marxism-Leninism and socialism in China, Hu Shih, in his famous essay "More Study of Problems, Less Talk of Isms," published in *Weekly Critic* on July 20, 1919, leveled the charge of irresponsibilty, lazy-mindedness, and impracticality at intellectuals like Li Ta-chao and Ch'en Tu-hsiu who espoused fundamental, radical solutions to China's problems.

> The great danger of "isms" is that they render men satisfied and complacent, believing that they are seeking the panacea of a "fundamental solution," and that it is, therefore, unnecessary for them to waste their energies by studying the way to solve this or that concrete problem.[33]

Hu, reflecting his commitment to American pragmatism, advocated gradual social reform through the examination and investigation of each individual problem, "drop by drop and bit by bit." He warned presciently that if the advocates of fundamental solutions had their way, it would mean the "death sentence for Chinese social reform."[34] Subsequent historical developments, in fact, proved Hu correct: Social reform did give way to revolution.

Hu's attack on "isms" drew fire immediately from Li Ta-chao. Pointing to the Russian Bolshevik Revolution, he argued that, given China's semicolonial and semifeudal status, a fundamental solution of economic problems could never be achieved without a mass political and social revolution. Without this, solutions drawn up by studying concrete and individual social problems could never be translated into reality.[35] Li defended the discussion of "isms" because this could develop among the poverty-ridden masses the type of consciousness that would enable them to relate their individual problems to those of society as a whole. Provide the masses with an "idealism," Li urged, and they will be motivated to act together. Show a "common direction" through which their efforts could be channeled toward an integrated solution of all social problems. Hu, the pragmatist, was the impractical one: "Your exhaustive study of social problems has no relation to the majority of people in society. Therefore, there can never be any hope of solving these social problems, and your study of social problems can have no practical influence."[36]

A year later a second round of debates took place between Ch'en Tu-hsiu and the syndicalist socialist Chang Tung-sun. It centered on the question of whether or not a capitalist stage was necessary for the development of Chinese socialism, and in this sense the debate may be seen as part of the continuous effort by non-Marxist intellectuals to stem the tide of Marxism-Leninism in China. Chang based his critique of Marxism on the ideas of John Dewey and Bertrand Russell. Socialism, he maintained, presupposed a viable proletarian class, but at the present time "Chinese factory workers are too few and too weak to take over political and economic responsibilities." In order to create the conditions for socialism, the urgent task of Chinese society was to develop capitalism under a strong central government rather than eliminate it.[37]

Ch'en Tu-hsiu and a number of young Marxists in Shanghai stepped forward to rebut this view. Ch'en argued that Chinese capitalism was merely the agent of foreign capitalism in China, the main source of China's poverty, and detrimental to the growth of the proletarian class. No strong central government was possible without the overthrow of this class which served the interests of the imperialists. Had not the Russian experience proved that a rapid transition from feudalism to socialism was within reach?

However, the most sophisticated counterattack against Chang's view came from Li Ta-chao. Li addressed himself to the question of how to sinicize Marxism in the concrete social conditions of China.

> If one asks whether or not the economic conditions
> of present-day China are favorable for the realiza-
> tion of socialism, it is first necessary to ask whether

or not present-day world economic conditions are tending toward the realization of socialism, because the Chinese economic situation really cannot be considered apart from the international economy. The contemporary world economy is already moving from capitalism to socialism, and although China itself has not yet undergone a process of capitalist economic development such as occurred in Europe, America, and Japan, the common people [of China] still indirectly suffer from capitalist economic oppression in a way that is even more bitter than the direct capitalist oppression suffered by the working classes of the various [capitalist] nations. . . .

If we look again at the international position of China today, [we see] that other nations have already passed from free competition to the necessary socialist-cooperative position, while we are still juveniles; others have walked a thousand *li*, while we are still taking the first step. . . . I fear that we will be unable to succeed unless we take double steps and unite into a socially cooperative organization. Therefore, if we want to develop industry in China, we must organize a government made up purely of producers in order to eliminate the exploiting classes within the country, to resist world capitalism, and to follow [the path of] industrialization organized upon a socialist basis.[38]

Li's argument rested on his notion of a "proletarian nation," advanced in his essay "An economic explanation for the causes of the changes in modern Chinese thought," in January 1920. By "proletarian" Li Ta-chao actually meant "propertyless," referring to both a material condition and state of mind shared by the exploited people in noncapitalist societies and the industrial workers in the advanced societies. Having undergone decades of economic exploitation by the Western and Japanese imperialist bourgeoisies, Chinese society had been gradually transformed into a "proletarian" society, and as such was part of the world proletariat. Li asserted that China was therefore fully qualified to take part in the world proletarian revolution. China's struggle against Western capitalism in China was inseparable from the world struggle by the proletariat against international capitalism. Li overcame the theoretical problem posed by the relative smallness of China's proletarian class through his optimistic and regenerative concept of a "proletarian nation," which assigned the Chinese nation a place in the worldwide process of proletarian revolution. The realization of socialism in China, therefore, did not hinge on the presence of a strong "real proletariat" (literally defined) developed in a capitalist era.

The development of a proletarian culture, as Li defined it, depended on three factors. First, since Chinese society was becoming more and more integrated into the substructure of the world capitalist system, the working-class culture of those advanced nations could be taken as a point of reference for Chinese proletarian culture. Second, the budding Chinese proletarian culture should draw on traditional Chinese peasant culture. Despite its backwardness, peasant culture contained many elements which would serve to reinforce the modern proletarian culture. Thus while the Chinese urban proletriat was still numerically weak, it could develop through a political and cultural alliance with both the broad masses of the world urban proletariat and China's peasants. The creative integration of these two cultures according to Marxist-Leninist principles was the third and final factor in the development of a vigorous and viable proletarian culture. Li felt that as the nation's impoverishment by foreign exploitation became more and more acute, the way was open for the development of China's proletarian culture. His notion of a proletarian nation, however, should be distinguished from the concept of a semicolonial nation which was the basis of Sun Yat-sen's vision of national revolution. Both Sun and Li employed the phrase *kuo-min* (all the people of the nation) in speaking of the Chinese. But as a Marxist, Li regarded the proletariat as the leading class with the peasantry as its major ally. These two classes constituted the backbone of the proletarian nation. Explicitly excluded from this concept were the bureaucrats, the gentry, the bourgeoisie, and the compradors.[39] But these main targets of internal class struggle in Li's schema were for Sun the most important classes in a semicolonial nation. This difference clearly marks off the republican Sun from the Marxist Li, and the respective ideologies of the KMT and the CCP.

Li's unorthodox but highly creative and insightful adaptation of Marxism to China inaugurated the populist tradition of Chinese communism which was soon to be greatly developed by one of his disciples, Mao Tsetung. In envisioning China's revolution, Li turned naturally to the vast peasantry of rural China as a reservoir of manpower, supplementing the numerically weak working class concentrated in the coastal provinces. The capitalists, on the other hand, dominant in the coastal cities, turned to the overseas Chinese community and the international capitalists as their rear social base. This contrast, reflected in Li's concept of a proletarian nation, foreshadowed the approaching confrontation between the KMT, based in the coastal areas, and the CCP in the interior. It further suggested the future intimate involvement of both the Western bourgeoisie and the Communist party of the Soviet Union in the long struggles between the CCP and the KMT.

Yet inevitably even Li's innovative synthesis bears signs of the persisting influence of the Confucian tradition which intellectuals of his generation so bitterly attacked. On the critical question of *how* the latent political consciousness of the common people is to be awakened, Li writes that this is the "historic duty" of the revolutionary intellectual. Because of his intellect and virtue, Li believed, it was the revolutionary intellectual whose mind and conscience were sharp enough to perceive and articulate the proletarian consciousness. Li defined the major task of the revolutionary intellectual not as developing the material preconditions for socialism through capitalism but as living and working among the peasants, untrammeling their abundant spiritual energy and latent socialist consciousness.[40] Elements of consciousness common to the landless peasant in the countryside and the propertyless industrial worker in the city should be reinforced.

Closely related to Li's views of the revolutionary intellectual and the peasantry was his tendency to stress consciousness and action rather than impersonal economic forces. This intellectual bent, perhaps reinforced by the activist and voluntarist strains in Marxism, in some sense resembles Lenin's, but there is an essential difference: While Lenin drew on the Hegelian origins of Marxism and his own Russian populist tradition to reinforce his faith in the powers of human will, consciousness, and action,[41] Li's appreciation of Marxist activism and voluntarism reveals features characteristic of the Confucian *ching-shih* tradition. In a manner reminiscent of the Confucian conception of *jen*, Li found socialist consciousness inherent in all human consciousness. He had faith in the force of moral action in human history, and tended to idealize the peasantry. In Li's writings, born out of the period marked by the decline of the old tradition and the slow birth of the new, Confucian ideas with agrarian, socialist overtones seem to have slipped unnoticed into concepts presented in Marxist terms. Indeed, it was quite natural for Chinese intellectuals emerging from centuries of an ethically oriented Confucian tradition to view the strategic and tactical problems confronting proletarian revolution through an ethical and political prism. Impelled by the deepening nationalist sentiment aroused in them by China's plight, these ethically minded intellectuals could often more easily be converted to the proletarian cause than to the capitalist one.

Hu Shih's invitation to his American teacher, John Dewey, to come to China in late 1919 and Liang Ch'i-ch'ao's and Chang Tung-sun's invitations to Bertrand Russell in 1920 and 1921 reveal the interrelationship between the debates of Chinese intellectuals of this time and ideological struggles being waged in the international arena. It is hardly coincidental that Dewey and Russell were from the United States and Britain, for the intellectual climate in these two countries was very critical of socialist Russia during these years. Both Dewey and Russell lent their personal support to their Chinese followers to counter the rising vogue of Russian influence and Marxism-Leninism in China. Despite their prestige and eloquence, however, Dewey's gradual reforms by "inches and drops" and Russell's program of nationalized capitalism were largely irrelevant to China's catastrophic situation.

The May Fourth period was indeed a major turning point in modern Chinese history. Ironically, in its wake, liberal followers of Hu Shih turned to the study of the national heritage—to archeological investigation, to textual criticism of traditional literature, and to the pursuit of problems in ancient Chinese philosophy and history. They largely ignored the burning national and social issues they had once urged as objects of the "piecemeal" approach. Although they had dreamed of ultimately replacing China's cultural heritage with Western bourgeois culture and its emphasis upon science and individualism, their efforts in politics and social reform met repeated frustration because of their alienation from the masses. Their bookish bent put them in a paradoxical situation: They feared the growing strength of the proletarian culture and the ever-mounting national crisis, but they refrained from actively participating in social and political movements. This detachment, an attitude deeply rooted in the liberal intellectual tradition of the West and reinforced by the persisting influence of the Confucian tradition of Empirical Research, erected a wall between them and Chinese society. But the process of searching for ideas to save China ended in the discovery of Marxism-Leninism as a guiding ideology. It promised a just and affluent society; its critique of the imperialist nature of Western bourgeois culture revealed the roots of the present ordeal; and its worldwide concern for the oppressed masses enabled the Chinese to identify their own national salvation with a universal cause. The conversion to Marxism of many Chinese intellectuals of bourgeois and landlord origins was aided by the confidence that the Russian example made the prospect of final victory much greater.

Thus, by the end of the May Fourth period, Communist intellectuals led by Ch'en Tu-hsiu and Li Ta-ch'ao, filled with a sense of rebirth and direction, confidence and dedication, embarked upon the application of Marxism-Leninism to China. Highly motivated young Communists like Mao Tsetung, Ch'ü Ch'iu-pai, and Teng Chung-hsia mingled with the masses of workers, peasants, and coolies to investigate their problems and organize them. Their work led to the establishment of the CCP in July 1921, and with its birth Chinese history moved into the second phase of the New Democratic Cultural Revolution.

SECOND PHASE

The First Civil War: 1921–27

The second phase of the New Democratic Cultural Revolution witnessed the development of a joint political struggle waged by the proletariat and the bourgeois classes, represented by the newly established CCP, and the reorganized KMT against the weakening landlord class, represented by the divided landlords. During this phase the CCP, working closely with leftist members of the KMT, was able to establish mass organizations, carry out workers' strikes, and investigate the nature of rural society. Domestic class struggle at this time, however, was greatly complicated by the direct and indirect involvement of Western imperialists, Japan, and Russia. Each nation sided with the political force compatible with its own interests: Japan with certain warlords, Russia with the CCP, and the British and the Americans with other warlords. (Sun Yat-sen's leftist tendencies discouraged any close relationship with Britain and America.)

Against this political background two debates flared up between the liberals and Confucian scholars who still defended the landlord culture. (The Communists and the

Nationalist ideologists, immersed in political struggles, remained largely uninvolved.) Shocked by the savage internecine strife among the imperialists during the First World
War, Liang Ch'i-ch'ao and Liang Sou-ming argued that
modern Western civilization based on science was declining.
Unlike Li Ta-chao who saw in the decline of Western
bourgeois culture the hope of China's rebirth through a
proletarian revolution, Liang Ch'i-ch'ao as early as 1919
called for the restoration of China's spiritual civilization on
the basis of Confucianism.

A second controversy in 1923 between Confucianists
Carsun Chang and Liang Ch'i-ch'ao and liberals Hu Shih,
Ting Wen-chiang, and Wu Chih-hui over metaphysics and
science further illustrates the nature of these debates. By
drawing upon Confucianism and such Western thinkers as
Bergson, Eucken, Driesch, and Urwick, the Confucianists
argued in favor of a view of life based on intuitive consciousness rather than on logical principles. The liberals
countered by appealing to the theories of Dewey, James,
and Pearson, maintaining that only scientific methods could
lead to true knowledge.

In such intellectual controversies, seemingly so peripheral
to China's immediate needs, it is nevertheless clear how the
process of searching for wealth and power led Chinese intellectuals to the very bases of modern Western civilization
and Chinese civilization.

The growing acceptance of science and democracy among
Chinese intellectuals naturally encountered fierce resistance
from conservative scholars unable to break out of the inner-
outer dualistic thinking. But in both these debates the Confucian scholars found little public receptivity to their
arguments. Chinese bourgeois culture was becoming
stronger; the intellectual debt of Chinese liberals to French
and Anglo-American bourgeois culture was growing.

During this same period, Sun Yat-sen was preparing his
final formulation of KMT ideology. Inspired by the Russian
Revolution and deeply disappointed by the continuing
aggression of the Western imperialists, Sun arrived at a

conclusion similar to that of the Communists: Learn from Russia. For the first time Sun adopted a clear anti-imperialist position. In a series of lectures delivered in 1924, he made communism and the *ta-t'ung* society the ultimate goal of the KMT, to be achieved through regulated capitalism. He bluntly equated his third principle, People's Livelihood, with socialism or communism, though he continued to reject the notions of class struggle and historical materialism. Sun's principles were essentially a mixture of ideas from the traditional culture of the landlord class, the bourgeoisie, and the proletariat, synthesized into an eclectic concept of a republican state. The KMT ideology, seemingly radical but with strong conservative strains, embraced all the prevailing intellectual currents of Sun's time without any attempt to distinguish the class bases of these ideas. In fact, so peripheral were the socialist elements in Sun's theory that liberals and right-wing elements in the KMT were able to dismiss them quickly after his death in 1925.

Chiang Kai-shek, the commander of the Nationalist Army, carried out a massive onslaught against the Communists in 1927 when the army reached the stronghold of Chinese and foreign capitalists, the lower Yangtse valley. Loyal to the interests of the bourgeoisie, Chiang compromised away even the mildly socialist principles in Sun Yat-sen's program. The first united front between the KMT and the CCP thus ended in disaster for the latter, with the KMT effecting a fragile unification of China by defeating the Peiyang warlords in 1928. These two events brought the second phase of the New Democratic Cultural Revolution to an abrupt end.

THIRD PHASE
The Second Civil War: 1927–37

With the removal of the landlord class as an independent political force through the defeat of the Peiyang warlords, the KMT sought to carry on the bourgeois revolution by building the economic base and superstructure of a bourgeois society. Still, the political power of the KMT was far from stable. The victory of the KMT over the Peiyang warlords was to a large degree the result of compromise and political maneuver. The defeated feudal elements, with their personal military forces and political influence still largely intact, continued to play a major role as influential bureaucrats or powerful military warlords. Warlordism and bureaucratism, rather than vanishing, persisted in a viable form, surviving within the bourgeois class but serving as deterrents to the establishment of the bourgeois order.

The most serious challenge to the KMT came from the CCP. When the Northern Expedition was drawing to a close in 1927, the KMT, in an action which culminated in five military encirclements, attempted to crush them once and for all. So intense was this political attack by the KMT on the CCP that the KMT refused to confront Japan's increasingly aggressive actions in Manchuria and North China.

Paralleling this campaign of military encirclement was a cultural one undertaken by pro-KMT liberals (Hu Shih, Hsü Chih-mo, Liang Shih-ch'iu) under the auspices of KMT ideologists such as T'ao Hsi-sheng. Attacking Lu Hsün, Li Ta and other leftists, their polemics dealt with a wide-ranging number of subjects, including Chinese society, history, philosophy, literature, the arts, and questions of cultural identity. The debates of the time over Chinese society and the periodization of Chinese history reveal an intense effort on the part of leftist intellectuals to find the laws of China's social development and, in them, guidelines for political action. In the area of literature, leftists argued that since content was conditioned by class, literature must serve the revolution and be written in the interests of China's workers, peasants, and soldiers. Liberals, however, contended that it should be politically detached—literature for literature's sake.

This attack on leftist intellectuals in the late 1920s left KMT ideologists, ultimately, with nowhere to turn but to revert once again to the Confucian tradition. Liang Sou-ming and Feng Yu-lan advanced the theory that the endless domestic chaos of these years was the result of a "loss of national cultural identity" since the May Fourth period. Seeking to rally the nation to a cause that transcended class differences, they tried to invoke a spirit of patriotism that idealized the past glory of the Confucian tradition. Although the thought of Feng and Liang was traditionalist and conservative, even liberals like Sa Meng-wu, Ho Ping-sung, and T'ao Hsi-sheng joined the revival. In 1935 they called for a reevaluation of Confucianism, attempting to construct a Chinese culture on the basis of the Confucian *ta-t'ung* society. Other liberals, such as Hu Shih, were appalled by this revival, however, and bluntly condemned it.[42]

The most influential and enthusiastic advocates of Confucianism were Chiang Kai-shek and his followers like Tai Chi-t'ao and Ch'en Li-fu. Assuming his position as superintendent of the Whampoa Military Academy in 1924, Chiang urged his students to emulate the feudal T'ung-chih statesmen, especially Tseng Kuo-fan, target of the fierce attack of the Taiping peasant revolutionaries.

The KMT movement toward Confucianism was tied to changes in the structure of the party after Sun's death in 1925. At this time, some of the senior party ideologists and bureaucrats led by Hu Han-min and Wang Ching-wei wanted to subordinate the army, commanded by Chiang Kai-shek, to the leadership of the party. But Chiang, wishing to keep the KMT under his personal control, made it subject to the power of the army. In the late 1920s and early 1930s, Chiang deprived Hu and Wang of their power and influence. The change in party leadership from civilian to military led to an emphasis on the conservative strains in Sun's Three Principles and their combination with elements of a fascistic ideology.

Yet the Confucian revival was merely a reflection of an insoluble dilemma in which the KMT found itself caught. The KMT was essentially a party of the bourgeois class, but bourgeois culture, developed by liberals like Yen Fu, Hu Shih, Hsü Chih-mo, and Liang Shih-ch'iu in the Anglo-

American tradition, could not provide a value system capable of justifying the KMT military dictatorship and its claim of party tutelage. Thus the KMT leaders had no alternative but to follow the same course as earlier revisionist Confucianists. By the late 1930s the sacred status of the four Confucian books and the image of Confucius had been restored, the moribund Confucian ethical system and Wang Yang-ming's neo-Confucianism had been reinstated as official doctrine. In 1934 Chiang launched a nationwide New Life movement to redefine Confucian virtues for a republican society. Chiang on the one hand sought to use Confucianism as a foil for his fascist ideology, while at the same time trying to gain liberal support through his emphasis on republicanism.

Chiang's resurrection of Confucian traditions must also be understood in the light of contemporary developments throughout East Asia. In the early 1930s the Japanese militarists had begun to impose their own brand of Confucianism on occupied Chinese territory. This was actually a combination of Chinese neo-Confucianism and Japanese Shinto concepts. For example, the Japanese restored the long-dethroned Manchu emperor Henry P'u-i in Manchuria, and compelled all school authorities in public, private, and mission schools to lead the children in worship, first at the Confucian temples in an artificial bid for a new "Manchu" nationalism, and in a later phase at Shinto shrines as a sign of loyalty to the emperor of Japan.[43]

During the early 1930s Chiang Kai-shek had succeeded in driving the Communists from their base. The Long March of the CCP from 1935 to 1936 led to the eventual establishment of a new base in northern China.

FOURTH PHASE (1937–45) AND
FIFTH PHASE (1945–49)

With the outbreak of the Sino-Japanese war in 1937, hostilities between the CCP and the KMT ended and a second united front began. The New Democratic Cultural

Revolution then moved into a fourth phase, in which there were three different life-styles contending for the favor of the Chinese people—Mao's Yenan way, Wang Ching-wei's Nanking way, and Ching Kai-shek's Chungking way.

Mao's Yenan way was undoubtedly the implementation of the mass line. It was through the work-styles developed in Yenan that the CCP, avowedly a workers' party separated from its urban base, succeeded in sinking roots in rural China. By creatively combining the principles of Marxism-Leninism with the traditional customs, values, and institutions adhered to by millions of peasants in northwestern China, Mao succeeded in cementing a solid worker-peasant alliance. In remote Yenan, intellectuals driven from the southeastern urban centers by the Japanese occupation learned to integrate themselves with peasants who had remained essentially unexposed to the influences of Western culture. It was on the basis of a grass-roots egalitarianism and diligent study of Marxism-Leninism that party cadres and army members achieved this integration with the peasants. A modified land-reform program was carried out; women's liberation was supported. Threats to these activities, whether from the KMT blockade or from Japanese military pressure, were dealt with by the policy of self-reliance. Taken together, all these characteristics of life in Yenan constituted what Mao called "New Democracy" and they continue to this day to be fundamental qualities of Chinese proletarian culture.[44]

Mao, in his late forties when he settled in Yenan, grew to intellectual maturity during his eight years there. It was in Yenan that he wrote the central essays "On Contradiction," "On Practice," "On New Democracy," and "Talks at the Yenan Forum on Literature and Art," and created the basic framework of the ideology later known as Mao Tsetung Thought. China's past, present, and future, the foreign and the Chinese, intellectuals and masses, the leaders and the people, the army and society, men and women were all given a proper place in his theoretical framework. This

CCP ideology even attracted a large number of critical writers and artists who were petty bourgeoisie. Their efforts and energies were successfully channeled into the task of the Resistance War and the armed struggle against the KMT.

In contrast to the Maoist mass line, Chiang Kai-shek and Wang Ching-wei prided themselves on maintaining an élitism that gave precedence to the interests of the bourgeoisie, the remaining feudal elements, the Japanese militarists, and even Western imperialists at the expense of the interests of the overwhelming majority of the people. When Chiang and Wang spoke of China's national interests during these years, it was invariably in conjunction with the interests of those foreigners who gave them support. This was in marked contrast with the CCP. Though there were many Soviet-educated students active in the CCP, they were not powerful. Mao's adaptation of various elements of foreign ideologies constantly gave precedence to the demands of the Chinese situation. Chiang and Wang were too indebted to their foreign supporters. The deeper the influence of the Japanese or British and American patrons went, the more alienated Wang and Chiang became. Growing numbers of the petty bourgeoisie and other patriotic Chinese felt they had no alternative but to support Mao.

Chiang's revival of Confucianism, moreover, inevitably conflicted with the republican policy of his party, outraging many of the liberals. Chiang attacked both liberalism and communism in his book *China's Destiny* (1943). In turn, though they themselves were virtually isolated from the masses, the liberals criticized Chiang for his despotic personal rule and the absence of the traditional bourgeois civil liberties. Their criticism undoubtedly weakened Chiang's government. Though he appeared strong, during these years Chiang was very vulnerable. As his alienation grew, moreover, the essential realism of the Maoist Yenan way became more and more clear. The seemingly never-ending, deepening impoverishment of Chinese society, exhausted by eight years of war against Japan and another four years of civil war, had indeed created a society close to what Li Ta-chao spoke of as a "proletarian nation."

No bourgeois culture growing out of the urban centers could hope to solve China's massive rural problems. Western bourgeois culture, confronting its own impasse after the Second World War, was unable to inject vigor into its Chinese counterpart. There was, in fact, nowhere in Chinese society a dynamic alternative to the growing popular culture fostered by the CCP in the rural areas. The victory of the CCP in 1949 was merely a culmination of these deep-seated trends. It brought unity to China and an end to the pattern of centrifugal disintegration which had marked Chinese society for over a century.

THE SOCIALIST CULTURAL REVOLUTION 1949–58

The founding of People's China formally ended the political power of the bourgeois class and ushered in the era of socialist construction. It marked the end of China's semifeudal, semicolonial status and the "removal of the three gigantic mountains—imperialism, bureaucratic capitalism and feudalism—from the shoulders of the Chinese people."[45] "China stands up," Mao proclaimed to the world on October 1, 1949. For the first time in the modern era, China obtained a genuine political independence from external domination.

Yet it would be a mistake to believe that in these conditions bourgeois culture died of its own accord in China. Following Chiang's retreat to Taiwan, it persisted tenaciously in the urban sector of the coastal provinces, traditionally the strongholds of KMT influence and control. It remained influential in the broad cultural fronts, as well as in the bureaucracy and the commercial and industrial sectors. The continuing strength of bourgeois culture in these areas of society posed a formidable obstacle to the development of a new socialist culture. Each attempt to deepen the revolution after the seizure of state power in 1949 was met by tenacious opposition from those members of the former privileged classes who had reluctantly sided with the revolution only when it became clear that the KMT would lose. The CCP had welcomed them into the folds of the new society, and to win their active support for the task of national reconstruction and economic recovery, it even went to considerable lengths to protect their social and material privileges.

But bourgeois technocrats and intellectuals, while admitting the need for social reform and the stabilization of Chinese society, feared a thoroughgoing social revolution, and thus increasingly clashed with party leadership in the struggle to define the political, economic, and cultural framework of the new society. This ongoing struggle to prevent the reemergence of the bourgeoisie found its fiercest expression in the cultural realm, where the strength of the bourgeois class was still relatively intact and dominant. From 1949 to 1957 the struggle passed through the following phases: the anti–Sun Yü campaign in 1951; the anti–Yü P'ing-po and anti–Hu Shih campaigns in 1954 and 1955; the Hundred Flowers movement in 1956 and 1957; and the antirightist campaign in 1957.

Developments in the Chinese cultural sphere took place in a dramatically changed domestic and international context following the victory of the revolution. After 1949, particularly with the signing of the Korean armistice in 1953, the major motivation for the sweeping cultural changes of the past decades were removed. National survival, humiliation by aggressive foreign powers, ceased to be the burning national issue. China could at last channel all her energies into achieving the long-unattained goal expressed by the T'ung-chih statesmen in the 1860s as the "wealth and power" of the nation. Building up the productive forces and changing the productive relations in Chinese society were the immense tasks facing the newly unified country.

Although China had finally "stood up," the new nation faced a largely hostile world that inevitably exerted pressure on Chinese society. The effects of China's policy, in the 1950s, of "leaning toward one side" are well known.[46] China in these years sent thousands of students, scientists, and scholars to Russia, while the Soviet Union dispatched thousands of technicians and engineers to China as advisers. The Russian experience was so thoroughly studied and applied by the Chinese in the areas of education, military affairs, the arts, and particularly economic construction, that in many ways the socialist culture of China seemed a duplication of Russia's. Amidst the boom, the concern for cultural identity seemed to have faded into the background. Pro-Russian bureaucrats, intellectuals devoted to the Russian model of socialism, swelled the ranks of the party. For a time the CCP's long tradition of independence from the CPSU (Communist Party of the Soviet Union) seemed to have been compromised. It was against this background that the cultural struggles in the early years of Chinese socialism took place.

The political offensives launched on the cultural front against the bourgeois class were both complex and subtle, and closely related to each advancing step in the socialization of Chinese society. It was not accidental that movies glorifying gradual reformism appeared simultaneously with the nationwide campaign to complete revolutionary land reform. The most striking example of this type of movie was Sun Yü's biographical film on the life of Wu Hsün, a late-nineteenth-century peasant reformer. The real-life Wu Hsün was a poor peasant who started out as a beggar in Shantung Province and through diligence and wise investment ended up a well-to-do landlord. He also established a reputation as a zealous educator-reformer of the poor. In the movie, Wu Hsün, an illiterate who suffers cruelly under landlord oppression, one day wakens from a dream and, having perceived that the real source of the poor's misery is illiteracy, sets out to beg money from landlords to begin a free school for the poor. It is Wu Hsün's belief that a proper Confucian education can raise the poor out of ignorance and poverty. Thus Sun Yü depicted Wu Hsün as a cultural hero who "intended to liberate his class culturally; was the great pioneer of the oppressed and the exploited laboring people; served the laboring people through the promotion of education by begging; and symbolized the noble virtues of industry, bravery and wisdom of the Chinese people."[47]

It was Mao himself who first published a critical analysis of Sun Yü's *Life of Wu Hsün*. He questioned the situation on the cultural front which allowed for glowing reviews of Sun's *Life of Wu Hsün* in newspapers and cultural journals throughout the land. A movie advocating reformism and class surrender, and thus implicitly rejecting violent revolutionary change and class struggle, should instead have been soundly repudiated, he said, especially during a time of revolutionary upsurge. Art and literature should help the masses to liberate themselves from the shackles of the old society, not tie them to it. Furthermore, the popularity of this film in big cities like Shanghai and Peking indicated to Mao an urgent need for an ideological campaign to equip the people with political attitudes that would enable them to distinguish revolutionary from counterrevolutionary art and literature.

From 1953 to 1957, the period of the first Five-Year Plan, agricultural cooperatives were established, individual land-ownership was abandoned, and capitalist commerce, industry, and the individual handicraft industry were socialized. To assure that these far-reaching economic changes were properly reflected in the superstructure, the CCP inaugurated three nationwide rectification movements. The first of these was the criticism of Yü P'ing-po, commentator on the famous novel *The Dream of the Red Chamber*. The criticism of Yü's interpretation began in September 1954. Although the novel was highly critical of feudal society and therefore contained a positive political message, critics pointed out that Yü had failed to bring out this political implication, concentrating simply on a textual analysis of isolated details which did not elucidate the novel's theme of the decline of the bureaucratic landlord class.

The ultimate source of Yü's errors was traced to the idealistic philosophy of Hu Shih.[48] Indeed, it was a logical step to make Hu's thought the next target of attack in 1955. Though he lived in exile in the United States at this time, Hu Shih's ideas and the philosophy of pragmatism had influenced several generations of scholars in the areas of classical literature, history, education, and the social sciences. To Communist intellectuals, this philosophy represented the idealistic mode of thought of the Chinese comprador capitalist class as well as the lingering influence of Anglo-American bourgeois ideas which had taken deep root in China's academic world since the late nineteenth century. Therefore, the CCP urged the academic world to carry out a thorough and nationwide criticism of Hu Shih. The intensity of this ideological campaign can be seen in the quantity and diversity of the essays written to criticize Hu Shih, a total of eight volumes covering numerous major intellectual areas.

The anti–Hu Feng campaign in 1954 and 1955 was a further development in the party-led struggle against bourgeois culture. In July 1954 Hu Feng, an independent leftist literary critic and student of Lu Hsün, submitted a 300,000-word cultural manifesto to the Central Committee in which he set forth his own theory of art and literature as an alternative to Mao's "Talks at the Yenan Forum on Literature and Art." In his cultural manifesto Hu repudiated the application of Mao's line on literature and art by party cultural leaders. He opposed the concept of party leadership in literature and art on the grounds that it was stultifying to creativity. He decryed the "five daggers at the heads of the writers," dissenting from the proposal of the party that writers should study Marxism, live among workers, peasants, and soldiers, remold their bourgeois world view, draw selectively from the Chinese traditional forms to create a national culture, and actively serve politics.

The publication of Hu's manifesto stimulated a virtual assault on the party's cultural policies by Hu's friends and disciples, many of whom were themselves party members in high places in cultural and educational circles. Not surprisingly, Hu and his followers provoked a strong rebuttal from the Central Committee, and criticism of Hu Feng crescendoed with the alleged discovery of a counterrevolutionary clique organized by Hu Feng and linked to the KMT. However, unlike the anti–Yü P'ing-po and Hu Shih campaigns, which were aimed at the non-Marxist intellectuals, the Hu Feng incident was mainly directed at the rightist writers and artists in the party who shared Hu Feng's views.

In step with the successful development of the socialist economy by 1956, the CCP deepened its ideological drives, now preparing for a movement against the entire non-Communist intelligentsia. Mao and his supporters argued that as the economic base underwent socialist transformation, the superstructure must also necessarily change. If not, the gains in the economic base would be lost. Following the intellectual tradition of sinicized Marxism-Leninism established by Li Ta-chao, Mao's theory placed great emphasis on the superstructure. It still bore the tremendous weight of millenniums of Confucian culture and a century of Western bourgeois liberal influences, Mao warned, and should therefore be an object of unflagging concern. For again and again Chinese thinkers and statesmen (Chang Chih-tung, K'ang Yu-wei, Liang Ch'i-ch'ao, Yuan Shih-k'ai, Hu Shih, Chang Tung-sun, Chiang Kai-shek) had pointed to China's lack of an advanced culture and the persistence of feudal Confucian culture in opposing radical ideological positions. This very phenomenon became Mao's rationale for the necessity of uninterrupted revolution in the cultural area. In Mao's view, it would be risky to idly wait for the "spontaneous" cultural breakthrough as a result of the quantitative changes in material conditions. If radical elements let things drift freely, supporters of the old culture would vigorously oppose such elements. People would cling so strongly to their old ways of life that the process of change would eventually be brought to a standstill, and even the new cultural elements evolved out of this process would be stabilized, consolidated, and turned into the status quo, finally becoming conservative.

With an extraordinarily keen insight into thousands of years of Chinese history, Mao insisted that the CCP, guided by the historical laws embodied in Marxism-Leninism, must consciously and through radical means make the cultural realm conform with the transformed economic base. Mao's thinking, in fact, bears some similarities to the traditional practices of past dynasties which attempted to uphold through conscious human effort the subtle balance between the inner and the outer in the Confucian framework. Recognizing the primacy of the inner over the outer, and apprehensive of the reaction of the outer upon the inner, the Confucian rulers put great emphasis on controlling human consciousness. In so doing, they sought to tap the moral forces of the inner realm to control the changes in the outer realm. In this way human consciousness could prevent changes in the outer realm from upsetting the crucial balance between the two realms.

Organically linked to Mao's theory of the dialectical relation of superstructure and base is his concept of class struggle. For Mao it is political, ideological, ethical, as well as economic. Even after the economic base has undergone socialist transformation, class struggle will continue on the political and cultural fronts. For until the proletarian world outlook universally prevails, the existence of the proletarian dictatorship cannot be regarded as secure. In the wake of the basic socialist transformation of China's productive relations, therefore, an equally intense class struggle in the realm of consciousness was necessary. Such was the struggle which Mao initiated in the Hundred Flowers movement of 1956.

On May 2, 1956, Mao announced in the Supreme State Conference the famous cultural policy "Let a hundred schools of thought contend, let a hundred flowers bloom."[49] The former applied to the areas of natural and social sciences; the latter to the world of arts and literature. Lu Ting-i, director of the Propaganda Department, urged even the scientific and cultural workers of petty bourgeois origin to join in the campaign, exercising the freedoms of "independent thinking, debate, creativity and criticism, expression of one's own opinion, and the insistence upon or reservation of one's own opinion."[50]

Clearly these general debates were not conceived by the CCP as mere academic exercises, but in terms of class struggle: "Contending and blooming" were peaceful ways to resolve the contradictions among the people in the superstructure. By allowing ideas of those opposed to socialist ways to come forth publicly, some could be changed through criticism, others attacked and, if unbending, overthrown. Indeed, those bourgeoisie, landlords, and others who took advantage of this opportunity to renew their attacks on the socialist system would be dealt with as "poisonous weeds." The way could thus be cleared for the rapid growth of the "fragrant flowers" of the newly emerging proletarian culture.

Mao's views on the nature of class struggle in the superstructure during the "contending and blooming" period are well expressed in the notion of redness and expertise (*hung-chuan*). In essence this movement was a struggle between the red outlook of the proletarian class and the expert outlook of the bourgeoisie. Here again, Mao's theory bears an affinity with old Confucian ideas, in this case Chang Chih-tung's *t'i-yung* formulation. Both *hung* and *t'i*, for example, refer to the prevailing ownership system. *Hung* represents the then emerging collective-ownership system in China, based on rural cooperatives and the joint public-private ownership of enterprises in the cities. *T'i* on the other hand, refers to a collapsing private-ownership system based on the family or clan. As behavioral guides both of these concepts suggest purpose, motivation, and a set of class values. *Hung* meant the study of Marxism-Leninism, serving the people, going to the people, doing manual labor, and devotion to the construction of socialism. Likewise, *t'i*, the study of Confucianism, meant sacrificing oneself for serving the imperial house and the landlord class, promoting "benevolent" rule over the people, doing mental labor, and defending the Confucian order. Both *chuan* and *yung*, which characterized the lower or outer realm, refer to natural and economic laws, and technical knowledge external to the ethical realm.

The tension between *t'i-yung* (the inner and the outer) in Chang's Confucian schema is similar in nature, but at a different level from that between *hung-chuan* (the superstructure and the base). In Chang Chih-tung's case, as a result of the failure of the inner to contain the outer, *yung* was about to upset *t'i*. In Mao's theory, however, consciousness is capable of harnessing the modern productive forces in the lower realm by challenging and essentially controlling them. Thus, while the Confucianists had been unable to cope with the specialized bourgeois intellectuals in the late nineteenth century, Communist cadres in the Fifties and Sixties were able to deal effectively with the professionals despite their often intense conflicts with them. For the first time in modern China, moral values achieved initial success in reigning over modern science and technology—a task that Confucian bureaucrats like Tseng Kuo-fan and Chang Chih-tung had been utterly unable to accomplish.

The ideal personalities envisioned by Mao and Chang also bear certain similarities. Both saw a personality maintaining a balance between red and expert (*t'i* and *yung*) but placing primary emphasis on the red or *t'i* (ethical) component of the balance. The difference between the model Communist and the model Confucianist, however, lay in the fact that the former, in addition to being ethically minded, was required to grasp the objective laws of history through a study of Marxism-Leninism. The Confucian scholar did not possess such tools of analysis. The study of Confucianism revealed to him a human history propelled mainly by spiritual or moral forces. The emergence of the red-expert concept around 1957, therefore, indicates that the nation's development had finally reached the point where Western science and technology could be organically integrated into Chinese society on the basis of socialism.

Not surprisingly, the response of the non-Communist intellectuals to the CCP's call for "contending and blooming" was lukewarm and apathetic. Many had had painful personal experiences in earlier campaigns. In addition, the defeat of threatening foreign powers made concern for national survival a less intense motivating force.

Previously, many from landlord or bourgeois backgrounds had sacrificed their personal or class interests and converted to the causes of republican or communist revolution. With the improvements in their lives since 1949, however, intellectuals who occupied prestigious positions were more inclined to preserve their status, or to harbor hopes of trading their expertise, indispensable to the construction of socialism, for a privileged way of life.

Finding the intellectuals reluctant to answer the call to "bloom and contend," the CCP launched in early 1957 a rectification campaign directed at party members. A policy of "mutual supervision and long-term coexistence" with various democratic parties was proclaimed. In this way the CCP sought to demonstrate its sincere commitment to a period of general relaxation. In early spring, Mao personally urged the intellectuals to speak out so as to help the CCP rectify its mistakes.

> In recent years, pushing movements have made people very tired. Quite a few people have been hurt by thought reforms and purges of counter-revolutionaries, and thus harbored resentment in their hearts. Let everyone express his resentment.[51]

Thus reassured by Mao, intellectuals began, not without suspicion and reluctance, to address themselves to three groups of problems: China's cultural heritage; the current cultural, educational, and economic policies; and current political issues.

In the discussions of cultural heritage, concern for cultural identity once more came to the fore. As national survival ceased to preoccupy the Chinese people and with the modern mode of production basically established, the question of cultural identity had begun to emerge more clearly in the minds of party cultural workers and intellectuals. As Hu Shih and Ku Chieh-kang had led the liberals in the 1920s to interpret China's traditional culture from a Western bourgeois point of view, the CCP now urged intellectuals to take a radically new look at the concept of class struggle in the cultural sphere. Through debate, the CCP sought to remold the world outlook of these intellectuals so that a correct proletarian attitude toward their specialized fields could emerge. This concern was expressed in the key slogans of the period—"emphasize the present and de-emphasize the past," (*hou-chin po-ku*); "Use the past for the present" (*ku-wei chin-yung*); and "Use the foreign for the Chinese" (*yang-wei chung-yung*). The guidelines of the debate were so general, however, that intellectuals could easily interpret them to suit their own interests. How, in actuality, to correctly combine the old and the new, the past and the present, the Chinese and the foreign was a question which would be answered in the future.

In the second category of problems, debate centered on the question of the party's leadership in specialized professions. Many intellectuals vigorously protested the CCP's interference in specialized work and demanded greater professional independence. They argued that though the party cadres were good at carrying out class struggle and political activities, they were laymen on the academic and economic fronts.[52] Professors held that the universities should be left to them; party cadres should be kept largely off campus.[53] In the factories, engineers and technicians insisted on keeping politics away from their specialized fields, arguing that the process of production was governed by impersonal economic laws, not by politics dealing with human affairs. The resistance of both groups to "politics in command" was bound to rise up and become stronger as the revolution deepened in these areas.

The last category of problems was the most explosive. A number of scholar-politicians, educated in Britain and the United States, launched a severe attack on the five great movements and three socialist transformations that had been carried out in the early Fifties. Led by Chang Po-chün and Lo Lung-chi, they challenged the CCP's leadership and called for a "rotating rule of China," to be shared equally among the various democratic parties. They vehemently criticized the proletarian dictatorship and the aid given to China by the Soviet Union. Some even attributed the CCP's system of democratic centralism to China's failure to pass through the Western parliamentary stage.

In the two months of "blooming and contending," "poisonous weeds" had certainly emerged. In response to their attacks, the CCP launched a fierce counterattack and in June 1957 began the Anti-Rightist movement. The aim of this movement was to purge only those who totally condemned the socialist system, and to try to work with the others. The launching of the Anti-Rightist movement was an event of great significance. It marked the start of an era in which the proletarian and bourgeois world outlooks, earlier defined as a non-antagonistic contradiction, became an antagonistic one. A stunning blow was dealt to the non-Communist political parties which had their base in remnants of the bourgeoisie. With the elimination of the bourgeoisie as a viable political force, the contradiction between the proletarian class, led by the Maoists, and the revisionists, represented by the Liuists, emerged as the major internal class struggle in the era of the Proletarian Culture Revolution.

THE PROLETARIAN CULTURAL REVOLUTION

In 1957 China's modern cultural struggle entered a historic new stage where the source of opposition to the proletarian class and its culture shifted from the social base of the old bourgeoisie to a newly identifiable social strata and ideology centered in the Communist party itself: "revisionism." A series of pivotal questions may help us understand the development of this ideological confrontation, which continued over twelve years until the end of the Great Proletarian Cultural Revolution in 1969. What was revisionism at this stage? How was it first identified? Where lay the roots of the political power of the revisionists? Did the revisionists form a separate class, distinct from the proletarian class? What is the nature of the contradiction between the "genuine" and "sham" Communists? And finally, was this contradiction antagonistic or nonantagonistic?

As early as March 1957, Mao defined revisionism in the following terms:

> It is dogmatism to approach Marxism from a metaphysical point of view and to regard it as something rigid. It is revisionism to negate the basic principles of Marxism and to negate its universal truth.
>
> Revisionism is one form of bourgeois ideology. The revisionists deny the differences between socialism and capitalism, between the dictatorship of the proletariat and the dictatorship of the bourgeoisie. What they advocate is in fact not the socialist line but the capitalist line.[54]

Revisionism, Mao warned his comrades, was "in the present circumstances, more pernicious than dogmatism," and he asked them to regard the criticism of revisionism as "one of our important tasks on the ideological front."

Revisionists, as Mao began to perceive them at this time, could be identified neither as capitalists nor as proletariat. They composed a distinctive social strata, rather than a class, with a sort of "double nature" combining both proletarian and bourgeois characteristics. Their predilection for bourgeois values, however, was such that they became, in fact, a substitute for the capitalists as class struggle continued under conditions of deepening socialism. It is for this reason that Mao has tended to regard revisionism as one form of bourgeois ideology, and why revisionists are generally condemned as "capitalist roaders" and not as capitalists *per se*. In theory as well as practice, then, the battle against revisionism, although in the beginning it is limited to the rectification of incorrect rightist tendencies, has the potential to develop into class struggle, involving both the party and the entire society.

The Maoist struggle against the revisionists was in many ways more intense, complicated, and protracted than the struggles of the early Fifties against the old bourgeoisie and landlord classes. For the revisionists, unlike the capitalists and landlords after 1949, held immense power in the party. Indeed, the nature of this struggle against revisionism, Mao commented in 1966, had been so new and perplexing that at first he had found no ready method to resolve it. For nine years conventional democratic methods used for decades to settle conflicts over ideology, policy, and tactics within the party all failed completely to stem the steady rise of revisionist ideology. Mao, confronting this reality, concluded finally that the only path to resolution was a violent one.

In retrospect, the course which led, ultimately, to Mao's choice of revolution as the weapon against revisionism may be traced according to the following phases: first, 1958–59; second, 1960–61; third, 1962–64; fourth, 1964–65; and finally, 1966–69, the Great Proletarian Cultural Revolution.

It was with Mao's identification of a new social group standing in the way of China's developing proletarian culture that the first phase of the first Proletarian Cultural

Revolution was initiated. Throughout the three decades of struggle preceding the founding of the socialist state, Mao had rested his political power on the vast constituency of poor and lower-middle peasants in the countryside and toiling people in the cities. Though early campaigns had immensely improved the living conditions of these masses, the former exploiting classes still occupied a highly favorable position in Chinese society during the first years of socialism. Through such early policies as "putting politics in command," however, Mao steadily pushed forward the cause of the masses, defining the correct line of the party always in accordance with their interests. Yet in 1959, Mao estimated that thirty percent of the Chinese population still stood in the way of these goals.

> Among the several hundred millions led by our cadres, 30 percent, at the very least, are positive activists. Perhaps 30 percent of our people are negative and obstructionist, including former landlords, rich peasants, counterrevolutionaries, evil elements and hidebound bureacracts. But the poor and lower-middle peasants of the mainstream represent 40 percent.[55]

Included along with the former exploiting classes in this "obstructionist 30%," were a numerically small but highly privileged strata of managers, technicians, scientists, artists, writers, professors, and schoolteachers. Though few in number, these people derived strength and social prestige from their specialized knowledge indispensable for increasing production. By merging with, seeking political protection from, and identifying their interests with certain cadres in the party, they exercised influence in every area of China's national life. These party cadres, in return, rested their political power on them.

It was on this social base that the political line which advocated giving precedence to expertise became prominent. It was this amalgamation of nonparty and party intellectuals that precipitated the unprecedented split of the Chinese Communist Party at this period into the revisionist and proletarian ranks.

The confluence of factors leading to the emergence of the revisionist ideology and a new social stratum in the late Fifties can be traced to roots in party history, to persistent influences from China's past, and to changing components in China's domestic and international situation. In the first place, a rough distinction in the social background of CP members was visible in the party from the beginning. Originally the social composition of the Communist party was determined largely by two groups: those from worker, or poor and lower-middle-class peasant origins who were of limited education and strongly native-minded; and those from bourgeois families along the coast or landlord families in the interior, many of whom had received Russian training and were inclined to be foreign-oriented in their thinking. In the Thirties and Forties, because of this difference in social and educational backgrounds, those party members of the first type generally worked in the "red area" in the countryside, while the others penetrated the "white area" in the coastal cities. After 1949 this distinction persisted, with the first group—the Maoists—prevailing in the largely peasant PLA and society at large, while the latter—the Liuists—gained great influence in the party and state organs.

Despite the striking differences in their backgrounds, the momentous tasks of fighting imperialism, feudalism, and bureaucratic capitalism before 1949, and of socialist construction immediately after, provided Maoists and Liuists with ample grounds for cooperation until the late Fifties. After 1957, however, the Russian-oriented outlook of the Liuists, previously instrumental in the basic process of organizing the socialist state, began to emerge as a major stumbling block on the path to deeper socialist transformation of productive relations and human consciousness. As the Maoists were to comment years later, the Liuists, like the dragon-loving Lord Yeh who was terrified by the appearance of a real dragon, seemed so alarmed by the living socialist reality that they began to resist and even to attempt to sabotage successive movements aimed at continuing the revolution. From the period of the Hundred Flowers and Anti-Rightist movements (1956–58) through the Three Red Flags (the General Line, the Great Leap Forward, and the Commune, 1958–59) and the Anti–Modern Revisionism (after 1962), the confrontation between Maoists and Liuists grew increasingly fierce.

Institutionally, the weight of centuries of the Chinese bureaucratic tradition reinforced the growing revisionist tendency. As traditional Confucian scholars once monopolized knowledge and bureaucratic skills, so, too, party intellectuals found themselves able to easily dominate China's political, cultural, and economic worlds. Moreover, China's lack of an advanced economic base made foreign-trained intellectuals indispensable in many areas of society. Although China after 1949 had become a people's democratic dictatorship in theory, in practice both political and cultural power came to be widely distributed among scholarly or bureaucratic intellectuals who commanded vast influence and prestige in Chinese society.

New developments in the domestic and international scene in the late Fifties also had their impact on the rift opening up between the revisionists and the Maoists. Domestically, the traditional contradiction between the coastal areas and the interior, for example, underscored the difference between the two groups. The First Five-Year Plan had served to strengthen, rather than decrease, the old gap between coast and interior by giving priority to the development of heavy industry. In the coastal cities, once the heartland of imported Western bourgeois culture, the influence of Soviet culture was strong. After 1958, however, the Maoists began a movement to reintegrate the industrial coastland with the agrarian hinterland, which was beginning to undergo accelerating industrialization.

In the international arena the balance of power between the capitalist world and the socialist bloc was being substantially altered. Earlier in the Fifties the remarkable Soviet success in building up strategic weaponry—missiles and thermonuclear bombs—and the launching of sputniks had signaled a strengthening of the socialist world epitomized by Mao in his slogan "The east wind prevails over the west wind." Under the leadership of Khrushchev, however, the Soviet Union embarked on its path of seeking détente with Western imperialist nations, advocating parliamentary politics for the world communist movement and trying to establish a bipolar world order dominated by the United States and the U.S.S.R.

Maoists and Liuists diverged sharply in their assessment of these international developments. In response to the Soviet Union's change of color, Mao adopted a radical new posture in both the socialist and international community. Modifying their previous *"Bandung* spirit" of peaceful coexistence, the Maoists now emphasized liberation wars against imperialism in Asia, Africa, and Latin America. The once cordial atmosphere with the Soviet Union, too, became clouded with suspicion and distrust as Mao led China away from the policy of "leaning toward one side" and espoused "equality among all socialist nations and independent and creative application of Marxism-Leninism to their specific social and cultural conditions."[56] The tension was further strained as the Maoists began a criticism of Soviet revisionist influence in every area of Chinese national life, in the arts and literature, education, science, economic development, and even ideology. Just as he had groped for a Chinese way of seizing political power in the period of the New Democratic Cultural Revolution, Mao now sought a Chinese way to achieve socialist construction, breaking with the almost uncritical use of Soviet models in the period of the First Five-Year Plan. The Liuists, however, continued to bow to Soviet leadership in the world communist movement and to accept its ultimate authority in communist ideology. For the Russian-oriented Liuists, to challenge the Soviet revisionist line as the Maoist were doing was going just too far.

Against this background, how was the split between Maoists and Liuists reflected ideologically? What was the ideological content of revisionism? By contrast to the period before 1949, when the outcome of intellectual debates had been so powerfully determined by foreign wars, the ongoing course of China's economic development seems to have been the strongest force influencing the development of ideological struggles under socialism. In the first phase of the Proletarian Cultural Revolution, for example, it was in heated controversies over economic planning that ideological differences between the Maoists and Liuists first began to emerge clearly.

How could China's economy, after the initial success of the First Five-Year Plan in 1957, continue to lift itself out of its deep-seated material backwardness? Both Maoists and Liuists agreed on the necessity for carrying out economic revolution after the proletarian class had seized political power. Nonetheless, they disagreed sharply about how to carry this out. Fundamental to their disagreement was the Liuist view, a basic component of revisionist ideology, that class struggle had basically come to an end. Since the completion of the three socialist transformations in 1956 and the successful Anti-Rightist movement in 1957, Liuists had argued that the line between the proletariat and its class enemies had become blurred. The changes in China's class structure, the rapid growth of the working class after 1949, and the need to overcome material backwardness all led the emerging revisionist elements to propose their theory of productive forces. Class, they argued, should from now on be seen as a purely economic concept, since the bourgeoisie and landlord class no longer existed as a viable political and social force. As Liu Shao-chi proposed in 1957,

> Now the internal enemies have been basically eliminated; the landlord class has long been destroyed, the capitalist class has been basically wiped out, and anti-revolution can also be reckoned as smashed. . . . When we say that the major internal class struggle

has basically come to a close or been solved, we
mean that the contradiction between us and the
enemies has basically been resolved.[57]

For Liu, henceforth, China would move toward socialism
through peaceful transformation rather than radical change.
In so declaring, Liu spoke for an influential constituency in
Chinese society, people with vested interests, both inside
and outside the party, who desired stability and the maintenance of the status quo.

In answer to the Liuist reformist emphasis on peaceful
change, Mao developed his radical theory of economic
development, based on his understanding of contradiction,
a central notion of Mao Tsetung Thought. In developing
these ideas, Mao went one step further in unfolding the
vision of uninterrupted revolution which has been his
guiding vision for the course of Chinese society in the
twentieth century. In socialist and communist societies,
Mao held, the superstructure and the economic base will
be in a constant state of contradiction, manifested in both
economic and noneconomic forms.

> Some naive ideas seem to suggest that contradictions
> no longer exist in a socialist society. To deny the
> existence of contradictions is to deny dialectics. The
> contradictions in various societies differ in character,
> as do the forms of their solution, but society at all
> times develops through continual contradictions.
> Socialist society also develops through contradictions
> between the productive forces and the conditions of
> production. In a socialist or communist society, tech-
> nical innovations and improvement in the social
> system inevitably continue to take place; otherwise
> the development of society would come to a stand-
> still and society could no longer advance.[58]

Revolutionary optimism and a burning desire to transform
man and refashion his social and natural environment infuse this passage on contradictions. In response to the con-

servative concern for the status quo in the revisionist world view, Mao sees as utterly natural a state of perpetual flux in society and the universe itself. Contradictions, gestated infinitely, press toward resolution through infinite revolutions in all spheres of human society: economic, political, cultural.

To place China's economic development in a framework of uninterrupted revolution was not mere subjective conceptualization on Mao's part. His view accurately reflects the material conditions of China and the people's deep longings and aspiration for change. As Mao stated,

> China's 600 million people have two peculiarities: they are first of all poor, and secondly, blank. This may seem like a bad thing, but it is really a good thing. Poor people want change, want to do things, want revolution. A clear sheet of paper has no blotches and so the newest and most beautiful words can be written on it.[59]

To make a virtue out of necessity and to see good aspects in bad things is a characteristic of Mao's dialectical thinking. As his theoretical mentor, Li Ta-chao, found hope of China's regeneration in the bleak scene during China's semicolonial status, Mao sees in China's poverty and blankness a constant demand for revolution, transforming China into a strong and prosperous socialist nation.

Nor is Mao's stress on uninterrupted revolution simply an attempt to carry on China's tradition of peasant revolution. For there is a powerful economic viability to this theory which sees man as the most important factor in economic production, just as he is the central protagonist in the political domain. In man, the producer, motivation derives from consciousness, which in turn comes from social practice. Motivation is the source of moral energies, such as dedication, devotion, determination, faith, frugality, industry, and simplicity. Consciousness and motivation reinforce each other, and can be transformed into material force through man's labor. Here, as in so many of Mao's other ideas, Western Marxist rationalism and the seemingly incompatible concerns of China's ancient, ethically oriented traditions are meaningfully synthesized.

In the specifically cultural spheres of literature and the arts, the start of the Proletarian Cultural Revolution was marked by a phenomenal burst of creativity in popular culture reflecting the economic developments of the Great Leap Forward and the Communization movement. Revisionist authors who blindly followed Soviet socialist realism were attacked, in order that revisionist literature could be replaced by a growing "people's literature" guided by the theme of "combining revolutionary romanticism and realism." Encouraged by the Maoists, the masses wrote prose and poetry. With the help of young intellectuals, they wrote histories of their villages, mines, factories, and communes. The creative writings produced from January through October 1958 are said to total 880 million. In short, simultaneous to the establishment of small and medium-size industries indispensable to lifting the poor and lower-middle peasants out of their traditional poverty, culture was also brought to them through Mao's call for the intellectuals to go to the countryside.

Paralleling this Maoist-inspired cultural movement was an official "socialist cultural revolution" launched by Liu Shao-ch'i to sweep away illiteracy; spread primary and secondary education; reform Chinese language and the arts of the minorities; do away with superstition and transform custom and habits; develop socialist arts and literature; and cultivate new intellectuals.[60] This cultural revolution was launched to support the technological revolution. Aimed at lifting the level of scientific knowledge of the Chinese population, it clearly reflected Liu's practical temperament and his technological approaches to economic growth.

The revival of confidence and pride on the part of Chinese intellectuals in their culture, visible in the 1957 rectification campaign, continued to be a theme in these activities.

Chinese cultural workers began to establish their own Marxist theories and criticism, seeking models in traditional Chinese culture that could be used to develop a "great socialist culture." For instance, Chou Yang maintained that people could find inspiration for revolutionary romanticism and realism in the works of writers like Ch'ü Yüan:

> One of the greatest poets in the history of our nation, Ch'ü Yüan was a very great romantic, while among later poets was Li T'ai-po who achieved remarkable results as a romantic. In their works both show close relations to folk literature. When more than a thousand years ago Liu Hsieh commented on Ch'ü Yüan's style by saying that a true poet "dips into the marvelous without losing the truth and appreciates the fanciful without sacrificing substance," it was, one could say, the very first simple idea of the combination of fantasy [huan-hsiang] and reality [chen-shih] in literature in our country.[61]

Along with Ch'ü Yüan, and Li T'ai-po, other ancient writers—like Kuang Han-ch'ing, T'ao Yüan-ming, Ch'en Tzu-ang, even Chu-ko Liang, noted for his sagacity and magic powers—were also favorably discussed. This rehabilitation extended to other areas of China's past literature and arts—drama, plays, music.

Needless to say, the attempt to adapt the feudal culture of the former ruling class to modern proletarian culture was no less difficult than earlier efforts to absorb Western bourgeois and Russian revisionist culture. Conditioned by their class education, specialization, and divorced from people's culture, old intellectuals both within and without the party often twisted Mao's guidance to fit their own purposes.

By the end of 1959 the Three Flags movement on the economic front had shaken the old economic structure in the rural area like an earthquake, leaving in its wake what some Maoist critics described as an "awful mess." Mao, however, regarded the situation as "very good indeed. It is not a mess at all. It is anything but an awful mess." The orderly minded revisionists, obsessed by "imperative" economic laws and appalled by disorder, called the Maoists' Great Leap policies "leftist rashness and impetuosity." The Maoists, they warned, "were going too fast." If people do not "get off the horse quickly," the "worker-peasant alliance will be in danger." The Maoists, in turn, likened the revisionist attitude to an old woman "tottering along with bound feet," a person "fearful of the dragon ahead and tigers behind." They vehemently denounced those who invoked the Soviet model of economic development to defend their "ideas of moving at a snail's pace." For the Liuists, who still recognized Moscow's ideological leadership, Mao's approaches to class struggle on the economic front were anachronistic. To Mao, the Liuists' attempt to reduce class struggle to purely economic terms was too simplistic.

The short-term difficulties arising from Mao's economic revolution were perhaps the calculated risk he was willing to take in order to overcome, in the long run, the centuries-old economic discrepancies between the city and the countryside, the rural area and the coastal area. Nevertheless, the "awful mess" perceived by some in the wake of the Maoist measures lent a degree of credibility to those questioning the premises of Mao's idea of continuing revolution in the economic domain. Growing numbers of party cadres and professionals, originally not attracted to the Liuists' cause, began to express serious doubts about Mao's leadership. So strong were these voices of doubt, and so critical the general economic situation by 1959, that Mao was apparently forced to "retreat to the second line," handing over the chairmanship of the state to his political opponent, Liu Shao-ch'i, ostensibly to have more time to study theoretical problems. The fact that the leading critic of Mao's Leap theory, P'eng Te-huai, and his colleague, Huang K'o-ch'eng, were then army chiefs suggests that Mao's retreat was perhaps also closely related to strong pressure from the army.

The extent of Mao's political setback in the intraparty power struggle in 1959 can only be compared to that in

1927 when, as a result of his leadership in the disastrous Autumn Harvest Uprisings in Hunan, he was accused of "military opportunism or adventurism" and removed from all his posts in the party hierarchy. With Mao's concession of part of his power to Liu Shao-ch'i in 1959, two power centers came into existence at the highest level.

Mao's political defeat was followed by a series of natural calamities from 1959 to 1961 that caused further material and human losses. Worse still, the already extremely strained economic situation was exacerbated by the sudden withdrawl of Soviet scientific and technical assistance, and by direct Soviet intervention in China's domestic politics by lending support to Mao's leading critic, P'eng Te-huai. From the South came the pressure of Western imperialism, led by the United States, exercised indirectly through the Chiang Kai-shek regime on Taiwan, and governments in neighboring countries such as Vietnam, Japan, Korea, and particularly India, which initiated a border dispute against China in 1962. At the same time, Russia continued with increasing enthusiasm to seek détente with the United States and European nations, hoping to prevent other potential powers in the once monolithic socialist bloc, like China, from challenging their hegemony. Their support and commitment to the world communist movement was relegated to secondary importance.

Concurrent with these international developments in the period 1960–61, was the growing power of the Liuists both in the party and society. To consolidate their recent gains, revisionists under Liu's leadership began in 1960 to gradually put the party firmly under their control by making Mao "a living Buddha," highly respected but with no real power. Mao's political retreat was accompanied by retreat on his economic line. The Great Leap Forward was abandoned, the communes, though retained, were considerably moderated. In their place was Liu's revisionist economic line, marked by what was called by Western China observers the "liberalization of the economy," including such capitalistic economic policies as free markets, individual plots for peasants, independent management of enterprises and permitting individual households to retain a certain amount of produce for their consumption or sale, apart from the fixed quota delivered to the state. Developments in the cultural area clearly reflected the above developments in the political and economic spheres. Mao's critics in the West launched a blunt attack on his Leap theory and policies, their voices swelling into "a great anti-Chinese chorus," as the Maoists later complained; Soviet ideologues criticized the Maoists' rashness and impetuosity, and flatly ridiculed China's readiness to enter the stage of communism. This hostile world climate seemed to confirm the Liuists' argument for cautious, gradual, and practical approaches to China's domestic socialist construction. Mao's domestic critics, once denigrated by the Maoists as "ghosts and monsters," now felt free to join the international anti-Maoist chorus,[62] "coming out of their confinement in great numbers to spread poison everywhere."[63]

In the area of party ideology, Yang Hsien-chen, a top revisionist ideologue, argued for Liu's theory that class struggle was dying out. Drawing upon the notion of "two-in-one," which emphasizes the unity rather than the contradiction in Marx's theory of contradiction, Yang asserted that class struggle was no longer needed in socialist China. As for Liu Shao-ch'i himself, as leader of the revisionist struggle against Mao's radicalism he republished in 1962 the revised edition of his book *How to Be a Good Communist,* written in 1939. In it Liu endorsed Yang's conciliatory supraclass position, intentionally played down the role of Mao Tsetung Thought, de-emphasized class struggle and the role of proletarian dictatorship, and attempted to revive the defunct Confucian tradition.

Encouraged by the revisionists, Sun Yeh-fang, one of China's leading economists, stepped forward with the theory of "economism." Sun stressed the role of imperative economic laws, material incentives, and free-market forces in promoting production. The revisionist tendencies in the area of education were equally evident. In 1962 Lu Ting-i suggested learning from Russia, the United States, and England. Lu was later accused of having tried to turn Peking University into Moscow University. Along with Chou Yang, Wu Han, and Chien Po-chien, Lu pushed an educational policy that deemphasized Mao Tsetung Thought and put expertise in command. He opposed half-work/half-study education and put emphasis on grades whereby students of bourgeois background would be much more favored than students from the families of the workers, peasants, and soldiers. Most important of all, he separated production from study, thus nullifying the very heart of Mao's educational line.

The strongest revisionist wind, however, blew in the areas of fine arts and literature, history, philosophy, and the study of cultural legacies. Greatly encouraged by the rehabilitation of the rightists, old intellectuals like Chou Ku-ch'eng, Chu Kuang-ch'ien, and many others urged that literary and artistic creation be guided by human emotion, intuition, or sentiment, as opposed to political views. Chou, for example, proposed the idea of an epochal spirit which represents the converging of the ethos of all classes rather than the expression of one leading class. Shao Ch'üan-lin proposed the concept of "deepening realism," which held that artists and writers should focus attention on average people instead of creating imaginary heroes. In essence, all these theories attempted to substitute class reconciliation in the place of class struggle.

Closely related to literary and artistic creations of this period were extensive efforts by these intellectuals to reevaluate past cultural legacies. In harmony with the prevailing climate of class reconciliation, writers and artists under the leadership of Chou Yang devoted themselves to traditional subjects, such as "ancient emperors, kings, great generals and ministers, famous talents and beauties, and even ghost stories," all of which represent the past ruling classes. According to statistics given in an editorial in *Liberation Army Daily*, December 25, 1964, among vernacular plays performed in East China only seven percent were modern plays in 1960, seventeen percent in 1961, and none in 1962. Over fifty percent were historical plays reflecting the life of the capitalist class. Some writers, like Hsia Yen and T'ien Han, enthusiastically urged the restoration of the literary tradition of the 1930s, portraying the life and ideas of the petty bourgeoisie, to counter the Yenan literary tradition of the 1940s.

As for history, the revisionist viewpoints were endorsed by such prominent historians as Wu Han, Chien Po-tsan, Liu Ta-nien, and Hou Wai-lu. In his historical essay "Hai Jui Upbraided the Emperor," and his play *Dismissal of Hai Jui*, Wu implied that history is propelled forward by *ch'ing-kuan* (honest officials), members of the ruling class who formulated a policy of class reconciliation. Likewise, Chien emphasized that "in the study of history, apart from the concept of class, there should be the place for historicity," and opposed the study of history by objective historical laws. Similarly, in the area of philosophy, during the seminar on Confucianism held in November 1962 under the auspices of Chou Yang and apparently backed by Liu and P'eng, some of the noted scholars on classical China, like Feng Yu-lan and Lü Chen-yü, again took the opportunity to lay emphasis on the positive contribution of Confucius to Chinese culture on the basis of "abstract inheritance." Along with Wu Han, these philosophers held that some of the good aspects of the feudal morality of the exploiting classes can be inherited and transformed into the morality of the working class today.

All these ideas, according to the Maoists, were contrary to Mao's theories that the masses and the class struggle through violence are the motivating forces of human history, and that the proletarian class possesses its own morality, distinctive from that of the exploiting classes.

The most sensitive and explosive controversies between

the Maoists and the Liuists, however, consisted in the latter's personal attack on Mao and acrimonious criticism of current state affairs. Learning from earlier experiences, Mao's critics, though backed by Liu's power, sought to express their protest and dissent in more disguised or academic forms, as fables, allegories, satire. Wu Han's 1959 essay, "Hai Jui Upbraided the Emperor," and his historical drama, *Dismissal of Hai Jui* in February 1961, Wu Nan-hsing's and Teng T'o's satiric essays, "Notes by Three Family Villages" and "Evening Talk at Yen-shan," are classic examples. They illustrate how skillfully the revisionists could use to their advantage Mao's directives "Emphasize the present and de-emphasize the past," or "Use the past to serve the present." They also indicated the seriousness of the opposition to Mao which had developed at this time. Aware that he must act before it was too late, Mao moved to counterattack, bringing the Proletarian Cultural Revolution to its third phase, marked by intensified struggle along two party lines.

By 1962 overall economic conditions had substantially improved. To reverse the strong anti-Maoist currents on both the domestic and international fronts, Mao moved with unmatched revolutionary vigor and consummate strategy and tactics to counterattack in all major areas. His comeback formally began at the Tenth Plenum of the Eighth Party Congress, held in September 1962. Drawing upon the concept of "one-into-two," Mao urged, "Class struggle is inevitable. This is a historical law long expounded by Marxism-Leninism which we should never forget." Mao further pointed out that this class struggle was bound to be reflected in the party. Therefore, "while fighting against the class enemy in the country, Chinese Communists must remain on alert at all times and resolutely opposed to the various ideological tendencies of the opportunists in the Party."[64]

A critical step in support of Mao was taken by Lin Piao,

then still loyal, who took over command of the army in 1959 from P'eng Te-huai and then consolidated control by intensifying political education. As part of the educational effort, Lin in early 1964 extended the army's political department to the civil commercial, financial, and industrial sectors, a crucial step for bringing the revisionist-inclined professionals under discipline. Urging the entire country to learn from the PLA, Lin stepped up a nationwide campaign to study Mao Tsetung Thought, stressing the cult of personality. To parallel Lin's steps in the army, Mao, making use of the socialist education movement, rebuilt the poor and lower-middle peasants' association in the countryside. By strengthening these political bodies with a view to carrying out class struggle against the rich peasants, the potential allies of the Liuists, Mao reassured his traditional mass base. All these measures were designed, as we know now, to put pressure on the Liuists and prepare for a possible showdown with them. Mao was clearly aware that, short of support from the PLA and the broad masses, he would never be able to overcome the Liuists who controlled the party and the state machinery.

It should be noted that during this period the general economic situation steadily developed in Mao's favor. With a steady rise in production, the early economic crisis came to an end. In Mao's view, therefore, Liu's liberalization policies were to be seen merely as temporary expedients, not normal order, to be discontinued as soon as circumstances no longer required them. The time had come to reassert the Maoist economic line, characterized at this time by emphasizing self-reliance. Communization was slowly reasserted, and despite his concern for rapid industrial growth, Mao laid more stress on the development of agriculture. The model for China's agricultural development was the remarkable experiences of the Tachai Brigade, where through bold application of Maoist approaches barren mountain faces had been transformed into fertile fields. Despite severe national disasters, the Tachai Brigade had succeeded in raising the standard of living of all its members, expanding sales of its surplus grain to the state instead of demanding relief, accumulating reserves against bad years, reconstructing housing, and establishing community projects to supplement agricultural income. This was contrary to the experience of the T'ao-yüan Brigade, located in Shangtung, which was endorsed by Liu.

Along with his counterattacks in these areas, Mao was even more enthusiastic and active in the area of arts and literature. Abandoning his previous reserve in commenting on revisionist tendencies in the literary and artistic worlds, Mao addressed himself directly to these problems in November 1963:

> There are quite a few problems in all forms of art such as the drama, ballads, music, the fine arts, the dance, the cinema, poetry and literature; the people engaged in them are numerous; and in many departments very little has been achieved so far in socialist transformation. The "dead" still rule today in many departments. . . . The social and economic base has already changed, but the arts as part of the superstructure, which serve this, still remain a great problem today. Hence we should proceed with investigation and study and attend to this matter in earnest.
>
> Isn't it absurd that many communists are enthusiastic about promoting feudal and capitalist art, but not socialist art?[65]

Sparked by Mao's counterattacks, the two-line struggle in the party flared up and grew in intensity. As the confrontation deepened, Mao issued a second directive in June 1964:

> Most of those associations and their publications (it is said that a few of them are good) have basically (but not all of them) not carried out the party's policy in the last fifteen years. They are officials and conduct themselves like lords, neither going near workers, peasants and soldiers, nor reflecting social-

ist revolution and construction. In recent years, they
have even slid down the brink of revisionism. Unless
they are seriously reformed, they will one day, in
the future, merely become organizations like the
Petöfi Club of Hungary.[66]

Mao's mention of the Petöfi Club was particularly meaningful, for it implied a political purge if the revisionist tendencies continued unabated. In support of Mao's verbal
warnings, Chiang Ch'ing, apparantly under Mao's guidance,
fought to revolutionize the traditional Peking opera by
creatively introducing modern Western musical instruments
and encouraging the depiction of the lives of workers, peasants, and soldiers. This was aimed at developing the proletarian culture while at the same time fostering a radical
climate to counter the revisionist current in the literary and
artistic worlds. Mao and Chiang Ch'ing also hoped to prepare opinion for a seemingly inevitable political purge on
the broad cultural front.

Despite the strenuous antirevisionist efforts by Mao,
Chiang Ch'ing, and Lin Piao, the resistance of their opponents, entrenched in the party and state organs, was too
strong to be crushed. Each move by the Maoists was followed
by a countermove by the Liuists. When Mao formulated a
draft "Decision by the Central Committee of the CCP
with regard to certain problems of the current rural work"
in 1963, Liu shortly put out his own "Regulation on several
policies of the socialist education movement in the countryside." As Mao called for "learning from Tachai," Liu
appealed to the country to take the "T'ao-yüan experience"
as the model for agricultural development. As these moves
and countermoves escalated, the tension between the Maoists
and the Liuists rapidly mounted.

By July 1964 Mao saw no alternative but to launch a
cultural purge lasting till the autumn of 1965. This constituted the fourth phase of the Proletarian Cultural
Revolution. To carry out this purge, a five-man "Cultural

Revolution Group" was formed. During the purge—a prelude to the Cultural Revolution in the following years—the Maoists selected a large number of intellectuals for criticism: ideologists (Yang Hsien-chen and Feng Ting); philosophers (Feng Yu-lan); economists (Sun Yeh-fang); artists and writers (Yang Han-sheng, Shao Ch'üan-lin, Hsia Yen). However, revisionists acted quickly to limit the effects of the purge. P'eng Chen interpreted it as simply a "self-examination" by scholars, writers, and artists of their writings, compositions, and performances. P'eng promised, moreover, that "if errors or defects were corrected they would be all right."[67] P'eng clearly downplayed Mao's directives in carrying them out. In fact, as the Maoists later asserted, it was largely due to Liu's and P'eng's machinations that they failed to include in the list for purge at this time P'eng's protégés, Wu Han, Teng T'o, and Liao Mo-sha, who had in fact delivered the most damaging and severe attacks on Mao and his policies.

By the middle of 1965 the highest echelons of the CCP authority were sharply divided by two centers contending for power in order to push forward their own ideas and policies. One center, led by Mao, had its base in the vast hinterland and the support of the poor and lower-middle peasants, the working people in the cities, and the powerful PLA. The other, revolving around Liu, had its roots in the coastal areas, supported by the powerful functional class of intellectuals and specialists and also by rich peasants in the countryside.

Given the depth of the confrontation, it is not surprising that when Mao, hoping to deepen the current purge, chose Wu Han as the next target, his suggestion was voted down by the Central Committee in September 1965. The Maoists had apparently become a minority in the party, their will effectively checked by its legal mechanisms. Mao was therefore forced to go to South China to build the staging base for his counterattack. With this move, the contradiction between the Maoists and the Liuists reached unprecedented magnitude and the Proletarian Cultural Revolution moved to its final and most violent phase around late 1965. The political forces in China now aligned in a two-line struggle within the CCP itself, rather than around various democratic parties as in the presocialist era when they were contending for the heavenly mandate. The question was: Should China follow Mao's theory of uninterrupted revolution, or Liu's theory of the dying out of class struggle, marked by gradual and peaceful transformation, in attaining its perennial ideal of *ta-t'ung* society?

THE GREAT PROLETARIAN CULTURAL REVOLUTION

Mao's decision in late 1965 to attack the revisionists came at a time when the United States was escalating its aggression in Vietnam. As the contradiction sharpened between the Maoists and the Liuists concerning how to cope with the American threat from the south, a sense of national crisis was generated among the Chinese people, paralleling that of 1898, 1919, or 1950 when China's destiny was at stake. Modern Chinese anti-imperialist nationalism was revitalized and, coupled with the upsurge of socialism, provided an indispensable momentum for continuing the revolution, as it has throughout the Chinese revolution. The imminent threat of all-out war with the United States helped to justify radical domestic steps Mao deemed necessary for preparing China for such a confrontation. The escalation of the Vietnam War and the fall of Sukarno in Indonesia in 1965 immensely strengthened Mao's radical domestic course.

When the purge began in November 1965, the Liuists under the leadership of Liu Shao-ch'i and P'eng Chen tried every means within the party's tradition of democratic centralism to circumvent it. They relied on their entrenched "legal" positions within the party to withstand the Maoists' frontal attack, while probably also resorting to various "illegal" means to depose Mao. The intensity of Liuist resistance was clearly reflected by the change in titles employed to designate the Cultural Revolution. On April 14, 1966, the vice-minister for culture, Shih Hsi-min, referred to it as the "Great Socialist Cultural Revolution," a name once used to denote the cultural revolution launched in 1958. The "May 16 Notice" of 1966 juxtaposed the notions "to destroy and to foster" and "to eliminate capitalist ideas and to enhance proletarian ideas" which had been used in 1958's socialist cultural revolution. On June 6, 1966, however, the *Liberation Army Daily* called it the "Great Proletarian Cultural Revolution." Two months later the Tenth Plenum of the Eighth Party Congress of the CCP for the first time used this title in "Decisions Concerning the Great Proletarian Cultural Revolution." The change in title was not a trivial affair. The earlier one meant that the contradiction between the Maoists and the Liuists, however acute, remained nonantagonistic, "a struggle among the people." The latter implied that the contradiction was antagonistic, a class struggle between the people and the class enemy. Thus between June and August 1966, the Maoists concluded that the ten-year ideological struggle between the revisionists and themselves had assumed the nature of class struggle and the magnitude of a revolution.

Unlike the periods of civil war, the center of turmoil in this Cultural Revolution was urban rather than rural China. Urban society, with its workers, intellectuals, youth, was swept up in "great revolutionary storm and waves." This was a process of "struggle-criticism-transformation" on three levels: an extremely intense struggle for "seizing power" at the local level; a nationwide campaign against the "four olds" (old ideas, old culture, old custom, old habit); and a drive for a "great union" or "three-in-one" (the combination of PLA, cadres, and the revolutionary masses). In early June 1966, the Maoists first characterized the Cultural Revolution as a struggle between two antagonistic world outlooks, the capitalist and the proletarian; and in November, as the revolution deepened, defined its essence as a class struggle between the *kung*-oriented and the *ssu*-oriented world outlooks.

Indeed, so prevalent was the uncompromisingly ethical and moralistic tone of the Cultural Revolution that it can be regarded as a great ethical campaign analagous in some ways to what Lu Hsün called for in the May Fourth period in 1919. The ethical spirit is clearly revealed by the notions of *p'o-ssu li-kung* ("to eliminate the notion of selfishness and to foster the notion of collective") and *tou-ssu p'i-hsiu* ("to combat selfishness and to repudiate those in power who take the revisionist or capitalist road").[68] The central concept in these two slogans is that of collectivity and its opposite, selfishness. The Maoists often spoke of the Cultural Revolution as aimed at crushing selfishness and replacing it with collectivity. It was an ethical and ideological struggle between altruism (the moral foundation of socialism) and self-interest (the moral foundation of capitalism and revisionism).

Throughout the Cultural Revolution the Maoists used the concepts of *kung* and *ssu* on a structural and behavorial level. Structurally, *kung* and *ssu* were defined according to their institutional origins in the class structure of society. Thus, in the light of Marxism-Leninism the Maoists defined *ssu* as *ssu-yu kuan-nien*, the consciousness of private ownership, deriving from the centuries-old private-ownership system of the feudal as well as the capitalist societies. It manifests itself in the superstructure in the forms of the "four olds." The meaning of *kung*, on the other hand, is *kung-yu kuan-nien*, the consciousness of collective ownership, a reflection of the collective-ownership system of the socialist societies. It manifests itself in the superstructure in the form of the "four news"—new ideas, new culture, new customs, and new habit.[69]

The Maoists also used the terms in the behavioral sense. From the viewpoint of motivation and purpose, they understood *kung* as *wei-kung* (for the collective) and defined it as "Strive not for reputation or gain; fear no hardship, have no fear of death; do nothing for self-interest, but always work for others; have total devotion to revolution and the people; wholeheartedly serve the Chinese people and the people of the world."[70] Here the meaning of *kung* is close to *li-ta chu-i* (altruism). The opposite notion of *ssu* they understood as *wei-ssu* (for oneself) and defined as follows: "Think only of oneself, care only for oneself; be eager for reputation, gain, power, position and fame; forget about the millions of Chinese people and the tens of hundred millions of people around the world."[71] Frequently the Maoists' understanding of *ssu* is hardly distinguishable from a negative concept of extreme individualism, translated by the Maoists as *li-chi chu-i* (self-interestism). Thus the *kung-ssu* dichotomy has both a structural and a behavioral meaning.

The notions of *kung* and *ssu* appeared before the Cultural Revolution in Chinese Communist literature in connection with *feng-ke* (style), *p'ing-ke* (moral character), *tao-te* (morality), and *hsiu-yang* (self-cultivation). The word *kung* was often understood as synonymous with collective spirit, proletarian idea. Its opposite, *ssu*, connoted self-interest, selfishness, and individualism which was the source of such mistakes as unprincipled disputes, factional strife, sectarianism, departmentalism, conceit, individual heroism, showing off, etc.[72] As early as 1928, in order to correct the undesirable ideas prevalent in the Fourth Red Army, Mao selected individualism as one of his chief targets of criticism. In 1938, during the period of national resistance against Japan, Mao for the first time juxtaposed notions like *ta-kung wu-ssu* (absolute impartiality) and *k'o-chi feng-kung* (self-denial in the interest of the collective).

> Hence, such things as selfishness and self-interest, inactiveness and negligence in work, corruption, degeneration and vainglory are merely contemptible; while the spirit of *ta-kung wu-ssu*, of active and hard work, of *k'o-chi feng-kung* and of complete absorption in arduous work commands respect.[73]

Here Mao treated *kung*, though not without emphasis, simply as one of several moral qualities a Chinese Communist Party member should possess in order to play an exemplary role as vanguard in all spheres of work in the national front—composed of the Nationalists and other democratic parties. It was due to this noble moral quality— i.e., the spirit of doing everything for others' benefit and nothing for his own—that Doctor Bethune, a Canadian who died in China after long service there, was highly commended by Mao in 1939 as a true Communist.

Yet only during the Cultural Revolution was this idea of collectivity really developed for the first time into an ideological and moral foundation for China's socialist society. Mao spoke of the Cultural Revolution as a necessary and crucial stage in China's march toward communism precisely because the ultimate threat to the proletarian dictatorship under socialist conditions came not so much from the visible enemies, such as the Americans and the Russians from without and the remaining landlords and the bourgeoisie from within, as from the invisible one—*ssu*— who dwells in everyone's soul. Mao and his followers thus argued that the surest guarantee of the proletarian dictatorship was the consciousness of collective.

The central problem of the Cultural Revolution, the Maoists argued, was power. They saw the primary task of the Cultural Revolution as a struggle against those officials in the CCP taking the capitalist road. But its purpose was to solve the problem of world outlook and to eradicate revisionism. Mao argued that a thorough solution of power required the elimination of the consciousness and motivation of the old society and the establishment of correct socialist consciousness and motivation in accord with the new socialist economic base. Only in this way could the proletarian dictatorship be consolidated. This is why the Maoists defined the Cultural Revolution as a political revolution in the realm of consciousness.

In the "Sixteen Points" of August 1966, the Maoists described the Cultural Revolution merely as the struggle of the "four news" against the "four olds." Victory in this regard would release an immense power promoting the growth of productive forces. Thus "to destroy four olds and to foster four news" and "to grasp revolution and to promote production" became two popular slogans throughout the nation.

In November 1966 the Red Guards, then the vanguards of the revolution, opened up another battlefront, "seizing power." Out of the "great revolutionary storm and waves" emerged the purpose of the Cultural Revolution.

> What is the essence of old ideas, old culture, old customs, and old habits? After all, the essence of all these old things can be ascribed to the notion of private ownership, and summarized in one word, *ssu*. Since the beginning of human culture the thousand-year-old human societies have all been class ones; their common feature is the private-ownership system. All old culture aimed at justifying the private-ownership system and served it. In order to establish the public-ownership system, we must destroy the old culture and various kinds of private-ownership ideas. The notion of private ownership is the root of capitalism and revisionism. The more thoroughly the notion of private ownership is destroyed the more firmly the proletarian dictatorship will be established, and only then will the socialist economy be able to develop.
>
> The new ideas, new culture, new customs, and new habits of the proletarian class can be summarized in one word, *kung*. In order to consolidate the public-ownership system, to establish socialism and communism, we must advocate the notion of total devotion to public service and the word *kung*.[74]

By early 1967 the Maoists faced the growing problem of factionalism and in this new situation they spoke of *ssu* in the forms of individualism, sectarianism, reputation-seeking, anarchism, and élitism. The Maoists thus linked the

struggle for strengthening unity among the young revolutionary successors with the struggle for doing away with
man's entrenched selfish desires.

> The most fundamental task in this revolution is to
> solve the problem of power. . . . If self-mindedness
> increases and keeps developing, people will follow
> the capitalist road. In order to consolidate the power
> of the working class, we must first of all consolidate
> the power of *kung* in our minds.[75]

The decisive battle against revisionism, therefore, had to be
fought in the very depths of one's soul.

> Comrade Mao Tsetung repeatedly told us that the
> Proletarian Cultural Revolution is a revolution
> touching everyone to his soul. Again, he said that to
> carry out this revolution we must use struggle by
> reasoning, not struggle by violence. What people
> call soul is thought, consciousness, popular culture,
> and various customs and habits attached to people's
> thoughts and consciousness. All of them are problems
> within people's minds. . . . To use the simple
> method of struggle by violence can only touch
> people's flesh and skin, not their souls, and cannot
> expose fully before the masses the ugly faces of
> demons and monsters and their reactionary poison.[76]

The debates over public and self, private and public
ownership are as old as China's philosophic tradition. Indeed, the Maoist concept of collective and the role of culture invokes highly ethical, political, social, and economic
values long debated by representatives of various classes
throughout Chinese history. These earlier debates provide
a context for appreciating the use of these terms in the
Great Proletarian Cultural Revolution.

Some of the close ethical-economic links underlying the
Chinese philosophic tradition are evident in two quite
different philosophies—Confucianism and Moism. Confucianism represented the culture of the ancient ruling

classes, while Moism sank its roots in the ancient laboring masses. Mo-tzu, who came from a class of prisoners or slaves, emphasized love and hate (*ai* and *wu*) rather than *i* and *li*, the outlook of the slave-lord and landlord classes. For the Moists, love expressed the desire of the oppressed for emancipation from bondage, and the dedication of individuals to that cause. For the Confucianists, however, "righteousness" was of benefit mainly for the ruling class.

The nature of China's agrarian economy led both groups to argue over virtues like frugality, industry, and simplicity.[77] Though the Confucianists endorsed such virtues, they still favored significant expenditures in areas of cultural and social activities. To overcome the economic hardship of the masses, the Moists denounced as waste and luxury such social activities as music, mourning, and other cultural mores that were essential parts of Confucian etiquette. They urged people to live at a modest level. But that was only possible, Mo-tzu argued, if there was peace in the land. Thus revolution or violence could only bring material damage to everyone. The alternative was universal love and an ascetic, unselfish, dedicated existence.

Thanks to modern productive methods, the modern Chinese proletariat have radically departed from their ancient predecessor by working to increase production through revolution and by substituting the concept of economic growth for the concept of a finite subsistence economy. The close link between economics and ethics remains, but now the moral incentive is that all people will gain as production rises, and become increasingly involved in the decision-making process. The public ownership of the means of production is the basis for this approach to China's development.

Closely tied to this ethical attitude toward economics is the relation between self and community. The transition from private ownership, characterized by the pursuit of individual material gratification, to collective requires the realization of inherent moral attributes of collectivity. This involves a struggle between public- and private-oriented world outlooks within the soul of every individual. The Maoists believe that man's moral potential is very great, but that its preservation and fulfillment can only be achieved through the community. Consequently, their argument concerning the moral self parallels that of Confucianism and Moism. The Confucian doctrine of *jen* (humanism), implied that ideally man was a social being whose meaning came from his association with others, but in practice these moral qualities applied only to the "gentleman." The complementing Confucian doctrine of *shu* (reciprocity) meant that for a "gentleman" others always precede oneself. "Self" can only be defined, therefore, in relation to others and what unites them. The Moists went even further than the Confucianists. They espoused universal love and affection regardless of class origins. But both still asserted that the preservation and fulfillment of self lies only in some form of community. The more integrated one is with the community, the more one's moral potential is realized.

Though their class content was totally different, some of the ways "self" and "community" are understood in Confucianism and Moism are clearly a reflection of China's general material and economic conditions. Both outlooks evolved in North China, an area with backward means of production, poor in land and livestock. Both assumed a static economy. Thus these thinkers faced the question of how to divide the existing material wealth in a way that would avoid starvation and privation. The pursuit of profit and economic self-gratification were condemned because, given free rein, they would lead to such extremes of wealth that the peace of the nation would be undermined. Both Confucianists and Moists, therefore, condemned selfish seeking of profits at the expense of others. The only way to ensure a bare subsistence for the people was by restraining man's economic self with his spiritual and moral qualities. Man's inner world was thus conceived as an infinite reservoir of moral potential capable of controlling the pursuit of economic self-interest. Both Moists and Confucianists endorsed the virtues of sharing and working with others and condemned seeking profits at the expense of others. But the Confucianists' espousal of sharing, of course, was confined to their own class and they sought vigorously to prevent traders and certain landlord groups from undermining it. The Moists, on the other hand, spoke for the oppressed slaves and called for sharing all wealth among the people.

Some historians argue that "the sages did everything to confine and inhibit the energies latent in the individual" and that "Chinese ethics achieves its purpose only by diminishing the energies of all—by a subtraction on all sides."[78] Such an argument, however, only confuses the issue. What Chinese sages intended to "inhibit" or "subtract" was the blind and greedy economic self. Under conditions of extremely limited surplus value and antagonistic class relations, any tapping of man's "promethean energies" could not create material abundance for all, only chaos inimical to the great majority. Both Moism and Confucianism concluded, therefore, that the primacy of community over self was the essential prerequisite for society's survival.

One feature of productive relations in traditional China illustrates this point quite well. The meaning of "private" did not refer to the individual but to the family or clan which was the basic unit of productive and social relations in the agrarian economy. "Private ownership" was actually clan or family ownership. Indeed, the Chinese traditionally identified themselves economically with their families or clans. They believed that a comfortable sum of family or clan wealth was the best guarantee of their own economic interests. For the Chinese people, therefore, the transition from private to collective values is largely a question of linking economic development with suprafamilial collectives such as productive brigades or communes under socialism, where under feudalism it had been linked to family or clan. These organizations were what the Maoists meant by "collective." Despite its significant defects, this specific feature of traditional China's social institutions has smoothed the passage of modern Chinese society from a feudal agrarian society to modern industrial socialism.

In addition, when the Maoists attributed the threat to proletarian power partly to man's selfishness (*ssu*), they did so in the context of a cultural tradition that emphasized the necessity for moral and ethical consciousness to restrain man's greed and striving for personal profit. The opening passage of the *Book of Mencius* says:

Mencius went to see King Wei of Liang. The King said: "Venerable sir, since you have not counted it far to come here, a distance of a thousand li, may I presume that you are likewise provided with counsels to profit my kingdom?" Mencius replied, "Why must Your Majesty use that word, profit? What I am likewise provided with, are counsels to benevolence and righteousness, and these are my only topics. If Your Majesty says, 'What is to be done to profit my kingdom?' the great officers will say, 'What is to be done to profit our persons?' " Superiors and inferiors will try to snatch this profit the one from the other, and the kingdom will be in danger. In a kingdom of ten thousand chariots, the murderer of his kingdom shall be the chief of a family of a thousand chariots. In a kingdom of a thousand chariots, the murderer of his principle shall be the chief of a family of a hundred chariots. To have a thousand in ten thousand, and a hundred in a thousand, cannot be said not to be a large allotment, but if righteousness be put last, and profit be put first, they will not be satisfied without snatching all. There never has been a man trained to benevolence who neglected his parents. There never has been a man trained to righteousness who made his sovereign an afterthought. Let Your Majesty also say, 'Benevolence and righteousness, and these shall be the only theme.' Why must you use that word—profit?"[79]

Mo-tzu, too, saw the disorder of his time in ethical terms, though his different class base led him to emphasize "love" rather than "righteousness."

> If everyone in the world will love universally, states will not attack one another; houses not disturb one another; thieves and robbers become extinct; emperor and minister, father and son, all be affectionate and filial—if all this comes to pass the world will be orderly. Therefore, how can the wise man who has charge of governing the empire fail to restrain hate and encourage love? So when there is universal love in the world, it will be orderly, and when there is mutual hate in the world, it will be disorderly.[80]

The dichotomies of Mencius's righteousness-profit and Mo-tzu's love-hate converge, despite their different class bases, on one basic point—correct motivation and correct attitude were the source of political stability and economic well-being. Both Mencius and Mo-tzu endorsed the exaltation of virtue and condemned selfish seeking of profits at the expense of others. Only righteous-minded rulers can manage state affairs in a way to benefit the people. The Confucian classics are full of eulogies for such rulers, even though their ideology of "peace and harmony" largely resulted in the consolidation of their own position as a ruling class. For Mo-tzu as well, whether the rulers were righteous or not was a matter of life and death for the people.

> But how do we know Heaven desires righteousness and abominates unrighteousness? For with righteousness the world lives and without it the world dies; with it the world becomes rich and without it the world becomes poor; with it the world becomes orderly and without it the world becomes chaotic.[81]

CONCLUSION

Mao's concern for the pivotal role of consciousness and superstructure developed within this cultural context which for centuries had seen "ethics" as the source of political stability and economic well-being. Indeed, the intensity of debate over ethics and consciousness at each stage of China's revolution reveals a certain continuity in the way problems have been posed throughout the course of Chinese history. The historical process since 1840 can in some ways be seen as a series of cultural revolutions struggling to create the correct consciousness and ethics for building a new China, and the Great Proletarian Cultural Revolution as a dramatic new stage in that struggle. Mao's emphasis on superstructure and consciousness and the way it is understood in Mao Tsetung Thought, one of his great contributions to Marxism, joins Mao and revolutionary thinkers like Li Ta-chao and Lu Hsün with the concerns of Chinese civilization since its earliest days.

NOTES

I am especially grateful to Brett Nee for her suggestions and editorial advice.

1. Mao Tsetung, "Hsin min-chu chu-i lun" [On new Democracy], in *Mao Tsetung's Selected Works* (Peking), pp. 689–91; written in 1940.
2. Fang Yao, Ting Tsung-en and Lieh Yü-k'ou, *Hsin min-chu chu-i ti ke-ming yü ch'ien-t'u* [The new democratic revolution and its future], *ibid.*, 1940, p. 92.
3. Chiang Po-ch'ien, *Shih-san-ching kai-lun* [Introduction to the Thirteen Classics] (Shanghai, 1944), p. 459.
4. Chien Yu-wen, *Taiping chün Kuangsi shou-i* [History of the Taiping uprisings in Kwangsi] (Shanghai, 1946), pp. 66–67.
5. Fan Wen-lan, "Chi-nien Taiping T'ien-kuo ch'i-i i-pai-wu-shih chou-nien" [In Memory of the one hundred and fiftieth anniversary of the Taiping Uprisings], in *Taiping T'ien-kuo ke-ming hsing-chih wen-t'i t'ao-lun chi* [Essays on the problem of the nature of the Taiping Revolution], ed. Lin Yen-chiao and Ching Heng (Peking, 1961), pp. 10–11.
6. Yang Yung-kuo, *Chung-kuo ku-tai ssu-hsiang shih* [The intellectual history of ancient China], 1st ed, 1954, 2nd and 3d eds., 1973, pp. 9–14.
7. The split within the Confucian *ching-shih* tradition began with Hsün-tzu (298–238 B.C.?). Chinese Communist ideologists and historians in the early 1970s treat these left-wing Confucianists

identically with the genuine legalists, like Shang Yang (d. 330 B.C.) and Han Fei (d. 233 B.C.).

8. Tseng Kuo-fan, *Tseng Wen-cheng-kung ch'üan-chi* [The complete works of Tseng Wen-cheng-kung], 3:1b.

9. Mary C. Wright, *The Last Stand of Chinese Conservativism* (New York, 1957), pp. 21–43.

10. The first edition of the book was published in 1844, i.e., four years after the Opium War, the second in 1849, and the third in 1852.

11. Feng Kuei-feng, "Chi yank-ch'i i" [On the adoption of Western learning], in *Personal Protests from the Study of Chiao-pin*, 2:69a–70b.

12. Ch'ou-pan i-wu shih-mu [A complete account of the management of barbarian affairs: the T'ung-chih reign] (Peiping, 1929–31), 47:241–25b.

13. *Ibid.*, 48:1a–4a.

14. Since the Emperor Wu of the Western Han dynasty, when Confucianism was instituted as the state philosophy and legalism was subsumed in the Confucian framework, the line between Confucianism and legalism had been considerably blurred. In actuality, those reformist scholars or scholar-officials who professed as Confucianists were either legalists or legalist-inclined. The latter category of Confucianists are called here revisionist Confucianists, for they were reluctant to identify themselves as legalists.

15. Ma chien-chung, "Shang Li Hsiang-po yen ch'u-yang kung-tu shu" [Report to Li Hung-chang on the part-time study abroad], written in 1877, in *Shih-k'o-chai chi-yen chi-hsing* [Notes from the Shih-k'o-chai studio], 1896, vol. 2; Wang T'ao, "Hsing-li" [Promotion of profits], in *T'ao-yüan wen-lu wai-p'ien* [Supplement to the collection of T'ao-yüan], (Hong Kong, 1882), vol. 2; Hsüeh Fu-ch'eng, "Shang-cheng" [On trade administration], in *Ch'ou-yang ch'u-i* [Rough discussion of the management of foreign affairs], 1879.

16. Ku Hung-ming, *The Story of a Chinese Oxford Movement* (Shanghai, 1912), p. 19.

17. *Ibid.*, p. 16.

18. *Ibid.*, p. 5.

19. Mou An-shih, *Yang-wu yun-tung* [Movement for foreign affairs] (Shanghai, 1956), pp. 145–53.

20. Ku Hung-ming, "Reminiscences of a Chinese Viceroy's Secretary," trans. "Ardsheal," *Journal of the North China Branch of the Royal Asiatic Society*, vol. 46, 45 (1914–15), p. 106.

21. Hao Yen-p'ing. *The Comprador in Nineteenth-century China: Bridge between East and West* (Cambridge, Mass., 1970), p. 184.

22. Sergei Leonidocivh Tikhvinskii, *The Reform Movement of China and K'ang Yu-wei* (1959), trans. Chang Shih-yü, Liang Chao-hsi, Lü Shih-lun, and Chiang Chen-ying (Peking, 1962), pp. 85, 116–27.

23. Chang Hao, *Liang Ch'i-ch'ao and Intellectual Transition in China, 1890–1907*, (Cambridge, Mass, 1971), pp. 151, 203–13.

24. Su Yü, Preface to *I-chiao ts'ung-pien* [The collection of writings for promoting sacred teachings] (Hunan, 1898), p. 1b.

25. Chang Chih-tung, "Ch'üan-hsüeh pien" [Exhortation to study], in *Chang Wen-hsiang-kung ch'üan-chi* [The Complete Works of Chang Wen-hsiang-kung], 202:1–2.

26. *Ibid.*, 203:48.

27. *Ibid.*

28. *Ibid.*, 202:23–24.

29. Chu Chih-hsin, "Lun she-hui ke-ming tang yü cheng-chih ke-ming ping-hsing" [That social revolution should be realized with political revolution], in *Chu Chih-hsin chi* [Collection of Chu Chih-hsin], ed. Chien-she She (Shanghai, 1928); 1st ed. 1921, p. 19.

30. Li Ta-chao, "Yu ching-chi shang chieh-shih Chung-kuo chin-tai ssu-hsiang pien-tung ti yüan-yin" [An economic explanation of the changes in modern Chinese thought], in *Li Ta-chao hsüan-chi* [Selected works of Li Ta-chao] (Peking, 1959), pp. 47–53.

31. Lu Hsün, *Selected Works of Lu Hsün* (Peking, 1956), 1:8–12.

32. *Ibid.*

33. Hu Shih, "To yen-chiu hsieh wen-t'i, shao t'an hsieh 'chu-i'" [Study more problems, talk less of "isms"], in *Hu Shih wen-ts'un* [Collected essays of Hu Shih], 2:484.

34. *Ibid.*

35. Maurice Meisner, *Li Ta-chao and the Origins of Chinese Marxism* (Cambridge, Mass., 1967), p. 106.

36. *Ibid.*, pp. 105–6.

37. Chow Tse-tsung, *The May Fourth Movement* (Cambridge, Mass., 1960), p. 236.

38. Li Ta-chao, "Chung-kuo ti she-hui chu-i yü shih-chieh ti tzu-pen chi-i" [Chinese socialism and world capitalism; March 20, 1921], in *Li Ta-chao ch'üan-chi*, pp. 356–57.

39. Maurice Meisner, *Li Ta-chao and the Origins of Chinese Marxism*, p. 145.

40. Li Ta-chao, "Ch'ing-nien yü nung-ts'un" [Youth and the rural area], in *Li Ta-chao hsüan-chi*, p. 146.

41. *Op. cit.*, p. 200.

42. Kuo Chan-po, *Chin wu-shih-nien Chung-kuo ssu-hsiang-shih* [An intellectual history in the last fifty years] (Peiping, 1935); enlarged ed., Hong Kong, 1965. p. 342.

43. John K. Fairbank, E. O. Reischauer, and A. M. Craig, *East Asia: The Modern Transformation* (Boston, 1965), pp. 544–46, 765–66.

44. Mark Selden, *The Yenan Way in Revolutionary China* (Cambridge, Mass., 1971), pp. 208–12.

45. Liang Han-ping, *Chung-kuo hsien-tai ke-ming shih chiao-hsüeh ts'an-k'ao t'i-kang* [The teaching outlines on contemporary chinese revolutionary history], p. 204.

46. Mao Tsetung, "On People's Democratic Dictatorship," in *Mao Tsetung's Selected Works*, p. 1477.

47. Wang Chang-ling, *Chung-kung ti wen-i cheng-feng* [The literary rectification campaign of the Chinese Communist Party] (Taipei, 1967), pp. 80–81.

48. Li Ta, *Hu Shih fan-tung ssu-hsiang p'i-p'an* [Criticism of Hu Shih reactionary ideas] (Hankow, 1955), p. 1.

49. *People's Daily*, May 27, 1956.

50. *Ibid.*

51. *Central Daily News*, Taipei, May 30, 1973.

52. I Feng, "T'an-t'an nei-hang yü wai-hang" [A discussion of expert and layman], *People's Daily*, August 4, 1957.

53. "Ch'ien Wei-ch'ang yü-cheng hsin-ch'ang t'an mao-tun" [Ch'ien Wei-ch'ang discusses contradiction with heavy hearts], *People's Daily*, May 17, 1957.

54. Mao Tse-tung, "Tsai Chung-kuo kung-ch'ang-tang ch'üan-kuo hsüan-ch'uan kung-tso hui-i shang ti chiang-huao" [Talk at the Chinese Communist Party's conference on propaganda work], in Mao Tsetung and Lin Piao, *Post-revolutionary Writings*, ed. K. Fan (New York, 1972), p. 209.

55. Robert S. Elegant, *Mao's Great Revolution* (London, 1971), p. 33.

56. Editorial in *People's Daily*, November 7, 1957.

57. Liu made this remark to the party cadres of Shanghai on April 27, 1957. See "Kuan-yü wen-hua ta-ke-ming ti hsüan-ch'uan chiao-yü yao-tien" [Regarding the essential points of propaganda education about the Great Cultural Revolution], *Liberation Army Daily*, June 6, 1957.

58. "On the historical experience of the dictatorship of the proletariat," editorial in *People's Daily*, April 5, 1956. It was believed to have been written by Mao himself.

59. Mao Tsetung, "Introducing a Farm Coop," *Red Flag*, June 1, 1958.

60. Ch'en Ch'i-wu, *Lun wen-hua ke-ming ho ssu-hsiang ke-ming* [On cultural revolution and thought revolution] (Shanghai, 1958), p. 6.

61. D. W. Fokkema, *Literary Doctrine in China and Soviet Influence, 1956–1960* (New York, 1965), p. 197.

62. William Hinton, *Turning Point in China: An Essay on the Cultural Revolution* (New York, 1972), p. 30.

63. Yao Wen-yuan, "P'ing hsin-pien li-shih chü Hai Jui pa-kuan" [A criticism of the new historical play, the dismissal of Hai Jui], *People's Daily*, November 30, 1965.

64. "Wu-ch'an chieh-chi chuan-cheng hsia chin-hsin ke-ming ti li-lun wu-ch'i" [Theoretical weapon for waging revolution under the proletarian dictatorship], editorial in *Red Flag*, no. 10 of 1967, reprinted in *People's Daily*, October 20, 1967.

65. Mao's instruction, dated December 12, 1973, published in May 1967, *Red Flag*, no. 9 of 1967, pp. 8–9.

66. "Kao-chü Mao Tse-tung ssu-hsiang wei-ta hung-ch'i pa wu-ch'an chieh-chi wen-hua ta-ke-ming chin-hsing toa-ti kuan-yü wen-hua

ta ke-ming ti hsüan-ch'uan chiao-yü yao-tien" [Hold high the great red banner of Mao Tse-tung thought and carry out the Great Proletarian Cultural Revolution], *People's Daily*, June 6, 1966.

67. P'eng Chen, "Tsai ching-chü hsien-tai kuan-mu yen-ch'u ta-hui shangti chiang-hua" [Talk at the rehearsal of modern Peking opera], *Red Flag*, no. 14, July 1964.

68. "Tou-ssu p'i-hsiu shih wu'ch-ang chieh-chi wen-hua ta ke-ming ti ken-pen fang-cheng" [To combat self and repudiate revisionism is the fundamental policy of the Great Proletarian Cultural Revolution], editorial in *People's Daily*, October 6, 1967.

69. "Tsai lun t'i-ch'ang i-ko kung-tzu" [Again on promoting one word, "kung"], editorial in *People's Daily*, November 3, 1966.

70. "Hsüeh-hsi wei jen-min fu-wu" [Learn to serve the people], *Liberation Army Daily*, reprinted in *People's Daily*, December 1, 1966.

71. "Tou-ssu p'i-hsiu shih wu-ch'an chieh-chi wen-hua ta ke-ming ti ken-pen fang-cheng," *People's Daily*, October 6, 1967.

72. Liu Shao-ch'i, "Lun kung-ch'ang-tang-yüan ti hsiu-yang" [How to be a good Communist], in *Liu Shao-ch'i hs'üan-chi* [Collected works of Liu Shao-ch'i] (Tokyo, 1967), pp. 39–57.

73. Mao Tsetung, "Chung-kuo kung-ch'ang-tang tsai min-tsu chan-cheng chung chih ti-wei" [The role of the Chinese Communist Party in the national war], in *Mao Tse-tung's Selected Works*, p. 510.

74. "Tsai lun t'i-ch'ang i-ko kung-tzu," *People's Daily*, November 3, 1966.

75. Wang Yung-chün, "Wo tung-te liao ch'üan ti cheng-yao" [I realize the importance of power], *People's Daily*, May 19, 1967.

76. "Yung wen-tou pu yung wu-tou" [Struggle by reasoning not by violence], *People's Daily*, September 5, 1966.

77. Manabendra Nath Roy, "A Marxist Interpretation of Chinese History," in his *Revolution and Counterrevolution in China*, (1946); reprinted Boston, n.d., pp. 19–20.

78. Benjamin I. Schwartz, *In Search of Wealth and Power* (Cambridge, Mass., 1964), p. 60.

79. Mencius, *The Works of Mencius*, trans. by J. Legge (New York, 1970).

80. Mo-tzu, *The Works of Mo-zu*, trans. Y. P. Mei (London, 1929), pp. 78–80.

81. *Ibid.*, p. 136.

REVOLUTION AND BUREAUCRACY: Shanghai in the Cultural Revolution

Victor Nee

A seemingly paradoxical development of Chinese revolutionary history was the emergence of the most powerful, centralized national state in China's history after the foundations of its ancient bureaucratic civilization had finally been destroyed. China, on the eve of her tumultuous Cultural Revolution, was governed by a broadly based party government that played the indispensable and vital role of coordinating and administering all facets of the political, cultural, and economic life of the country. Its record of achievement had been singularly impressive. In just sixteen years it successfully led China's economic recovery and revitalized the war-ravaged, inflation-ridden economy left stagnant by a century of civil chaos and imperialism; radically reorganized the fabric of Chinese society; awakened in the Chinese people a new sense of hope, national purpose, and direction; and masterfully defended the still young revolution against the combined threats of domestic and international counterrevolution. The new Chinese state, led by a revolutionary party dedicated to serving the interests of the people and to exercising ironclad dictatorship over the old exploiting classes, was fundamentally different from all previous states that have risen and fallen in China's long history. Yet this state, emerging from a political culture deeply rooted in a long and complex bureaucratic tradition, could not but reflect certain aspects of that tradition. Moreover, consciously modeled after the Soviet state system, it shared common features with the Soviet bureaucracy.

By the early 1960s the Chinese critique of the Soviet Union and a growing concern for the danger of revisionism in China led Mao Tsetung to an increasingly negative evaluation of the borrowing from Soviet institutional and organizational models. Uncritical borrowing in the period of "leaning to one side" had contributed to a party-state system in deepening contradiction with the goals of social revolution. As the machinery of the state grew and continued to swell in size and complexity, so did the party organization which sought to maintain its control over the state. As the party became an integral part of the state system it grew increasingly separate from the masses. Swollen bureaucracies, moreover, fostered a milieu that encouraged attitudes and styles of work associated with the traditional bureaucracy. Centralization of power in state bureaucracies tended to discourage initiative and activism by the masses. Nascent tendencies toward bureaucratic inertia, privilege, and class differentiation threatened to undermine the dynamism and vigor of the revolution.

Just as the establishment of the new Chinese state was a climactic event in the long course of the Chinese Revolution, so was the outbreak of the Great Proletarian Cultural Revolution. Whereas the victory of the revolution in October 1949 led to the establishment of a vast new party-state system patterned after the Soviet state, the Cultural Revolution saw a massive popular assault against that system. This unprecedented revolution within a revolution, led by the founding father of the People's Republic, Mao Tsetung, was inspired by revolutionary ideas and symbols that have deep resonances with the populist traditions of the Chinese peasant uprisings, Chinese revolutionary history, and the great revolutions of the West: the American, French, and Russian revolutions. In the Cultural Revolution the Chinese struggled to restructure their state system in a manner that would allow for participation of the masses in state affairs.

They sought to create a new public spirit that would rule against privilege and wealth as motivation for assuming official responsibility. And they experimented boldly in political measures that would make party and state officials directly accountable to the masses.

At no time in the Cultural Revolution were the issues concerning the fate of the Soviet-styled state system so clearly articulated and so sharply defined as in Shanghai during the turbulent period of the January Revolution in 1967. As the Cultural Revolution swept through city after city in China, the Shanghai party machine, under the onslaught of rebel attacks, initiated a city-wide strike that threatened the total collapse of the city government and industrial system. Had the strike succeeded in bringing this great port city and sprawling hub of industry to its knees, party bureaucrats opposed to the Cultural Revolution could have exerted unbearable pressure on the central leadership in Peking, effecting the sabotage of the Cultural Revolution.

The rebel response to this strike in Shanghai was the direct take-over of its political, cultural, and economic system by popular forces. An alliance of industrial workers, radical students, and a restive stratum of lower- and middle-level party cadres, together with representatives from the Central Cultural Revolution Group in Peking, formed the decisive political coalition that ultimately rose to power in the Cultural Revolution in Shanghai. During the January Revolution, workers attempting to restore Shanghai to full production erected temporary leadership committees in factories and plants all over the city. The temporary structures were first necessitated by the collapse in management that followed the December walkout strike of factory directors, party officials, management cadres, and technical personnel. They were popularly elected committees of rank-and-file workers (and/or party cadres from the working class) who had emerged as leaders in the course of the Cultural Revolution. The committees were elected at ad hoc factory-wide meetings called to discuss the directives sent down from the city's new revolutionary leadership and to organize new production schedules and the allotment of work responsibility.

Because of the crisis situation, during which rebel workers were working in at least double shifts, leaders once elected found themselves as often as not on the production line with other workers rather than in the office set up by the workers' committee. The skeleton staff that remained in the office functioned as a nerve center, relaying messages, posting schedules, and doing accounting work. These temporary leadership committees were the nascent form of what later became one of the most important political fruits of the Cultural Revolution in Shanghai, the revolutionary committee.

It was the local, though centrally coordinated, actions of hundreds of thousands of rebel workers, students, and lower- and middle-level party cadres that delivered Shanghai from the brink of total civil and financial collapse and established the basis of a new revolutionary municipal state system. The prevalent mood of Shanghai's rebel workers during the January Revolution was captured in the popular saying heard among the industrial workers: "We liberated ourselves and managed ourselves!" Perhaps the most powerful rallying symbol for Shanghai citizens during the January Revolution was that of the Paris Commune of 1871. Study sessions of the commune had been carried out in Shanghai since the summer of 1966, and it was this historic precedent of proletarian government that emerged naturally as a model for Shanghai in the course of debate and discussion during the exciting days that followed the seizures of power. Through the symbol of the Paris Commune, Shanghai workers gained a powerful critique of bureaucratic rule and inspiration for undertaking the ultimate responsibility for the governing of the city.

But immense practical problems awaited the rebels who had seized power in the January Revolution. How could they create a city government that incorporated and consolidated the gains of the January Revolution while continuing to provide the type of stable and orderly government essential for rapid industrial growth? Seemingly indispensable to such economic progress was the maintenance of an efficient bureaucratic and managerial system in some form. Moreover, in a developing society still poor and at an early stage of industrialization, a high degree of political centralization and discipline would be required to maximize scarce capital and limited resources. Could these requirements be reconciled with the uncompromising democratic idealism of the January Revolution?

Thus, while the old order had been overthrown by the January Revolution, the search for a new order was both difficult and complex. While the symbol of the Paris Commune could provide a critique of bureaucratic rule and a historic model suggesting the direction of transformation, the new forms for revolutionary political organs had to emerge from the revolutionary practice of the masses in the course of the Cultural Revolution. They were to be tempered in the storm of revolutionary struggle, and the ideas that inspired them were to be tested and adapted to the present conditions and history of the Chinese Revolution. The Cultural Revolution upheld Mao's dictum that learning from the experiences of foreign revolutions was essential for the Chinese Revolution, but such learning must not be carried out mechanically and without imagination.

SHANGHAI BEFORE THE JANUARY REVOLUTION

In autumn 1966, the eve of the January Revolution, China's largest city anxiously awaited the full force of the political tempest Mao had fanned from the inner party circles to schools, factories, newspaper offices, and municipal bureaus throughout the country after the dramatic June national broadcasting of Nieh Yüan-tzu's famous Peking University big-character poster (*ta-tzu-pao*). Fed by successive waves of Peking Red Guard groups who had come to Shanghai by train to stir the flames of revolution, the Shanghai student movement had just begun to shift the spearhead of its attack from campus "capitalist roaders" and "bourgeois authorities" to high-ranking muncipal party officials—Ch'ang Hsi-p'ing, director of education, and Yang Hsi-kuang, the acting director of propaganda. While some of these rebel students joined Red Guards from all over the nation who were making their way to Peking, others plunged into the mounting storm in Shanghai, organizing city-wide student alliances, searching homes of the former ruling class for "counterrevolutionary evidence," or spilling out into factories throughout the city to agitate and link up with rebel workers' groups.

Although in most other cities it had been Red Guard students who first sparked the formation of rebel groups in factories, in Shanghai factories a full-blown, independently formed workers' movement awaited the students. Organized originally by a nucleus of lower- and middle-level cadres and young workers who had been quick to respond to the Peking University poster, factory rebel groups, like those from the universities, had spent the summer first in carrying out wall-poster attacks against their own factory party committees, and then in bitter confrontation with work teams sent down by the municipal bureaus to hold them in check. Out of these small groups of rebels in key factories and plants of the city emerged the first independent workers' movement in Shanghai since liberation. In Autumn 1966, attempting to coordinate and provide overall leadership for the movement, worker leaders began to meet secretly in the city to discuss the formation of an all-city rebel workers' organization. Scattered groups of journalists and staff members in Shanghai's leading newspapers added their forces to the growing rebel movement.

Late in October, five young journalists from Shanghai's leading newspaper, the *Wenhuipao*, organized a group called "The Spark that Sets the Prairie Fire" to carry out the Cultural Revolution on the city's press front.

The circle of rebel political activism in Shanghai expanded steadily through weeks of relentless confrontation with the upper levels of the municipal bureaucracy, building up a siege mentality among party officials holding positions of responsibility in the city. Ch'en P'ei-hsien, the First Secretary of the East China Bureau and concurrently the First Secretary of the Shanghai Municipal Party Committee, and Ts'ao Ti-ch'iu, the mayor of Shanghai, through skillful behind-the-scenes political maneuvering and manipulation had maintained at least a modicum of leverage and control over the Shanghai Cultural Revolution. Ch'en and Ts'ao still commanded the loyalty of the overwhelming majority of the city's party and government cadres. They had succeeded in placing an effective check, however temporary, on the politically inexperienced Red Guards by organizing their own city-wide Red Guard unit, the General Headquarters of Red Guards from Shanghai Schools and Colleges, and setting it in opposition to the student radicals. When more than 20,000 rebel workers from 200 of the city's 800 factories announced the formation of the Shanghai Workers' Revolutionary Rebel General Headquarters at a mass rally in Culture Square on November 9, Ch'en and Ts'ao responded quickly. They rejected the rebels' demands and immediately set out to organize their own workers' contingent, one loyal to the party machine and able to contend with the rebel workers' organization.

The Anting Incident in mid-November dealt the Shanghai Municipal Party Committee its first shattering blow. On November 10, the day following the Culture Square inaugural rally for the Workers' Rebel Headquarters and the rejection of their demands for official recognition and financial and logistical support, 2500 rebel workers descended on the Shanghai Railway Station, seized command of a northbound train, and started out to Peking. They hoped to meet with Mao and report the repressive tactics of the Shanghai party leadership.

As soon as the Municipal Party Committee got word of the event, they issued an order to halt the progress of the train. In Anting, a small station outside of Shanghai, station workers alerted by a telephone call switched the tracks of the oncoming train and brought it to a halt on a side track. Alarmed at the effect on production should large numbers of the nation's workers leave their factories to travel to Peking, the central leadership in Peking shared the Shanghai party officials' concern that the rebel workers in Anting return immediately to their factories. Chen Po-ta, then a leading member of the Central Cultural Revolution Group, sent a telegram to Shanghai to this effect, and Chang Ch'un-ch'iao, also a member of the Cultural Revolution Group, flew down from Peking and proceeded directly to Anting where he met and talked at length with Workers' Rebel Headquarters leaders. Chang, however, while urging workers to return to production, supported their rebellion against the local party leadership and, by signing the demands issued by the rebel workers, legitimized the existence of the Workers' Rebel Headquarters and affirmed the right of the Shanghai workers to oppose the Muncipal Party Committee. This was a critical blow to the Shanghai party leadership because, from that point on, seasoned industrial workers, and not youthful students, formed the dominant oppositional force in the Shanghai Cultural Revolution.

After the Anting Incident, political turbulence directed against the Shanghai party machine mounted steadily. In the early hours of the morning of November 30, radical students broke into the *Liberation Daily* building on Nanking Road and demanded that the newspaper staff stop the presses. They announced to the surprised newsmen that they would not leave until the newspaper agreed not only to print their tabloid, the *Red Guard Dispatch*, but distribute it as a flyer to the paper's regular subscribers.

Their action was immediately censured by the Municipal Party Committee. The Workers' Rebel Headquarters, however, acclaimed the Red Guard action and promptly dispatched a large detachment of rebel workers to help the Red Revolutionaries defend the building's seizure against large numbers of protesting moderate workers milling about outside the occupied building. Serious violence broke out between the two sides on December 3 and 4. But the support of the Workers' Rebel Headquarters, combined with the fear that party files would be purloined and party secrets exposed, forced the Municipal Party Committee to capitulate. On December 5 two high-ranking secretaries of the Municipal Party Committee, Sun Shi-wen and Wang Yi-p'ing, signed the list of demands issued by the Red Revolutionaries and the Workers' Rebel Headquarters. The next day the moderate workers, covertly organized by the Muncipal Party Committee in early November, finally came to the surface. Their leaders announced the formation of a new workers' mass organization, the Workers' Scarlet Guards for the Defense of Mao Tsetung Thought. From its inception its purpose was to wage battle with the Workers' Rebel Headquarters and by so doing safeguard the Shanghai party officialdom.

Confrontation between the two rival workers' mass organizations grew more frequent and more intense in the weeks following the *Liberation Daily* building's occupation. It reached its climax in late December at the Battle of Kunshan where rebel workers and Scarlet Guards workers fought what proved to be the decisive battle of Shanghai's Cultural Revolution. On December 28 and 29 there was wide-scale fighting between the Scarlet Guards and Workers' Rebel Headquarters in front of the East China Bureau Secretariat on Kanping Road in the old French concession. The fighting involved considerable violence and bloodshed and terminated in the defeat of the Scarlet Guards. On December 30, 60,000 to 70,000 of its members left Shanghai en masse and proceeded on foot and in trucks to Peking to lodge formal complaints of rebel violence before the Central Committee. In Kunshan, a small farming town thirty miles northwest of Shanghai, a numerically superior force of rebel workers caught up with the Scarlet Guards and a pitched battle ensued. Despite the support given them by the local citizens of Kunshan, the workers' Scarlet Guards again were defeated. The violent defeat of the Scarlet Guards in Kunshan compelled party officials in Shanghai to resort thereafter to even more desperate tactics.

THE JANUARY REVOLUTION

In a speech to an Anhwei delegation held in Peking's Great Hall of the People in October 1967, Chang Ch'un-ch'iao described the state of Shanghai on his arrival at the beginning of the January Revolution: "The old Municipal Party Committee had then been paralyzed. Many factories, including vital industrial plants, had stopped production. . . . The piers and railway stations were also immobilized, causing severe dislocations."[1] The Shanghai party bureaucrats, faced with a political crisis they could no longer control or even contain by conventional political countermeasures, had in the closing days of December 1966 resorted to tactics that sought to divert a mounting political revolution into struggles for individual material gain.

One tactic, labeled "economism" by the Maoists, was an attempt to buy off the Shanghai working class (including peasants from communes in the outskirts of the city who worked as temporary or contract laborers) by freely dispensing wage increases, bonuses, and cash handouts. In this attempt to divert political struggle and controversy away from themselves, they not only sought to appease Shanghai workers through monetary bribes but hoped to lure them away from Shanghai, to Peking and other cities in China, with generous travel allowances and extended leaves of absence from work.[2] This was more than a way to pass upward the political pressure they felt; it was a way to discredit the Cultural Revolution. The severe disruption of the Shanghai economy caused by massive desertion of factories and by the fiscal anarchy brought about by the policy of "economism" could only serve to undermine the conditions in which the Cultural Revolution could be successfully carried out.

In addition to these efforts, party bureaucrats also sought to organize, covertly, a walkout strike of cadres, technicians, and workers still loyal to the old party leadership. Their overall objective was to paralyze the city, cutting off its power and water supply, disrupting its transportation system, halting production in factories, inducing anarchy in its financial institutions, and thus in a dramatic manner show that the Cultural Revolution could not continue without incurring extraordinarily high costs.

The response of Shanghai's rebel forces to this crisis was the January Revolution. Unexpectedly, this period of hastily improvised emergency measures, designed to break the city-wide paralysis, developed into the central experience of the city's Cultural Revolution.

The political act that launched the January Revolution took place in the office of Shanghai's influential party newspaper, *Wenhuipao,* early in January. A group of journalists and staff workers seized control of the newspaper on January 3, claiming it as the mouthpiece of rebel workers and students.[3] Their act was not a random one; it had been coordinated with the broader national strategy of the central leadership in Peking and with the activities of local rebel organizations. On January 1 the *Wenhuipao* rebel group had sent a delegation to consult with the Cultural Revolution Group in Peking and had received Premier Chou En-lai's approval of their plan to seize power at the *Wenhuipao.* The delegation also established a permanent liaison center at the office of the Cultural Revolution Group in order to facilitate direct communication between the party center and Shanghai.[4]

A striking feature of the January Revolution in Shanghai was the presence, from its very early stages, of representatives from the central leadership in Peking. Within a day of the *Wenhuipao* take-over, Chang Ch'un-ch'iao and Yao Wen-yuan, of the Cultural Revolution Group, had arrived in Shanghai to rally rebel forces to cope with the emergency in the city. Although Chang and Yao, with the approval of Mao, assumed leadership of the rebel forces later in the month, it seems clear that their initial dispatch was conceived of rather as an emergency measure, to cope with the unexpected crisis in Shanghai. Their immediate concern was to revive the city from the state of near-collapse brought on by the strike. "In the early stage of the 'seizure of power' in Shanghai, we never thought of the 'capture of power' nor did we use the words 'January Revolution,' " recalled Chang Ch'un-ch'iao. "What was uppermost in our minds was what we were going to do. After discussing the situation as a whole, we set about putting the vital departments such as the docks, railway stations, waterworks, power plants, broadcasting stations, postal offices and banks under our control."[5] With so large a percentage of the city's cadres and industrial technicians, as well as hundreds of thousands of moderate workers, out on strike, Chang and Yao instinctively turned for support in this task toward workers and cadres in the rebel faction, led by the Workers' Rebel Headquarters, and to Red Guard student groups.

Two days after the take-over of the *Wenhuipao*, with the approval of Mao and the party center, the newspaper published its historic "Message to All the People of Shanghai." Drafted and signed by the Workers' Rebel Headquarters and eleven other rebel mass organizations, the "Message" fired the opening salvo of the January Revolution: "Comrades, revolutionary workers! . . . Whose interests are you serving? . . . Wake up quickly, return to your post in production and return to the proletarian revolutionary line. We, comrades of the revolutionary rebel groups, will certainly warmly welcome you back to make revolution with us. . . ."[6]

The events of the January Revolution followed in a rapid series of bold and creative political actions. On January 6, Chang Ch'un-ch'iao presided over a mass televised rally of over one million participants at People's Square at which a number of officials were stripped of their authority and instructed to write confessions. Among these were First Secretary Ch'en P'ei-hsien, Mayor Ts'ao Ti-ch'iu, two secretaries of the East China Bureau (Wei Wen-po and Han Che-yi), and all members of the standing committee of the Municipal Party Committee (among them Ma T'ien-shui, Wang Yi-p'ing, Liang Kuo-p'in, and Wang Shao-yung). All other party officials and functionaries were ordered to continue with their customary work, albeit under the direct supervision of the Workers' Rebel Headguarters.

The joint publication on January 9 of the "Urgent Notice" by *Wenhuipao* and a radicalized *Liberation Daily* reported to the citizens of Shanghai the rapid flow of events and issued specific instructions for coordinated city-wide measures to curb the crisis. An immediate pickup of the "Urgent Notice" by the national newspapers and the Central Radio Station in Peking (which had broadcast the "Message to All the Shanghai People" a few days earlier) and the news that the "Notice" had been personally approved by Mao enhanced the legitimacy and authority of the Shanghai rebel leadership. The "Notice" stressed the crisis situation in Shanghai. It reported a city-wide "breakdown in factory production and railway and road traffic." The Shanghai harbor had been disrupted and dockers incited to stop work. Cadres in charge of the city's financial institutions had caused a serious run on the banks by "arbitrarily increasing wages and material benefits" for workers and by "granting all kinds of allowances and subsides without limit" and encouraged workers to leave their factories "to exchange revolutionary experience" in the fashion of the youthful Red Guards. Public buildings and facilities in Shanghai had even been offered up by cadres to workers as new housing allotments, "stirring people to take over public buildings by force." The "Urgent Notice" therefore issued the following instructions to the people of Shanghai:

1. Rebel workers and cadres, including student members of rebel organizations, were to follow Mao's instruction to "grasp revolution and promote production" and remain "fast at their production posts." They were urged to "appeal to all revolutionary rebels throughout the country" to persuade Shanghai workers, cadres, staff members of enterprises and apprentices "who are exchanging revolutionary experience in other parts of the country to return to Shanghai immediately." All certificates which authorized these departures for exchanging revolutionary experience were declared "null and void."

2. The circulating funds of all government offices, organizations, and financial institutions were frozen, with the exception of what was "necessary expenditure on production, wages, the Cultural Revolution, office administration," and other "appropriate purposes." Questions concerning wage adjustment, back pay, and other material benefits detracted from the issues of the Cultural Revolution and were to be dealt with later. Higher wages were not to be given to students for work in factories because this "stirred up dissatisfaction among the workers" and strained the worker-student alliance.

3. Public buildings and houses that had been confiscated from capitalists were not to be seized by workers. Those who had incited workers to seize public buildings were to be punished according to the law, and those who had moved in illegally were to move out within a week's time.

4. Lastly, those who sought to undermine the Cultural Revolution by sabotaging production were to be arrested by the Public Security Bureau [police department], and all offenses involving criminal assault, robbery, or larceny were similarly accountable to the law.

The "Urgent Notice" was signed by the Shanghai Workers' Rebel Headquarters along with thirty-one other rebel organizations, many of which were liaison centers of Red Guard units from other cities in China.[7]

In order to provide central coordination for the task of restoring the city's functions, establishment of a new city-wide leadership body was an urgent priority. On January 8 a rebel organ was set up to take charge of the economic management of the city. This new leadership body consisted of fifty representatives nominated by the Workers' Rebel Headquarters from factories, the municipal finance bureau, and the economics departments of Shanghai universities. The new organ, called the Fighting Line Command, was described as a "brand-new organization . . . fundamentally different from the original organs in charge of the economic programs under the Shanghai Municipal People's Council."[8] Its primary characteristic, according to newspaper accounts at the time, was that it was a nonbureaucratic administrative structure which was revolutionary and which "put politics in command." As a *Hsinhua* correspondent described it, "It is not a cumbersome and unwieldy organization divided into bureaus, departments, sections and subsections" and its staff "is not even as large as that of a section of certain departments of the former Municipal People's Council. Instead of confining themselves all day long to their office, poring over documents, listening to summary reports, or making telephone calls, the staff of this new organization goes deep among the masses to solve problems where they are located and do things after consulting with the masses."[9] With its nonbureaucratic operational style, its compact size, and its emphasis on "on-the-spot" problem solving, the new municipal organ was a prototype of the reformed administrative structures later to be born out of the Cultural Revolution.

How did the Shanghai rebels structure their new administrative organ? The new municipal body was divided into four sections: a steering committee, a propaganda section, a liaison section, and a section in charge of secretarial work. The steering committee was made up of representatives of the Workers' Rebel Headquarters and staff members from the economic bureaus of the former municipal government. This "nucleus group" formulated the overall strategy for the Fighting Line Command and was the decision-making organ. The propaganda section published a newssheet that disseminated information and new policies to the public at large. The liaison section sent its staff into factories, plants, transportation centers, and other basic-level units "to conduct investigation and study," giving whatever assistance was necessary to the workers' committees that ran the factories and to other basic-level units.

The overall breadth of responsibility assumed by the Fighting Line Command apparently included the whole of Shanghai's complex industrial, marketing, and transportation systems. According to *Hsinhua* news reports, this responsibility was borne by industrial workers, lower- and middle-level cadres, radical economics students, and staff personnel from the city's finance bureau who had had no previous experience in city-wide economic management.

The Shanghai Railways Station, the biggest rail junction in East China, was one of the most strategic municipal facilities that Shanghai rebels first sought to restore to normal function. Since December 30 all rail transportation had been completely paralyzed, including the two main rail lines linking Shanghai with Hangchow and the important industrial city, Nanking. All the controls in the control office of the railway station had been switched off. All train conductors had left their jobs to join the strike, apparently bribed by the Shanghai Municipal Party Committee which allegedly handed over thirty million yuan to the railway administration to distribute to workers as wage hikes or bonus pay.[10]

On January 9 rebel workers sent a twelve-member delegation of rail workers with previous experience in train control to assume management of the control office. There they ordered the chief controller to resume work under their supervision. They recruited as many train conductors as would join their ranks and began the work of disentangling the clogged rail lines and directing train movement. The rebel train workers then hastily formed a political alliance of the eight different railway workers' rebel groups involved in the seizure of power and "elected a leading body by general elections modeled on that of the Paris Commune, and set up a command office to direct the labor force."[11]

The significance of the broad rank-and-file workers' participation in the new administrative structure impressed the *Hsinhua* correspondent covering the event, who commented: "The establishment of new, revolutionary order required an enormous amount of organization and this was all done by those who were formerly looked down upon as 'nobodies' such as train conductors, engine-drivers, switchmen, signal-men, lathe-turners, ticket inspectors. The leader of the railway rebel organization is an ordinary bench-worker, who was branded as a 'counterrevolutionary' for writing the first poster to expose the party people in authority in his factory."[12]

The rebel workers, with the assistance of thousands of college students who manned the ticket booths and entry points to train platforms, succeeded in clearing the lines and in getting the rolling stock moving again. One outcome of reopening the rail lines was that critically needed coal could be transported once again to waiting factories and power plants in Shanghai; thus the fuel crisis caused by the strike, in a city overwhelmingly dependent on coal as its source of energy, was overcome.

Another success for the rebel forces was at the Shanghai docks. Power seizure there followed similar lines as that at the railway station. Since late December, the wharves had been at a standstill as a result of the wave of "economism" organized by the party machine, which had given raises and bonuses to workers at the harbor. Large numbers of longshoremen and dock workers had left their jobs. As ships of various national flags lay moored in the harbor, waiting with growing impatience for their cargoes to be unloaded, China's principal port quickly became congested, its wharves jammed with freight. On January 2, however, a mass meeting of dock workers was held by the Revolutionary Rebel Detachment of the Workers of the 5th District to discuss the crisis situation at the harbor. Speeches were delivered condemning the party authorities responsible for the mess. "They want to buy us over with money in order to save their offices," said one dock worker who had been a coolie before liberation. "This would be more difficult than ascending to heaven."[13] Rebel leaders organized dockers, many of whom were recently illiterate, to write posters denouncing the party authorities.

In an effort to get Scarlet Guard workers to return to their posts, a detachment of rebel dock workers was reported to have sped out of Shanghai and caught up with and boarded a ship steaming up the Yangtze River. It had been commandeered by dockers who left their posts to exchange revolutionary experiences. Fighting broke out between the rebel dock workers and the strikers, but after several days of earnest effort the rebels managed to persuade the strikers to return to their jobs, and trucks were sent to carry the workers back to Shanghai.

Because so many of the skilled dock workers had left their loading machines, rebel workers attempting to move cargo relied on makeshift measures, using such primitive loading devices as handcarts and wheelbarrows. Encouraged by the support given by Peking to rebel activities in Shanghai, rebel dock workers of the 5th District of the Shanghai Harbor Bureau finally began on January 11, to seize "all party, government and financial powers" and took control of the harbor administration. They then sought to reopen the wharves as quickly as possible with the help of tens of thousands of volunteer students and teachers from practically all of the secondary schools in Shanghai. Chang Ch'un-ch'iao, who went frequently to inspect the progress at the wharves and to talk with rebel dockers and students, mentioned in a later speech being particularly impressed by the sight of these high-school students busy at the piers helping to load and unload cargo. Although rebel dockers were reported to have worked sixteen- to twenty-four-hour shifts nonstop, it was not until January 21 that the harbor returned to a state approaching normal operations.

In establishing new political organs during the January Revolution, the historical model workers cited was the Paris Commune of 1871.[14] The mood of the January Revolution was indeed close to that which surrounded the emergence of the two historic prototypes of workers' self-government—the Paris Commune and the workers' councils of the October Revolution of 1917. The democratic idealism that fired the vision of the founders of the Paris Commune echoes in the words with which Shanghai workers described their committees. As workers in one factory wrote, their committee was "a political committee, production committee, and workers' committee self-consciously organized by the masses. . . . It is a committe born of the full election system of the Paris Commune."[15]

The fiercely antibureaucratic spirit that characterized the Paris Commune and the Russian Soviets of 1917 also had its parallel in the January Revolution. Russian workers of the October Revolution demanded that all cadres "be obliged to perform annually at least three months of physical labor in the factories, mills, or mines, or coal pits," and live "under the same conditions as the workers did."[16] Their call for elected councils of workers to manage factories and their staunch opposition to the establishment of "one-man management" were also revived by Chinese workers who criticized their former management system, one directly adapted from the Russian "one-man management" system.[17] Workers of the Shanghai Glass Machine Plant wrote:

> Over thousands of years, the ideology of the exploiting classes has ruled the minds of the people.

Even down to this day, the idea of lording it over the people by becoming a government official is still entrenched in the minds of some people. They are immensely interested in becoming bureaucrats. During the past 17 years since the Liberation, power-holders within the Party who take the capitalist road have treated the masses as "babies" and themselves as "wise old men." They practiced "tutelage by cadres" and pursued an "obscurantist policy." As a result, some industrial and mining enterprises, while appearing to be "State-operated" and "socialist in form" have essentially become capitalist in character. The volcano has finally erupted! The "revolution and production committee" has appeared with a brand-new outlook. Its members remain fast at their production post. Along with the masses, they are ordinary laborers whose faces are stained with grease and whose bodies smell of oil. Bourgeois aristocrats! Do you want to take advantage of us people of tough bones? You are dreaming.[18]

It was the broadness of scale of the power seizure by workers and lower- and middle-level cadres that lay at the heart of the January Revolution's significance to Shanghai's working class. By the latter part of January, the strike had been broken and this attempt to sabotage the Cultural Revolution defeated. In expressing his appreciation for the deeds of the Shanghai working class during the January Revolution, Mao, who understood well the spirit and significance of the revolution, said to a group of foreign visitors in Peking in the summer of 1967, the "January Storm, for instance, was raised by the workers of Shanghai. Since then workers and peasants all over the country have arisen." Intellectuals and students, Mao pointed out, had launched the first phases of the Cultural Revolution through their criticism of the "bourgeois reactionary line," but the "power seizures in the January Storm were accomplished by the masters of our time."[19]

Toward a New Order

In contrast to the period immediately preceding the Cultural Revolution, the most striking change brought to Shanghai by the January Revolution was a remarkable advance in the degree of popular familiarity with and participation in the higher levels of municipal politics. At the height of the Liuist period, the Shanghai polity had begun to develop signs of considerable alienation of the government from the lives of its ordinary citizens.[20] It had revealed tendencies toward close identity of the party with the state, rule by bureaucrats increasingly detached from the masses and from productive labor, and a lack of concern for promoting popular participation in the critical processes of the polity. The "storm" in Shanghai repudiated these tendencies which, left unchecked, would have led to a form of bureaucratic socialism similar to that of the Soviet Union. The storm awakened the political aspirations of Shanghai's citizens. The seizures of power gave them direct practice in the exercise of state power and an unparalleled degree of participatory democracy.

The following section will attempt to elucidate briefly the significance and purpose of the Paris Commune symbol as it was initially raised in the Cultural Revolution, and to understand the fate of the symbol when, in the difficult days following the January Storm, the citizens of Shanghai attempted to transform their vision into reality.

The Paris Commune, to which there was little reference in Mao's theoretical writings before 1957, received its first significant attention in the context of the widening Sino-Soviet rift that followed the Great Leap Forward. Between 1958 and 1964 it emerged prominently in Chinese critiques of the Soviet Union as a symbol of the continuing necessity for armed revolutionary struggle in contrast to the Soviet path of "peaceful evolution." In 1966, however, as the atmosphere of political crisis preceding the Cultural Revolution heightened, there was a sudden and dramatic development in the interpretation of this symbol, a shifting of emphasis away from the context of the international Communist movement toward the relevance of the Paris Commune as a model for political reform directly applicable within Chinese society itself.[21]

By far the most significant theoretical development of this second interpretation was the essay "The Great Lesson of the Paris Commune" published in *Red Flag*, April 1966, by the historian Cheng Chih-szu. While Cheng's essay dutifully pays its respects to the classical Marxist interpretation of the commune, areas where the interpretation is strikingly original reveal the perspective from which the Chinese were reexamining the commune at this stage in their own history. Distinctive in Cheng's analysis of the commune is his attempt to evaluate it in terms of the Chinese mass-line experience, leading him to place the greatest emphasis on the integration of government officials and the masses in the commune over all its other features. Cheng hailed the commune for having "done away with all the privileges of state functionaries. We know that states ruled by the exploiting classes invariably offer their officials choice conditions and many privileges so as to turn them into overlords riding roughshod over the people. Sitting in their high positions, enjoying lucrative salaries and bullying the people—such is the picture of the officials of the exploiting classes."[22] For Cheng, at the heart of the significance of the Paris Commune was the existence of popular control over every aspect of political life:

> The masses were the real masters of the Paris Commune. While the Commune was in being the masses were organized on a wide scale and they discussed important state matters within their respective organizations. Each day around 20,000 activists attended club meetings where they made proposals or advanced critical opinions on social and political

matters great and small. They also made their wishes
and demands known through articles and letters to
the revolutionary newspapers and journals. This
revolutionary enthusiasm and initiative of the masses
was the source of the Commune's strength.[23]

A major portion of Cheng's essay deals with the specific
measures through which the Paris Commune achieved its
high level of popular control over the government. He
describes the commune's election system, by which all posts
were filled on election based on universal suffrage, and the
citizens' right to recall these officials at any time. A second
method developed by the commune to prevent government
officials from becoming a privileged stratum alienated from
the people was the practice of limiting government salaries
to the same level as those received by ordinary workers. In
the Paris Commune, Cheng wrote, the fixing of wages
" 'sufficient to maintain the well-being and dignity of the
one who carries out its functions' [at the wage level of
skilled workers] turned the conduct of state affairs simply
into one of a worker's duties and transformed functionaries
into workers operating 'special tools.' "[24]

For Cheng, however, the interest of these methods is more
than purely historical. The system of election and recall,
particularly, are clearly seen by him as models directly
relevant to Chinese society in its current stage of transition.
As he concludes unequivocally, "The provisions for the
replacing and recalling of elected representatives who betrayed the interests of the people were not empty words."[25]
The fact that rebel groups in several cities attempted in early
1967 to establish governments incorporating the system of
election, recall, and limited government salaries is testimony
to the fact that Cheng's sense of the applicability of these
aspects of the Paris Commune to China had come to be
shared by many others at that time.

A final and most intriguing aspect of Cheng Chih-szu's
study of the Paris Commune and its significance for the
Chinese Revolution is the ambiguity of his reference to the

structure and role of the Communist party. Cheng accepted the Marxist interpretation that the fundamental cause of the crushing defeat of the Paris Commune was the fact that Marxist revolutionary theory had not achieved a dominant position in the Parisian workers' movement. In *The Civil War in France* Marx had chided the leaders of the Paris workers' insurrection for not effectively mobilizing the armed forces of the Parisian working class, the National Guards, to deal powerfully with the French bourgeoisie and ruthlessly suppress the counterrevolution by marching on to Versailles while M. Thiers was still recruiting his army. Instead the anarchist-led Central Committee, Paris's provisional government, busied itself in preparing for the election of the commune and allowed Thiers the necessary time to strengthen the forces of reaction in Versailles.[26] Lenin, commenting on the same point, went on to draw from the defeat of the Paris Commune the lesson that a powerful proletarian state could only be consolidated through a highly centralized and tightly disciplined vanguard party that could effectively exercise the dictatorship of the proletariat on behalf of the working class.[27]

Cheng, however, does not refer to Lenin's concept of the vanguard party in analyzing the defeat of the Paris Commune. Instead of reiterating the need for a Bolshevik-type party organization, with its widely known tendencies for ironclad centralism and élitism, Cheng uses the more ambiguous phrase "Marxist political party": "They pointed out that because the commune did not have the leadership of a Marxist political party and the guidance of Marxist theory, it was therefore not a complete or mature proletarian dictatorship."[28] This ambiguity, in the context of his discussion of the Paris Commune, suggested a degree of doubt about the Leninist party, which had provided no direct method for the people to elect their own leaders or effective checks to prevent authoritarian abuses of power.

The publication of Cheng Chih-szu's article in *Red Flag* in the critical weeks preceding the outbreak of the Cultural

Revolution at Peking University can only have meant that a significant portion of the early Cultural Revolution leadership (*Red Flag* editor Chen Po-ta, for example) was seriously advocating application of the Paris Commune as a model for political reform in China. Mao's own public comments on the Paris Commune pointed directly to its relevance for the Cultural Revolution, and Article 9 of the definitive "Sixteen Points" policy statement for the Cultural Revolution passed by the Central Committee reiterated the themes developed in the *Red Flag* essay and raised the Paris Commune as a model political form:

> It is necessary to institute a system of general elections, like that of the Paris Commune, for electing members of the cultural revolutionary groups and committees and delegates to the cultural revolutionary congresses. The lists of candidates should be put forward by the revolutionary masses after full discussion and the election should be held after the masses have discussed the lists over and over again.
>
> The masses are entitled at any time to criticize members of the cultural revolutionary groups and committees and delegates elected to the cultural revolutionary congresses. If these members or delegates prove incompetent, they can be replaced through election or recalled by the masses after discussion.[29]

Yet in writings on the Paris Commune published in this period, subtle variations in interpretation were visible. It was Wang Li—the young coeditor of *Red Flag* who would later be purged from the Cultural Revolution Group as a leader of an ultraleft faction—who coauthored with Chia Yi-hsueh and Li Hsin one of the most politically provocative interpretations of the Paris Commune and its relevance for the Cultural Revolution:

> The masses have the right to criticize and raise suggestions about Party and state policies and every aspect of the state apparatus. *The masses have the*

*right to criticize leading cadres at all levels no matter
how meritorious their service, how high their position or how senior their qualifications* [emphasis
added]. A system of general elections, like that of
the Paris Commune, is [sic] introduced without exception for all organs of power leading the cultural
revolution. The masses have the power to replace
through election or recall any elected member at
any time.

Wang Li's statement, published in *Red Flag* in December
1966, later provided the theoretical basis for the rise of an
ultraleft trend of thought which found its crystallization in
the popular Red Guard slogan "Suspect all, overthrow all."

Perhaps the most systematic presentation of the ultraleft
interpretation of the Paris Commune can be found in a
pamphlet published in January 1968 by the Hunan province
anarchist collective, the *Shengwulien*, which called for the
formation of a Hunan commune that could be part of a
national Chinese People's Commune.[30] According to their
interpretation, the dictatorship of the proletariat had never
been established in China. Moreover, sixteen years of the
People's Republic had led to the formation of a "new
bureaucratic bourgeoisie" who constituted ninety percent of
China's leading party and state officials. This "red capitalist class," led by no other than Chou En-lai, had to be overthrown by the armed masses because they "impeded the
progress of history"; and a new proletarian state, modeled
directly on the Paris Commune, was to be constructed after
the "smashing" of the old bureaucratic-military apparatus.

Thus, for the ultraleft, the purpose of the Great Proletarian Cultural Revolution was to establish for the first
time the dictatorship of the proletariat in China. The ultraleft carried the ideas of the Paris Commune to their extreme
conclusion, calling for a mechanical application of the
commune model in China. In order to establish the "Chinese People's Commune," the *Shengwulien* called for the
violent overthrow of the People's Republic through a
strategy of "protracted people's revolutionary warfare."

The Founding of the
Shanghai People's Commune

It is not surprising that the January Revolution in Shanghai, so deeply infused with the enthusiasm that swept China in the early stages of the Cultural Revolution, gave rise to a popular movement to establish a new municipal government along similar lines as that of the Paris Commune of 1871. But while certain similarities existed in the moods of the Paris Commune and the January Revolution, important historical and cultural differences separated the two workers' struggles for emancipation. The Paris Commune was erected as a crisis government to defend Paris from the Prussian Army which stood poised for attack before the gates of Paris. Threat of imminent conquest, and anger stirred up against the French bourgeoisie for its repeated attempts to capitulate, greatly reinforced a sense of solidarity among citizens of Paris. Moreover, it encouraged the formation of a critical alliance between the Parisian working class and petty bourgeoisie, both of whose interests would have suffered the most as the result of surrender to Bismarck. In Shanghai, however, this sense of unity born of resistance to foreign invasion was lacking.

Factionalism, moreover, could not be controlled once the Cultural Revolution began, and became rampant in the workers' movement following the brief period of rebel unity during the January seizures of power. This factionalism worked to undermine attempts in Shanghai to found a new government modeled after the Paris Commune. By the third week in January, factional strife had resumed in Shanghai, this time with the rebel groups jostling for positions vacated by toppled party officials. The Workers' Rebel Headquarters had been a confederation of smaller groupings of workers' rebel organizations from hundreds of factories and plants all over the city, each with its own leadership and following of workers. These workers' rebel factions, led by dynamic young workers and worker cadres, had been able to band together in alliance when they were branded as counterrevolutionaries by the old Municipal Party Committee and when confronted with the crisis of the walkout strike and "economism." But once Shanghai was back in running order and the Municipal Party Committee had been overthrown, reasons for cooperation began to recede and petty jealousies and ambitions were aroused. Severe infighting broke out in their ranks and the leadership coalition within the Workers' Rebel Headquarters soon fell apart.

To compound the problems created by factionalism, a mood of retaliation swept over the city against those who had not participated in the January Storm. Starting from mid-January and lasting to the end of the month, party officials were driven every day through the streets of Shanghai in open trucks with placards hung over their heads and surrounded by fifty or more chanting rebel workers and Red Guards. Rebel hostility was extended even to the moderate and conservative workers, technical and managerial personnel who had followed these party officials on the walkout strike. Excluded from participation in the new leadership organs and subjected to this rebel distrust, nearly half of Shanghai's working class and most of its technical, administrative, and managerial personnel remained alienated from the new power constellation. Moreover, many leading party officials, ordered to return to their posts under rebel supervision, continued to oppose the spirit of the Cultural Revolution and sought to benefit from the new factional strife.[31]

The factionalism in Shanghai was to some extent exacerbated by the simultaneous appearance of factions in the party center leading the Cultural Revolution in Peking, with whom various local groups aligned. It is clear, for example, that while leaders like Wang Li, Kuan Feng, Mu Hsin, Lin Chieh, Ch'i Pen-yü, Chiang Ch'ing, and Chen Po-ta, all members of the Cultural Revolution Group, pushed for the most radical outcome in Shanghai, key national leaders like Chou En-lai, alarmed by the fact that virtually all of Shanghai's leading municipal cadres had been overthrown by the seizures of power, sought instead to check the excesses of the January Revolution.

While it is difficult to ascertain just what Mao's own position was in these critical days after the January Revolution, it is likely that his sentiments stood between those of Chou En-lai and his wife Chiang Ch'ing, who was among the most outspoken of the radicals in Peking. Mao was disturbed both by the sweeping overthrow of established party leaders in Shanghai and by the emergence of the ultraleft trend of thought "suspect all, overthrow all." Yet he was committed to the broad underlying principles of the Paris Commune as interpreted by Marx and Lenin. In keeping with his theoretical essay "On Practice" and its emphasis on the necessity of "leaps" from practice to theory, and from theory back to practice, Mao probably wanted to see what would come of the experiment to apply the Paris Commune model in China. He sought a new form of proletarian government suitable for China, which would emerge through radical experimentation that allowed for the creative interaction of theory with the revolutionary practice of the masses.

The breakdown of rebel unity, emergent splits in the national leadership coalition, and continued opposition of deposed party officials and their followers placed enormous pressures on Chang Ch'un-ch'iao and Yao Wen-yuan, who emerged as the highest-ranking party leaders in Shanghai after the January seizures of power. Chang, whose stated primary concern in the seizures of power was to restore Shanghai's vital functions, from this time concentrated his energies on the task of political consolidation. This necessarily began to direct him to curb some of the extremes of the January Revolution so that the base of support for the emerging new order would be broadened, especially among key administrators and managerial personnel. Chang's close ties with Mao, stemming from the assistance he and Yao Wen-yuan had given Mao in launching the Cultural Revolution from Shanghai, facilitated his exercise of leadership in these weeks following the January Storm.[32]

Rather than back away from the movement to establish a Shanghai Commune, which men of lesser leadership talent and less broadness of political vision might have been tempted to do, Chang's brilliance was to identify himself with the idea of establishing a commune, and in this manner outmaneuver a rising ultraleft faction. As the first steps in preparation for the establishment of the Shanghai Commune, Chang set out to forge a "great alliance of proletarian revolutionaries" to build the broadest base of rebel support for the commune and to check the factional strife. Meeting frequently with leaders of Red Guard organizations and workers' rebel mass organizations, he soon managed to weave together the beginnings of a "great alliance." It included young worker cadres like Wang Hung-wen of the Workers' Rebel Headquarters, whose support he had enjoyed since the Anting Incident in November 1966, and Red Guard groups from Shanghai (including a number of liaison centers representing Red Guard organizations based in Peking, Wuhan, Tientsin, Harbin, and Sian). Also of critical importance was support from Shanghai's leading newspapers and the commanders of the Shanghai garrison of the People's Liberation Army, called on by Peking to support the Left.

The challenge presented to Chang by opposing factions, however, was immense. Although he had sought to avoid the limelight and instead work quietly in the background, his position as the highest-ranking party official and his reputation as a leader of national standing quickly gave rise to resentment and jealousy among ambitious local rebel leaders and to suspicion among Red Guards influenced by the ultraleft trend of thought, "Suspect all, overthrow all."[33]

The most powerful and persistent opposition to Chang and the Shanghai Commune were the rebel workers' organizations led by Keng Chin-chang and Ch'en Hung-kang. Both Keng and Ch'en were party members and were leaders in the rebel coalition which made up the Workers' Rebel Headquarters before the January Revolution. The First, Second, and Third regiments of the Northern Expedition, which Keng Chin-chang led, had gained a reputation as the most militant and assertively independent of the workers' factions in the Workers' Rebel Headquarters and were responsible for much of the violence at Kanping Road and later at the Battle of Kunshan. Following the January seizures of power, the First, Second, and Third regiments split away from the Workers' Rebel Headquarters in a bold bid for city-wide leadership. Among their important Red Guard allies was the Shanghai Liaison Center of the Tsinghua University Chingkangshan Headquarters, which by that time was intimately involved with Wang Li and the rising "ultraleft."[34] Since January 6 the deposed party chieftains, Ch'en P'ei-hsien, Ts'ao Ti-ch'iu, and almost the entire Standing Committee of the Municipal Party Committee had been residing in a large mansion at 922 Huashan Road, the new headquarters of the Second Regiment. Although they were held there as hostages, it seems conceivable, as Chang Ch'un-ch'iao charged, that Keng compromised himself to these deposed party officials in order to gain their assistance in his attempt to overthrow Chang and Yao and discredit the Workers' Rebel Headquarters to become the dominant figure in Shanghai.

By February, Keng Chin-chang claimed control of seven municipal departments of the city bureaucracy as well as four of the ten municipal districts. He had built the First and Second regiments from 500 to 520,000 workers in a little more than a month's time. He had established his own "great alliance" with fourteen separate Red Guard and workers' mass organizations.[35]

During the latter part of January and the first week of February there were five reported attempts by these rebel workers' and Red Guard groups to seize control of the offices of the Municipal Party Committee and the Municipal People's Council in their bid for power and authority.[36]

None of these attempts were recognized by Chang Ch'un-ch'iao, nor were they acknowledged in Peking. Chang proceeded with his plans for the Shanghai Commune and called a preparatory meeting to convene on January 26. Delegates from all rebel workers' organizations and Red Guard groups were invited to participate in this meeting which was to lay the foundation for the Shanghai Commune. Keng, sensing he would be excluded from playing a leading role, brought his workers from the Second Regiment and disrupted the meeting. Then, on January 30 and 31, he led the Second Regiment in lightning raids against the South Shanghai branch of the Workers' Rebel Headquarters, in an attempt to squash the rebel group which blocked his rise to power in Shanghai. These attacks were reported to have led to serious fighting, but the Workers' Rebel Headquarters succeeded in repelling the brunt of Keng's assault.[37]

In the midst of the most intense battering from opposing factions, Chang pushed through plans for the commune and announced the founding of the Shanghai People's Commune on February 5. The Shanghai Commune was proclaimed as a new organizational form, "a local organ of the proletarian dictatorship" based on the "system of centralized democracy taught by Chairman Mao." The Provisional Committee, which was to temporarily lead the commune, was described as a "3-in-1 alliance" of representatives chosen from rebel mass organizations, commanding officers of the PLA garrison stationed in Shanghai, and leading cadres—Chang Ch'un-ch'iao and his lieutenant, Yao Wen-yuan. The responsibility of the Provisional Committee was to assume full executive and legislative powers from the defunct Shanghai Municipal Party Committee and Municipal People's Council. At an appropriate time, it was to call and administer a municipal election to elect members of the Formal Committee. Following the election of the Formal Committee of the Shanghai People's Commune, the Provisional Committee was to disband.[38]

In the "Declaration of the Shanghai People's Commune,"

the new municipal leaders issued and reaffirmed the mass line as the fundamental policy of the new city government. The Shanghai Commune, it declared,

> must hold high the great red banner of Mao Tse-tung Thought, give prominence to politics, resolutely carry out the mass line laid down by Chairman Mao, implement the working method "from the masses, to the masses," trust the masses, rely on the masses, mobilize the masses, respect the creative spirit of the masses, accept the supervision of the masses and listen to the opinion and advice of the masses. All personnel of the Shanghai People's Commune have as their duty to serve the people, but absolutely have no right to become officials and squires. Whoever departs from the masses, acts for his own individual interests, suppresses the masses, or acts arbitrarily must be replaced or eliminated.[39]

At the time of its inauguration, nearly half of Shanghai's rebels, belonging to twenty-five mass organizations, still stood outside the Shanghai Commune in defiant opposition. In a gesture designed to overcome factional rivalry and jealousy, Chang Ch'un-ch'iao, as First Secretary of the Shanghai Commune, nevertheless made provisions in the Commune's charter that "approved" delegates of these twenty-five mass organizations could sit in the commune's Presidium at the Inaugural Meeting along with delegates from the thirty-eight "proposing" units. He further stipulated that the Shanghai Commune must remain open to all rebel mass organizations, though only "after subjecting them to gradual stages of screening."[40] Even when the "Declaration of the Shanghai People's Commune" was published in *Wenhuipao*, Chang gave discreet instructions not to publish the list of names of the proposing units in the "Declaration." In this manner Chang sought to ensure the broadest base of rebel support for the commune, while at the same time isolating Keng and Ch'en from their base of support.

The establishment of the Shanghai People's Commune can be seen as a success for Chang, since he did set up a government that ultimately outlived Keng's rival headquarters and received central support. The close identity of the commune with Chang Ch'un-ch'iao and the Workers' Rebel Headquarters, however, gave it the appearance of being a factional power center.[41] Also, as we shall see, the influences of the differing political cultures and historical circumstances separating the Paris Commune of 1871 from the events in China would prove decisive in the Chinese attempt to remake their state system.

THE LIMITS OF REBELLION

The political task of leading the Cultural Revolution from Peking after the January Revolution was not an enviable one. For it required extraordinary powers of discernment to grasp the complex currents and countercurrents that lashed powerfully across the nation in the wake of the upsurge of the Shanghai working class. In every province and every municipality, rebels rose up to seize power from stubbornly entrenched party officials in provincial and municipal party committees. However, since they lacked the political sophistication and maturity of the Shanghai workers, their attempts to seize power led to widespread civil chaos and disorder. Massive organizations of students and workers, linked with embattled cliques and factions within party and state bureaucracies, threw their tentacles across the nation in a frantic search for factional alliances to bolster their local power and prestige.

In January, when repeated factional clashes and battles were bringing the nation precariously close to the brink of civil war, divisions of the People's Liberation Army were called in for the first time to support the rebels and avert large-scale, quasi-military battles between opposing factions. Not only had it become exceedingly difficult to disentangle the myriad threads of factional alliances spun out by mass organizations and cliques at every level throughout the land, it had also grown nearly impossible to distinguish ultraleftists from leftists, conservatives from leftists, and unrepentant revisionists from revolutionary cadres. Everybody seemed to call themselves "rebels" and fought under the same political slogans. Moreover, uprisings in other municipalities were sometimes accompanied by destruction of state property and valuable cultural treasures, bloodletting, even loss of life, and humiliation of party and state officials.

What Mao thought and how he reacted as the Cultural Revolution went through its various phases can only be the subject of speculation. But as his 1970 interview with Edgar Snow suggests, the degree of violence and chaos unleashed by the rebel movement at different points seems to have been unanticipated by Mao and even to have struck him with a certain sense of dismay and shock. Whether the first of such reactions came in response to the above events or not is difficult to know, but in February 1967, on the heels of the first introduction of PLA units to maintain order in turbulent power seizures, a striking new element appeared in editorials of the leading newspapers and journals. On February 1, *Red Flag*, which in the preceding months had enthusiastically urged wide-scale mass assaults on party committees, abruptly issued a warning to rebel forces to maintain "strict proletarian discipline" and to guard against excesses of "ultra-democracy," "anarchism," the "mountain-stronghold mentality," and the "small group mentality."[42] Another editorial voiced a similar call for restraint: "To regard all persons in authority as untrustworthy is wrong . . . to oppose, exclude, and overthrow all indiscriminately runs counter to the class viewpoint of Marxism-Leninism, Mao-tsetung Thought."[43]

For the next few months, a concern for maintaining civil

order figured prominently in the press. This seems to indicate that at this point, as in later phases of the Cultural Revolution, Mao's response to anarchic disorder and factional violence was to pull back from his most radical statements and restrain extremists of the right and left. Disturbed by the unexpectedly violent course of events in seizures of power in certain parts of the country, Mao seems to have become apprehensive that out-and-out rebellion against all authority would sweep away the very underpinnings of the nation's social order.

At the same time, the crisis of authority that erupted in China in the wake of the January Revolution may be seen as a manifestation of certain critical problems in the early definitions of the Cultural Revolution. Article 5 of the "Sixteen Points" clearly stated that ninety-five percent of the cadres were basically good, but it provided no clear guidelines on how to determine which cadres were among the five percent who were to be overthrown. The "Sixteen Points" merely said, "In the course of normal and full debate, the masses will affirm what is right, correct what is wrong and gradually reach unanimity."[44]

This placed great confidence in the collective wisdom of the masses, the prerequisite for political democracy. But the Chinese masses, as masses elsewhere, are made up of highly diverse and complexly motivated individuals. How could these individuals agree unanimously on which cadres were revolutionary or revisionist?

There were hints of an answer in the published discussion and statements on the Paris Commune: that leaders should be elected by the people and subject to their immediate recall. But the debate on the Paris Commune as a model for the Cultural Revolution had left unclear the crucial question concerning the method of party leadership. While the "Sixteen Points" affirmed the principle of party leadership, in August Mao withdrew and repudiated party work teams, the accepted method of leadership in all previous rectification campaigns. Moreover, Mao did not propose a clearly defined alternative mode of party leadership to re-place the work teams; the "Sixteen Points" simply instructed cadres to abandon "outmoded ways and regulations" and "break away from conventional practices." "In the Great Proletarian Cultural Revolution, the only method is for the masses to liberate themselves and any method of doing things on their behalf must not be used. Trust the masses, rely on them and respect their initiatives. Cast out fear. Don't be afraid of disorder."[45] Party committees through-out the country soon became paralyzed, rent with internal dissension and confusion, and incapable of providing leader-ship. In order to deal with this crisis, Mao, Chou En-lai, Lin Piao, and the Cultural Revolution Group issued a joint decision instructing the PLA to support the left and provide stability in power seizures.[46] Military control committees as well were quickly set up in virtually every province to replace defunct party committees.

It was against the background of these events that the Paris Commune came to be regarded as unfeasible as a national model. The ambiguous implications of the com-mune symbol *vis-à-vis* the role of a vanguard party proved to be the decisive factor. As Mao posed the dilemma: "If everything were changed into the commune, then what about the party? Where would we place the party? Among Commune Committee members [in Shanghai] are both party members and nonparty members. Where would we place the Party Committee? There must be a party some-how. There must be a nucleus, no matter what we call it. Be it called the Communist party, or Social Democratic party, or Kuomintang, or I Kuan Tao, it must have a party. The commune must have a party, but can the commune replace the party?"[47] The Paris Commune, after all, had been defeated. "Communes," Mao also commented, "are too weak when it comes to suppressing counterrevolution."[48]

Thus, as the Cultural Revolution unexpectedly escalated into a crisis in which the very stability of Chinese society was threatened, Mao moved to side with Chou En-lai to drop the Paris Commune as the model proletarian government for the nation. In the *People's Daily* on February 10, it was not the new Shanghai People's Commune, which had overthrown the entire Municipal Party Committee and Municipal People's Council of Shanghai (with the exception, of course, of Chang Ch'un-ch'iao), that Peking upheld as a national model, but the far less dramatic and less well-known seizure of power in the strategic border province of Heilungkiang. The salient feature of the Heilungkiang seizure of power was that it included the First Secretary of the Heilungkiang Provincial Party Committee (P'an Fu-sheng), the commander and vice-commander of the regional PLA garrison (Wang Chia-tao and Chang Wan-ch'un), and two Red Guard leaders in a five-man leadership coalition. The lesson *People's Daily* drew from this was that leading cadres of provincial party committees and government organs "can be the backbone and leadership of the struggle to seize power," and that commanders of regional or provincial PLA garrisons were needed to maintain stability and discipline.[49]

It is interesting to note that Chou En-lai played a central role in the Heilungkiang Cultural Revolution and to a large degree defined the new Heilungkiang provincial leadership organ.[50]

Chang Ch'un-ch'iao Speaks to the People of Shanghai

The task of conveying the dramatic change of policy to the people of Shanghai fell to Chang Ch'un-ch'iao. On February 23, two weeks after the announcement of the Heilungkiang Revolutionary Committee, he and Yao Wen-yuan flew back from eleven days of conferences in Peking to a suspense-ridden city.

For Chang, who had left the city at the height of controversy and enthusiasm following the formation of the Shanghai People's Commune, it was a delicate reunion. At

a massive televised rally held the next day in Culture
Square and attended by over one million rebel workers and
students, he appeared in his rumpled cadre's uniform to
address the people of Shanghai and convey the instructions
of the Center for the next stages of activity in Shanghai.

"For a long time we have not sat together for discussion
of problems," he began, then went on to tell of his meeting
with Mao on February 12 and subsequent meetings of the
Central Committee where the question of Shanghai and
other problems had been discussed. Chang first assured the
listening crowd of Mao's positive evaluation of the January
Revolution and its achievements, then gradually moved on
to the points Mao had recently brought up in editorials in
Red Flag. The Cultural Revolution, said Chang, "is a
revolution under the dictatorship of the proletariat, one
which has been organized and started by ourselves."[51] He
pointed out that the conditions of the Cultural Revolution
were therefore different from those which surrounded the
formation of the Paris Commune, in which the com-
munards were at the first stages of seeking to establish the
dictatorship of the proletariat over the bourgeoisie. In the
Cultural Revolution, he explained, alliances are the best
way to seize power effectively, and the most effective alliance
is in the "three-in-one" combination form. Chang said Mao
had pointed out to him, for example, that without the support of the army, the seizure of power in Shansi could not
have been accomplished. The reactionary Shansi Provincial
Party Committee had sent plainclothes secret agents with
guns to repress the revolutionary rebels. "It was because
the army stationed in Shansi steadfastly supported the revolutionary rebels that the unarmed revolutionary masses
were able to seize power."[52]

As a second point, Chang went on to stress that from the
beginning Mao had never meant the Cultural Revolution
to lead to the overthrow of all leading cadres, but only to
their remolding through mass criticism and debate.
Only the small handful of capitalist roaders in the party

who refused to accept mass criticism and reform themselves in the course of the mass movement were to be dismissed from office. Although the workers had made significant contributions to the Cultural Revolution, Chang pointed out a practical problem: If one turns over to the workers a city such as Shanghai or a province such as Kiangsu, their lack of experience would pose many difficulties in managing it. "A worker may be more adept at managing one workshop." Therefore, he asked, "Can we do without revolutionary leading cadres?" Chang answered his own rhetorical question: "No!"[53]

Chang then outlined revisions that would have to be made in the structure of the Shanghai People's Commune so it would conform to national policy. "The Shanghai People's Commune has obtained a certain authority," he said, but "in the future its authority will have to be strengthened."

To accomplish this the commune would have to admit heads of municipal bureaus and departments. There were 600 bureau chiefs and 6000 department heads in the city of Shanghai. Asked Chang: "How can we fail to find candidates for 'three-in-one combinations' from among these 600 and 6000 cadres?" The Chairman had said ninety-five percent of the cadres would follow the proletarian revolution, and for this reason, Chang said, the "idea of 'suspect all, overthrow all' is a reactionary one." Those who persisted in this notion were "bound in the end to transform themselves into their very opposites and to be overthrown themselves." Chang gave great importance to overcoming the bitter hostility that had divided rebels and leading cadres of the city. "So it is important not only to unite with those who hold opinions similar to ours, but it is also essential to be good at uniting with those who hold opinions different from ours. In addition, it is necessary to be good at uniting with those who have opposed us and who have been proven wrong by practice."

Chang was, of course, aware of the very real resentments that remained in the wake of the strife and knew that overcoming them would not be easy. He admitted that the different sides now "are not on speaking terms," but urged rebels to return to their units and ask cadres to join them. Cadres, he cautioned, "particularly leading cadres," must "not bear grudges" even though they might have been "unfairly treated" at the hands of the rebels. "A revolution will always demand a price, and how can we refuse to pay a price for such a great revolution which is without precedent in history? Our price is not great and is insignificant compared with the price exacted by the British and French bourgeois democratic revolutions."[54]

Chang then told his audience that although Mao had decided it wouldn't do to call new power organs "communes," the Chairman, out of respect and great admiration for the achievements of the Shanghai working class, would permit the Shanghai Commune to stand as the only exception. Mao and the Central Committee had agreed to send "separate directives" to Shanghai, apart from those sent to all the other provinces where power seizures had been less successful. Chang suggested that it would be preferable, however, for the Shanghai rebels to bow to the rest of the nation and change the title of the Shanghai People's Commune to the Shanghai Municipal Revolutionary Committee. "Would you feel isolated because yours is the only commune in the whole country?" The *People's Daily* "could not publish the news of the establishment of the Shanghai People's Commune," he added, "for if it published it, all would follow suit, and the series of problems just mentioned would arise."[55]

Chang Ch'un-ch'iao's speech took more than two hours— and concluded the period of the January Revolution. The title "Shanghai People's Commune" passed into history, the Provisional Committee acquired a new name—the Shanghai Municipal Revolutionary Committee—and a new stage was begun in the Shanghai Cultural Revolution.

CONSOLIDATION AND ORDER

The Heilungkiang Provincial Revolutionary Committee was officially established on January 31, 1967, and from that day the nation became embroiled in the politics of establishing revolutionary committees. In many places this involved a long and arduous two-year struggle.

In Shanghai, Chang, First Secretary of the provisional Municipal Revolutionary Committee, moved quickly and forcefully to strengthen its authority and political legitimacy by seeking to expand its base of popular support and addressing it to solving the long list of problems which beset the city. Shanghai had been left unsettled by the factionalism that followed the January Revolution. Factional conflict was a constant worry, always threatening to spill over again and disrupt the life of the city. In the factories, work discipline was lax. There were strivings for autonomous workers' control, a tendency that came to be known as the "mountain-stronghold mentality," and a dangerous sectarianism among groups and cliques of workers. While industrial production had not been seriously disrupted during the revolution, it had not surged forward. From January to February there had been only a 3.4 percent advance in production over the previous year, which, though better than a drop, needed to be greatly increased.[56] The formerly spotless city was badly littered and a wave of crime had broken out for the first time since 1949.

Efforts to solve these problems often met with stubborn obstacles, for in the months ahead the forces of national and local political currents continued to collide, producing tortuous twists and turns in the Shanghai Cultural Revolution. One example of this was the ticklish and sensitive process of uniting the city's rebel forces with party officials and functionaries in three-in-one combinations in every municipal bureau, district, county, neighborhood, factory, store, public facility, and school. The process had barely begun when a national crisis was created by deposed right-ists who tried to reinstate themselves in their former positions, a development known as the "February Adverse Currents."[57]

As soon as these rightist currents had peaked, a leftist wave began to sweep through the country again. From the spring of 1967 through the summer and fall and into 1968, there were widespread outbreaks of ultraleftist disturbances and violence, directed largely against the newly constituted revolutionary committees.[58]

Amidst these currents and countercurrents, Chang and Yao sought to consolidate the new proletarian government of Shanghai and to steer the revolution between the Scylla of the right and the Charybdis of the ultraleft. Largely to the credit of their skillful and subtle leadership, Shanghai never experienced the level of disorder and violence that shook China in 1967 and 1968.

Three-in-One Alliance

The new leaders of the provisional government threw themselves immediately to the task of forging "three-in-one alliance" revolutionary committees throughout the city. Their goal was the consolidation of the January Revolution and a sweeping reconstruction of Shanghai. The existence of a strong center, the Shanghai Municipal Revolutionary Committee, with a broad mandate for social change and with its three pillars of support—popular rebel leaders, leading cadres, and commanders of the land and naval branches of the PLA—would, they felt, provide the stability and order necessary for revolution "from the bottom up" in municipal bureaus, districts, counties, and basic-level units. The provisional government first called upon the city's rebel mass organizations to hold meetings of representatives from all rebel groups of workplaces, residential quarters, and district and county administrative offices to discuss and analyze the problems of setting up revolutionary committees. They instructed rebel mass organizations to "decide whether power should be seized, how it should be seized, and how it should be exercised after its seizure" in units that had not yet experienced seizures of power; or where power seizures had degenerated into "mountain-strongholds" controlled by single rebel groups for factional aims; or where workers' committees were co-opted by party bureaucrats eager to reinstate themselves in their old positions.[59]

Of immediate concern to the new government was the task of reconstructing district, county, and municipal bureau administrations. In the winter and spring of 1967, meetings were held in the city's ten municipal districts at which representatives of rebel mass organizations discussed and debated the concrete steps of setting up district revolutionary committees. At these meetings there was extensive discussion of which class had held power in the former district party committees, how drastic the turnover of party cadres ought to be, which party cadres were revolutionary, and, in the case of those who were not, which ones could be reformed. The resulting district revolutionary committees were fashioned in the image of the Municipal Revolutionary Committee. Like the Municipal Committee, district revolutionary committees were built from three bases of support—popular local leaders who genuinely represented the people of the district, leading cadres from the old District Party Committee, and officers of the PLA or representatives of workers' armed militias.

The actual turnover of leading cadres in district committees was not as sweeping as it was at the highest level of municipal government. For example, Chang Ching-piao, the First Secretary of the Yangpu District Party Committee, after undergoing mass criticism and reform became the chairman of the Yangpu District Revolutionary Committee.[60] This was partly because all district and county revolutionary committees had to be approved by the Municipal Revolutionary Committee which was, by that time, eager to ensure the presence of capable and experienced city administrators in leading positions of new district power organs.

In the spring and summer, revolutionary committees were also established in the ten suburban counties where more than three million Shanghai peasants live. Like their city counterparts, county revolutionary committees were based on the three-in-one alliance of poor and lower-middle peasant leaders, leading cadres from the former county party committees, and representatives of the PLA or People's Militia. During this same period, provisional power organs in the municipal bureaus were likewise speedily pushed forward. Unlike the revolutionary committees in the districts and counties, the provisional leadership organs in the municipal bureaus (Bureau of Education, Transportation, Commerce, etc.) did not include PLA cadres or representatives of people's militias. Instead, revolutionary committees in municipal bureaus were structured according to a three-in-one combination of leading party officials, middle-level cadres, and representatives of staff workers.

The process of integrating leading cadres in municipal bureaus into revolutionary committees may have been even more sensitive and controversial than it was elsewhere. As Chang Ch'un-ch'iao pointed out in a speech delivered before the Municipal Revolutionary Committee in May 1967, in the early stages of the Cultural Revolution leading cadres in municipal bureaus "did not see the need for the Great Proletarian Cultural Revolution" and instead sought to suppress it through the work teams.[61] Moreover, some leading cadres continued "unwittingly to evince their old attitudes. . . . This is why the young fighters say that they can't trust the cadres, which is quite reasonable."[62]

Since heads of bureaus were among those most aggressively opposed to the Cultural Revolution, relatively few were reinstated in leadership positions. In the No. 2 Commercial Bureau of the Finance and Trade System, for example, the rebel organization finally admitted just five leading cadres into the bureau's revolutionary committee, after submitting them to what appears to have been an elaborate process of review. These leading cadres, none of whom were bureau heads, were asked "to expose, criticize, and refute the bourgeois reactionary line" at a rally held in the bureau and "express their stand before the masses." They were also invited to attend smaller forums where they were asked to clarify their thoughts, discuss their political views, analyze the present situation of the Cultural Revolution, and answer questions.[63] Even so, the rebel groups admitted they "were apprehensive about accepting power-holders" for fear that they might be seen by other rebel organizations as a conservative "royalist" group. Moreover, there was widespread concern about whether the leading cadres (all department heads) would "put all powers in their [the leading cadres] hands" or "return to their old selves" after being admitted to the revolutionary committee.[64]

The Role of the People's Liberation Army

In contrast with the rest of China, Shanghai's Cultural Revolution was characterized by an extremely limited involvement of the PLA. As a rule, civilian measures were attempted first in dealing with difficult problems, and only when these failed did the provisional government call in the PLA to play a support role. Overall leadership in Shanghai always remained clearly in civilian hands.

The most pressing and urgent problem facing the Shanghai provisional government was the persistent factionalism among rebel workers' groups in factories, municipal power plants, and transportation and communication centers. It was in response to this problem that the Municipal Revolutionary Committee first dispatched work teams of PLA political cadres. They were sent to strategic plants and public facilities to prevent breakdown of vital services, to arbitrate between sparring factions, and help establish or reestablish great alliances. These PLA work teams went unarmed, and because of the high prestige of the PLA they appear to have gained the respect of workers in units where they were sent. Although the party work teams which had preceded them had often encountered bitter opposition in factories, there were few if any incidences of serious conflict between PLA teams and rebel workers in Shanghai. To some degree this was because the Cultural Revolution was directed against the party bureaucracy; PLA work teams in Shanghai had no strong reasons to feel threatened by the revolutionary activism of workers and students.

The role of PLA work teams in resolving factional strife in the Shanghai harbor illustrates the nature of their involvement in the city in the month following the January Storm. During the January Revolution, eight rebel mass organizations of the 6th District of the Shanghai harbor had formed the first "great alliance," which had seized financial and political power from the port authority in mid-January. Within a month's time, however, this alliance had broken down, as disputes arose between leaders of these eight rebel organizations over the distribution of power and positions in the newly erected workers' committee. Initial squabbling and bickering in the workers' committee grew into wall-poster debates, heated quarrels between members of the different workers' factions, and finally into a "civil war." The principal combatants were the two largest workers' factions, the Rebel Battalion and the East Is Red Rebel Detachment—both from the Workers' Rebel Headquarters. The war apparently lasted for several weeks.

The first introduction of PLA cadres took place early in March. On March 21, acting jointly in a work team half composed of public-security cadres, the PLA cadres directed the formation of a second great alliance, and then the formation of a "preparatory group" for the Revolutionary Committee of the 6th District. Leaders of the eight rebel dockers' organizations, however, continued to jealously guard their groups' advantage. As rebel dockers commented, the " 'civil war' went on, waged not with wall posters, but across the table." In the end, the preparatory group, too, seems to have splintered, and it was ordered to disband following an investigation by representatives from the Municipal Revolutionary Committee.

With the arrival of more PLA personnel from the naval station to support work in the harbor, the PLA work team proceeded to conduct a rectification campaign. PLA men spent long hours chatting with workers and setting examples by personally unloading and loading ships at the docks. They led rebel leaders to make public statements of self-criticism for their unwillingness to halt factional strife at the harbor. They conducted mass discussion to "eradicate self-interest," which was described as the primary cause of factional strife, and appealed to the dockers to promote instead the public interest.

Through painstaking political work, peace between the rival factions was finally achieved. Middle-level cadres were carefully recruited into the rebel fold. Finally, a third great alliance was established in the Shanghai harbor's 6th District.[65]

Grasp Revolution, Promote Production

The task of keeping Shanghai's economy in a more normal running order was a critical one for the provisional government. Although economic considerations were prominent, political factors as well were central to the emphasis on maintaining production. Political and social reforms sparked by the Cultural Revolution were considered successful only when they proved compatible with the needs of rapid economic growth.

In keeping with this principle, Chang and the Provisional Committee called upon rebel workers to act as models in both revolution and production. Poor and lower-middle peasants in the many communes encircling the city on its outskirts were urged to do a good job in spring plowing, strengthen their leadership over production teams and brigades, and promote agriculture. Educated youths who had left places as far off as Sinkiang Province to return to their homes in Shanghai and participate in the city's cultural revolution were reminded that they had never received official sanction to leave the rural areas to which they had been assigned and were instructed to return immediately to their units.[66]

Restoration of work discipline in the factories was essential to the industrial upsurge that the new municipal leaders hoped to spark. In 1967 there had been a slight drop in industrial production.[67] "One of the most important reasons why production in some units does not increase is that anarchism is playing evil," remarked a *Wenhuipao* editorial as late as August 15, 1968. "The condition of many units shows that this anarchism in production is often related to the fact that responsible persons of these units do not pay any attention to their work." Describing the situation at the Shanghai Fabric Mill, its newly established revolutionary committee reported that workers in the mill had "the practice of coming late to work and leaving early." The committee complained that when meetings were called, "the workers came together but left in the middle of the meeting." Moreover, some "even left their work-post without permission, and they defied interference by anybody." The mill's revolutionary committee also had problems in gaining the cooperation of cadres who had been dismissed. It reported that some "capitalist roaders" simply "worked passively or stood idle. They resisted supervision over their work. They also sowed dissension among the workers . . ."[68] The revolutionary committee concluded that "this situation seriously impeded the progress" of industrial production.

The Shanghai Rubber Mold Factory, a small workshop formed as an amalgamation of twenty-odd neighborhood factories set up during the Great Leap Forward, reported the existence of a wide gulf between the rebel faction that controlled the factory revolutionary committee and the workers of the "conservative" faction. When the revolutionary committee called factory meetings, workers of the opposing faction "boycotted the meetings or played chess and poker at the meeting, talked and laughed loudly and carried out sabotage so that the meeting could not go on."[69] The lack of cooperation was attributed to a certain "bad element" who had spread false rumors among workers of the conservative faction that the revolutionary committee was preparing to parade conservative leaders through the streets in an effort to disgrace them. During production breaks, this "bad element . . . instigated some youths to play flutes, sing songs, dance, and talk about picnics."[70]

The new municipal leaders urged rebel workers to strengthen committees concerned with production and put production plans back on a realistic basis, economize on the use of raw materials, and ensure product quality. Rebels in charge of the transportation system were instructed to assure under all circumstances the smooth flow of cargo and passengers. All industrial units and business enterprises were instructed not to change the wage system or promote economic benefits in any way. Shanghai workers who had been assigned to construction projects in other regions of China were instructed to return to their jobs. Temporary workers, part-time workers, and workers on limited contracts from agricultural sectors outside Shanghai were forbidden to agitate for permanent work in Shanghai factories.

While emphasis was placed upon restoring industrial production to normalcy, workers and staff members of the city's cultural, educational, and health institutions, including researchers and staff members of scientific research centers, were also called upon to resume their normal work load while at the same time carrying through the Cultural Revolution in their respective units. Revolutionary committees in all units were authorized to invoke disciplinary measures on those who left their posts without permission and those who loitered on their jobs. Full restitution was demanded of state property which had been used without proper authorization; and in cases where state resources had been used up, thorough investigations and accounting were to be made at a later date. Future violations concerning unauthorized use of state property and resources would be dealt with as sabotaging the socialist economy.[71]

The Dictatorship
of the Proletariat

Marx in *The Civil War in France* and Lenin in *The State and Revolution* made the observation that a primary factor in the defeat of the Paris Commune had been its failure to forcefully exercise the dictatorship of the proletariat. Both these works were widely read in Shanghai during the Cultural Revolution, and the importance of exercising the dictatorship of the proletariat became an influential idea among newly formed revolutionary committees. Conscious that the Public Security, Judicial, and Procuratorial bureaus had been rendered inoperative by bureaucratic infighting, the Municipal Revolutionary Committee set out to establish two new organs—the "civil offense, armed defense" Workers' Militia and "mass-dictatorship organs"—in order to augment PLA and civilian law-enforcement and judicial agencies.

The Workers' Armed Militia was organized in July and August 1967 as a city-wide organization directly responsible to the Municipal Revolutionary Committee. Although it received its training from the PLA and followed military lines in its internal organization—divisions, regiments, and battalions—the Workers' Armed Militia was independent of military control. Its more than 20,000 members, all industrial workers from factories and plants throughout the city, usually remained on the production lines and were called into active duty only when the need arose. In December 1967, for example, the Municipal Revolutionary Committee asked the Workers' Armed Militia to help in its campaign to suppress counterrevolutionaries and assist finance, trade, communications, and public-security cadres to check rising black-market activities in the city. When members of the Workers' Militia were not active in broader municipal public-security functions, their own factory's revolutionary committee assigned them to handle local incidences of criminal disturbances and maintain workers' vigilance in the effort to prevent sabotage of production sites. As its name suggests, the "civil offense, armed defense" Workers' Militia, like the PLA, relied primarily on ideological and political work to carry out its assignments.[72]

The counterpart of the Workers' Militia in the city's residential quarters was the "mass-dictatorship organs" in newly established neighborhood revolutionary committees. These mass-dictatorship organs were set up in the spring and summer of 1967, along with the three-in-one-alliance neighborhood revolutionary committee made up of elected representatives of urban communities, cadres from street and lane administrative stations, and public-security cadres. In the mass-dictatorship organs, residents actively shared with public-security and street and lane cadres the responsibility for maintaining civil order in their own neighborhoods. Formerly this responsibility was held by the neighborhood public-security station and street and lane committees; although residents were asked to assist in the maintenance of law and order, they did not participate in the decision-making bodies of this lowest level of municipal government.[73]

During the municipal campaign waged in 1967 and 1968 to uncover "traitors," Kuomintang secret agents, as well as hard-core criminals, mass-dictatorship organs throughout the city organized neighborhood public trials.[74] At these trials the accused stood before their peers, and after public discussion and debate of their cases, the neighborhood revolutionary committee arrived at sentences for the accused. In the more complicated cases, sentences were subject to review at higher administrative levels, while the most serious cases were reviewed personally by Chang Ch'un-ch'iao.[75] Apparently, there was a general inclination to sentence only the most serious offenders to jail; public nuisances continued to live in their own neighborhoods, but since everybody knew who they were, neighborhoods could keep a watchful eye over any with histories of petty crime.[76]

No doubt these new citizens' organs made mistakes in exercising their "dictatorship" and injustices were committed against innocent individuals. Neighborhood "judgment rallies" in some cases were nothing more than kangaroo courts that selected scapegoats or unpopular neighbors for public vilification. In order to minimize such excesses, the Municipal Revolutionary Committee issued strict guidelines and repeated calls for city-wide study of Mao's essay "On the Correct Handling of Contradictions among the People." In this essay Mao distinguished between two types of social contradictions in socialist society: "those between the enemies and ourselves and those among the people themselves."[77] Only contradictions with the people's enemies—bureaucrat capitalists, landlords, and the Kuomintang—were "antagonistic" to socialism, while those arising among the people—workers, peasants, intellectuals, cadres, and the national bourgeoisie—were "nonantagonistic." Mao argued that the dictatorship of the proletariat could only be applied against the people's enemies. "Dictatorship does not apply within the ranks of the people. The people cannot exercise dictatorship over themselves, nor must one section of the people oppress another."[78]

In keeping with this principle, Shanghai's proletarian dictatorship was directed primarily at the problem of weeding out "renegades" and "secret agents" from among capitalist roaders in the Communist party, in newly established revolutionary committees at every level of the municipal structure, and in rebel mass organizations.[79] In February 1968, Wang Shao-yung, formerly a member of the Standing

Committee of the Municipal Party Committee and now a leading member of the Shanghai Municipal Revolutionary Committee, announced that 2086 suspects, of which 284 were bureau chiefs, had been investigated for their past records.[80] As evidence of the importance placed on the campaign to uproot renegades and secret agents in the Communist party and new leadership organs, Chang Ch'un-ch'iao personally presided over all aspects of the "special case" investigations. To impress on the people of Shanghai the concern of the new municipal government to weed out counterrevolutionaries and check the wave of crime, several televised "public judgment" rallies were held in Culture Square at which counterrevolutionaries and criminal elements were publicly sentenced. Following these rallies, executioners from the Public Security Bureau led out the few counterrevolutionaries who had received death sentences, and according to reports these counterrevolutionaries were immediately executed.[81]

Workers' Rebel
Mass Organizations

A legacy of the January Revolution was the presence of numerous rebel mass organizations scattered in disarray throughout Shanghai. As Chou En-lai remarked in a meeting with Red Guard leaders in Peking: "The present state of affairs cannot be allowed to go on forever. A factory is now usually divided into several factions, each stretching its hands into all parts of the country like an independent kingdom of several thousands of years ago." Chou quipped that the Chairman had told him "several days ago that we were like a country divided into eight hundred princely states."[82]

In order to reduce the confusion inherent in this situation, the Municipal Revolutionary Committee first sought to curb the broad-ranging activities of these groups. Known and active counterrevolutionary organizations like the

United Action Committee and Red Flag Army were banned and their leaders severely punished when caught. Warnings were issued against rumored ultraleft attacks on the PLA garrison to seize arms and ammunition. Would-be raiders on the Shanghai airport, broadcasting stations, prisons, detention centers, secret-documents rooms, and other party documentation filing centers were warned that they'd be severely dealt with. All raids under any circumstances against other rebel mass organizations, the abduction, detention, and beating of hostages, and the setting up of kangaroo courts and torture chambers were also strictly forbidden and all violations, when discovered, were to be handled according to state law. The Municipal Revolutionary Committee issued directives informing rebel mass organizations that they were no longer permitted to dispatch workers' militias at will.

In addition, mass organizations at basic-level units were instructed to disband their full-time secretarial staff and personnel, returning them to the production lines. They were forbidden to use factories they controlled for factional purposes, and they were likewise reminded of the new laws promulgated against the unauthorized use of state property and resources. Membership in workers' rebel organizations was scaled down to include only workers of the same trade or in the same factory; while intellectuals, students, artists, doctors, and municipal party and government cadres who had been recruited into workers' mass organizations were asked to return to their own units. The Red Guard Army and other organizations of demobilized soldiers, all nationwide organizations, and all special-interest groups organized to further specific economic goals, such as new housing allotments and higher wages, were declared anathema to the spirit of the Cultural Revolution and ordered to disband. Members of these organizations were then encouraged to join mass organizations in their respective units.

On a broader scale, mass organizations in the city were

called on to conduct self-rectification campaigns: to carry out criticism and self-criticism, accept criticism and suggestions from nonactivists, rectify their work-style, and purify their ranks. They were further instructed to implement the spirit of the call to form "great alliances of proletarian revolutionaries" and unite with opposing workers' factions in their respective units; and at the same time to oppose anarchism, ultrademocracy, the mountain-stronghold mentality, the small-group mentality, and sectarianism.

In September 1967 great alliances of rival workers' factions were reported to have been formed throughout the city. In November a unified organization of Red Guard groups in colleges and universities of Shanghai was established. In February 1968 Wang Hung-wen, a leading member of the Municipal Revolutionary Committee representing the No. 17 Cotton Mill, announced that 99.9 percent of the city's more than 800 factories had formed great alliances and 75 percent had formed three-in-one-combination revolutionary committees.[83] In order to raise the level of political consciousness and understanding of the events that were taking place, the new municipal leaders issued reading lists of Mao's writings to the city's rebels for study and consideration throughout the duration of its cultural revolution.

When Mao visited Shanghai in September 1967 on his inspection tour of North, Central-South, and East China, which included stays in Honan, Hopei, Hunan, Kiangsi, and Chekiang provinces, he commented to Chang Ch'un-ch'iao and Yao Wen-yuan on how remarkably calm and stable Shanghai seemed in comparison to the rest of China.[84] Mao's continuing high regard for their leadership capability and their handling of the Cultural Revolution in Shanghai, the most successful of any city in China, would later catapult the middle-aged Chang and his young colleagues Yao Wen-yuan and Wang Hung-wen to the highest levels of power and influence in China.[85]

On Revolutionary Committees and the New Policy

The revolutionary committee emerged as a compromise solution to the problem of advancing democratic control of state organs after the most radical period of the Cultural Revolution had passed. Characteristic of Mao's leadership from the start was his ability to draw from both the theoretical summations of the world revolutionary experiences and the concrete experiences of the Chinese Revolution to come up with a bold new revolutionary synthesis at the critical stages of the Chinese Revolution.

The main features of Mao's new political synthesis as it emerged in Shanghai were:

1. *Working-class supervision of the superstructure.* Active and sustained working-class supervision of the state apparatus and other areas of the superstructure, such as cultural and educational institutions, seems to have been a major lesson that Mao and his followers drew from the Paris Commune.[86] For Mao the presence of workers in three-in-one revolutionary committees at all levels of the new municipal system, especially in factories and industrial plants, would ensure and promote the maintenance of working-class government infused with the spirit and politics of a revolutionary proletariat. It was in Shanghai, China's largest and most advanced industrial base, that working-class supervision of the superstructure was realized to its furthest extent. In other municipalities the more limited degree of actual and direct workers' participation in state organs and other areas of the superstructure was defined to a large degree by the comparative youth of the working classes of these cities and by the relative smallness of their industrial bases.

2. *Mass-line politics.* Revolutionary committees ideally constituted a "nucleus of leadership" composed of the most

vigorous, alert, and politically conscious activists in a particular unit who emerged in the course of the Cultural Revolution as leaders and who maintain close and active links with the masses. In the revolutionary committee these activists were seen as forming a compact, tightly integrated leadership body, which owing to its small size would be capable of functioning as a decisive, efficient, revolutionary executive organ. As in Yenan, all members of the revolutionary committee as well as the party committee would take part in physical labor along with workers or peasants on a regular and frequent basis in order that they not grow alienated from the reality and lives of the laboring people, and to ensure that all their actions and policies would be infused with the concrete needs and concerns of the masses they led. Furthermore, to enhance continued mass supervision over leaders, "open-door rectification campaigns" would be held periodically, at least once a year, in every unit to enable the masses to review critically their leaders' activities and programs, as well as provide a method for the recall of unwanted leaders.

3. *Better troops and simpler administration.* Like the administrative reforms carried out in Yenan during the *cheng-feng* rectification campaign in 1942, the Cultural Revolution led to a drastic slashing of the municipal administrative apparatus.[87] The formerly separate bureaucracies of the party and state were amalgamated into one streamlined and integrated administrative system which was put under the unified control of the revolutionary committee in each unit, thus eliminating the independent status of government and management. Administrative personnel were then sent down from municipal and district administrative organs to basic-level units. As in the Yenan revolutionary base area, this downward shift of administrative cadres strengthened the role of basic-level leadership organs. It also had the effect of narrowing the alienation of the state from society, since, increasingly, key

administrative processes were carried out in "grass-roots" units, such as the residents' and workshop revolutionary committees, rather than in central municipal bureaus.

After the administrative reforms had been completed, the city's revolutionary committees maintained only small staffs of cadres to perform daily administrative tasks. Office work was trimmed to a bare minimum, while as many office cadres as possible were transferred down to the production line. Thus, through the revolutionary committee, Mao sought to evolve an antibureaucratic administrative system for the cities.

4. *Unified party leadership.* Party committees in Shanghai were carefully rebuilt with the launching of a party rectification campaign in the summer of 1968. The most politically mature rebels, if not already party members, were admitted into the party and incorrigible capitalist roaders were sloughed off. Emphasis was placed on recruiting young workers into party committees at all levels of the city. In Shanghai the party emerged from the Cultural Revolution reinforced and revitalized as a vanguard party of the working class, with its "revisionist" deadwood cast away. New worker cadres, together with veteran cadres, became the core leadership groups which exercised unified and centralized party leadership over the revolutionary committee. Thus the leadership role of party committees was actually strengthened by the Cultural Revolution, as they were after the *cheng-feng* rectification campaign of 1942.

The changes brought about by the Cultural Revolution which most immediately and directly affected the people of Shanghai were those that occurred in their places of work. But of broader significance were the administrative reforms carried out in the structure and process of municipal government. The remaining part of this analysis of revolutionary committees will discuss the changes brought to the city's factories, where nearly all of its 1,200,000 industrial working class works. We will then turn to a brief examination of the Shanghai Municipal Revolutionary Committee, and the sweeping administrative reforms implemented at both the municipal and submunicipal levels. What is the continuity between the workers' committees and the revolutionary committees that were formed from them? How does the revolutionary committee deal with the contradiction between centralism and democracy, party leadership and popular control, unity and factionalism? What changes were made in the management of factories and in the administration of the city to solve the problem of swollen bureaucracies and élite control? What are the continuing tensions between administrators and workers, and how are they dealt with within the framework of the revolutionary committees?

Revolution in the Factories

In most cases the original core of rebel leaders who erected workers' committees in factories during the January Revolution managed to maintain their leading positions. They guided the subsequent revisions which incorporated leading cadres from the former party committee, management personnel, industrial engineers, women, and members of the opposing workers' faction. This was especially true in factories where a few middle-level cadres had joined the rebel ranks and participated in the workers' committees of the January Revolution. The revolutionary committee of the No. 17 Cotton Mill, for example, had in 1972 twenty-nine members: five were veteran cadres and twenty-four were rank-and-file workers, one of whom represented the factory's workers' militia. There were no representatives of the PLA owing to the lack of factional violence in this mill during the Cultural Revolution. All but one of the five veteran cadres rose from the ranks of the mill's lower- and middle-level cadres who, along with rebel rank-and-file workers (all party members), sparked the Cultural Revolution in this fifty-five-year-old British-built mill.

Workers in the mill reconstructed for my wife the events

of the early stages of the Cultural Revolution, as follows. On June 6, 1966, in response to the Peking University big-character posters, six rebel party members posted the first wall posters criticizing the mill's party committee. The party secretary immediately mobilized the mill's party organization in an effort to isolate the six rebel party members. Branding their attack on the mill's party committee an attack on the Chinese Communist Party and on socialism, he labeled the rebel party members counterrevolutionaries and "antiparty elements." On June 20, a work team from the Municipal Textile Bureau arrived at the mill and soon joined the mill's party secretary in the effort to suppress the rebellious cadres. Simultaneously, the work team selected a list of 400 workers and workshop cadres as "safe" targets for the mill's cultural revolution. This, however, only drove these workers and cadres to the rebel faction.

In early June the rebel group in the No. 17 Cotton Mill had numbered only thirty workers and cadres. But as the repressive tactics of the work team and party committee became increasingly blatant, more and more workers joined their ranks, until by November 1966 the rebel faction numbered 3000 workers and worker cadres. On November 9, 1000 rebels from the mill participated in the massive Culture Square rally that founded the Workers' Rebel Headquarters. Wang Hung-wen, the leader of the mill's rebel workers and a middle-level cadre in charge of the mill's Welfare Department, played a prominent role at this rally, becoming a cofounder and leading member of the Workers' Rebel Headquarters. The next day, 380 workers from the mill took part in the Anting Incident. As in many other mills and factories in Shanghai, the seizure of power in the No. 17 Cotton Mill was precipitated by the general strike in January. More than 3000 of the mill's 8000 workers walked out, along with leading cadres, engineers, and the majority of the middle-level cadres. Rebel workers and cadres, responding to the call of the "Urgent Notice," then threw themselves into production, working double shifts while hastily electing a workers' committee to coordinate their activities and replace the defunct factory party committee and management. When the call was made in February to admit leading cadres into the workers' committee, the mill's rebel workers simply promoted their middle-level cadres, admitted a leading cadre, a representative of the Workers' Militia, and members of the conservative workers' faction. On April 11, 1967, the formation of a three-in-one combination revolutionary committee was announced.[88]

Today Wang Hung-wen—who began as a worker in the mill and was only thirty years old in 1966 when the Cultural Revolution began—is a vice-chairman of the Shanghai Municipal Revolutionary Committee, vice-secretary of the party branch of Shanghai, a member of the Central Committee in Peking, and one of the five vice-chairmen of the Chinese Communist Party (along with Chou En-lai, Kang Sheng, Yeh Chien-ying, and Li Teh-sheng). Tang Wen-lai, a woman weaver, is a workers' representative of the Municipal Revolutionary Committee, deputy secretary of the Textile Bureau of Shanghai, and party secretary of the mill's party branch.

The No. 17 Cotton Mill's revolutionary committee may be the most successful in the city, but it is also representative of what happened in many of Shanghai's important factories and plants which were supporting units of the January Revolution and whose rebel leaders rose to leadership positions in the Workers' Rebel Headquarters.

Because only one of the twenty-nine members of the No. 17 Cotton Mill's revolutionary committee had been a member of the former party committee, a less dramatic case might be the Shanghai Diesel Engine Plant's revolutionary committee. Unlike the No. 17 Cotton Mill, the Diesel Engine Plant, situated on the outskirts of the city along the Whangpu River, had experienced bitter and violent factional strife in which at least one worker (and probably more) lost his life. Rebel workers told me that in this respect the Diesel Engine Plant was considered to be one of the worst in the city. It was also a center of the city-wide ultraleftist uprising in the spring and summer of 1967 which sought to overthrow the Municipal Revolutionary Committee and bring about a "second great chaos" in Shanghai. On September 29, 1967, the plant's revolutionary committee was finally established with the assistance of the PLA. In 1972 the revolutionary committee had thirty-two members: twenty-five workers' representatives, three PLA soldiers, and four leading cadres. Five of the workers' representatives were women, five were from the conservative workers' faction, and eight were nonparty activists. All four of the leading cadres were members of the former factory party committee, and they were all leading members of the eight-member standing committee of the revolutionary committee.

The important differences between the Diesel Engine Plant and the No. 17 Cotton Mill experiences in the Cultural Revolution can be partly explained by the fact that, unlike the Cotton Mill, the Diesel Engine Plant had only been a small farm-equipment repair workshop before liberation, jointly owned by American and Chinese interests, and did not have a history of workers' political activism. Most of the Diesel Engine Plant's 8000 workers were recruited after 1952, when the original workshop greatly expanded to become a major manufacturer of diesel truck engines; thus almost all were in their twenties and thirties. When the Cultural Revolution came to the plant, few if any of the workers had ever participated in revolutionary politics. The Diesel Engine Plant never did establish a workers' committee during the January Storm. In November 1966, after six months of intense debate and contention, the two workers' factions—the rebel East Is Red and the work-team-organized United Rebel Headquarters (which later switched from its early conservative stance to ultraleft opposition)—locked horns. Their violent struggle turned the plant into a virtual battleground in which contingents of helmeted workers flew at each other with stones, iron rods, and spears. Production ground to a halt and only gradually resumed in March 1967, when a detachment of PLA soldiers arrived to end the violence and begin the slow process of healing factional wounds and forming a great alliance.[89]

Although the method of selecting members to the revolutionary committee varied from factory to factory, it does seem clear that concern was especially given to making the leadership body representative according to the guiding formula of the three-in-one combination. Not only was it to be constituted of leading cadres, representatives of the Workers' Militia or PLA, and workers' representatives, it also had to include leaders from both workers' factions, women, engineers, and old, middle-aged, and young factory personnel—with the latter two categories forming the clear majority.

In factories where strong workers' committees were set up during the January Revolution, rebel leaders, themselves elected by fellow rebel workers, appear to have simply recruited cooperative leading cadres; then, following a period of consultation with workers in the factory, expanded the leadership group in order to make it more representative of all the categories of workers.

In factories where there was not a strong workers' committee, rebel leaders and/or leading cadres conducted a factory-wide election to establish a provisional revolutionary committee. In the Diesel Engine Plant, members of the revolutionary committee told me that the core leadership of the East Is Red rebel organization repeatedly canvassed and consulted with workers of the entire factory in the process of selecting a list of candidates. During this period of consultation, apparently every worker had the right to speak out or write open letters discussing the qualifications of each proposed candidate. After careful consideration was given to the question of representativeness, making sure that adequate representation was given to all of the plant's eight workshops, the final list was presented to the factory for ratification. This was done by secret ballot in which workers marked "yes" or "no" beside each candidate's name. The same type of election was conducted in all factories to decide the membership of the revolutionary committee.

In the three-in-one combination, the most active and definitive roles are played by the leading cadres and workers' representatives. Workers' representatives remain as full-time workers on the production line and fulfill the role of exercising worker supervision of the factory management and the activities of the leading cadres. In the revolutionary committee, they represent and advocate the interests and sentiments of the workers, participate in discussion and debate on all aspects of the factory's management and operation, and help formulate annual production plans and factory policies. At the same time, as the active link between the revolutionary committee and the masses, their responsibility is to assure that workers actively support and implement policies and commands issued by the revolutionary committee.

Leading cadres, on the other hand, function primarily in a leading capacity and form the "backbone" of the revolutionary committee. Although they work on the production line at least once a week, and in the course of a year perform one to two months of physical labor, leading cadres remain full-time administrators with the responsibility of implementing plans and decisions issued by the revolutionary committee.

The role of the PLA or Workers' Militia representatives, however, lacks clear definition. It seems that where PLA representatives were present, their primary responsibility was to infuse the committee with the martial discipline of the PLA and maintain public security. While this role demanded active participation during the Cultural Revolution, once stability was reestablished in the factories the PLA representatives were either withdrawn or remained in a nominal capacity.[90]

While the revolutionary committee has brought workers into a position of exercising supervision over factory management, party leadership in the revolutionary committee is nevertheless scrupulously maintained. In the late spring and summer of 1968, the Shanghai Municipal Revolutionary Committee launched a city-wide party rectification campaign. Previous to this rectification campaign, the relationship between the revolutionary committee and the still defunct party committee had been left unclear. If anything, it was generally assumed that the revolutionary committee would be the center of power and authority. Yet, in launching the rectification campaign, *Wenhuipao* published editorials bearing the exhortation that "Party power is the core of political power. It is the power of powers. Party development is the basis of development of political power."[91]

Naturally, this news caused considerable anxiety among nonparty workers' representatives and rebel leaders. Many grew "worried by the rectification and found it disagreeable to them," and there was "tension between rebels and cadres, each suspecting the other."[92] At the No. 17 Cotton Mill a rebel worker on the revolutionary committee made the popular suggestion that all rebels in the factory should be admitted into the newly resurrected party branch. Wang Hung-wen, however, quickly repudiated this suggestion, arguing that it would only serve to dilute the strength and leadership capability of the party branch.[93] It seems probable therefore that the party rectification campaign made crystal clear the relationship between newly reconstituted party committees and the revolutionary committee.

The party was reorganized according to the three-in-one formula of the revolutionary committee. As a smaller and more compact group, its role was to lead the revolutionary committee. The reorganization of the party sparked a recruitment drive to bring into the party the most outstanding of the nonparty members of the revolutionary committee. In Shanghai this led to an intensive campaign to recruit workers into the party and to promote worker cadres into leadership positions. By May 1973 more than 40,000 industrial workers were reported to be holding leading positions in factories, plants, and higher-level municipal organs in Shanghai.[94]

In the revolutionary committee the specific mechanism of party leadership is exercised through the party committee, the membership of which is nearly identical to that of the standing committee of the revolutionary committee. The standing committee is the center of power and is the ultimate seat of decision making since its members assume direct control over the factory management, meet on a more frequent and regular basis, and have the right of final approval of all important decisions passed by the revolutionary committee. Nonetheless, its actions and decisions are held accountable to the workers' representatives who form the dominant majority in the revolutionary committee and who hold the right of "revolutionary supervision."[95] In this manner a system of checks and balances is maintained in the revolutionary committee.

Once established, revolutionary committees launched factory-wide meetings and smaller workshop meetings where they encouraged workers to make both general and specific criticisms of the former management system. They led workers to integrate their criticisms of the factory management to the larger criticism of Liu Shao-ch'i's revisionist line. In factory after factory, workers voiced critiques echoing those made in the manifestos issued at the time of the January Revolution. They criticized the "theory of the production party" in which workers were told simply to master their techniques, work hard, and behave as obedient cogs on the production line. They criticized the factory

management for single-minded concern for increased production, uncritical reliance on material incentives, and for
discouraging workers from participation in political study
and activism. They attacked the old management system,
run by experts under the leadership of the party committee, which "hampered workers' activism and creativity" by ignoring their opinions and suggestions.[96] In
Shanghai factories there was resentment of engineers, technicians, and management cadres for their condescending
attitudes toward workers. Widespread support was voiced
for Mao's suggestion to drastically cut the management
personnel, sending cadres, engineers, and technicians to
production lines to be "reeducated" by the workers.[97]

After these meetings, the revolutionary committee distilled the opinions and suggestions of the workers and
threw itself into the task of presiding over sweeping management reforms. So extensive were these reforms that
repeated editorials issued from *Wenhuipao* urged factory
revolutionary committees to be sure to remember to consult and report to the Municipal Revolutionary Committee
the important changes taking place in their factories:

> Some comrades often neglect and slacken the seeking
> of advice and making of reports under the excuse of
> their being busily engaged in work. This is incor-
> rect. Being busy is a normal phenomenon in revolu-
> tion. It is precisely because we are busy and the work
> is complicated that we should all the more strengthen
> the system of seeking advice from and making reports
> to a higher authority. In this way, we can be busy
> without getting confused and we can do all our work
> in accordance with Chairman Mao's revolutionary
> line.[98]

The *Wenhuipao* editorial concluded by requesting that
"each report should be limited to 1000 words or so." In
special cases, "it should not exceed 2000 words at the most."

The broad thrust of management reforms was to eliminate
"functional dualism," a system adapted from the Soviet one-

man management system, and replace it with the collective leadership and control of the revolutionary committee.[99] The revolutionary committee merged the formerly separate offices and staffs of the party committee with that of management. Paring the combined administrative personnel to the bare bone, they sent extra cadres down to the production line where they would work as full-time workers while continuing as lower-level cadres with certain administrative responsibilities under the workshop revolutionary committee. This simultaneously served to decentralize factory administration by transferring a large portion of administrative work down to the production line. They then radically reorganized the remaining management personnel, eliminating redundancy and overlapping of administrative roles and unnecessary division of labor. Their objective was to make management more streamlined, more efficient, and more rational.

At the Shanghai Aimin Candy Factory, for example, the revolutionary committee reported that, under the former management, "workers worked busily in production," economizing on time, while some administrative personnel had so much free time that they stood around "spinning yarns."[100] The original management staff of thirty-eight cadres, fifteen percent of the factory personnel, was slashed to twenty-two full-time administrative cadres. Its six three-tiered functional administrative divisions were reduced to three—a political group, production group, and logistics group.

As these reforms were carried out in the candy factory's management staff, groups of experienced workers were sent up to the management offices to conduct study and investigation. Upon completion of their research they made concrete suggestions, based on their technical experience on the line, for changes which should be made to eliminate irrational or excessive regulations and rules, particularly those involving approval for technological innovations pioneered by workers. A *Wenhuipao* reporter, writing on the experience of a worker research team at the East Is Red Shipyard, observed: "In a factory, there are many things which the leadership does not know about, but which the workers know and understand very well."[101]

While the revolutionary committee sought to mold its management staff into a more compact and streamlined unit, sending cadres down to the production line, it also reorganized factories' engineering and technical staff. They were urged to leave their desks and go to the workshops to be reeducated and form cadre-worker-engineer three-in-one combinations. The objective was to speed up the process and quality of technological innovations, which were stressed after the Cultural Revolution.[102]

In the structure of the revolutionary committee there is a clear conflict of interest between full-time administrators in the standing committee (veteran cadres and newly recruited leading cadres) and the workers' representatives. Workers' representatives advocate and defend the interests of the rank-and-file workers and seek to exercise worker control over the factory; while leading cadres (even though most are recruited from the working class) must exercise party leadership and represent the interests and the centralist concerns of the state.

This problem is accentuated in the relationship between veteran cadres and workers' representatives. Because in many factories veteran cadres and workers' representatives were formerly bitter combatants in the Cultural Revolution, there frequently existed a visible line of tension between veteran cadres and workers' representatives. Veteran cadres were inclined to feel some resentment toward the workers' representatives for exercising "revolutionary supervision" over them. Probably out of apprehension over the soundness of direct worker participation in management, veteran cadres had the tendency to push tasks of lesser importance to workers' representatives, reducing the content of their participation, even ritualizing the role of workers' supervision.

Repeated warnings were therefore issued by *Wenhuipao* urging veteran cadres to overcome their condescending attitudes toward representatives of the masses, and, instead, encourage their full participation in the revolutionary committee; otherwise, the editorials warned, the old order would gradually be restored and the revolutionary committee, as well as the Cultural Revolution, would fail.

Not only were leading cadres called upon to adhere rigorously to the mass line, but the representatives of the masses were urged to stand up to defend Mao's "proletarian revolutionary line" and tenaciously insist on the right of supervision to assure that leading cadres act as servants of the people and not their masters. A *Wenhuipao* editorial exclaimed, "You must express your attitude, your attitude toward this side or the other."[103]

Because the balance of power is tilted to the side of the leading cadres, it seems that the revolutionary committee's long-term success in realizing workers' control is largely dependent upon the collective strength and high political consciousness of the representatives of the masses. Since the workers' representatives in Shanghai factories appear to be primarily younger workers "between 20 and 30 years old" who emerged as the leaders of the workers, the revolutionary committee was also structured to combine the "high-spiritedness and vitality" of youth with the experience and maturity of the older veteran cadres, who form a very slim minority. A report filed by a *Hsinhua* correspondent of an on-the-spot investigation conducted in June 1968 at the Kehsin Electric Motor Plant in Shanghai described the tension between veteran cadres and young workers' representatives:

> The representatives of the masses in the revolutionary committee are characterized by their clear-cut stand and point of view and their courage in persisting in and debating matters of principle. In the first few days of the revolutionary committee, the meeting often took on the form of heated debates, and

some of the old cadres on the committee shook their heads in doubt, saying "Such debates are too heated." This made the young cadres dissatisfied, and they complained, "The old cadres are trying to smooth things over."[104]

Not only are there centralizing tendencies structured into the revolutionary committee, which left unchecked would restore the one-man leadership of the party secretary or factory director, but an editorial in *Wenhuipao* pointed out the possibility that the new workers' leaders might themselves become corrupted by power and gradually assume bureaucratic airs and detach themselves from the masses:

> Though they have joined the three-in-one organ of power, they also must persistently keep in close contact with the masses and "remain one of the common people while serving as an official." Otherwise, if they are divorced from the masses, as time goes by, their affection for the masses will subside and they will speak less in the language of the masses and more in the tune of an official. If so, how can they maintain their vigor, vitality, and revolutionary spirit? To be revolutionary forever and to make revolution continuously, we must never be divorced from the masses but must always strike root among the masses.[105]

There appear to be four institutionalized checks provided by the revolutionary committee to militate against the degeneration of new leaders.

First, workers' representatives as well as leading cadres must constantly study and analyze the classic works by Marx and Lenin. In the early 1970s they were studying the *Communist Manifesto* (Marx and Engels), *The State and Revolution* (Lenin), *The Civil War in France* (Marx), the *Critique of the Gotha Program* (Marx), *Anti-Dühring* (Engels), and all of Mao's political writings.

Second, with few exceptions, workers' representatives who do not receive any additional wages or fees for their work on the revolutionary committee continue to work on the production line as full-time workers and thus are subject to the direct supervision of the workers they represent.[106] The *Hsinhua* correspondent reporting on the situation at the Kehsin Electric Motor Plant described the revolutionary atmosphere at the factory, and concluded:

> This is due to the fact that with the exception of a few of them, the committee members at the plant and workshop levels are all full-time workers in the shop. Visitors to the plant find that no special offices are assigned to the workshop revolutionary committee, and that notices on the doors of the shops indicate where the members of the committee are. Inquiries reveal that the members of the workshop committee see no necessity to have an office since they work side by side with workers and problems can be solved on the spot.[107]

The third institutionalized check appears to be annual "open-door rectification meetings" at which workers of the entire plant review the record and performance of all the members of the factory revolutionary committee. They then write big-character posters making specific criticisms or suggestions for improvement of leadership work-style or factory policies. At these meetings, leaders of the revolutionary committee, leading cadres and workers' representatives, must "pass the gate" of worker supervision, address themselves to the criticisms, and evaluate themselves critically before the worker audience. Leaders who have degenerated and who fail to "pass the gate" may be sloughed off, and new leaders chosen to replace them. Similar rectification meetings are held twice a year in each of the factory's workshops where the record and performance of the workshop's revolutionary committee are opened to the same critical review by workers in the workshop.

Although the open-door rectification meeting seems to provide the mechanism for recall of leaders,[108] it should be noted that it is not clear whether the party committee can retain unpopular leaders despite their rejection by the masses. However, elections held every year in party branches—and every other year in party committees of basic-level units—provide an additional, though more indirect mechanism for maintaining popular control over leadership.[109] Unpopular or incompetent leaders can be voted out of positions of responsibility at these party elections.

Proletarian Municipal Government

There is little that citizens of Shanghai do in their day-to-day life that isn't influenced by or related to the policies of their municipal government. Their places of work, the stores at which they shop, the schools where their children are educated, the newspapers they read, the banks where they deposit their savings, the theaters and restaurants they frequent for entertainment, and the hospitals to which they go for medical care are all run by revolutionary committees. Indeed, the whole of Shanghai, the largest city in the world with a population of 1,820,000,[110] is organized as a broadly flung confederation of the city's revolutionary committees.

These committees, while following the centralized leadership of the Municipal Revolutionary Committee and the Central Committee in Peking, encourage active public participation in community and municipal politics and provide a channel of communication that reaches up to the Municipal Revolutionary Committee and beyond to Peking. The decentralization of control and the downward flow of state power into basic-level units, such as the neighborhood and residents' revolutionary committees, facilitates a high degree of dynamism, initiative, and flexibility at the basic levels. Citizens, through their active participation in these community organizations, can exercise a new degree of control over the administrative processes that directly affect their communities.

What is the nature of this municipal government, and in

what way does it represent the people of Shanghai and their interests?

The Shanghai Municipal Revolutionary Committee is located in a squat, drab-gray building that faces the mud-colored Whangpu River along the famous Shanghai bund. When in session its First Secretary, Chang Ch'un-ch'iao, and its Second Secretary, Yao Wen-yuan, preside over a large meeting of 150 members: 21 are leading cadres of the city (14 percent), 102 are representatives of the masses (70 percent), and 24 are representatives from the PLA garrison in Shanghai (16 percent). The representatives of the masses come from various backgrounds and occupations throughout the city and its far-flung suburban counties: 43 are rank-and-file workers from the city's factories and public facilities, 21 are peasants from the suburban communes, 8 are Red Guards from universities and colleges, 16 are intellectuals from leading newspapers and cultural and educational institutions, and 14 come from a miscellany of backgrounds, including salesmen and clerks from the city's department stores and shopping centers. There is also a broad range of different age groups: 40 are below 30 years old (26.7 percent), 80 are between 31 and 45 years old (53.3 percent), and 30 are over 46 years old (30 percent).[111]

The Municipal Revolutionary Committee thus seeks to be representative according to the widely promulgated three-in-one combination.

When the Municipal Revolutionary Committee is not in full session, a twenty-member standing committee executes its policies. This includes responsibility for managing and coordinating the work of the administrative staffs of the different municipal departments and bureaus which run the day-to-day affairs of the city government and of the city as a whole. The standing committee is similarly structured according to the principle of the three-in-one combination and has approximately the same percentages of the different representative categories that constitute the revolutionary committee.

The members of the Municipal Revolutionary Committee were not elected in the same fashion as the leaders of the Paris Commune, in an open, city-wide election. Instead, members were chosen through a careful process of consultation, screening, and election by ratification. During the Cultural Revolution the city's rebel mass organizations sent delegations of representatives to consultative meetings called by Chang Ch'un-ch'iao and the core group of rebel worker leaders and cadres of the Provisional Municipal Revolutionary Committee (basically the same group that formed the Provisional Committee of the Shanghai Commune). At these meetings the different delegations submitted lists of candidates. Then, in closed meetings of the core group of twenty-odd rebel leaders and cadres, the candidates were extensively discussed and individually evaluated for their record of performance through the whole process of the Cultural Revolution. Particular consideration was given to the question of representativeness—whether the different trades and occupations, the municipal districts, the communes on the outskirts of the city, the different age groups, women, and all the major components of the three-in-one combination were proportionately represented.

When a tentative list was finally arrived at, an enlarged meeting of all the representatives was reconvened to discuss and debate the list, and following this meeting subsequent revisions were made by the core group in closed sessions. The revised list was then carried back by the rebel delegations to their respective mass organizations and basic-level units where the candidates' qualifications were further discussed and debated. An election by opinion poll was then conducted throughout the city; on secret ballots, people marked "yes" or "no" to the different leaders proposed as candidates. Letters voicing specific grounds for disapproval of certain candidates could also be sent at this time to the core leadership group of the provisional government.

The results of this city-wide poll were carried back to an

enlarged consultative meeting where there was further discussion of each candidate in light of the opinion poll. The final list was then announced to the city after another closed session of the core group, which consulted with Peking before arriving at its decision. In this manner there was an "integration of democracy with centralism."[112]

Members of the Municipal Revolutionary Committee receive no additional salary beyond what they earned before they were selected, and continue to receive their pay from their original units. However, there seem to be no provisions for periodic city-wide general elections and no procedure for immediate popular recall of leaders. In this sense it should be seen as a relatively stable leadership group which drops or admits members according to the internal processes and decisions of the party branch of Shanghai. Elections are held at party congresses, which meet every three years according to the revised Party Constitution. Drastic turnover of leadership, however, appears unlikely except in the context of another cultural revolution.

As is the factories and revolutionary committees of basic-level units throughout the city, party leadership is also maintained in the Municipal Revolutionary Committee through a party committee. In January 1971 the party branch of Shanghai convened its Fourth Municipal Party Congress at which a new municipal Party Constitution was passed and seventy-six party members elected to a newly reconstituted Municipal Party Committee (according to the three-in-one formula). The new Municipal Party Committee, composed of fifty-nine full members and seventeen alternates, in turn elected a sixteen-member standing committee which, like that of the previous Municipal Party Committee, is the center of power and decision making. Most members of the party committee are also members of the revolutionary committee, and all members of the party standing committee are members of the standing committee of the Municipal Revolutionary Committee. Thus the party committee and its standing committee were selected to mirror the Municipal Revolutionary Committee and constitute its core leadership group.

The same system of checks and balances described in the factory revolutionary committee also operates in the Municipal Revolutionary Committee. Like the factory committee, there are centralizing tendencies inherent in the structure of the municipal committee. And here they are even stronger since the political distance between the standing committee of the Municipal Revolutionary Committee and the masses is greater than that which separates leading cadres from the masses in basic-level units. Thus the mechanism for maintaining accountability and popular supervision are proportionately weaker in the municipal committee.

It is largely for this reason that leading cadres of the municipal committee are required to do longer periods of physical labor. Each year, leading municipal-level cadres are supposed to perform several months of physical labor in Shanghai factories, plants, communes, or May 7th Cadre Schools. All representatives of the masses work in basic-level units once a week, usually on Thursday, and perform from one to three months of physical labor each year. In addition, apparently no matter how busy they are, members of the Municipal Revolutionary Committee spend their mornings from 10 to 12 A.M. in study groups reading and discussing selections from the classic works from the Marxist tradition, with particular emphasis on those dealing with the problem of proletarian government. Furthermore, each representative of the masses is held accountable by the standing committee for the situation in their basic-level unit; thus representatives maintain active ties and continue to play a leadership role in their original units. Representatives of the masses also are expected to specialize in their particular line of industry, occupation, or trade, and therefore spend a considerable portion of their time visiting and investigating conditions in other basic-level units in their fields.

This same division of labor is also operative in the standing committee, where each member specializes according to his background and assumes overall responsibility for his area of specialization. To keep abreast with their line of responsibility, they too spend considerable amounts of time visiting and inspecting units at the basic levels.

Of the many administrative reforms implemented by the Municipal Revolutionary Committee, the ones of the broadest significance involve the merging of party and state bureaucracies into one administrative unit under the Municipal Revolutionary Committee. While the bureaucracies were merged, the party still maintains its role as a policy-making leadership organ. Before the Cultural Revolution, the Municipal Party Committee and Municipal People's Council maintained entirely separate bureaucracies. Party committees, serving as watchdogs over the activities of state bureaucrats, paralleled the three-tiered national structure of the state apparatus—central government, provincial and municipal government, and basic-level units—keeping separate offices and staffs of functionaries. This formal separation of party and state was rationalized as necessary to preserve the party's purity as an organization whose purpose was to function as the cutting edge in the struggle to narrow the alienation of the state from society. In this role the party saw itself as a policy-making body that ought not to compromise its leadership capability in the morass of daily bureaucratic procedure involved in policy execution. But under the revolutionary committee the party has sought to combine the formerly separate party-government bureaucracies in one compact administrative structure in which policy making and execution are united in one system of command, so that "policies and systems can be implemented through to the end."[113]

Significantly, this remarkable and far-reaching administrative reform afforded a greater degree of centralization of power in municipal revolutionary committees under the "unified" and "centralized" leadership of the party led by Mao's "proletarian revolutionary line." Under Ts'ao Ti-ch'iu, the Municipal People's Council had become an independent center of power which rivaled that of the party and worked at cross-purposes to Mao's leadership of the revolution. In an important article written by rebel cadres of the People's Council, the former mayor was harshly criticized for having upheld what had been a rarely questioned assumption. "It won't do to mix the Party with the government."[114]

Ts'ao, who allegedly said, "Even guidelines and policies need not completely come from the party," had apparently assumed independent policy-making powers distinct from that of the party's and thus transformed the People's Council into a "watertight" independent kingdom.[115] He was further attacked for having advocated, along with Liu Shao-ch'i, the "theory of many centers" and the "theory of vertical leadership." "If things were done according to the theory of vertical leadership of China's Khrushchev and his agent Ts'ao Ti-ch'iu in Shanghai, then many centers of 'vertical leadership' would appear in all parts of the country and many centers would amount to no center at all."[116]

Moreover, during his tenure as mayor of Shanghai Ts'ao had woven a clique of bureaucrats, bound by an extensive web of personal ties and loyalties, which extended across the country and was linked at the highest level to Liu Shao-ch'i. He "put his trusted men in important positions, gathered together minions who would serve him, and formed a clique for private ends."[117]

It is interesting to note that the descriptions of Ts'ao's bureaucratic clique bear striking resemblance to the cliques of scholar-officials whose feuds and infighting for so long dominated China's Confucian bureaucracy. The Ts'ao clique's national ties and alliances cemented by strong personal bonds and loyalties also bespeaks the structure of China's traditional bureaucratic politics of clique intrigues and maneuvering. By merging party and state bureaucracies, Mao sought to smash this "watertight" independent kingdom and exercise unified and centralized party leadership over the administrative apparatus of government. At the same time, by setting the government under the direct supervision and control of the Municipal Revolutionary Committee, he sought to establish "revolutionary supervision" by representatives of the masses over the state bureaucracy.

Of equal importance, the merging of party and state bureaucracies facilitated a drastic slashing of administrative personnel and the elimination of gross redundancy and overlapping in administrative tasks and assignments. A *Wenhuipao* editorial commented that with the existence of the two separate bureaucracies, "there are several systems, many different groups of men, many organs with a big staff at many different levels; meetings are held excessively, contradictions are numerous and troubles are frequent. . . . In this way, 'there are one thousand threads at the higher level but there is only one needle at the lower level.' Leaders are high above, assuming the airs of officials and overlords."[118] Rampant growth of the municipal bureaucracies accompanied by the emergence of a bureaucratic stratum of party and state officials—which was in certain respects reminiscent of China's long tradition of scholar-official bureaucratic ruling class—and a prevailing "bureaucratic style of work" were directly attributed to Liu Shao-ch'i's revisionist line.[119]

In the course of the Cultural Revolution, however, at least three-quarters of the former administrative staffs of the two municipal bureaucracies, if not more, were eliminated simply by merging party and government staffs and reorganizing the combined staffs with a ruthless eye for paring away any redundancy, overlapping, or unnecessary division of labor. As in the factory-management reforms, the Municipal Revolutionary Committee sought to mold the remaining staff with an overriding concern for streamlining and efficiency. Their objective was to arrive at a more compact and rational municipal administrative system in accordance with Mao's policy of "better troops and simpler administration."

A final aspect of the sweeping administrative reforms designed to impose popular checks on the power of the state was the policy of sending municipal cadres to the "grass roots" where the bulk of administrative work was to be processed. "If they stay in their offices all the time, they will by and by be covered with the dust of being divorced from the masses," explained a *Wenhuipao* editorial.[120] The editorial urged cutting down on "excessive paper work, routinism and the influence of old habits." A cadre thus stripped of the security of his office and official distance, we may expect, would be more readily accountable to the people. The presence of cadres in basic-level units, moreover, would strengthen community organizations and workplace revolutionary committees. On this basis, the state could gradually narrow its alienation from society and be made more responsive to the masses, while its activities would shed their aura of mystery as people became more familiar with the local municipal cadre and the daily routine of his responsibilities. By enhancing the significance of community and workplace leadership bodies, in which citizens play an active role in decision making and in carrying out key administrative processes, sending cadres to the "grass roots" might have the long-term effect of transferring more and more of the responsibilities of the state into the hands of ordinary citizens. As Lenin pointed out, "The more the functions of state power devolve upon the people as a whole the less need is there for the existence of this power."[121]

At the Yangpu District Revolutionary Committee there were formerly thirty-one separate administrative departments in the District Party Committee and the District People's Council with a combined staff of 312 functionaries and officials. Following the administrative reforms, there are now only five groups, two offices, and eighty-four staff members. Only one staff member remains in each of the five administrative divisions to man the office, while the others leave every morning to their assigned units at the "grass roots." Field cadres, after investigating and researching problems in basic-level units, return to the District Office periodically to discuss and analyze the most difficult problems. After dividing the work load they return to the basic-level unit, sometimes accompanied by another cadre, to solve the problem. Solving problems at the site is apparently more efficient than the former system because it is task-oriented and avoids the passing of paper through numerous hands from one administrative level to another.

Since it is a new system, however, a number of difficulties have yet to be ironed out. For example, cadres, after prolonged stays at the grass roots, have been known to find various pretexts for returning to the home office; and leading cadres, feeling swamped by their own paper work, frequently transfer cadres back to the office. These tendencies are fought in the context of the continuing struggle between the two lines.

Another problem, from the masses' point of view, is that through this system municipal cadres are in a position to become oppressive agents of the state. Should the state turn repressive, the rich backlog of personal information and the network of personal contacts accumulated by the field cadres could be at its disposal. The prolonged presence of cadres in the community is undoubtedly viewed with suspicion and caution by some citizens, who are fearful that personal information might be used against them in future political campaigns. Such anxiety probably still corrodes efforts directed at establishing a new relationship between the cadres and the masses.

Aware that such problems exist, Mao had warned the Chinese people of the dangers of fascism should their revolution halt midway and bureaucratic control become dominant. For Mao the revolution must be a continuous, uninterrupted process that will ultimately bring about the withering away of the state. But during the period of transition, Mao feels that the repressive face of the modern state can best be held in check by the vigorous and sustained exercise of popular supervision.

Contained within the revolutionary committee were the very contradictions between the interests of the state, the collective, and the individual, between democracy and centralism, between leadership and led, between bureaucracy and the masses, which the Cultural Revolution sought to resolve, but which could not be resolved by one cultural revolution alone. As Mao himself said, China was "paying a very high price in the current Great Cultural Revolution. The struggle between the two classes and two lines cannot be settled in one, two, three, or four cultural revolutions, but the results of the current Great Cultural Revolution must be consolidated for at least fifteen years."[122] Since "two or three cultural revolutions should be carried out every hundred years," revolutionary committees were defined as a "transitional form of political power" which Mao felt should be further transformed and revised by subsequent cultural revolutions in the course of an uninterrupted revolutionary process. Revolutionary committees thus crystallized the essence of the new stage of the Chinese Revolution, embodying its continuing contradictions, compromises, and still unrealized promises.

No other revolution has pushed the limits of theoretical and practical understanding of state power further than has the Great Proletarian Cultural Revolution. Among Mao's most original contributions to the theory of revolution has been that classes, class contradiction, and class struggle will persist throughout the entire historic period of socialism; and as a corollary, that the state, the "product and the manifestation of the irreconcilability of class antagonisms,"[123] will continue to be the focus of class struggle and revolutionary politics.

This theory of the state is the basis of Mao's great heresy in the minds of party leaders who govern the vast and oppressive Soviet bureaucracy, and it is why they find Mao's Cultural Revolution so dangerously subversive to the legitimacy of the Soviet state system. Mao pointed to an emerging bureaucratic stratum of new mandarins who, in the name of the revolution and the masses, rationalized a system of élite rule and bureaucratic control which dichotomized socialist society into two distinct and separate groupings, the bureaucratic élite and the masses. The masses labored with their hands, producing the material sustenance and the wealth of the nation. The bureaucrats labored with their minds, coordinating and administering the activities of the masses. This division of labor, the primary impetus of new class formation in a socialist society, was for Mao the very precondition for revisionism. Mao feared that Chinese party officials and state bureaucrats, left on their own, would, like their Russian counterparts, seek to accumulate all the privileges of power and in time become a ruling stratum not unlike that which ruled China for thousands of years through the imperial bureaucracy of the Confucian state.

Through the Cultural Revolution, the veil of mystery and secrecy that enshrouded the party-state was torn away, revealing in the light of popular criticism and debate its contradictions and internal processes. The Cultural Revolution replaced the Soviet-style state system with one that was both innovative and yet in some ways strikingly harmonious with traditional forms of the Chinese state. But it also set in motion the protracted process of the "withering away of the state," which Mao believes will extend through the entire period of socialism. As he wrote in 1949 when the revolution first came to power:

> When classes disappear, all instruments of class struggle—parties and the state machinery—will lose their function, cease to be necessary, therefore gradually wither away and end their historical mission; and human society will move to a higher state. . . . K'ang Yu-wei wrote *Ta T'ung Shu* or the *Book of Great Harmony*, but he did not and could not find the way to achieve Great Harmony.[124]

Ta-t'ung, or great harmony, "a society based on public ownership, free from class exploitation and oppression," symbolizes Mao's broadest vision of the society of the future.

As a vision of a stateless society in which man lives in harmony with his collective, through which he realizes his full creative and human potentials—in politics, culture, and productive labor—the ideal of great harmony both encompasses Marx's hope for the communist society of the future and strikes a deep resonance with Chinese classical political thought.

The way to great harmony, however, will be a centuries-long process punctuated by repeated and intense periods of class struggle as demanding and torturous as the first Cultural Revolution. Through the historic experience of the Great Proletarian Cultural Revolution, Mao has demonstrated that a revolution conducted within a revolution is both possible and necessary to sustain the forward momentum of socialist revolution and prevent it from ossifying in the morass of bureaucratism and statism.

NOTES

I am grateful to James Peck, Mark Selden, Martha Winnacker, and especially my wife Brett for careful criticism and editorial advice. Sam Noumoff kindly read the galley proofs.

1. *K'uang-ying Hung-ch'i* (Canton Printing Red Flag), no. 2, November 23, 1967, in *Survey of China Mainland Press* (hereafter *SCMP*), no. 4145, March 25, 1968, p. 2.
2. "Wo chien-chüeh ting-chu le ching-chi-chu-yi de yin-feng," *Hung-ch'i* (Red Flag, hereafter *HC*), no. 2, January 16, 1967; *Kuang-ming Jih-pao*, January 25, 1967; *New China News Agency* (hereafter *NCNA*), December 29 and 30, 1967; *NCNA,* January 13, 1968.
3. *Wenhuipao* (hereafter *WHP*), January 4, 1967, p. 1; in *Union Research Service* (hereafter *URS*), Volume 46:114. For an account of the *Wenhuipao* two-line struggle see "Liang t'iao ken-pen tui-li de ching-chi chien-she lu-hsien," *Jen-min Jih-pao* (People's Daily) August 25, 1967. For description of Wenhuipao rebel takeover see *HC* no. 2, February 1, 1967.
4. *Hung Chan-pao* (Red Combat Bulletin), no. 10, October 10, 1967; in *URS*, 49:111.
5. *SCMP*, no. 4145, p. 2.

6. Translation available in Joan Robinson, *The Cultural Revolution in China* (London, 1969), pp. 96–101.

7. *Ibid.*, pp. 101–105.

8. *NCNA*, February 10, 1967.

9. *Kuang-ming Jih-pao*, February 10, 1967; also in *NCNA*, February 9, 1967.

10. *NCNA*, February 21, 1967.

11. *NCNA*, February 9, 1967.

12. *Ibid.*

13. "Hai-kung de ming-yün yu wo-men tzu-chi lai chang-wo" [Let us hold the destiny of the seaport in our hands], *HC*, no. 2, February 1, 1967, p. 54.

14. Interview with young workers at the No. 17 Cotton Mill in Shanghai. In the spring of 1972, my wife and I were granted a three-month visa by the People's Republic of China to travel and study. In Shanghai we had the opportunity to meet and interview a broad selection of citizens. Brett visited both the No. 17 Cotton Mill and the Fungchen Residents' Revolutionary Committee and carried out extensive interviews there. I spent my time primarily at the Shanghai Diesel Engine Plant in order to get a more in-depth account of the Cultural Revolution in one factory. We also had a long series of interviews with a representative of the Shanghai Municipal Revolutionary Committee.

15. "Tsan 'ke-ming sheng-ch'an wei-yuan-hui'" [Praise the 'revolution and production committee'], *Jen-min Jih-pao* (hereafter *JMJP*), January 23, 1967, p. 3.

16. Cited in Daniel Bell, *The End of Ideology* (Toronto, 1965), p. 381.

17. See Franz Schurmann, *Ideology and Organization in Communist China* (Berkeley and Los Angeles, 1966). Schurmann's chapter on "management" gives analysis of the introduction of Soviet management techniques into Chinese factories in the early 1950's. The management system which emerged after the Great Leap Forward was an adaptation of the Soviet "one-man management system."

18. *JMJP*, January 23, 1967.

19. *SCMP*, no. 4200, June 18, 1968, p. 3.

20. Interviews with workers and personnel at the Shanghai Diesel Engine Plant and the no. 17 Cotton Mill. See also Lynn White, "Leadership in Shanghai, 1955–69," in *Elites in the People's Republic of China*, ed. Robert Scalapino (Seattle, 1972), pp. 327–46.

21. See John Starr, "The Paris Commune through Chinese Eyes," *China Quarterly*, no. 49 (January–March 1972), pp. 116–20.

22. Cheng Chih-szu "The Great Lessons of the Paris Commune—In Commemoration of Its Ninety-fifth Anniversary," *Peking Review*, no. 16 (April 15, 1966), p. 24.

23. *Ibid.*, p. 25.

24. *Ibid.*, p. 24.

25. *Ibid.*, p. 23.

26. Lissagaray, *History of the Commune of 1871* (New York, 1967), pp. 88–170. See also Marx, *The Civil War in France* (Peking, 1970), pp. 54–63.

27. See V. I. Lenin, *"Left-Wing" Communism, an Infantile Disorder* (Peking, 1965).

28. Cheng, *Peking Review*, no. 16, p. 23.

29. "Decision of the Central Committee of the Chinese Communist Party Concerning the Great Proletarian Cultural Revolution" (adopted on August 8, 1966), *Peking Review*, no. 33, August 12, 1966, pp. 6–11.

30. "Whither China?", *K'uang-ying Hung-ch'i*, no. 5, March 1968, reprinted in *SCMP*, no. 4190, June 4, 1968, p. 1.

31. This fact lends credence to Chang Ch'un-ch'iao's later charge that to a large degree factionalism between rebel groups in the city was exacerbated and even instigated by deposed capitalist roaders. See *SCMP*, no. 4088, December 28, 1968, p. 9.

32. As director of propaganda in the Shanghai Municipal Party Committee, Chang had given critical support in 1965 to Chiang Ch'ing's reform of the Peking Opera. Yao Wen-yuan, a brilliant young Shanghai literary critic, had written what has been credited as the opening shot of the Cultural Revolution, an essay criticizing Wu Han's historical play "Hai Jui's Dismissal from Office," published in *Wenhuipao*, November 10, 1965.

33. The best study of the ultraleft influence on the Red Guards is William Hinton's account of the Cultural Revolution at Tsinghua University, *The Hundred Day War* (New York, 1972). See also Victor G. and Brett de Bary Nee, "Peking no interi wa nani o kangaete iru ka" [Intellectuals at Peking University], *Chuo Koron*, Tokyo, September 1972.

34. Hinton, *Hundred Day War*, pp. 105–37.

35. It may have been, as Neale Hunter has argued, that Keng Chinchang had a greater degree of "grass-roots" support than did Chang Ch'un-ch'iao and Yao Wen-yuan. Nevertheless, it appears that the channels through which this support was built were precisely those most available to the former party machine which Ch-en P'ei-hsien and Ts'ao Ti-ch'iu continued to control and which the January Revolution had bypassed. Whether or not there had been actual collusion between them cannot be proven by the available evidence. But the effect of Keng's opposition to the Shanghai Commune could only have benefited Ch'en Pei-hsien and Ts'ao Ti-ch'iu, and Keng's lack of open criticism for these two capitalist roaders during the period following the January Storm was conspicuous. See William Hinton, *Turning Point in China* (New York, 1972), pp. 78–79. Hinton gives a critique of Hunter's interpretation of the Shanghai Cultural Revolution.

36. Interview with Wu Sui-wu of the Shanghai Municipal Revolutionary Committee and *SCMP*, no. 4156, pp. 3–5.
37. Hunter, pp. 244–45.
38. "Long Live the Victory of the January Revolution!—The Declaration of the Shanghai People's Commune," *WHP*, February 7, 1967, in *URS*, 47:191.
39. *Ibid.*, p. 192.
40. *SCMP*, no. 4156, p. 7.
41. Hunter, pp. 244–67.
42. "Lun wu-ch'an chieh-chi de ke-ming chi-lü he ke-ming ch'üanwei," *HC*, no. 3, February 1, 1967.
43. "Lun wu-ch'an chieh-chi ke-ming-p'ai de to-ch'üan t'ou-cheng," *HC*, no. 3, February 1, 1967, p. 13.
44. *Peking Review*, no. 33, August 12, 1966, p. 8.
45. *Ibid.*
46. "Decision Concerning the PLA to Give Resolute Support to the Masses of Revolutionary Leftists," CCP Central Committee, State Council, Central Military Affairs Committee and Central Cultural Revolution Group.
47. *Joint Publications Research Service,* no. 61269-2 (February 20, 1974), Miscellany of Mao Tse-tung Thought (1949–1968), pt. 2, pp. 451–5.
48. Mao Tsetung, (February 1967) in *Chairman Mao Talks to the People*, ed. Stuart Schram (New York, 1974), p. 278.
49. "Wu-ch'an chieh-chi ke-ming-p'ai to-ch'uan t'ou-cheng de yigo hao fan-li" [Good example in the struggle by proletarian revolutionaries to seize power], *JMJP*, February 10, 1967, p. 1.
50. Margie Sargent, "The Cultural Revolution in Heilungkiang" in *The Cultural Revolution in the Provinces* (Cambridge, Mass., 1971), pp. 24–34.
51. *Tsu-liao Chuan-chi* [Special issue of reference material], February 10, 1968, in *SCMP*, no. 4190, June 4, 1968, p. 1.
52. *Ibid.*
53. *Ibid.*
54. *Ibid.*
55. *Ibid.*
56. This figure was supplied me by the Shanghai Municipal Revolutionary Committee.
57. *WHP*, March 29, April 5, and April 11, 1968.
58. For an interpretation of the events of spring and summer 1967 from an ultraleftist point of view, see "Whiter China" by the *Shengwulien*.
59. "Situation and Tasks of the Current Great Cultural Revolution in Shanghai" (Draft Resolution Made by the Shanghai Municipal Revolutionary Committee for Discussion and Execution by Various Revolutionary Committees and the Revolutionary Masses), *NCNA*, February 27, 1967.
60. "Experience of a Shanghai Cadre in the Cultural Revolution," *NCNA*, March 22, 1968.

61. *Hung-ch'i T'ung-tsun*, no. 5, 1968; in *SCMP*, no. 625, pp. 11–12.
62. *Ibid.*
63. *WHP*, March 6, 1967.
64. "Wo-men chieh-chueh le 'san chieh-ho' chong de ssu-ge wen-t'i," *JMJP*, March 10, 1967.
65. "Shih-hsien ke-ming de lien-ho pi-hsiu ta-tao tzu-chi." [Get Rid of ego in order to achieve revolutionary alliance], *HQ*, no. 11, 1967, p. 36.
66. "Immediately Return to the Countryside to Make Revolution!" *WHP*, February 12, 1967, p. 4, in *URS*, 47:168.
67. Industrial production steadily increased after 1967. The total increase in the value of industrial output in Shanghai between 1966 and 1970 was 68 percent greater than that between 1960–65. Shanghai has reaped continuous bumper harvests in her agricultural sectors for the past nine years, with grain output increasing 33 percent from 1966–70 as compared with increases gained between 1960 and 1965. Living standards have also improved gradually since the Cultural Revolution. From 1966–70 there was a 16 percent increase in total retail sales as compared to the period 1960–65. These figures were supplied to me by the Shanghai Municipal Revolutionary Committee. Thus while the first years of the Cultural Revolution were mildly disruptive to the Shanghai economy, the overall effect of the Cultural Revolution seems to have stimulated the rate of economic growth.
68. *WHP*, February 13, 1968; in *SCMP*, no. 4135, pp. 5–6.
69. *Ibid.*
70. *Ibid.*
71. "Draft Resolution," *NCNA*, February 27, 1967.
72. Interview with a member of the workers' militia at the no. 17 Cotton Mill; see *WHP*, March 26, 1968, in *SCMP*, no. 4169, pp. 11–13.
73. Interview with residents of the Fungchen Residents' Revolutionary Committee in the Yangpu District.
74. *WHP*, May 4, 1968.
75. *Wen-ko Tung-tsun* [Cultural revolution bulletin] no. 13, March 1968; in *SCMP*, no. 4166, pp. 12–13.
76. Interview with residents of the Fungchen Residents' Revolutionary Committee.
77. Mao Tsetung, "On the Correct Handling of Contradictions among the People," *Selected Readings from the Works of Mao Tse-tung* (Peking, 1971), p. 433.
78. *Ibid.*, p. 436.
79. See "Shanghai Worker Rebel News" no. 157, August 17, 1968, p. 2 (published by Shanghai Workers' Rebel Headquarters); in *URS*, 52:317. This document gives very detailed guidelines which specify categories of political crime in the Cultural Revolution. 1. Only former Kuomintang officials who were in the army, government, and police forces, secret agents or gendarmes, Kuomintang Youth League leaders and Kuomintang district party

branch committee members could be considered to be in the category of counterrevolutionaries. People who had past associations with the Kuomintang or who were only ordinary members of Kuomintang organizations were to be handled as contradictions among the people. 2. Counterrevolutionaries who had already made "clear" confessions were not to be confused with those who had managed to slip through the public-security net and were only uncovered in the Cultural Revolution. 3. A careful distinction was to be maintained between capitalist roaders in the Communist party who only wrote or spoke revisionist thoughts, and those who had actually engaged in planning counterrevolutionary activities during the Cultural Revolution. 4. Special care was to be given to handling counterrevolutionary cliques. A distinction was to be drawn between those cliques that had merely planned or conspired to carry out counterrevolutionary activities and those that had executed their plans and engaged in acts of sabotage. Only the leaders of these cliques were to be severely punished. Ordinary members, members who had not participated in counterrevolutionary activities, and people who had associations with the clique, but who were not members, were to be dealt with more leniently. 5. Those accused of being "traitors" to the party and of being "secret agents" were to be handled with caution. Only those Communist party members who had actually joined up with the Kuomintang during the period of the Revolutionary War, or who had cooperated with the Kuomintang after being captured and betrayed their comrades in the Shanghai party underground, could be considered "renegades" or "traitors." But party members who had penetrated Kuomintang organizations as counteragents were to be carefully detached from this category. In the 1930s and 1940s Communists had attempted to infiltrate the Kuomintang-controlled workers' unions. These people were not to be treated as "traitors" or "secret agents." 6. Only those of Shanghai's 88,000 citizens of bourgeoisie background who had actually engaged in "rightist" activities were to be investigated. These categories reveal a very careful attempt to narrow the target of mass struggle to Kuomintang secret agents, which was the emphasis especially in the later part of the Cultural Revolution.

80. *Wen-ko T'ung-tsun*, no. 3, March 1968, *SCMP*, no. 4167, p. 14.
81. *WHP*, April 11, April 28, 1968.
82. *SCMP*, no. 4088, pp. 1–19.
83. *Wen-ko T'ung-tsun*, no. 13, March 1968; in *SCMP*, no. 4166, pp. 12–13.
84. Interview with Wu Sui-wu.
85. Chang Ch'un-ch'iao was the secretary general of the Presidium of the 10th National Congress of the Communist Party of China, a member of the Central Committee, the Politburo, and the Standing Committee of the Politburo. Yao Wen-yuan is a member of the Central Committee and its Politburo. Wang Hung-wen

was the vice-chairman of the 10th Party Congress, a vice-chairman of the CCP, member of the Central Committee, Politburo, and its Standing Committee.

86. Yao Wen-yuan, "The Working Class Must Exercise Leadership in Everything," *Peking Review*, no. 35, August 30, 1968, pp. 3–6.

87. For a study of the Yenan revolutionary base area, see Mark Selden, *The Yenan Way in Revolutionary China* (Cambridge, Mass., 1971). Selden points out the importance of the political ideas and organizational techniques developed in Yenan in the Great Proletarian Cultural Revolution.

88. Reconstructed from interviews held at the no. 17 Cotton Mill.

89. Reconstructed from interviews held at the Shanghai Diesel Engine Plant.

90. "Revolutionary Committees Are Fine!" *NCNA*, March 29, 1968. This editorial appeared simultaneously in *Renmin Ribao*, *Hongqi*, and *Jiefang Junbao*. It stimulated a long series of editorials on revolutionary committees in Shanghai's *Wenhuibao*. Also based on interviews in Shanghai factories.

91. *WHP*, June 16, 1968, in *SCMP*, no. 4246, pp. 13–17; and *WHB*, June 17, 1967, in *SCMP*, no. 4232, p. 5.

92. *Ibid.*, p. 15. See *WHP*, March 22, 1968, in *SCMP*, no. 4170, p. 13.

93. *WHP*, June 11, 1968.

94. *Peking Review*, no. 18, May 4, 1973, pp. 21–22.

95. Interviews at the Shanghai Diesel Engine Plant and no. 17 Cotton Mill.

96. Interviews at the Shanghai Diesel Engine Plant and no. 17 Cotton Mill. See also *HQ*, no. 11, 1967, p. 9.

97. Interview with Yang Cheng-han, an engineer, and workers at the Diesel Engine Plant. Yang Cheng-han is the brother of the Chinese-American Nobel Prize-winning physicist, Yang Chenning.

98. *WHP*, September 13, 1968, in *SCMP*, no. 4287, pp. 9–10.

99. See Steve Andors, "Revolution and Modernization: Man and Machine in Industrializing Society, the Chinese Case," Edward Friedman and Mark Selden, eds., *America's Asia* (New York, 1971). Andors presents an illuminating analysis of Chinese experimentation in factory management reforms in the Great Leap Forward. He suggests that the Great Leap Forward management experiments anticipated the new management system which emerged out of the Cultural Revolution. For a discussion of "functional dualism" see Schurmann, *Ideology and Organization in Communist China*, p. 292.

100. "Pa ta p'i-p'an ho pen tan-wei t'ou-p'i kai chih-ho chi-lai" [Combine big criticism with struggle, criticism, and transformation in each unit], *HQ*, no. 10, 1967, p. 69.

101. *WHP*, September 13, 1968.

102. Interview with Pao Yang-shong, leading engineer at the Diesel Engine Plant, and Yang Cheng-han.

103. *WHP*, May 6, 1968, in *SCMP*, no. 4190, p. 19.

104. *NCNA*, June 23, 1968.
105. *WHP*, April 22, 1968.
106. Interviews at the Diesel Engine Plant and no. 17 Cotton Mill.
107. *NCNA*, June 23, 1968.
108. Interviews at the Diesel Engine Plant and no. 17 Cotton Mill.
109. "Constitution of the Communist Party of China," *Peking Review*, no. 34–35, September 17, 1973, p. 28.
110. This figure was released in the 1972 *United Nations Demographic Yearbook*, Tokyo (2), New York (3), Peking (4).
111. Figures released to me by the Shanghai Municipal Revolutionary Committee in 1972.
112. Interview with Wu Sui-wu.
113. *WHP*, April 21, 1968, in *SCMP*, no. 4178, pp. 1–2. For an analysis of the pre–Cultural Revolution party see Schurmann, *Ideology and Organization in Communist China* (especially the chapter on the "party").
114. *WHP*, 1968.
115. *Ibid.*
116. *Ibid.*
117. *Ibid.*
118. *WHP*, April 21, 1968.
119. *WHP*, August 14, 1968.
120. *WHP*, April 2, 1968.
121. Lenin, *The State and Revolution* (Peiking, 1970), pp. 50–51.
122. Mao Tsetung (August 31, 1967) in *SCMP*, no. 4200 June 18, 1968, pp. 2–7.
123. Lenin, *State and Revolution*, pp. 5–13.
124. Mao Tsetung, "On the People's Democratic Dictatorship," in *Selected Work of Mao Tsetung*. IV. (Peking, 1969), p. 414.

MAOISM AND
MOTIVATION:
Work Incentives in China

Carl Riskin

Visitors to China invariably comment on the energy and zeal of the people they met there. Seymour Topping's impression that "the basic needs of the people are being met and the foundation is being laid for a modern industrial country" he ascribes partly to "the energy exhibited everywhere."[1] Business economist Barry Richman found that Chinese industrial executives had a "high need for achievement" and displayed "considerable zeal, dedication, patriotism . . . a deep sense of commitment and purpose."[2] These examples could easily be multiplied.

Yet by now even those whose acquaintance with the country stops at the name of its chairman have heard that the ordinary incentives (as we know them) to work hard and well have been drastically weakened in China. Moreover, this supposed fact is generally held responsible for a record of dismal failure in economic development efforts. As Edwin O. Reischauer put it: "I think Mao or else people close to him . . . just did not want to admit that people were people and were going to act like human beings. That is one of the great failings of communism everywhere. It has always tried to change people into something else, and then it finds it cannot."[3]

But if Mao ("or else people close to him") has failed in his understanding of human nature, it follows that all the Chinese managers with high need for achievement and all the workers and peasants laboring on despite the absence of incentives are either masochists or uniquely pliant subjects. In other words, these two commonly held and widely expressed views of the motivational atmosphere in China conflict with one another.

In this article, I will argue that the assumptions implicit in the experts' common wisdom regarding incentives in China are naïve and contradict well-known and easily available material on motivation and work; that motivation is a crucial variable in economic development although it is generally neglected by economists; and that the Chinese approach to motivation requires us to broaden our treatment of this concept as well as to understand its links with other variables, such as organization, leadership, and the distribution of political power.

I. China Watchers' Perception of Motivation

It is difficult to grasp precisely what the critics of Maoist incentive practices mean because of the vagueness with which the have habitually stated their arguments, as though the latter were self-evident and did not require careful exposition. Maoist policies are characterized as obsessed with ideology and with the use of moral rather than material incentives; these policies are normally leavened with a sufficient dose of individual material incentives to keep production going, but during periods of extreme emphasis upon ideology (such as the Great Leap Forward) the leavening disappears and morale and production consequently suffer. Such, I believe, is a fair short statement of the position of this school.

It is a position, however, that raises substantial questions. What is responsible for good (or at least adequate) work morale during "normal" periods—the material or the nonmaterial incentives, or both? Moreover, what is the analytical basis for distinguishing an "extreme" from a "normal" mix of material and moral incentives? Without specifying this, the argument reduces to the tautology that extreme reliance upon nonmaterial incentives causes morale and production to suffer, where "extreme" is defined as a state in which morale and production are observed to suffer.

One searches the literature in vain for satisfactory answers to these two questions. One writer, for example, asserts that "a minimum of incentives for the peasant population" consisted of location of the basic accounting unit no higher than production-team level, existence of "free plots," and functioning of rural free markets.[4] This is fair enough, being presumably an empirical generalization from recent Chinese history. But it lacks an underlying rationale, ignores the question of how individual incomes are distributed for *collective* labor, and fails to take into account some well-known disincentives in locating the basic unit at team level (e.g., that neighboring teams will differ substantially in level of income per member simply because of differences in soil fertility, or access to water—surely a cause for grumbling among poorer team members). Moreover, it is sustainable, if at all, only for the specific conditions of a given historical period. The most thorough study to date of the role of private plots in Chinese agriculture concluded that their function would end when the peasants acquired "enough confidence that the collective economy will supply their needs."[5]

A common manner of treating the incentives question is to describe with approving adjectives the values of Chinese "pragmatists," thus implying that the "extremists" (usually Maoists) oppose these same values. For instance, the pragmatists "apparently recognize that effective management, scientific and technical skills, and economic incentives are required for success in economic development and modernization."[6] The implication is that the Maoists wish to dispense with effective management, scientific and technical skills, and economic incentives.

Or, "The pragmatists—who doubtless include some of

China's leading administrators and technical bureaucrats—
have apparently been successful in demanding that economic policies take account of economic realities."[7] This
implies that the "ideologues"—who have little or no administrative or technical experience—demand in their turn
that economic policies ignore economic realities. Neither of
these points would be easy to support directly.

The penchant for criticizing undefined "extremes" is
illustrated in such statements as: "The anti-material incentive, anti-modern technology mentality, if allowed full sway,
will hinder the growth of economy in general and of the
modern sector in particular."[8] The difficulty with this statement lies not only in what I will contend below is a mistaken
view of the "mentality" concerned, but also in the meaning
of the picturesque term "full sway." The only passage in
which its author offers a more specific idea of what is being
criticized is the following, which refers to "those periods
when the policy gave priority to ideology":

> Since the accent was on an egalitarian spirit and self-
> sacrifice, wages were not used as a proper stimulant
> to improvement of skills and increased productivity.
> In rural areas, this egalitarian tendency took the
> form of foodgrain distribution on grounds mainly
> unrelated to either work input or output. These
> irrational measures always cause a drop or stagnation
> in production.[9]

The writer apparently means that when wages are not
structured to stimulate improvement of skills and increased
productivity, skills will not be improved and productivity
will remain dormant; and when food grain is distributed
in a manner unrelated to the peasant's work input or productivity, "a drop or stagnation in production" will ensue.
Yet there is no evidence that workers were not motivated to
upgrade skills during the "extremist" Great Leap. (Introduction of industrial technology to peasants during the
"backyard iron and steel movement" is one of the few

generally conceded virtues of that movement.) Moreover, the current practice in rural areas of distributing some food grain independent of work done[10] has not caused the predicted decline in production.

Much of the remainder of this paper will be devoted to showing that the quoted statements, far from being obvious, beg most of the important questions.

Perhaps the most thorough and specific critique of "ideological extremism" is that of Barry Richman.[11] According to Richman,

> Ideological extremism in Chinese industrial management seems to have four key prongs: These are (1) the Reds vs. expert dilemma or pendulum; (2) material incentives and self-interest vs. non-material stimuli, altruism and self-sacrifice; (3) "class struggle" and the elimination of class distinctions; (4) the amount of time spent on political education and ideological indoctrination.[12]

In normal periods, experts are given more authority than Reds, material incentives hold sway over altruism, class struggle is muted, and people spend less time meeting and studying instead of working. In "ideologically extreme" periods, the opposite propensities dominate.

Richman's approach is unusual in that he finds value in moderate progress toward the "ideological" ends of these "prongs." "Management participation in labor at Chinese factories does appear to have some favorable effects" in "breaking down" "deep-rooted antagonism and resentment" based on "class distinctions between managers and workers, the educated and uneducated and mental and physical labor."[13] But in general Richman treats "ideology and politics," on the one hand, and "economic, managerial and technical rationality," on the other, as two poles between which a "pendulum" constantly swings.[14] Moreover, he considers swings to the left of this pendulum to be the greatest single impediment to rapid industrial progress in China:

> The types of constraints—both external and internal to the enterprise—thus far discussed which tend to hamper managerial efficiency and industrial progress in China [such as lack of managerial skills, technical expertise, etc.] appear to be but mere midgets as compared to the giant constraints arising from ideological extremism.[15]

Although Richman finds some pragmatic value in the use of "ideology," more frequently he regards it as a utopian attempt to repeal "centuries of world history and experience" by performing the "miracle" of replacing "material gain" and "pure altruism" as the force motivating man.[16] Such a description, I suggest, inaccurately portrays both the real problem of motivation in China and the current approach to solving it.

Economics and Human Motivation

Despite its importance to economic theory, economists are uncomfortable with the subject of human motivation. Especially since the development of neoclassical economic theory in the late nineteenth century, economists have tended to shy away from serious consideration of the psychological and sociological assumptions and implications of their work.[17] Instead, they have attempted to paper over the problem by means of various treatments, which, however, turn out upon closer examination to have strong and often simplistic psychological assumptions at their roots.[18] While this may have been possible in some branches of economics, it is clearly not legitimate in development theory where it would remove the very essence of the development process. This is a basic reason why this sector of economics has vigorously called upon the aid of anthropology, sociology, and psychology in a rare display of interdisciplinary cooperation. However, the term "depsychologization" is indeed accurate insofar as it pertains to the failure of economics to inquire into (or utilize the results of others' inquiries into) the nature and causes of human motivation lying behind the choices with which economists concern themselves: between work and leisure, between saving and consumption, and between different combinations of goods and services. Instead of analyzing the increase or decrease in production and growth directly attributable to differentials in human commitment, resourcefulness, energy, and creativity, economic theorists have traditionally avoided this problem by assuming given supply schedules* of resources, including labor, and then calculating how to achieve the most efficient allocation of these resources among alternative uses.

There are grounds for believing that in making this choice economics has been guilty, by its own standards, of a cardinal sin: misallocation of professional resources. For empirical studies indicate that motivational factors are responsible for incomparably greater variations in actual economic performance than is allocational inefficiency. For instance, Harvey Leibenstein, upon reviewing several ingenious attempts in the literature to measure the loss in national income that arises from misallocation of resources, concludes that "empirical evidence has been accumulating that suggests that the problem of allocative efficiency is trivial."[19] "Yet," Leibenstein continues, "it is hard to escape the notion that efficiency in some broad sense is significant." This type of efficiency "in some broad sense"—a major element of which is "motivation"—he gives the mysterious title "x-efficiency."[20]

The dominant motivational component of "x-efficiency" is more familiar and less mysterious than the term implies. It has been observed that "if you have some quantitative measure of their contribution to the organization, you will probably find that the best person in each group is contributing two, five, or perhaps ten times what the poorest is contributing."[21] The assumption that a substantial part of such differences in performance among people doing the

---

* A supply schedule is a relation between the quantity of a good or service supplied and the price (or wage) offered it.

same kind of work reflects differences in their motivation has generated a voluminous literature on work motivation which will be briefly touched upon below.

An almost identical case is made by Jaroslav Vanek. Citing the same kinds of evidence used by Leibenstein, to establish that misallocation of resources is generally responsible for only negligible shortfalls in output, Vanek points out that even multiplying these shortfalls many times would not approach the huge variations reasonably attributable to motivational factors.[22] "And yet, let it be noted, the time and concern of economists devoted to the study of what we have identified here as effort is of the order of one-thousandth" of that devoted to the problem of allocational efficiency.[23] Apparently, in identifying man as the "most precious" resource, in concentrating upon activating the "boundless creative power" of the masses, in urging that "spirit can become matter," and in teaching that "it is people, not things, that are decisive," Mao has avoided the economists' misallocation of mental resources, and eschewed the "trivial" for the "significant." In other words, a key to the Maoist conception of the development process lies in its search for institutional forms of achieving the multifold increases associated with human creativity and effort, rather than the marginal increments associated with achieving optimal allocation of statically conceived resources.[24]

This formulation, of course, leaves open the question whether Maoist antipathy to individual material incentives, by contradicting human nature and the requirements of a modern industrial society, renders the Maoist objectives utopian and thus impossible to realize. The evaluation of this argument requires a brief digression into motivation theory, and then the development of a more adequate (if rudimentary) picture of work motivation in contemporary China.

II. INSIGHTS OF INDUSTRIAL PSYCHOLOGY

Economists still commonly regard work as an unpl...
trespass on leisure, necessitated by and supplied only bec...
of the need to earn income. From the viewpoint of th...
worker, work is thus a "negative good," to which "disutility"
is attached, and to overcome this disutility and coax work
out of workers, a more than countervailing amount of
"utility" must be offered them in the form of purchasing
power. Since, furthermore, the amount of "disutility" is
assumed to increase faster than the number of hours worked,
whereas the "utility" per additional dollar of income falls
as income increases, it is easy to see why keeping up work
efforts is thought to require a highly progressive payment
scheme.

This theory is not so naïve as to assume that "leisure"
(the desired state among workers) consists of sitting around
and doing nothing. Of course people have interests and
would like to be active, but except for the lucky few, such
interests from the viewpoint of the market must be considered "hobbies." The job of the market is to get people
to perform services that are "demanded," with due regard
for the wage differentials required by different amounts of
talent, skill, and training, as well as compensating differentials required by the varying attractiveness of jobs.

In the eighteenth century, a simpler and more extreme
version of this theory held that workers worked only to avoid
starvation, so that the utility attaching to increments of
income above the subsistence level was zero. In this case, no
wage increase, however large, could ever induce more work
from a laborer. The more he is paid, the less work he need
perform to earn his subsistence. The moral, of course, is
to pay as little as possible.

Given what we know about the alienation of workers
from their products in modern industrial environments, the

ness and monotony of mass-production jobs, and
re uction of labor to a commodity in the capitalist
th , the standard view would seem to be a not unreason-
model for, say, the United States over the last 150 years.
d, perhaps because of its plausibility, it is approxi-
ted by the recently dominant and still influential "scien-
fic management" school associated with the work of
Frederick W. Taylor. It is worth citing the assumptions of
"scientific management" at some length because of their
direct relevance to the standard view of Chinese practices.
They include the following propositions, as summarized by
Douglas McGregor:

1. Management is responsible for organizing the
   elements of productive enterprise—money, materials, equipment, people—in the interest of
   economic ends.
2. With respect to people, this is a process of directing their efforts, motivating them, controlling
   their actions, modifying their behavior to fit the
   needs of the organization.
3. Without this active intervention by management,
   people would be passive—even resistant—to
   organizational needs. They must therefore be
   persuaded, rewarded, punished, controlled—
   their activities must be directed.

As McGregor points out, several additional postulates underlie this conventional theory:

4. The average man is by nature indolent—he works
   as little as possible.
5. He lacks ambition, dislikes responsibility, prefers
   to be led.
6. He is inherently self-centered, indifferent to
   organizational needs.
7. He is by nature resistant to change.
8. He is gullible, not very bright, the ready dupe of
   the charlatan and the demagogue.[25]

If these assumptions call to mind those of the eighteenth century, the impression is justified. "It is clear that the psychologists and efficiency experts of this [the Taylorist] period had accepted the attitudes of management which arose during the early stages of the Industrial Revolution and these tended to form the background to all their investigations."[26] These same assumptions find expression (albeit in less blatant and extreme form) in the exclusive attention of the orthodox school of Pekingologists to external, individual, material incentives as if these were the sole or at least dominant sources of motivation to be considered.

Industrial psychologists do not deny the efficacy of external rewards and punishments or of other insights of the "scientific management" school. Its predictions are corroborated by many empirical studies,[27] and it is regarded as having a psychological basis in reinforcement theory.[28] But it is now regarded as based upon insights into a very limited aspect of human psychology, rather than upon "human nature" in some holistic sense. Worker behavior responsive to direct external stimuli "is *not* a consequence of man's inherent nature," but "is a consequence rather of the nature of industrial organizations, of management philosophy, policy, and practice."[29] The orthodox view of Chinese incentives derives only from one particular corner of "human nature."

Not only is the "carrot and stick" theory of motivation now rejected as inadequate psychology, it also does badly when measured against the yardstick of history. The historical archetypes of Western capitalist development are of course the classic English or American nineteenth-century entrepreneurs who, with creativity, diligence, and frugality deriving from their Calvinist fundamentalism, accumulated personal fortunes while they created the Industrial Revolution. "But," writes David McClelland, "could their chief motive be profit if they were expressly denied the possibility of enjoying material benefits?"[30] Indeed, as McClelland goes on to observe, in both East and West it has been the ascetic cultural or religious groups, not the secular hedonists primarily motivated by achieving high personal consumption, who have established entrepreneurial credentials.[31]

The newer views about work motivation have strong roots in the famous Hawthorne studies of the 1920s as well as in the theoretical work of A. H. Maslow.[32] The Hawthorne experiments are generally credited with the discovery that the economic functions of the factory (production of goods) and its social functions ("creating and distributing human satisfactions among the people under its roof") are inseparable.[33] From the work of Hawthorne's principal investigator, Elton Mayo, came conclusions such as: Work is a group activity; it is the primary locus of the adult's social world; recognition, security, and sense of belonging are more important determinants of morale and productivity than physical conditions of work; and informal groups exert strong controls on work habits and attitudes within the plant.[34]

Clearly, these insights greatly complicated the game of bribing workers.[35] From their initial assumption that "money is the most powerful incentive," many industrial psychologists now found abundant data tending to the conclusion that "money is one of the least important."[36] In one study, eighty percent of a random sample of 401 employed men in the United States said they would continue to work even if by chance they were to inherit enough money to live comfortably without working.[37] Clearly, working gives people "a feeling of being tied into the larger society, of having something to do, of having a purpose in life. These other functions which working serves are evidently not seen as available in nonwork activities."[38]

Evidence was developed which showed that such factors as enlargement of job variety and responsibility, decrease in hierarchical control, increase in felt influence over decision making, and increased opportunities for informal interaction all correlated with increased job satisfaction and decreased turnover.[39] The convergence of such evidence led to the development of a new school of "participatory management" theorists. In contrast to their "scientific" predecessors, they claimed to find in workers "potential for development, the capacity for assuming responsibility, the readiness to direct behavior towards organizational goals." Management's job, according to this school, is to "arrange organizational conditions and methods of operation so that people can achieve their own goals best by directing *their own* efforts toward organizational objectives."[40]

As one would expect of a school that "uncritically adopt[s] industry's own conception of workers as *means* to be manipulated,"[41] this position rests comfortably on the unspoken heroic assumption that employee goals and organizational objectives are fundamentally compatible. We need not accept this assumption in order to agree that the approach to motivation of the "participatory management" advocates, in its resourceful methods of maximizing the area of short-term compatibility, is considerably more sophisticated than that of the "scientific managers." One writer likens it to "the difference between treating people as children and treating them as mature adults."[42]

The orthodox view of Chinese incentives tends, as we have seen, to depend upon implicit assumptions parallel to those of the "scientific" managers. Yet it is hard to avoid the conclusion that the theoretical and empirical work of the "participatory" school has rendered obsolete these earlier assumptions as a possible basis for a general theory of work motivation.

III. Two Systems of Distribution

Collective Incentives

Treatments of Chinese incentive practices often equate material with private incentives, and nonmaterial with collective ones. A grain of truth exists in this confusion, for personal incentive systems do embody a more direct relation between individual work effort and individual income than do collective systems. Slight variations in an individual's output have a more perceptible effect on his earnings.

This advantage in sensitivity is widely assumed to prove the overall superiority of personal over collective incentive systems in motivating work effort, but this view is fallacious because it focuses on only one property of an incentive system. It is like arguing that the best brush for painting is invariably the finest. Imagine, for instance, that residents of a village believe that only by working together as a group can they transform the economy of their village and significantly improve living standards, and that they similarly feel that individual incentive payments would create divisions in the group and destroy its cohesiveness. Under these circumstances, the residents would opt for a relatively egalitarian payment scheme, and yet still be motivated by the expectation of material gain. Nor is it inconceivable that they would work harder than if motivated by the combination of individual incentives and the expectation of smaller overall gains in income. This is precisely the distinction between the power (or overall effectiveness in stimulating work effort) of an incentive system and its sensitivity.

In the above example the expectation of material gain motivates people effectively even though distribution is equal. Such a result, however, depends upon the social consciousness of the members of the collective. To see this more clearly, let us strip the problem to its logical essentials in the form of a simple "game" suggested by Amartya Sen.[43]

We begin by assuming that distribution is based roughly upon need. Each member of a particular group has four possible modes of behavior: (1) He is lazy when everyone else is diligent (call this situation LD); (2) he is diligent when everyone else is diligent (DD); (3) he is lazy when everyone else is lazy (LL); and (4) he is diligent when everyone else is lazy (DL).

The level of social consciousness of members is revealed by the order of preference in which they rank these situations. If each member is selfish, in that he prefers not to work hard whether his colleagues do or not, he will rank the possibilities like this: LD, DD, LL, DL. Notice that although each member will choose to be lazy given either kind of behavior by his colleagues, each also prefers everyone diligent (DD) to everyone lazy (LL), since universal laziness would be ruinous to all members. Despite the latter preference, it is easy to see that if each individual is left to make his own rational calculation, the result must be universal laziness. Individual choice leads inevitably to a result that is inferior, even by the individuals' own selfish preference rankings, to one that is unattainable by means of individual choice.[44]

This dilemma can be avoided if each member simply reverses his order of preference for the first two situations: Each now prefers to be diligent so long as the other members also work hard, but does not want to be taken advantage of by toiling for the common good while others malinger. In contrast to the first, "selfish" state of social consciousness, let us call this one "socialist" consciousness: DD, LD, LL, DL. Now it remains only to establish confidence in each member's mind that the others will pull their fair share, and he will choose to do the same. Common diligence will be the result.

Of course, if the members of the collective had a purely "selfless" state of consciousness, such that they each preferred diligence even if their colleagues were lazy (DD, LD, DL, LL), then common diligence would result automatically with or without confidence in the diligence of others.

If ideological education and propaganda can persuade group members that the proper way to behave is "socialistically" (or better yet, "selflessly") rather than "selfishly," even though they remain selfish at heart, then the result DD will obtain. This is preferred by all, even according to their true selfish values, to the result (LL) of choice based upon those values.[45] The same result, of course, follows even more forcefully if education actually can change true values in a "socialist" or "selfless" direction.

Where labor is still long, toilsome, and difficult, however, and where its immediate links with livelihood have been loosened (as when pay is relatively equal), won't there be a continuing tendency to slack off? Under these conditions, is it realistic to expect education and exhortation alone to cause people to behave *as if* they preferred more drudgery to less—let alone cause them actually to prefer it? Whether because of their own experience, or out of deference to the traditional Marxist (and especially Leninist) skepticism in this regard,[46] the Chinese do not by any means rely exclusively on education and propaganda.

Given underlying "selfish" preferences, the only other way of separating individual choices from individual preferences is to legislate or otherwise enforce desired individual behavior. If individuals recognize that the legislated outcome is preferable to the "free" one, they will accept—even themselves draw up—the legislation. Thus, for example, individuals will gladly accept a law that makes them pay fair taxes along with everyone else even though they would individually prefer not to pay any, if they know that without such a law nobody would choose to pay any and that consequently there would be no social services. But such an administered solution runs into serious problems when applied to work motivation. It is impossible in practice to define standards of reasonable diligence and creativity for different individuals and then to enforce them, and difficult even to make the attempt without alienating workers. As Sen argues, "The feasibility of using payments according to needs combined with vigorous supervision of work done is profoundly doubtful."[47] Indeed, such an attempt during the Great Leap Forward led to serious problems of "commandism" on the part of cadres, and caused at least a temporary abandonment of the system of distribution according to need ("free supply" system).

However, there is a method of supervision that may avoid this pitfall. If the group is small enough and has sufficient control of the fruits of its collective labor, then each member will realize that his welfare is dependent upon the diligence of all other members. In conjunction with a general social climate favoring selflessness, such perceived interdependence can lead to the exertion of powerful group pressure on laggards to measure up to their potential. "Vigorous supervision" is thus exercised not through hierarchic organs of control, with their inevitable offshoots of "commandism" and alienation, but by means of a diffused group morale based on each member's recognition of mutual interdependence with all other members. When the group's activities are the principal source of its members' livelihoods, a powerful material incentive will exist to exert such social pressure, even if distribution *within the group* is based upon need. Describing this form of distribution in Chinese communes, Arthur Galston writes, "Any worker 'goofing off' hurts his entire production team. You can imagine what kind of social pressure would be exerted against any chronic malingerer."[48] This is a hybrid solution, fusing local (within the group) egalitarian distribution with the retention of material incentives to motivate diligent work. It requires a relatively small group, a method of determining need regarded as just by group members, and a significant degree of control by the group over its net income. These prerequisites make the system more suitable to a rural work team, brigade, or commune, or even a *hsien* factory, than to a national-level enterprise. Such a system also requires a refined and widely disseminated method by which groups can treat the delicate problems of group-individual interaction. Finally, it does *not* require "selfless" participants, although it is certainly aided by a cultural climate favoring a high degree of social consciousness.

Because this incentive system implies a strong tie between collective output and collective welfare, it requires that groups which produce more, keep more (which indicates its affinity to "self-reliance"). Therefore, under this system, distribution of regional or national income *between* groups will tend to be "according to labor" even while distribution *within* groups is "according to need." It is the first feature that explains the continued existence of material incentives in the face of the second feature.

Having seen how the socialist principle can be retained as a method of collective distribution while personal income is distributed according to a different mode, we must recall that in China personal distribution as well is supposed to follow the socialist precept. Although it still does so to an important extent, the Chinese have tried to refine the principle of "to each according to his labor" in such a way as to reward not merely output *per se* but desired work behavior. Before discussing China's distribution practices in detail, we must briefly look into the logic of the socialist mode of distributing personal income.

Personal Incentives

The socialist principle "to each according to his work" was regarded by Marx as governing the distribution of income in the early stage of communist society "as it *emerges* from capitalist society."[49] By "work" or "labor" is meant the net value added by each individual worker's labor: "The individual producer receives back from society—after the deductions have been made—exactly what he gives to it."[50]

Marx was concerned to distinguish this form of distribution from the one that would eventually develop in "a higher phase of communist society": "from each according to his ability, to each according to his needs."[51] Therefore, his treatment separates the two principles sharply. The early principle is "still stigmatised by a bourgeois limitation," namely, that the right of producers to income is proportional to the labor they supply. Individuals differ in physical and mental ability and hence supply different amounts of labor. Therefore, the right to payment according to one's labor "is an unequal right for unequal labor." Moreover, even if individuals supplied equal amounts, they would still differ in their needs, for one would have many dependents, another few, etc. In sum, while the socialist principle of distribution abolishes exploitation, it cannot abolish inequality.

Lenin also drew a rigid line of distinction between the two principles, arguing that the distribution of income and allotment of labor among individuals continues under socialism to be governed by "bourgeois right," and that, accordingly, "differences, and unjust differences, in wealth will still exist" under socialism.[52]

Marx and Lenin saw these two modes of distribution as characterizing two distinct stages of development of communist society, and neither attempted to predict the actual process of transition from one to another. But they left no doubt that a principal reason for the preservation of "bourgeois right" under socialism was the inadequate development of social consciousness and the consequent need to retain material incentives to stimulate work. For instance, Lenin argued that the transition to communist distribution would occur when man's bourgeois compulsion to "calculate with the stringency of a Shylock whether he has not worked half an hour more than another, whether he is not getting less pay than another, is left behind."[53] Commenting on the principle of distribution according to labor, Lenin harshly brought out its motivational purpose: "Also a form of compulsion: 'He who does not work, neither shall he eat.' " And on the passage describing the higher, communist principle, he noted: "Work has become a necessity, there is no compulsion whatever."[54] Thus, Lenin saw the survival of the socialist principle as due to the continuing need under socialism to use the threat of withholding means of subsistence to stimulate work effort.

But how long does this need continue, what are the links between its disappearance and the development of the economic base, and how is its disappearance expressed in the evolving system of distribution? These questions, of prime importance to the actual practice of the socialist state, were ones that Marx did not take up, and the answers to which Lenin expressly stated "we do not and cannot know" in advance.[55]

Let us look more closely at the motivational features that grace the principle of "distribution according to work" and which explain its retention under socialism. There are several reasons why the productivity of individuals may vary:

1. Differences in the amount of machinery and equipment per worker
2. Differences in the amount of education and training per worker
3. Differences in natural endowments of strength, dexterity, or talent
4. Differences in the values of workers' respective physical outputs
5. Differences in organizational environments (e.g., in managerial quality, availability of raw materials, etc.)
6. Differences in attitudes toward work, making some workers more diligent and creative than others

Abstracting for the moment from the problem of skills or attitudes that must be inculcated so that workers will treat machinery properly, the differences in productivity due to number 1 are explained by the equipment with which labor works, not by behavior that responds to incentives. No reasonable, merit-based distribution system would treat one worker as more deserving than the next according to whether or not he has a better machine to work with. Nor will the supply of high-productivity workers with better machines be increased if they are paid more.

Number 2 is somewhat more complicated. If the acquisition of education and training is a private expense of the worker, then there might be a motivational need to repay this investment with higher earnings; otherwise there would be little incentive to acquire education and training. However, as Engels put it, "In a socialistically organized society, these costs are borne by society, and to it therefore belong also the fruits, the greater values produced by skilled labor. The laborer himself has no claim to extra payment."[56] Nor is there any a priori reason to believe, so long as education is regarded as having independent benefits of its own, that the demand for an education (all of whose costs are borne by the state) would be inadequate unless extra pay were proffered to the educated.[57]

It is likely that in a new socialist society some skills acquired in the past will have to be rewarded with incentive pay in order to be kept in service with reasonably good morale. This may be necessary even when the acquirement of such skills was financed by income derived from exploitation. But it is difficult to see why this practice need extend beyond the generation which makes the transition to socialism as adults.

The third factor (differences in native strength and talent) is analogous to variations in land fertility. From the point of view of merit, there is no more reason for the fortuitous owner of a six-foot frame or a genius for mathematics to be rewarded exceptionally than there is to so favor the owner of a particularly rich piece of land. With respect to motivation, the supply of such endowments cannot be sensitive to incentives, since by definition they are given by nature and do not develop in response to rewards and punishments.[58] Nevertheless, the *allocation* of natural abilities to appropriate employment is not independent of incentives. An individual with an aptitude for mathematics, for example, may fail to make his or her talents available to a job requiring them if the compensation system in that job does not reward them. Similarly, a job requiring physical strength may have to reward the productivity of such strength in order to attract strong workers, who otherwise could earn as much in another job without such a requirement. Thus, in the absence of a refined system for ascertaining talents and allocating them to occupations in a way that avoids arbitrariness and alienation, a case can be made strictly on grounds of efficiency for allowing the market a degree of latitude. Natural endowments would be given some differential reward as a means of ensuring their employment in jobs that can better utilize them.

The fourth factor (differences in the *values* of physical

outputs of different jobs) alerts us to the difficulty of applying the principle of "distribution according to labor" to workers with different types of jobs. There is no direct way of comparing, for example, a day of mechanic's labor with a day of farm labor. If the values of the outputs are used as the basis for comparison, then the prices upon which these values are based cannot in turn be founded upon the values of labor embodied in the respective products without the reasoning becoming circular. But if prices are not determined by labor values, then differences in measured worker productivity are partly arbitrary and cannot be taken as a guide to differences in work done. In practice, therefore, the principle of distribution according to labor is ambiguous except for workers in closely similar jobs.

The fifth factor (differences in organizational environments) can be ruled out as a valid basis for differential pay. Neither merit nor incentive considerations would dictate paying one worker more than another because his shop was better managed—unless he were also the manager. But in that case the reasons for the difference would be encompassed by one of the other categories.

Finally, in our search for a motivational basis for the socialist principle "to each according to his work," we come to the consideration of diligence and creativity stemming from attitudes toward work. Here, of course, we are on firm ground in expecting that differential pay will stimulate work efforts. Socialist man, "morally and intellectually still stamped with the birthmarks of the old society" (Marx), is indeed likely to respond to the rough justice of payment according to the amount of toil, sweat, and concentration he puts into his job. Also, to the extent that training costs must still be borne individually (e.g., in lost leisure for after-hours study), he will still tend to require the promise of later rewards to make it worthwhile to upgrade skills.

Of the several causes of variations in labor productivity, then, only that of category 6 and possibly category 3 justify differences in pay on incentive grounds. The trouble is, work as measured by the value of a worker's output is but a rough and imperfect indicator of these two factors, since differences in output value reflect differences between workers in the other categories as well, none of which warrant differences in pay. Hence a system of distribution according to work is not a very efficient system for realizing either allocative efficiency or the incentives that Marx and Lenin regarded as necessary until the full attainment of communism. It has the advantage, however, of being a relatively straightforward system that does not require deeper probing of individual "worthiness," or grappling with the thorny problems of how and by whom such an evaluation should be made.

To isolate natural capability and diligent, conscientious effort, and make distribution of income depend only upon these traits, would be no less "bourgeois." It would still entail the application of an equal standard of right to unequal individuals. The standard becomes that *part* of productivity due to the presence of these traits, leaving aside the residue of productivity due to other factors. But some workers will not be as strong or talented as others, or will possess talents not valued by plan or market, and so will earn less. Others, for reasons of psychology or social background, will be unable to work as diligently or conscientiously as others, and will earn less. Moreover, the single worker and the worker with six children to support will still be unequal under this standard.

However, the standard of capability and conscientiousness would probably on balance reduce inequality by eliminating some unequally shared and arbitrary characteristics as factors determining income. It would align income distribution more closely with widely held standards of merit, and thus achieve a greater degree of acceptability. Yet, by tying payment more specifically to desired behavior and needed abilities, without the interference of extraneous and irrelevant factors, it paradoxically would tend to sharpen material incentives.

IV. Work Motivation in China

We now have before us two systems of distribution, described in the abstract, both incorporating material incentives, although in different forms. The first consists of distribution between collectives according to labor, and distribution according to need among individuals within each collective.[59] The second is a refined form of distribution according to work, with "work" measured by individual productivity due to ability and conscientious effort.

The Maoist literature, of course, uniformly condemns *all* material incentives, without making any of these distinctions. Just as clearly does this literature insist on adherence to the socialist principle that payment correlate with work.[60] Yet, as we have seen, Marx and Lenin felt that the principle of payment according to work had to be retained in socialist society precisely in order to provide material incentives to stimulate work. The Chinese attempt to draw a sharp line of demarcation between the two principles causes some confusion, as in the following non sequitur:

> We working people have now become masters of our own country. We are no longer wage-laborers selling our labor power as a commodity. We work for the building of socialism, for the complete emancipation of the working people. Therefore, the wages we now get are no longer the value or price of our labor power but a kind of distribution of consumer goods to the workers by the state according to the socialist principle—"From each according to his ability, to each according to his work."[61]

If the premise "We work for the building of socialism, for the complete emancipation of the working people" were to be regarded as a statement of accomplished fact rather than of aspiration, then the socialist system of distribution to which it is linked in this passage would be regressive in terms of the Marxist-Leninist analysis. Because such statements are really in part ideological exhortations designed to strengthen desired values in the population, and therefore do not accurately describe current reality, we must dig deeper to uncover the operative characteristics of incentive practice in China.

Urban and rural income-distribution mechanisms have been described in detail elsewhere.[62] In this section I will show how recent trends in China's approach to income distribution seem to have incorporated the motivational principles described in Part II, to create a rather complex and sophisticated overall system of incentives. The evolving system seems to permit increasing equality of distribution to coexist with the retention of material incentives.

The Tachai System

For a model of the merit-oriented principle of distribution according to labor, consider the following criteria for allocating work points used by the famous Tachai Brigade:

> High skills, and abundance of enthusiasm for work, support from the community, honesty, and a high degree of class consciousness are important. A man's ability or labor power may be great or small. But if he works with heart and soul for the good of everyone he is respected and we will ensure him a secure life even if his labor power is limited.[63]

Tachai probably carries to the extreme the concept of rewarding merit rather than product.[64] But the practice itself is widely evident. At Hongqiao Commune near Shanghai, the criteria for payment to individuals are attitude toward work (encompassing a range of factors associated with a worker's ideological level), level of skill, and strength.[65] At Shashihyu Brigade in Hopeh Province, the criteria are attitude toward labor, time devoted to labor, quantity of work performed, and quality of work.[66] At Dragon Well Brigade near Hangchow, they are political behavior, attitude toward work, quantity and quality of work.[67] Commenting on the system at Evergreen Commune, Maria Antonietta Macciocchi writes, "The calculation is not based on the basic work day, which would have the effect of stimulating the peasants to work, but the flaw of differentiating among them according to their strength, their age, their technical level. . . ."[68] Many such reports from communes indicate practices that attempt to bring rewards more in line with desired behavior and to weaken other influences upon income. "Workpoints are given according to the behavior of each person. . . . Weak or strong, all that matters is whether one is able to work."[69]

The behavior encouraged within the collective is more than just diligence. It is also "selflessness"—the subordination of one's individual interests to those of the collective—as evidenced by a willingness to help others, devote extra labor and night soil to the collective fields in preference to the private plot, participate in group political, cultural, and welfare activities, etc., all without undue concern for personal gain or loss. If "selfless" behavior in this broad sense is encouraged by the use of work points, which by their nature appeal to the desire for self-gain, the contradiction between means and end[70] may evoke simulations of the desired attitudes. Chinese criticisms of such superficial behavior as reciting slogans by rote, talking volubly at meetings without having anything to say, and carrying the display of Mao pictures and buttons to extremes indicate that such a problem has existed. To the extent that simulated and mechanical manifestations of desired attitudes are exposed and fail, the payment system ceases entirely to be an active motivator of correct behavior. This is because the real goals by their very nature cannot be measured directly or otherwise quantified. A worker's enthusiasm for work, willingness to help others, and political seriousness, for example, cannot be assessed in such manner that an increase or decrease would lead to a corresponding change in pay. Therefore, the worker is not apt to change his behavior in response to such an incentive. In sum, the very generality of Tachai-type criteria of performance weakens the material-incentive element in the system of payment according to behavior.

Nevertheless, the Tachai system remains a "desert-based" system—that is, one based on the criterion of merit—distinctly different in this respect from payment according to need. As such it continues to play an important motivational role that the latter system could not play—namely, the passive, reinforcing role of preventing meritorious behavior from being penalized by losses in work points.[71] There are basically two reasons why this is so.

First, payment strictly according to work done requires relative evaluation of different kinds of work. But in agriculture the relative values of different tasks change continuously with the weather, the season, and the course of local development. No administered price system (such as a detailed work-point schedule) can as adequately represent need priorities on the local level as can the day-to-day perceptions of the local people themselves (unless the schedule were revised literally daily!). In the Fifties and early Sixties, the use of such a rigid work-point schedule resulted in oversupplies of workers applying for high-point jobs and the understaffing of low-point ones. Attempts to solve the problem by administrative assignment led to disgruntlement on the part of the unfavorably assigned workers.[72] Under the Tachai-type system, however, workers can volunteer for high-priority tasks without worrying about whether or not those tasks carry work-point values that reflect their importance. In general, under this system, being a good guy does not imply finishing last, and this weakens the motive of prudence for not being one.

Second, the attitudes of different individuals are interdependent. One worker may set an example for others and inspire them, or may help others to improve their skills and overcome problems. Or, he may demoralize them by means of his own behavior. Such "externalities"—to use the economists' term—create a gap between the worker's individual, direct contribution to output and his total social contribution, including the indirect contribution made through his influence on others' productivity. There is no way to measure the latter component; hence any payment scheme tied to productivity will tend to ignore it, thus underpaying the inspiring workers and overpaying the demoralizing ones. The Tachai-type criteria permit evaluation of a worker's total social role, and thus enable his interaction with others to be taken into account—even if only in a general way—when calculating his contribution.[73]

For both these reasons, then, general behavior-oriented criteria for work-point allocation lessen the tendency inherent in the earlier system—and indeed in any more specific system—for work-point allocation to conflict with, and thus to discourage, desired work behavior.

In industry, payment according to work may embody to some extent the same principles of merit and aptitude as in the rural communes, but it is harder to detect. Time wages, the chief method of payment in factories and mines since the Cultural Revolution, are an imperfect reflector of behavioral differences of any kind between workers. In state enterprises, wages conform to standards set by the state and differentiated by branch of activity. For ordinary workers the usual pattern is an eight-grade system, with the top wage averaging two to three times the bottom one. Each worker is assigned a grade according to his seniority, skill, and function.[74] Before the Cultural Revolution when bonuses were still being paid, they depended not only upon productivity but also upon "politics and aid to co-workers."[75] I have seen little indication of whether a worker's assignment to a basic wage grade also depends upon such criteria now that differential bonuses are no longer paid.[76] Therefore, it is not possible to judge the degree of "merit" reward on the basis of grade-assignment criteria.

The suggestion of merit system comes rather from the smallness of wage differentials associated with skill and status. In 8 of 38 industrial enterprises visited in 1966, Barry Richman found that workers were the highest-paid employees. In most of the 38 enterprises, the director's salary was only twice as high as the average enterprise pay, and this ratio never exceeed 3 to 1.[77] The average ratio of the salary of the highest-paid engineer or technician to the average enterprise wage was less than 2.7 to 1.[78] Moreover, this gap has probably been further reduced since Richman's visit in June 1966. For example, at Peking No. 1 Machine Tool Plant, Richman reported the chief engineer was getting 180 yuan in 1966, or some 3.6 times as much as the average enterprise wage (52 yuan). But visitors in August 1972 were told that engineers get a maximum pay of only 120 yuan, 2.2 times the average wage of 55 yuan.[79] The same visitors found technicians at the Fangezhuang Pit of the Kailan Coal Mines in Tangshan getting only 1.4 times the average wage for pit work (145 yuan as compared to 100 yuan), while at Shanghai's Construction Machinery Factory, technicians, cadres, and workers were all paid the same scale. A major part of the difference between high and low wages within a plant now seems to be accounted for by length of service.

Of course, such narrow differentials do not prove that enterprise pay follows the merit principle, but they do suggest that premiums due to fortuitous factors such as advantages of social background have been substantially reduced, which is consistent with this principle.[80]

The Collective Material-Incentive System

Coexisting with the merit version of personal distribution is the collective material-incentive system with payment according to need within the enterprise. This system, as we have seen, implies a rough correlation between group productivity and group income, and therefore a system of distribution *between groups* pegged to their productivities, if it is to retain its material-incentive feature. It is most evident therefore in the collective sector. Collectively owned enterprises set the level of their wages and welfare funds according to the level of their net incomes. Since their equipment is more backward and makeshift than that of state enterprises, and their workers' level of skill lower, the wages and welfare services they can generate are almost invariably lower than those of the state enterprises.

Visitors to the Peking February 7 Rolling Stock Plant in 1971, for example, found that regular workers in the main plant earned twice as much as dependents and women who worked in a collectively owned metalworking subsidiary earned "for similar work, of similar duration, effort and difficulty."[81] At the K'ung Chiang Workers' New Village in Shanghai, American political economists were told that former housewives making flashlight bulbs in the settlement's collective workshops earn only about 30 yuan per month, one-third less than the average pay of 45 yuan for such work in state factories. This wage will gradually rise as productivity increases. But within the shops the wages of the workers are remarkably similar, with very little spread between the highest wage (1.1 yuan per day) and the lowest (.9 yuan per day). The visitors were told emphatically that the women in this enterprise did not work for money but to serve the revolution, and it is evident that whatever material incentives exist there operate through expectations of increased community benefits. Yet, despite the adamancy of the hosts on this point, they also mentioned that during the Cultural Revolution the workers had demanded and won the right to have enterprise net income accrue to the neighborhood committee rather than to Shanghai municipality, because so little of it had been returning in welfare benefits to the community.

In the example of K'ung Chiang Village's flashlight-bulb factory, we see all the elements of the collective material-incentive system: dependence of wages and welfare fund upon productivity; resulting differences between enterprises in incomes generated; relatively egalitarian distribution within the enterprise; and workers motivated by the expectation of community development financed by their income. This system, as it were, transfers the bourgeois character of the principle "to each according to his work" to a higher level, so that inequalities occur between groups rather than between individuals. But it also accustoms individuals to working collectively in an atmosphere of relative equality, while it retains a material incentive for them to do so.

The resulting inequalities between collectives are temporarily tolerated because they do not immediately reflect and aggravate the *class* tensions still present in *intra*collective relations. Reduced income differentiation within groups weakens the tendency for class stratification to recur, while inequalities between groups cut across class lines and are less divisive in the short run. Later, however, the inherent tendency of such a system of "self-reliance" to generate group and regional differences might well become a more serious problem for government at all levels.

In the rural communes, egalitarian distribution is evident in the rejuvenated "free supply" system, reminiscent of—but more limited than—that of the Great Leap Forward. At Shashihyu Brigade, the most crucial item of all—food grain—has been distributed largely without reference to work performed. In 1971, for example, eighty percent of the total per capita supply was distributed "free" of work points earned. Visitors are told that families with more children and less labor power are thus assured sufficient food grain, that public welfare funds provide an additional such guarantee, and that the brigade in this way both implements the principle of "to each according to his labor," and guarantees livelihood for all. Note, however, that this system abandons the first principle in its strict Leninist form, "He who does not work, neither shall he eat." Myrdal and Kessle report a similar practice in another poor North China village,[82] but it is difficult to gauge just how common it is in the country as a whole.

Yet it is clearly only one part, albeit a dramatic one, of

a more general system of cooperative distribution that has been developing in the communes. The collective provision of free education, medical care, housing, and cultural facilities, financed mainly by collective income and from small premiums assessed on members, is another important and new component of this system. Thus, funds for the establishment and expansion of schools, hospitals, clinics, old-age homes, cultural and recreational facilities increasingly are coming from the incomes of the local units they will serve. In many cases the new cooperative services are the first of their kind available to the rural people. By permitting the teams and brigades to keep enough of their net incomes to take responsibility for such undertakings, rather than siphoning off this income in the form of taxes or price differentials to be reallocated centrally, the state provides the collective material incentives to spur socialism locally. The system constitutes, as Arthur Galston puts it, "an unusual combination of conditions promoting both unselfish, self-abnegating labor for the good of the group and work for personal gain."[83]

From where are the resources to come for such ambitious programs? In part from the expansion of agricultural production since the early 1960s. In part, as already indicated, from the forbearance of the central government, which has allowed much of the expanded output to remain with the units producing it.[84] Partly from other forms of subsidy, such as the *hsia-fang* and *hsia-hsiang* of experienced technical and administrative personnel to the villages, the circulation of mobile medical teams, the provision of free technical and scientific advice at experimental farms, the exchange of experience with advanced model work units, etc. And partly from the extra income earned through rural diversification, especially local industrialization.[85]

Ever since the Hawthorne experiments, it has been almost axiomatic in literature on management that providing workers with greater understanding of the significance of their work and greater influence over its design and purpose would stimulate productivity. In the Chinese case outlined above, this is accomplished by locating responsibility for improving the collective welfare and security in the grass-roots collective. Rather than have funds—and decision-making authority with them—flow to a remote central government, most questions of immediate relevance to the individual's material and cultural standard of life become subjective to his influence as a member of the collective. It requires no leap of the imagination to grasp that a farmer might work hard and with ingenuity to enable his work team to produce a surplus with which a teacher can be paid to educate his children. Nor are the reasons necessarily purely selfless. What is important is that the motivation stems from an understanding that the collective has the means and the authority to make significant contributions to the individual's welfare, and that the individual has a significant share of responsibility for determining the nature and size of those contributions.

In this motivational context, many policies associated with Mao take on new significance as designed to add to the means and authority of the collective, as well as to the psychological disposition of members to exploit them. For example, the great attention paid to experimentation and innovation at the factory or village level, to rural industrialization, and to agricultural diversification and mechanization acquaint the worker and farmer with the possibilities for improvement in his local condition, and create a heightened tension between the actual and the potential. Coupled with urgings to visit, study, and catch up with advanced units, such policies encourage a form of "demonstration effect" which stimulates savings and ingenuity even though part of the ultimate motive may be increased consumption.

Participatory Management in Industry

In industry, as in the communes, a floor is put under consumption by socially provided goods and services. From their welfare funds, industrial enterprises supply medical treatment, dining halls, transportation expenses for workers living far from the worksite, safety clothing, hardship allowances, pensions, and educational expenses. In enterprises visited by Barry Richman that had such funds, they averaged 12 to 13.5 percent of the enterprises' total wage bill. In one factory (Canton Chemical Fertilizer) whose welfare fund came to 13 percent of total wages paid, Richman was told that some 42 percent of the fund went for medical expenses, 15 percent for trade union operations, the rest for various educational, recreational, cultural, insurance, and social-security expenses.[86] In Shanghai's Hutung Shipyard, an amount equal to 36 percent of the total wage bill was spent for such purposes in 1971.[87] The American political economists who visited China in 1972 found the percentage of the wage bill devoted to welfare more in line with Richman's observations (12 percent at the Peking No. 1 Machine Tool Plant, and 8.8 percent at the Shanghai Construction Machinery Plant), and spent on similar undertakings. In addition to such welfare provisions, rent is heavily subsidized, as are public transportation and other goods and services deemed necessities of life by the state.

While the broad range of socially provided goods and services dulls the spur of feared deprivation, the relative modesty of the maximum income to which a worker can aspire puts a severe damper on personal income as an active source of work motivation. Moreover, distribution policy and the values instilled through education in China both discredit consumerism as an acceptable mode of behavior and remove the physical means for realizing it. As Richman points out, the Chinese industrial employee can clearly afford the basic necessities, and if a family contains two or more income earners it can afford the kinds of semiluxury items increasingly produced on a mass scale: radios, sewing machines, watches, cameras, bicycles. But beyond such goods there is little to catch the imagination—even one fired by Madison Avenue:

Cars, modern private homes, TV sets, washers and dryers, air conditioners, fine jewelry, works of art and rare antiques are either not available or beyond the financial means of even the highest-paid industrial personnel. Such items are typically purchased only by organizations or allocated to individuals: they are rarely bought by individuals. . . . this is likely to mean that monetary incentives and material gain lose some of their potency as potential motivating forces.[88]

But if substantial portions of income accrue to the industrial worker, as to the commune member, in the form of collectively provided goods and services unconnected with individual work effort, it is *not* the case that industrial workers are motivated by the same kind of collective material-incentive system. The individual and collective incomes of workers in a state enterprise do not appear to depend greatly upon the productivity of the enterprise. Indeed, some enterprises accept planned losses (as a means of subsidizing necessities), which does not imply that their workers earn less than in profit-making firms. Wages, as we have seen, are fixed by the state. The welfare fund, from which collective welfare benefits are paid, are financed from payments by the enterprise of a fixed percentage of the total wage fund.[89] However, to a variable extent, enterprises have been permitted to retain fixed percentages of their profits, and to use part of the retained portion for increasing workers' welfare provisions.[90] This practice, the current status and extent of which is unclear, is the only obvious way in which worker welfare is tied directly to plant performance in Chinese state industry. It is clearly a less important and substantial tie than that which exists in the collective sector of the economy.

To be an industrial worker in China is still to be in a privileged position, politically and economically. The industrial worker represents the future, is entrusted with the most advanced technology, enjoys the best working conditions and welfare benefits, has the highest wages outside the small group of very highly paid intellectuals and scientists. The élan that such a position entails may well substitute in part for the material incentives that still motivate work in the collective enterprises.

In the mushrooming local industries at the country level, industrial workers are even more in the position of pioneers, mastering for the first time scientific and industrial technology, playing the role of "leading factor" in the economic transformation of their localities. The county (*hsien*) is a small enough unit so that each new item produced, each increase in output, is not only noticeable but may change living standards significantly. In these factories, moreover, working conditions and welfare benefits depend much more directly on performance and growth than in the larger state-operated enterprises, since they must be provided for out of *hsien* revenues, the most rapidly growing source of which is local enterprise profits.

For all these reasons, merely being an industrial worker probably relieves work of some of its "disutility" and invests the worker's life with a sense of purpose and participation. Beyond this, and contributing to the same result, is the approach to enterprise management that the Chinese are still in process of forging.[91] By means of the principles tersely enunciated in the Anshan Constitution[92] (said to have been formulated by Mao himself in March 1960), China has been moving toward a system of reduced hierarchical distinctions between workers, managers, and technicians, in which the rank and file genuinely participates in setting enterprise goals and overseeing their fulfillment, and in which the enterprise itself becomes not merely an instrument of production but also the locus of education, welfare implementation, and social activity.

It is difficult to judge the degree to which Chinese industrial enterprises today realize these goals. The political and ideological level of the work force, not the mechanical system of procedures, is the crucial variable, and it is not subject to easy evaluation. For example, a principal method by which mass participation in factory management is implemented is the periodic mass meeting at which objectives are explained and worker opinions collected.[93] At one enterprise visited by the American political economists in August 1972, criticisms voiced at such a meeting had actually caused the enterprise plan to be reformulated. The mere existence of such a procedure, however, does not automatically imply the real substance of mass participation. As Mao put it, "Without mass consciousness and willingness, any work requiring mass participation is bound vainly to degenerate into formalism and fail."[94]

In the vigorous attacks carried out during the Cultural Revolution on such "revisionist" practices as "relying on specialists to run factories," and "concocting rules and regulations to bind the masses hand and foot," enterprise management probably was weakened and the importance of job competence belittled. Later articles put great emphasis on the principle that "any society has to be managed," and on the need to increase technical and managerial personnel, "define the scope of managerial authority," and establish a "clear-cut division of work and responsibility as regards who is responsible for each task or matter."[95] Thus, there has been a period of consolidation in enterprise management, during which some of the radical participatory practices that grew up during the Cultural Revolution have been altered in order to strengthen control and administration.

Whatever the short-run turns and twists, however, the long-term trend in enterprise management, as Steven Andors has shown, is to experiment with systems of sharing power and responsibility, in which jobs have significance beyond the pay they bring. Accorded a significant share of responsibility for formulating and implementing the tasks of the enterprise, for innovating, and for organizing the social and political life that revolves around the factory, the worker comes to regard his work to some extent as important and satisfying. The manifest fairness of the actual distribution of income helps persuade him to relinquish the need for direct material stimuli by strengthening his confidence that "no one else is benefiting more than he is by his own acceptance of egalitarian and cooperative behavior."[96] All this, it must be remembered, occurs in a context in which the state industrial worker already occupies a materially privileged position in society and is therefore relatively disposed to accept its ideological goals as his own.

The participatory management system in state enterprises, whose motivational elements are highlighted above in rather ideal and general terms, really amounts to a third type of incentive system. It features neither the close relation between group productivity and group income of the collective material-incentive system, nor the work-point system's practice of basing personal income upon meritorious behavior. Instead, it depends on the establishment of an environment in which work becomes an implicitly important and rewarding part of the workers' lives. As attempts to implement it come into conflict with the interests and ambitions of bureaucratic administrators on the one hand, and on the other, with the orderliness required for efficient planning and operation, greater or lesser compromises occur, reflecting both political and technological conditions.

External and Internal Incentives

Of the three models of motivational systems discussed so far—payment according to merit, collective material incentives, and participatory management—only the first embodies completely external incentives—i.e., incentives stemming directly from the reward offered.

External incentives can be either material or nonmaterial; the difference lies only in the nature of the reward, not in its relation to work. In the case of material incentives, individuals or groups receive higher pay, cash bonuses, and the like. In that of nonmaterial incentives, they get commendations, banners, honorary status, prestige. There are, of course, differences in the economic costs of the two systems, and in the values they seek to instill, but they are alike in that both rely upon external stimuli to motivate effort, rather than upon properties of the job itself.

Therefore, contrary to outward appearances, the degree of reliance upon moral incentives *per se* is not an index of social consciousness. In fact, the necessity of providing external rewards, *even of a nonmaterial sort*, to reinforce socially desirable behavior is a measure of the distance still to be traveled to achieve what Lenin understood by "communist labor":

> labor performed gratis for the benefit of society, labor performed not as a definite duty, not for the purpose of obtaining a right to certain products, not according to previously established and legally fixed quotas, but voluntary labor. . . . performed because it has become a habit to work for the common good, and because of a conscious realization (that has become a habit) of the necessity of working for the common good.[97]

Internal incentives are the motivating properties of a job itself. They may flow from the nature of the work, as in the case of arts, crafts, or sports, or from its significance. The boy who saved Amsterdam by putting his finger in the dike was neither enamored of the work nor expecting a bonus. He simply knew the importance of what he was doing. Lenin's description of communist labor implies internal motivation. But internal motivation does not necessarily imply "communist labor"; a good craftsman who loves his work may be oblivious to the needs of his fellows and work for himself rather than "for the common good."

The collective material-incentive system is an intermediate one, partly internal and partly external. Its incentive is internal in that the members of the collective perceive and are motivated by the significance of their labor in transforming their locality. The link between work and the anticipated increase in material welfare is organic, not simply a matter of earning an additional yuan by doing work for somebody else which has no intrinsic significance.

At the same time, because part of this significance comes from expected future income, and because part of the motivation for working is due to the collective morale and the desire to be well thought of by one's colleagues, the incentive under this system remains partly external. It is not yet purely a matter of "conscious realization (that has become a habit) of the necessity of working for the common good."

The participatory management system of state industries more substantially internalizes its incentives.[98] In part this is because industrial workers, among the most well-off members of the new society and enjoying a high level of material security, are in a relatively good position to "work for the common good" without fear of individual deprivation. But the management system in its ideal formulation also increases the intrinsic satisfaction to be derived from work. The movement for scientific experimentation and innovation, the attempt to create generalists or "all-rounders" who are competent at a number of tasks, to encourage comprehensive rather than highly specialized production wherever possible, and to break down the distinction between technicians and workers can all be seen as facets of what industrial-management specialists call "horizontal job enlargement" (an increase in the number and variety of operations performed on the job). Genuine participation by the rank and file in setting the goals of their enterprise and overseeing their fulfillment corresponds to what is called "vertical job enlargement."

Both of these forms of "job enlargement" lead to

heightened work motivation because they provide for meaningful feedback about job performance (information about the results of one's work), the use and development of abilities valued by the worker, and a high degree of control by the worker over his work goals and the means of achieving them.[99]

The internal incentives of Chinese industry, like the semi-internal ones of the collective, do not necessarily imply selfless "communist labor," however readily one might confuse them. If it is observed, for example, that wage differentials are unusually small and there are no bonuses or awards, it is easy to jump to the conclusion that people are being motivated by pure public-spiritedness. The alternative explanation—internal incentives—springs less quickly to mind because it cannot be directly observed and measured. Yet it appears to be very important in China today.

Finally, worksite incentive mechanisms must be evaluated in the context of the general social, economic, and political milieu in which people live. The degree of legitimacy enjoyed by the existing social arrangements (including work arrangements), insofar as this relates to workers' capacities for identifying with and helping to shape the goals of their work, is an important motivational factor. "Participation becomes a farce when it is applied as a sales gimmick or a device for kidding people into thinking they are important."[100] The crux of the issue is whether the basis for a convergence of individual goals and organizational objectives exists or not. If not, attempts to arrange organizational methods to fabricate an appearance of compatibility will ultimately be perceived as manipulation by the subjects and will have no significant motivational impact in the long run.

My emphasis on internal motivation and the metamorphosis of material incentives in contemporary China is not intended to disparage the evidence of a generally heightened social consciousness, as captured in the slogans

"Fight self" and "Serve the people." But I believe it does serve to put the question of the "emergence of a new Socialist man" in China into a less idealistic perspective by linking the qualities being encouraged directly to the forms of social organization and the distribution of political and economic power. China is a country in transition. That its motivational morality should also be in transition is not surprising. As Chairman Mao has said, "a voyage of 10,000 li begins with a single step," and China's progress toward a more satisfactory basis for motivating its people can justly be regarded as more than a single step.

NOTES

I am grateful to Perry Link and Mark Selden for close and penetrating criticisms of an earlier draft of this article. My intellectual debt to the work of Steven Andors, Jack Gray and Jack Gurley will be obvious to the reader. None of the above is responsible for remaining errors of fact or fancy.

1. *New York Times*, June 27, 1971.
2. *Mainland China in the World Economy*, Hearings before the Joint Economic Committee of Congress, Washington, D.C., 1967, pp. 73–74 (hereafter cited as *Mainland China*).
3. *Ibid.*, p. 22.
4. A. Doak Barnett, *China after Mao* (Princeton, 1967), p. 18.
5. Kenneth Walker, *Planning in Chinese Agriculture: Socialization and the Private Sector* (London, 1965), pp. 93, 98.
6. *China after Mao*, p. 23.
7. *Ibid.*
8. C. Y. Cheng, *The Economy of Communist China, 1949–1969*, Michigan Papers in Chinese Studies, no. 9, 1971, p. 45.
9. *Ibid.*, p. 37.
10. See Jan Myrdal and Gun Kessle, *China: The Revolution Continued* (New York, 1970), pp. 53–55.
11. See his *Industrial Society in Communist China*, New York, 1969; "Ideology and Management: The Chinese Oscillate," *Columbia Journal of World Business* (May–June 1971); testimony before Joint Economic Committee of Congress, *Mainland China*, pp. 50–115.
12. *Mainland China*, p. 82.
13. *Ibid.*, pp. 88–89.

14. See, e.g., *ibid.*, p. 66.

15. *Ibid.*, p. 82.

16. *Ibid.*, p. 90.

17. Benjamin Higgins, *Economic Development* (New York, 1968), p. 309.

18. See Herb Gintis, "Neo-Classical Welfare Economics and Individual Development," URPE Occasional Paper No. 3.

19. H. Leibenstein, "Allocative Efficiency vs. 'X-Efficiency,'" *American Economic Review* (June 1966), p. 392.

20. *Ibid.* For a more precise notion of the contents of "x-efficiency," see pp. 406–12.

21. Victor H. Vroom and Edward L. Deci, *Management and Motivation* (Baltimore, 1970), p. 9.

22. J. Vanek, *General Theory of Labor-Managed Market Economies* (Ithaca, 1970), p. 237.

23. *Ibid.*, pp. 237–38.

24. The point is eloquently made in John Gurley, "Maoist vs. Capitalist Development," in Edward Friedman and Mark Selden, eds., *America's Asia* (New York, 1971).

25. Douglas M. MacGregor, "The Human Side of Enterprise," in Vroom and Deci, p. 307.

26. J. A. C. Brown, *The Social Psychology of Industry* (Baltimore, 1954), p. 15.

27. See R. L. Opsahl and M. D. Dunnette, "The Role of Financial Compensation in Industrial Motivation," *Psychological Bulletin*, 66 (1966).

28. Vroom and Deci, p. 13.

29. MacGregor, p. 309.

30. Quoted in Higgins, pp. 299–300.

31. *Ibid.*

32. See, for example, Maslow's "A Theory of Human Motivation," in Vroom and Deci, especially p. 40.

33. Stuart Chase, quoted in J. A. C. Brown, p. 72.

34. Brown, p. 85.

35. On the question of the objectives of industrial psychiatry, Daniel Bell has written that Mayo and his followers "uncritically adopt industry's own conception of workers as *means* to be manipulated or adjusted to impersonal ends. . . . the social science of the factory researchers is not a science of man, but a cow-sociology" (*Commentary*, January 1947, quoted in Brown, p. 93). Miller and Form on this point write: "It is also a well-known fact that professors as well as researchers in 'good' colleges of business administration do not displease the business community. . . . These [Mayo's] researches were conducted to help *management* solve its problems. Therefore the status quo is accepted" (from *Industrial Sociology*, quoted in Brown, p. 93).

36. Brown, p. 187.

37. N. C. Morse and R. S. Weiss, "The Function and Meaning of

Work and the Job," *American Sociological Review*, 20 (1955), reprinted in Vroom and Deci, pp. 42–57.

38. *Ibid.*, p. 42.
39. V. H. Vroom, "Industrial Social Psychology," in Vroom and Deci, pp. 92–93.
40. MacGregor, p. 315, emphasis in original.
41. See note 35 above. For an incisive discussion arguing that scientific management remains the predominant system in American industry today, and that other approaches are confined to the secondary objective of habituating workers to their work, see Harry Braverman, *Labor and Monopoly Capital* (New York, 1974), especially ch. 6.
42. MacGregor, p. 316.
43. This part of the discussion is based upon A. K. Sen, "On Economic Inequality" (the Radcliffe Lectures delivered at the University of Warwick, 1972), mimeographed ms., pp. 110–14. The terminology is my own.
44. Those familiar with the theory of games will recognize this situation as "the Prisoner's Dilemma."
45. Sen, "On Economic Inequality," p. 112.
46. See, e.g., Marx, *Critique of the Gotha Program* (New York, 1938), p. 10; and Lenin, "State and Revolution," in *ibid.*, pp. 79–88; and "From Lenin's Notebook," in *ibid.*, p. 59.
47. Sen, "On Economic Inequality," p. 111.
48. Arthur Galston, "Life in a Chinese Commune," Hong Kong *Standard*, August 25, 1972, p. 7.
49. Karl Marx, *Critique of the Gotha Program*, p. 8.
50. *Ibid.* The "deductions" are for maintenance and depreciation, net investment, reserve fund for contingencies, administrative costs, funds for collective consumption, goods and services such as schools and hospitals, and welfare funds.
51. *Critique of the Gotha Program*, p. 10.
52. "The State and Revolution," in Marx, *op. cit.*, pp. 79–80.
53. "The State and Revolution," p. 82.
54. "Lenin on the Critique of the Gotha Program," in Marx, *op. cit.*, p. 59.
55. "The State and Revolution," in Marx, *op. cit.*, p. 85.
56. *Anti-Dühring* (New York, 1939), p. 222.
57. That a small educated élite might successfully seek such differential pay is a different matter.
58. A. K. Sen, "On Economic Inequality," pp. 117–18.
59. Note that the first system contains analogs at the level of groups to the arbitrary inequalities between individuals implied by distribution according to labor. Thus, groups with more fertile land, better equipment, and/or a more talented or educated membership will tend to earn more and grow faster than less favorably endowed groups.
60. See *Renmin Ribao* editorial, February 18, 1971.
61. "Essential Difference between Two Distribution Systems," by a

workers' group in Shanghai's Hutung Shipyard, *Peking Review,* no. 32 (August 11, 1972), p. 6.

62. See Charles Hoffmann, *Work Incentive Practices and Policies in the People's Republic of China, 1953–1965* (Albany, N.Y., 1967), and *The Chinese Worker* (Albany, N.Y., 1974); Christopher Howe, *Wage Patterns and Wage Policy in Modern China, 1919–1972,* Cambridge, 1973; Barry Richman, *Industrial Society in Communist China* (New York, 1969), and "Ideology and Management: The Chinese Oscillate," in *Columbia Journal of World Business,* 6, no. 1 (January–February 1971); Peter Schran, *The Structure of Income in Communist China* (Ph.D. diss. Berkeley, 1961), and "Unity and Diversity of Chinese Industrial Wage Policies," *Journal of Asian Studies* (February 1964); Chen Mae-fun, "Paying the Peasants," *Far Eastern Economic Review* (hereafter *FEER*) (November 3, 1966); A. Nathan, "China's Work-Point System: A Study in Agricultural Splitism," *Current Scene,* 2, no. 31 (April 15, 1964), and Martin K. Whyte, "The Tachai Brigade and Incentives for the Peasant," *Current Scene,* 7, no. 16 (August 15, 1969); Carl Riskin, "Worker Incentives in Chinese Industry," in U.S. Congress, Joint Economic Committee, *China: A Reassessment of the Economy* (Washington, 1975); "Constitution of Anshan Iron and Steel Company Spurs Revolution and Production," *Peking Review,* no. 16 (April 17, 1970); Gerald Tannebaum, "The Real Spirit of Tachai," *Eastern Horizon,* 10, no. 2 (1971); "Essential Difference between Two Distribution Systems," *Peking Review,* no. 32 (August 11, 1972). Many Chinese articles on the subject can be found listed in Hoffmann's bibliography.

63. Chen Yonggui, leader of Tachai Brigade, quoted in C. C. A. S., *China! Inside the People's Republic* (New York, 1972), p. 169.

64. The "high skills" that are rewarded at Tachai are no doubt largely the product of after-work study and other forms of self-training, rather than the result of formal education. As such, they are acquired at significant personal cost.

65. *China! Inside the People's Republic,* p. 169.

66. Obtained during my visit to Shashihyu, August 18, 1972.

67. M. A. Macciocchi, *Daily Life in Rovolutionary China* (New York, 1972), p. 255.

68. *Ibid.,* p. 246.

69. "Management Should Be Based on the Ideological Consciousness of Commune Members," *Chingchi Yenchiu,* no. 3, 1966, quoted in Macciocchi, p. 247. Several of the quotations in the above paragraph of the text imply that natural endowments are not properly subject to reward. I believe that this position, at least in its extreme form, was a short-lived manifestation of the Cultural Revolution. More recent articles in the Chinese press strongly endorse the principle of paying stronger commune workers more for the extra work they can do, for example.

70. Whyte, "The Tachai Brigade," p. 6.

71. To the degree that the criteria include quantity and quality of work done, of course, work points continue to play an *active* role as well.

72. The problem of work points causing an incorrect allocation of labor between tasks is discussed in Jan Myrdal and Gun Kessle, *China: The Revolution Continued* (New York, 1970), pp. 81–82; Tannebaum, p. 15; Whyte, pp. 3–4.

73. This aspect of the Tachai system, of course, raises the political and philosophical problem of how much of the individual's behavior ought to be subject to scrutiny, evaluation, and conscious influence by the organized representatives of society. This description of Tachai-type criteria and their properties should not be construed as an answer to that question. Also, our discussion ignores the question whether it is feasible to establish methods of evaluating workers according to such vague and general criteria, which are neither arbitrary (if imposed from above) nor divisive (if arrived at through group discussion).

74. Charles Hoffmann, *The Chinese Worker*, Ch. 4.

75. Barry Richman, *Industrial Society in Communist China*, p. 318.

76. Richman states that after promotion to grade two, which is more or less automatic, "there is typically no set pattern for basic wage increases, which are then based chiefly on skill, experience, productivity, and general performance, with politics playing a minor role, at least in relatively normal times." *Industrial Society*, p. 803.

77. *Industrial Society in Communist China*, pp. 804–805.

78. For Richman's entire sample of 38 industrial enterprises, the average ratio of top pay to mean enterprise pay was 2.5 to 1. For the 14 enterprises in which an engineer or technician was the top-paid employee, this ratio was 2.7 to 1. Therefore, in the other 24 firms, the ratio of top engineer's pay to average enterprise pay must have been less than 2.5 to 1. [Data from Richman, *op. cit.*, pp. 800–2, 804.]

79. Based upon an interview at Peking No. 1 Machine Tool Plant, August 11, 1972, by a group of American economists, including the author. For additional evidence of a narrowing gap between technicians and administrative cadres on the one hand and ordinary workers on the other, see Hoffmann, *op. cit.*, ch. 4.

80. Subsequent to the writing of this article, I explored the issues of this section further in "Worker Incentives in Chinese Industry" (see note 62).

81. *China! Inside the People's Republic*, p. 189.

82. See their *China: The Revolution Continued*, pp. 53–55.

83. "Life on a Chinese Commune," Hong Kong *Standard*, August 25, 1972, p. 7.

84. See A. Donnithorne, "China's Grain: Output, Procurement, Transfers, and Trade," Economic Research Center, The Chinese University of Hong Kong, 1971.

85. The general directions discussed above are documented in the following sources: Colina MacDougall, "The Chinese Economy: Pie in the Sky," *FEER*, no. 26 (1969) ; Myrdal and Kessle, *China: The Revolution Continued,* esp. pp. 52–56, 75–81, 109–15, and 139–72; E. L. Wheelwright and Bruce McFarlane, *The Chinese Road to Socialism* (New York, 1971); Carl Riskin, "Small Industry and the Chinese Model of Development," *China Quarterly,* no. 46 (April–June 1971), pp. 266–73.
86. *Industrial Society*, p. 807.
87. *Peking Review*, no. 32 (August 11, 1972), p. 7.
88. *Industrial Society*, p. 809.
89. *China's Economic System*, p. 213.
90. *Ibid.*, pp. 164–68.
91. See the excellent discussion of this subject by Steven Andors in *America's Asia*, op. cit.
92. "Keep politics firmly in command; strengthen Party leadership; launch vigorous mass movements; institute the system of cadre participation in productive labor and worker participation in management, of reform of irrational and outdated rules and regulations, and of close cooperation among workers, cadres and technicians; and go full steam ahead with the technical innovations and technical revolution." *Peking Review*, no. 16 (1970), p. 3.
93. See, for example, "Shanghai No. 17 Cotton Mill—'Red Bulwark of the Great Proletarian Cultural Revolution in Shanghai,' " *Peking Review*, no. 27 (1969).
94. "Take the Line as the Key Link and Carry Out Enterprise Management Well," *Hong Qi*, No. 4, April 1, 1972.
95. *Ibid.*
96. Andors, "The Chinese Factory," mimeo, p. 16.
97. Lenin, "From the Destruction of the Old Social System to the Creation of the New," quoted in Myrdal and Kessle, *China*, p. 60.
98. To the extent that this system coexists with wages differentiated according to merit, skill, or productivity, it also contains external incentives. To the extent that the enterprise welfare fund is tied to profits, it partakes of the mixed character of the collective material-incentive system.
99. V. H. Vroom, "Satisfaction: Its Determinants and Effects," in Vroom and Deci, pp. 93–95.
100. MacGregor, in Vroom and Deci, p. 317.

INDEX

NOTES ON CONTRIBUTORS

KUNG CHUNG-WU was born in Anhwei province, China. He went to Taiwan, where he received his M.A. in history from National Taiwan University. He is now completing his doctorate in modern Chinese history at Harvard and is working at the United Nations. He has published two books and written various essays in Chinese.

VICTOR NEE holds degrees in Far Eastern and American history and is now completing his doctorate in sociology at Harvard. He is the author of *Longtime Californ'* (Pantheon, 1973) with Brett de Bary Nee and *Cultural Revolution at Peking University* with Don Layman. From 1973 to 1975 he attended the Peking Language Institute and Peking University in the People's Republic of China.

JAMES PECK, who was formerly an editor of the *Bulletin of Concerned Asia Scholars* and a co-director of the Bay Area Institute in San Francisco, studied contemporary China and sociology at Harvard. He was an editor of *The Indochina Story* and is currently editor of the Pantheon Asia Library.

CARL RISKIN, who received his doctorate from the University of California (Berkeley), teaches economics at Queens College and is a research associate at the East Asian Institute at Columbia University. He is the author of numerous articles on the role of small industry in the Chinese model of development, the Chinese approach to work incentives, and the nature and size of economic surplus in pre-liberated China, and was a founding member of the Committee of Concerned Asia Scholars.